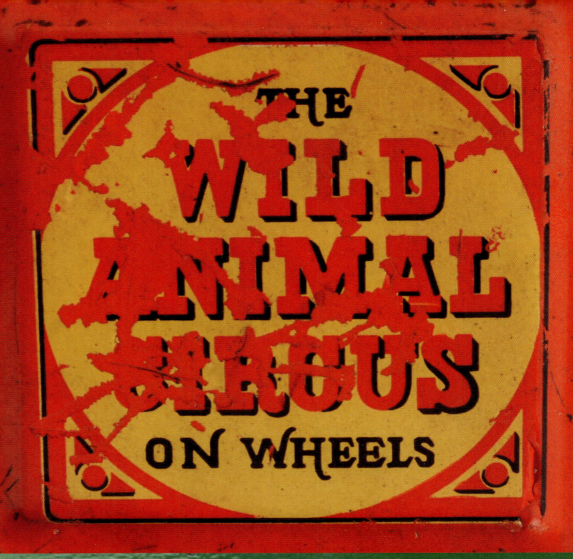

THE WILD ANIMAL CIRCUS ON WHEELS

CHAD VALLEY TOY

GREEN LINE

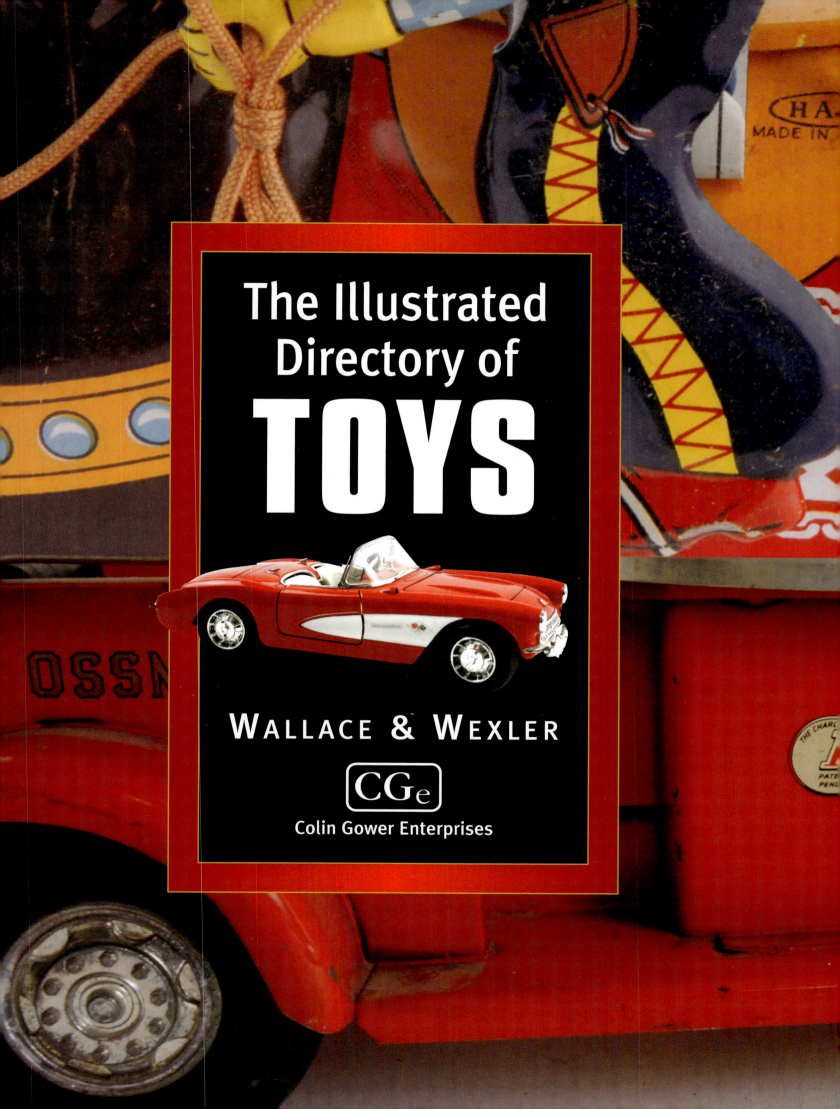

The Illustrated Directory of
TOYS

WALLACE & WEXLER

CGe

Colin Gower Enterprises

Colin Gower Enterprises Ltd.,
Cordwainers, Caring Lane,
Leeds, Maidstone, Kent ME17 1TJ
United Kingdom.
© 2007 Colin Gower Enterprises Ltd.

ISBN: 0-681-63614-9

Designed by Philip Clucas MCSD
Photography by J. P. Bell
Edited by Marie Clayton
Printed and bound in China

CONTENTS

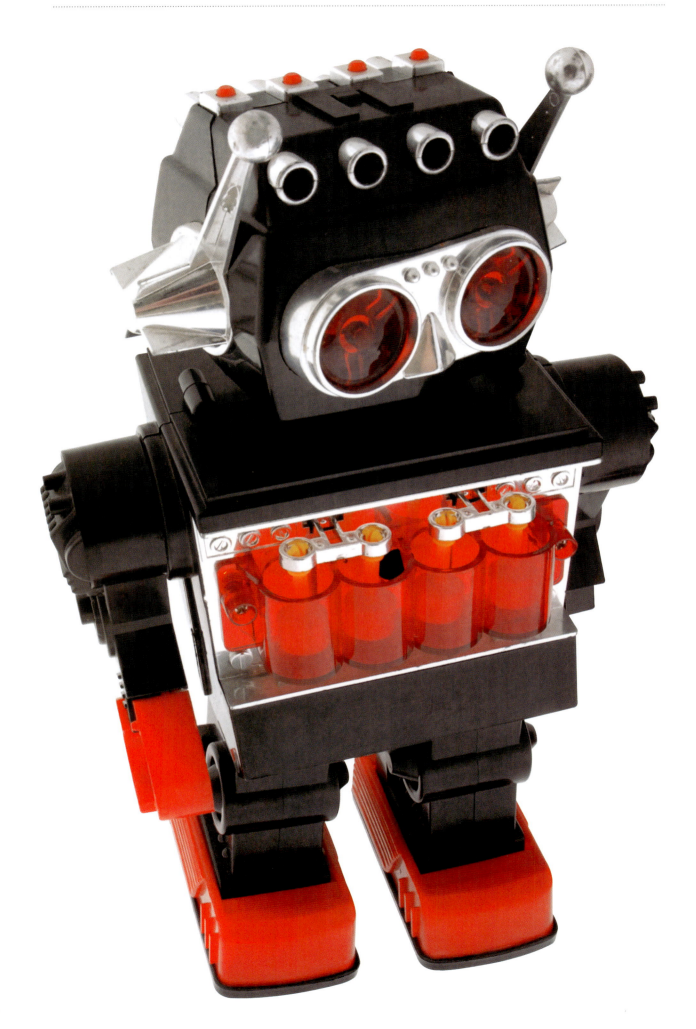

INTRODUCTION

This book does not presume to be a catalog of every toy ever produced, but aims to present a wide range of toy categories for the reader's interest and amusement. For that purpose, we went to toy expert Mr. Tom Beck at the World's Largest Toy Museum in Branson, Missouri. We accessed each of his display cabinets in turn, photographing the many toys he has thought to include in his definitive collection. The organization of the book is based on our journey around the museum. The book is not alphabetical, and the toys appear in more or less the same juxtaposition as they are displayed in the museum. Most of the toy descriptions are based on Mr. Beck's highly informative notes. To the best of our knowledge the descriptions are accurate, but with the passage of time and the absence of clear markings, similar types of toy can occasionally be mistaken for each other.

The rational behind Mr. Beck's wonderful collection is to present classic toys from all eras. This enables the Museum to bring alive the joy of childhood for visitors of every generation. Mr. Beck does not over-restore toys, but presents them in their original, "played with" condition, which keeps the authentic spirit of the toy. If a toy truck comes in with some "non original" bowling pins in the back, he keeps them together. The pins have become part of the toy truck's heritage.

Other private collectors have contributed greatly to the range and quality of toys cataloged in these 750 pages. David Wallace's fine collection of toy buses and cars deserves a particularly special mention.

The toys featured in the book range from the late nineteenth century, right up to the present day, and present the reader with a fascinating spectrum of well over a century of toy evolution. Toys have proved to be wonderful barometers of historical change and popular culture. Some of them are hugely evocative: the cast iron model "Hillclimbers" from the very early days of the automobile industry, the tin "nickel and dime" toys from the Great Depression years, the wooden toys made during World War II when metal was diverted to the war effort, the cowboy guns and Western gear of the 1950s, right up to the robot toys of the space age.

We hope the young at heart everywhere will enjoy our selection.

FOUR TIN GUN BOATS

The absence of markings on these fine examples of 1950s tin toys probably suggests that they are of Japanese or Chinese manufacture. Tin was still popular for toys at this time and was very affordable, and every child had a boat. The most impressive example here is the PT-107, a motor torpedo boat of the type that John F. Kennedy served on during World War II. It has a lot of pressed tin details on the deck, such as captain's bridge and cabin, a forward-firing cannon on the port bow, torpedo tubs either side of the deck and a gun in a turret mounted at the stern—all of which gives it a very realistic appearance. The key to the wind-up mechanism is built into the deck superstructure. The toy is finished in standard navy colors of gray and red,

with light blue details such as the lifeboats and anchor, which are intricately lithographed.

PT-109 celebrates the number of J.F.K.'s actual boat, but little resembles a PT boat. It is more akin to a landing craft, with deck-mounted tin pressings such as torpedo tubs and machine gun mounts. The rest of the detailing is lithographed, and the paint finish is Army green with yellow trim.

PT-10, finished in Navy gray and red, has no external components—all details are lithographed.

The U-12 gunboat is an amphibian, with an external, top-mounted machine gun, and is a wind-up toy.

Below left: The view underside the rear of PT-107 shows the four-bladed propeller, which was driven by the wind-up motor below deck.

The adjustable rudder shows signs of paint loss, which is a good provenance for a genuine toy that has been played with and not restored.

Below and bottom right: Two views of the toy that show the extensive deck fittings, which make it an extremely realistic representation of the boat for the young owner. The built-in key meant that it was not lost, as it was in many wind-up toys.

Above: The lithography was extremely intricate on this model and adds greatly to the overall impression of realism.

THREE TIN SPEEDBOATS

In the 1950s tin toys were still in fashion, prior to the onrush of plastic toys in the 1960s. Boats like the first two examples were made by T. Cohn Inc. in their Brooklyn, New York, factory. The company was probably most noted for its lithographed tin dolls houses; marketed as "Modern Metal Dolls Houses," they remained steady sellers throughout the 1950s. Many treasured examples are now reaching eBay, having been safely stored in attics for the past 50 years. The company gradually switched over to plastic moldings toward the end of the decade, as is evidenced by the change from metal to plastic for the key to the wind-up motor, which occurred between the dates of manufacture of the first two boats. T. Cohn

Inc. marketed plastic play sets featuring soldiers and tanks between 1955 and 1975, licensing plastic dies from the British Airfix Company.

The "Peggy Jane" is the earliest boat and is probably based on pre-war tooling, judging by the design. It is a tin wind-up with lithography detailing for the decking, windows, and a lifesaver. It has a spinning propeller and an adjustable rudder and is very charmingly finished in green and yellow with a red trim.

The blue, red and yellow boat is also by T. Cohn Inc, but is a later design, probably late 1950s or early 1960s. The red, white and blue boat is signwritten as a "Guard Ship." It is a tin wind-up toy manufactured by Daito in Japan, probably dating from the early 1960s.

The lithography on the Japanese-made boat is bright and colorful.

The overall design and lithography of the "Peggy Jane" has a pre-war charm.

Below: Although the two toys are of similar proportions they reflect the evolution in sport boat design from fore engine location to aft.

PEGGY JANE

The later boat has a blue plastic key to wind the motor.

Close-ups of the intricate lithography, which gives the toy its fine detail.

FOUR WOODEN BOATS

During the 1940s there was a conflict of interest between children's natural desire to play with military toys and the fact that many toy manufacturers were engaged in wartime production of essential products. Materials were short, particularly metals, so as a result many toys were fashioned from off-cuts of wood.

The brown, green and red boat is a wind-up toy, with a large cast key inserted into the upper deck. It has two wooden, forward-firing guns painted red, what looks like a rocket in a sliding track on the upper deck, and the added luxury of a couple of chrome embellishments, a capstan and bow capping.

The gray battleship was made by Keystone of Boston around 1950 when materials were still short, but compared to many toys of this era it has a remarkable amount of detail and moving parts. It has two forward-firing metal guns to shoot missiles activated by spring-loaded levers. The rear twin machine guns are missing from this example, but the gray square on the deck where they were is clearly visible. The mast is metal.

The gray submarine also features a spring-loaded mechanism to fire its red torpedo.

The small gray PT boat looks almost handmade, but was a toy for some small child in times of hardship.

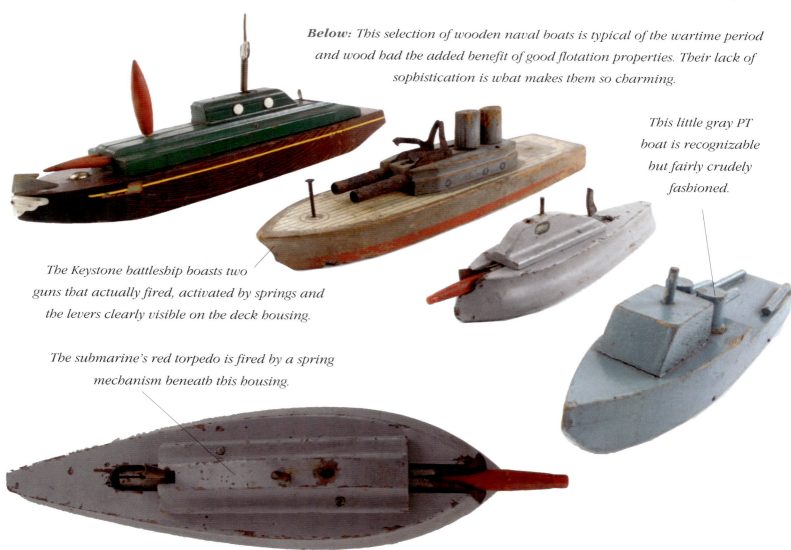

Below: This selection of wooden naval boats is typical of the wartime period and wood had the added benefit of good flotation properties. Their lack of sophistication is what makes them so charming.

This little gray PT boat is recognizable but fairly crudely fashioned.

The Keystone battleship boasts two guns that actually fired, activated by springs and the levers clearly visible on the deck housing.

The submarine's red torpedo is fired by a spring mechanism beneath this housing.

A substantial cast metal key winds the battleship's motor.

The deck is painted to look like planks, part of the standard detail on the Keystone battleship model range.

HILLCLIMBER SHIP

On November 2, 1897, Israel Donald Boyer patented the Locomotive Toy mechanism, which powered toys that came to be known as friction toys, momentum toys or "Hillclimbers." His invention led to four companies setting up in Dayton, Ohio, to manufacture such toys. One was David P. Clark, formerly a clothier from Miamisburg, Ohio, who is thought to have made this example, which dates from 1899. The D.P. Clark toy company operated from 1898 to 1909, becoming the Schieble Toy & Novelty Co. in 1909; Schiebel continued to manufacture toys right up to the Depression in the 1930s. The inertia toy mechanism was used to power

various types of toy, mainly cars, trucks and, more rarely, a battleship. It consisted of a heavy cast-iron flywheel and spring mechanism, which was wound up to power the vehicle and even allowed it to climb a fairly steep incline—hence its popular name. This charming toy boat is redolent of the Golden years as the 1800s came to a close, when steam-powered dreadnought battleships ruled the seas. It is not hard to imagine a small boy in a sailor suit playing with it over a century ago.

Below: The boat is made of sheet steel with detailed pressings, such as smoke stacks and lifeboats. It is painted gray and cream, with light blue lifeboats. It has metal wheels beneath the skirt of the hull.

Removable lifeboats, in what looks like original light blue paint finish, grace the upper deck.

Gray paint on the lower part of the hull simulates the waves beneath the waterline.

WOLVERINE SUBMARINES

The Wolverine Supply & Manufacturing Company was founded by Benjamin F. Bain and his wife in 1903 in Pittsburgh, Pennsylvania. The company's original range was of sandbox toys, which used the weight of the sand to power them, typically endlessly unloading sand or marbles from an elevated hopper. A range of girl's toys was added in 1918, announced at the New York Toy Fair in March of that year. The product range included tea sets, sand pails, washtubs, ironing boards, and miniature grocery stores as shown on page 370.

By 1929 the company had diversified into tin toys under the "Sunny Andy" and "Sunny Suzy" brand names. The company traded remarkably successfully throughout the Depression years and up to World War II, which is when these two submarines date from. They are wind-up toys with working propellers, finished in red

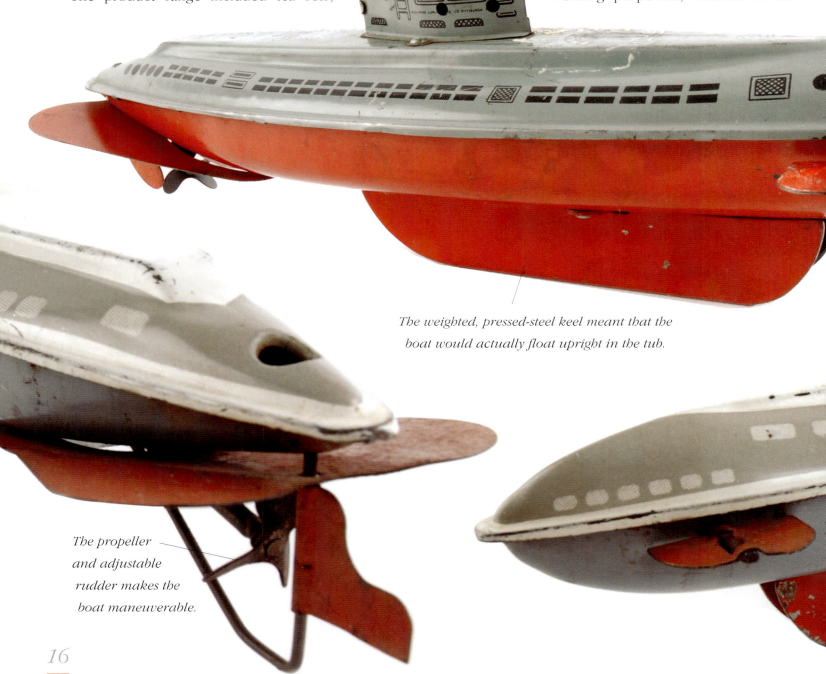

The weighted, pressed-steel keel meant that the boat would actually float upright in the tub.

The propeller and adjustable rudder makes the boat maneuverable.

and gray with detailed lithographed graphics depicting anchors and portholes. The two examples are produced from exactly the same tooling, but are finished in slightly different tones and color schemes. The design is not based on any recognizable submarine model, but has generic submarine characteristics such as a conning tower, keel, and vanes. These are very realistic toys on a pleasing scale and with some weight, which would make them great fun to play with in the days before plastic toys introduced even greater realism. However, toys of this era still have a charm of their very own.

Above right: *A view from the top of the prow area reveals remarkably untouched graphics and the access for the wind-up key in the deck.*

These adjustable vanes were designed to move to alter the dive plane of the boat.

The submarine was simply constructed out of two metal stampings, a top and a bottom, which are pressed together forming this rim around the toy. This gave a good strong waterproof seal.

THE FERRYGO TWIN

The Ferrygo Twin is a pull-along toy with a twin paddle wheel and four small rollers underneath, so it will glide over the floor. The original string pull fixing can be seen on the prow. Made of tin with colorful lithographed detailing, this toy is a charming piece patented on September 27, 1927, as printed above the windows on the cabin. When pulled along the rotation of the paddle wheels also causes a linkage to rock the beam on the upper deck for extra realism. The boat is 14 inches long overall. The style of graphics and manufacture has many of the hallmarks of the Wolverine range, so this may well be made by them although there are no visible brand markings.

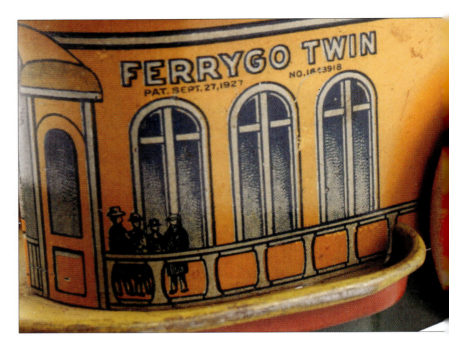

Above: A detail of the side of the cabin, showing intricate graphics depicting passengers standing at the railings, opulent arched windows, and the patent date and number #1643918.

This beam rocks as the boat is pulled along.

TWO METAL SUBMARINES

The "Sea Wolf" is made by Sutcliffe in England and uses similar stampings to the company's 1950s, Disney-licensed, Nautilus model, which was based on the sub that appeared in the movie of the Jules Verne classic Twenty Thousand Leagues Under the Sea. Here the deck superstructure has been updated, using red plastic moldings to provide a conning tower and rocket launcher. It comes with its original box. The same gold-edged lettering was used throughout the range, which included the "Unda-Wunda."

The larger submarine is blue-gray and red with a white tower, and numbered #571. It is a wind-up toy from the early 1950s and was manufactured in Japan, although it has no brand name.

A rocket launcher in red plastic shows this to be from the early 1960s.

The wind-up motor propels this sub quite fast in the tub. I know, I had one!

Above: *The body of the "Sea Wolf" is in remarkably good condition, retaining all of its original paint finish and graphics. This helps keep its value as a collector's item.*

This sub is well equipped, with vanes to adjust the diving angle fore and aft, adjustable rudder and twin propellers.

Above: *The stamping has great detail built into it—unlike many subs of this era, which had simple flat sections that relied on lithography to provide features.*

TUG BOAT

This black and red tug boat with white trim is truly representative of Japanese manufacturers' output in the 1960s: high quality models in molded plastic with metal fittings, offering an attention to detail that makes them almost of hand-built scale model quality. This example is battery-operated, tires protect the sides of the boat, nets are carefully stowed and life preservers are ready. There is a letter "B" on the stack and a light on the mast; the realism is complete. As well as looking good, these toys were very robust and practical, and could be sailed on ponds or lakes—although in the days before widespread remote control, with such a valuable toy you had to get to the other side of the pond pretty quick to reclaim it! A boating hook was essential for removing weed snagged around the propellers, and dragging the boat to safety if the batteries went flat.

Left: A close-up reveals brass-mounted portholes, klaxon horn and ladder, rubber tires as fenders, and lifeboat ready to be launched and dangling on two davits. All creating a toy at the pinnacle of realism.

The rope fender at the bow is made of woven thread, in exactly the same way a real, full-size item would be made.

Deck fittings and planking made to a very high standard of realism complete the job.

Above: *The finished toy is mounted on two purpose-built cradles in the same way that professional hand-built models are. It would form the centerpiece of any child's toy collection.*

The propeller means business, but the adjustable rudder is missing.

TORPEDO BOAT

Based on the U.S. Navy PT boats of World War II, this torpedo boat is battery operated and was made in Japan, probably in the early 1950s. This was a time when the Japanese toy industry was getting back onto its feet after World War II and the U.S. and Europe opened their doors to Japanese toys, which were well constructed and relatively cheap to purchase. Many U.S. manufacturers licensed a lot of their production in Japan from the 1950s onward. This example is typical of the quality Japanese production of the period. It is constructed of wood with metal fittings and has a remarkable amount of detail in its deck fittings, such as deck railings, capstans, rope cleats,

searchlights, torpedo tubs, machine gun turrets, and depth charges. The toy is powered by two electric motors, with separate switching controls, driving twin propellers. Painted in Navy colors of battleship gray, with red below the waterline and a black stripe, the finish is in good shape after 60 years of play. This toy can be appreciated as a practical boating plaything in the tub and on the pond, where the twin motors would have given it an impressive turn of speed like the real thing, and as a realistic model that evokes the spirit of the PT boats.

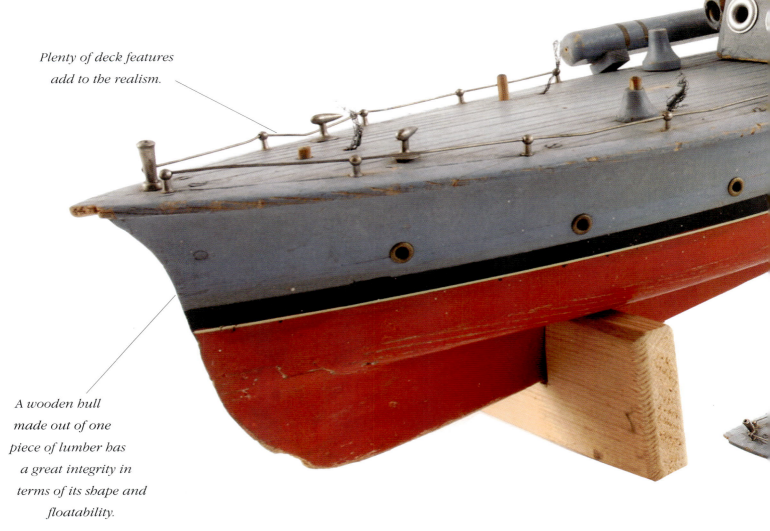

Plenty of deck features add to the realism.

A wooden hull made out of one piece of lumber has a great integrity in terms of its shape and floatability.

Below and bottom of page: *Two views of the PT-inspired boat demonstrate what an impressive toy this really was back in the 1950s. Although made in a time of austerity with only fairly basic materials at his disposal, the manufacturer has captured the detail beautifully.*

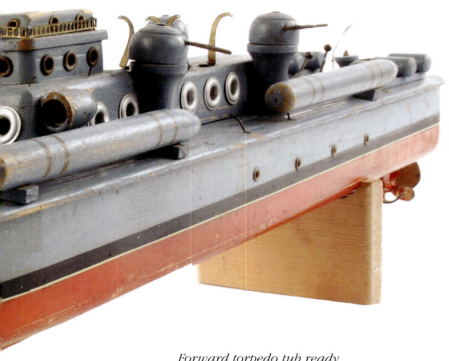

Above: *To avoid expensive tooling and keep costs down, the manufacturer has cleverly used standard metal grommets for the porthole edging.*

Forward torpedo tub ready for action!

WIND-UP TIN BOAT

This charming, small, ocean-going liner or ferry dates from the 1920s and is made in metal. The richness of the vintage color palette—bright blue, red and yellow—as well as the design of the hull and deck cabin, fixes it as an earlier piece. It has a fixed key to wind the motor, which consists of a bent steel rod located in the fore funnel. The power is delivered through a single propeller, steered by an adjustable rudder. There are two ferrule-type mountings on the deck, which would have held wooden masts originally. It is possible that the boat was equipped with sails too, as there are signs of a bowsprit mounting for a foresail and a cleat at the stern. This would have provided an alternate means of propulsion when the clockwork spring ran down half way across

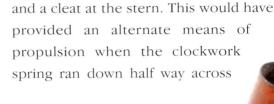

Deck fitments give a clue to the original fitting of masts and sails.

Paint missing from the hull is part of the patination process and is acceptable to most collectors.

The boat is stamped in two parts and is crimped together around this seam.

Above left: *Seen from above it is easy to see how simply the boat is made, but how realistic and pleasing a toy it is despite this. The sturdy metal construction means that very little has been damaged or lost in 90 years of play.*

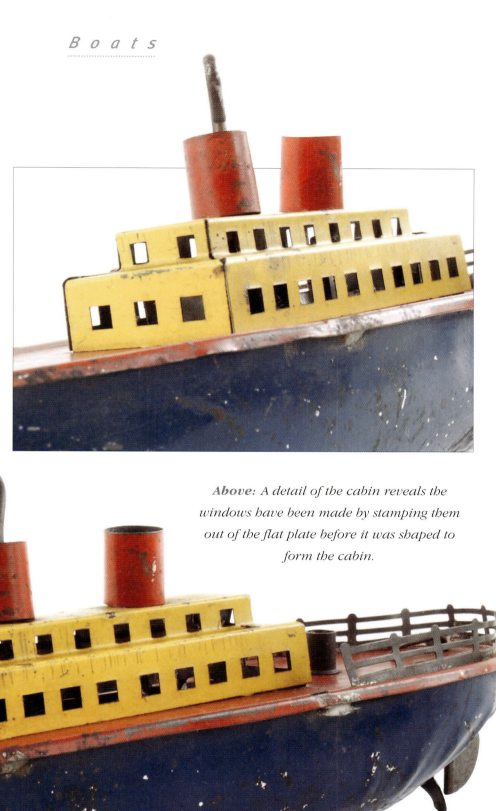

the pond. There are no markings on the boat, but we believe it probably to be of German manufacture, since both the style and the very robust quality of the construction are very similar to the locomotives of the German Bing Company.

Above: A detail of the cabin reveals the windows have been made by stamping them out of the flat plate before it was shaped to form the cabin.

The pressed metal hull remains in good shape despite plenty of immersions in tub and stream.

Above left: The part side view shows off the stern deck railings—remarkably uncrushed by parental feet—two proud red funnels and the simple, but effective, bent rod key.

STAR YACHT

Located in Birkenhead, a port near, Liverpool England, the Star Yacht Company is famous worldwide for its pond yachts, all of which, according to the company's logo, are "guaranteed to sail." This part of England has a great tradition of seafaring so it is hardly surprising that such a toy has emanated from there. There are several models in the range, including the lavish Excelsior MK/3-4 model, with realistic decking and a rudder, down to the basic, but still effective, SY/1. The sheer basic practicality of their manufacture—hull machined out of a single piece of hardwood, inset heavy steel plate keel, collapsible rigging—has

Above and above right: A detail of the working rigging on the yacht, which adjusted both sails and the swinging boom. All the cotton sails carry the distinctive Star stamp and the model number.

guaranteed the toy's survival in attics and garages, to be snapped up today by collectors on eBay.

Our example is an SY/1 made in the 1960s, but the company's product remained the same for over 30 years bearing out the axiom: if a design works don't fix it! The cotton sails are still in good condition, having been stored furled up, despite some rust staining from the metal ferrules. Every yacht came with full

instructions in a leaflet that also sets out the basic principles of sailing, which may have formed the foundations of many a young sailor's career. The wording of the instructions is from a bygone era, advising that: "Several publications can be obtained from any reliable bookseller, which give very useful information on the subject of model yacht sailing, and these are to be recommended to anyone sufficiently interested."

Above: *The colorful Star Yacht trademark, a decal that appears on the aft deck of every boat.*

Above: *Original 1960's dark blue paintwork with a light blue pinstripe adorns the solid hardwood hull.*

The solid metal keel is set into the wooden hull to keep the yacht upright under full sail.

STEELCRAFT BUS

As the name implies, Steelcraft produced a range of large, strong, toy vehicles fabricated in pressed steel. Like many toy manufacturers the company was based in the mid-west—in this case, the state of Ohio. This bus is from the 1920s and typifies the real-life buses of that era, with its long hood and very square lines. Its running board is very reminiscent of a rather overgrown car or perhaps an early example of a stretch limousine. Steelcraft also made many other toys, such as toy delivery trucks, oil tankers, pedal cars, dump trucks and a road roller, to name but a few.

Left: The long hood is a typical design feature of the 1920s.

Above: This Steelcraft Intercity bus is made from strong pressed steel.

Above: A toy that could be used and abused in the outdoors "down on the farm," or on the city streets.

TURNER BUS

Another example of a large pressed steel bus toy of the 1920s is this Overland Bus, manufactured by John C. Turner of Dayton, Ohio. It is of a similar appearance to the Steelcraft shown on the opposite page, and just as durable in the hands of a young omnibus operator in town or country.

The company made the usual range of automotive toys, from trucks to cars measuring up to 26 inches or more. A catalog of 1931 promises that the toys are "made of heavy auto steel, substantially constructed, beautifully finished in gay, flashy, colored enamels which are baked on." What more could a discerning child want?

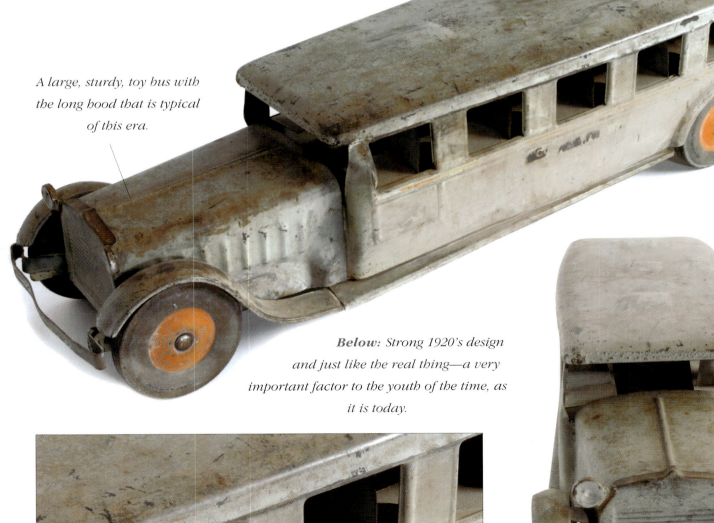

A large, sturdy, toy bus with the long hood that is typical of this era.

Below: *Strong 1920's design and just like the real thing—a very important factor to the youth of the time, as it is today.*

CHEIN ROYAL BLUE LINE BUS

Chein produced tin toys, often with wind-up mechanisms. Their products were much lighter than some of the other heavy, robust, pressed steel toys featured elsewhere in this book. They would not hold the weight of a young owner, since the steel was much finer—but as a result some of the detail was better. Their factory was in New Jersey and toys were made through into the 1970s.

This particular toy bus belonged to the Hercules series and was made in the 1920s; it also appeared in blue. Although a little play worn, it evokes the styling and nostalgia of the period. Chein produced several other toy buses—including a smaller version of this toy called a Junior Bus, with tin printed curtains, which was made in blue, green and yellow. They also made a lovely parlor coach in full Greyhound livery.

Right: *Strong, angular 1920's styling, with rectangular radiator and license plate showing 1K-10-30.*

Oval rear windows and warning sign that passengers are alighting.

Left: *The Coast to Coast Service is often advertised on toy buses from the 1920s to the 1940s.*

LARGE OVERLAND BUS

The bus shown here is an extremely large, imposing, and very robust toy—it is 20 inches long and 6 inches high—which was made in the 1920s by the Schieble Toy and Novelty Company of Dayton, Ohio. The typical 1920's design is very apparent here in the large wheels, long hood and square profile, and the running board is also evocative of the period, with its characteristic outsize-car look. The bus has a bright yellow body, with a green roof, black detailing for fenders, running board, wheels and fluted radiator, and little gold cup-shaped headlamps mounted on the fenders. Inside, the simple, shaped metal seats are also bright yellow in color. This is certainly another toy for tough play down on the farm, or hard play along city streets—the bus was so big that children would sit straddling it, pushing it along with their feet. It is amazing that this model has survived in such good condition.

The Schieble Toy and Novelty Company made a number of fine automotive toys, including several fire trucks, a sedan, a roadster, a racer, a dump truck and

Above: Note the large wheels, with headlamps mounted on the fenders, and the prominent, fluted radiator.

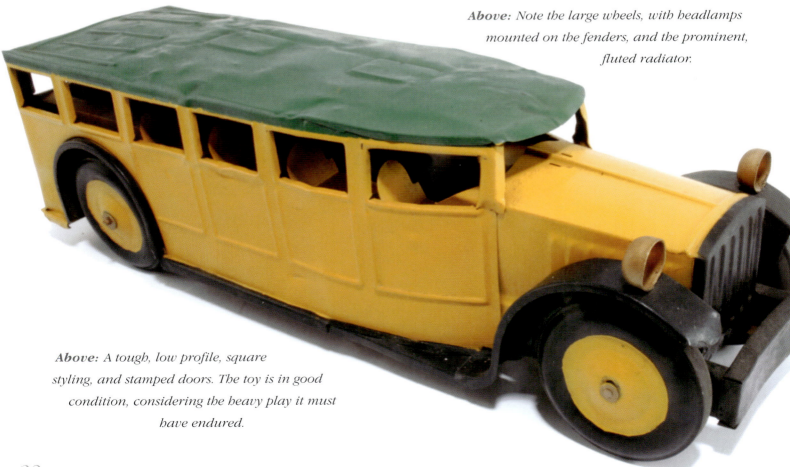

Above: A tough, low profile, square styling, and stamped doors. The toy is in good condition, considering the heavy play it must have endured.

a pick-up. Their toys were popular with small boys at the time, and today appeal to toy and car collectors alike. The boom years of the 1920s saw a period of strong sales, as for many other American toy manufacturers, but unfortunately the 1929 stock market crash resulted in bankruptcy for Schieble in 1931. Schieble's assets were purchased by the John C. Turner Co., also of Dayton, Ohio.

WYANDOTTE COAST TO COAST BUS

Wyandotte Toys, or All Metal Products, produced a wide range of toys for both boys and girls from 1921 to 1956. They made toy guns, games, water pistols, dolls prams—and of course a very fine range of pressed steel, enameled toy vehicles, of which this bus is an example. Like Arcade, the company often made the same vehicle in several different sizes so that parents with different budgets and living spaces could provide their offspring with an appropriate toy to fit.

This toy bus was manufactured in the 1930s and displays art deco streamlined styling with an unusual separate driver's cab that is further accentuated by the change of body color. The slope of the front fenders and the semi-concealed rear wheels add to the streamlined appearance. The strange snout-type hood and large "chrome" radiator at the front only add to its rather odd looks. This example is missing the stickers on the sides, which should read "Coast to Coast Bus Line." It is one of the larger models, at 21 inches long and 6 inches high.

Below: The strange art deco styling gives the bus an odd streamlined appearance.

Above left and above: *Note the rather pig-like snout and the very prominent chrome radiator grille.*

GREYHOUND SCENICRUISER

This is a beautiful tin toy, made in Japan in the mid to late 1950s by Daiya specifically for the U.S. market. It models the famous Greyhound GMC PD-4501 Scenicruiser of the mid 1950s, a one-and-a-half deck design that was a landmark in American cross-country bus travel and was very common on U.S roads throughout the late 1950s/early 1960s. It has been modeled many times by toy manufacturers, both in the U.S.A. and abroad.

This example measures just less than 15 inches long and features tasteful lithographed passengers and the impressive Greyhound dog logo. The toy is battery

The Scenicruiser had a one-and-a-half deck design.

Below: The long, sleek line was a landmark in bus design of the period. The real bus was common on the roads of America throughout the late 1950s/early 1960s.

Lithographed passengers make the toy particularly appealing.

Below: The driver seems to be concentrating very carefully on the road ahead!

operated from a compartment in the base and has an on/off switch. A round disc on the base with two small wheels enables the bus to change directions as it moves around. This toy bus is substantial enough to have pleased a child of the time, and to have given hours of amusement.

ARCADE SAFETY COACH

The Arcade Manufacturing Company was founded as the Novelty Iron Works in 1868 in Freeport, Illinois. This mid-western state was to become the seat of production for a number of toy firms, including Tootsietoy and Midgetoy. Freeport itself was almost a "mini Detroit" for the toy vehicle world. The Arcade name became pre-eminent in the early 1880s, with the production of toy coffee mills and the famous and successful yellow taxi toys. Arcade went on to produce a wide range of toys until World War II and was especially renowned for its cast iron vehicles. This Fageol Safety Coach was produced in four different

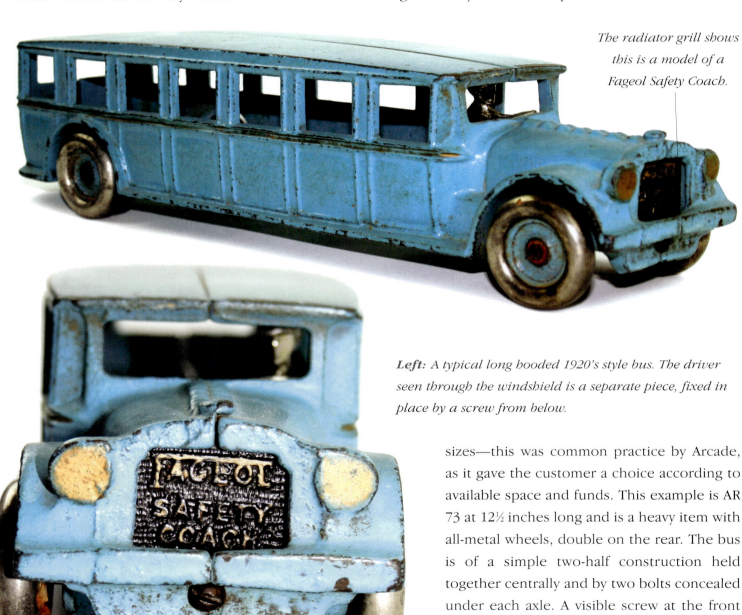

The radiator grill shows this is a model of a Fageol Safety Coach.

Left: *A typical long hooded 1920's style bus. The driver seen through the windshield is a separate piece, fixed in place by a screw from below.*

sizes—this was common practice by Arcade, as it gave the customer a choice according to available space and funds. This example is AR 73 at 12½ inches long and is a heavy item with all-metal wheels, double on the rear. The bus is of a simple two-half construction held together centrally and by two bolts concealed under each axle. A visible screw at the front holds on the radiator and the metal driver is rather "painfully" pinned to his seat by a screw from below.

ARCADE OPEN TOP DOUBLE DECKER

Another, but very different, Arcade bus. This attractive open topper with open rear stairs is typical of the kind of bus that was found on the streets of New York and Chicago from about 1910 to 1925. The double decker bus is commonly associated with Great Britain but many other countries, including the U.S.A., have operated them. Although the early New York and Chicago buses were green, this example is in blue with a gold trim and white all-rubber wheels with matching blue inserts. The construction is again very simple, with two halves, the rear stairs and the upper floor, and cast-in seats.

A rather crude finish to the exposed upper deck.

TRU-MINIATURES THRU-LINER

This Tru-miniatures bus is meant to represent the Flxible VL100 Thru-liner, which Trailways intended to put into operation to rival the super three-axle Scenicruisers of archrival Greyhound in the 1950s. In fact the real bus was never produced in three-axle form, but Flxible (yes, the spelling is correct) did make a two-axle bus, which was used by several other operators. This toy was probably made by Tru-miniatures to be used as a promotional model by Trailways and sold at their bus stations; it came in a lovely printed box that could be used as a toy bus station. It is made from hard plastic with a metal base and rubber tires and is over 17½ inches long. It has a neat revolving destination blind, which can be turned

A three-axle long wheelbase bus to rival the Greyhound Scenicruiser.

Left: The front of the bus shows the Trailways name and the revolving destination blind set to San Francisco.

to show a destination of any one of several major U.S. cities. The rear and side luggage compartment doors open for extra play value. This version is in Trailways red, silver and white livery but the model was also available in simpler color schemes: plain red, with Trailways lettering on the side in gold; plain yellow with red lettering; and white with a red band and lettering. The simpler versions did not have opening doors or a working destination blind.

Above: The more detailed version was perhaps produced as a promotional model, but the real bus was not destined to be seen on U.S. highways

BUDDY L YELLOW COACH

Buddy L toys started as part of the Moline Pressed Steel Company of East Moline, Illinois, in the early 1920s. The company first made automobile parts but the owner, Fred Lundahl, began making a few toys for his son, Arthur "Buddy" Lundahl. The bus shown is a reasonable model of a Yellow Coach 743 in Greyhound livery. It works via a fixed-key clockwork motor and an intricate series of cogs and wheels that make the bus stop and start. To brake, a retarder makes contact with one of the rear wheels and the floor, and as the bus stops a bell rings and a lever opens the door. The door closes again and the bus moves off.

The bus clearly shows the famous
Greyhound logo on each side.

Left: *The front shows it is a
Buddy L, while the rear shows
number X 4071. A battery
powers the red light on the rear.*

Above: *The large rubber
wheels and coiled spring
motor are clearly visible here,
as is the lettering
"Greyhound Lines."*

KEYSTONE GREYHOUND

Keystone Toys of Boston, Massachusetts, produced a wide range of toys from about 1922, using pressed steel and later plastic. A 1928 Butler Brothers' catalog shows a range of trucks, including several fire trucks, a tanker, a locomotive, an ambulance and some army vehicles, and a portly-looking man standing on one of the trucks claims they will support a weight of 200 pounds! A top-of-the-range fire truck could be purchased in 1928 for $8.75, while an army truck with canvas canopy could be rolled away at a mere $4.25.

This Greyhound bus measures 18 inches in length and is from the 1940s. It represents a "Silversides" of the period—the sides on this toy are blue but the all-ridged sides on the real buses were silver aluminum,

hence the term silversides. The Keystone Greyhound has the same operating mechanism and shares similar components with the Kingsbury Greyhound. The Kingsbury represents the earlier Super Coach, but modifications and similarities can be noticed. Keystone assumed production of this bus and several other toys when Kingsbury ceased toy making in the early 1940s.

Extra play value is provided via this opening rear section, allowing a child to drive smaller vehicles inside.

Above: *The tires are rubber and are stamped "Keystone Toys Boston Mass. U.S.A."*

Left: *Study pressed steel construction meant that a small owner could even sit on the toy.*

KINGSBURY GREYHOUND

Kingsbury was named after its owner and founder, Harry T. Kingsbury, who had been in toy making since the late nineteenth century in Keene, New Hampshire. The company is known for its sturdy toys with pressed steel construction and powerful spring motors. Great toys for use in rural or urban play areas, they were big, tough, and even able to take a small owner's weight if they were sat on.

This toy coach is a representation of a Greyhound Super Coach of 1937, with the streamlined paint application of the period. The fixed key is in part of the back axle under the toy, and a brake works on the rear wheels. It has rubber tires, which are stamped "Kingsbury Toys Keene NH U.S.A.," and the wheels have metal hubs. The number shown on the front of the bus is 228.

Above: *The sturdy pressed steel construction would allow for some "rough" treatment from little owners.*

The streamline paint finish is very typical of the real buses of the time.

WOODHAVEN ROBOT BUS

This Robot Bus was made by the Woodhaven Metal Stamping Company Incorporated of Brooklyn, New York. It is an extremely solid toy made of pressed steel, with thick sturdy rubber tires. The front wheels and axle turned by a cog system powered by the motor; a large fixed key on the base is turned to wind up the motor, which is then activated by an on/off switch on the base. The bus moves around in different directions—as it says on the box, it is: "the bus with the mechanical brain." This model was also available in blue with either a silver or brown roof.

Above: A happy and contented driver beside the cash machine for the fares.

The large rubber tires on the wheels, fixed on the rear and moveable on the front for "steering."

Above: Nearly 14 inches long, the bus
seats 44 and stands 22 small
passengers!

BELL PRODUCTS SCENICRUISER

The GMC PD-4501 Scenicruiser was a revolutionary design by Raymond Loewy and its 40-foot length meant that prevailing length restrictions had to be changed. Between 1954 and 1956, 1001 Scenicruisers were made. These new, long wheelbase, 3-axle buses heralded in a new era in parlor coaches, with their seating on two levels: 10 passengers on the lower level and 33 on the upper level. This superb plastic model was produced by Bell Products of St. Louis, Missouri. It is battery-operated, with an on/off switch on the nearside, and a rotating housing on the base with two wheels that cause the bus to change direction at random. The bus is 18 inches in length, and is an excellent representation of the real thing.

Left: The front headlight housing. The bus is battery operated, with two size "D" flashlight batteries in a compartment in the base.

Top right: The destination blind suggests an eastbound service to New York via Chicago.

Above: *The toy has a very realistic appearance—except for the greyhound,*
which is going the wrong way!

GREYHOUND SCENICRUISER

This is another substantial toy, also modeled on the landmark design of the GMC PD-4501 Scenicruiser, and made in Japan in the late 1950s or early 1960s. This version uses a little more license and as a result looks more like a toy, rather than being a good representation of the real thing; this is perhaps fair enough, since it was supposed to be a toy first and foremost. It measures a hefty 16½ inches in length, is made of lithographed tin and is battery operated—the battery compartment is unusually located, in the line

of vision in the roof. There is a round disc on the base with two wheels, which causes the toy to change direction as it moves rather like the one shown on page 36. As an additional feature, the lights on the roof flash as it goes. The toy features interesting lithography—especially on the back window, which shows attractively wrapped packages. It is carrying a guide with a microphone, as seen in the lower level side window below right, so it can be assumed that it is a tour bus and not just a normal service.

Above: The long lines of the Scenicruiser,
and the famous running dog logo.

Note the detailed wheel hubs
and rubber tires.

MADE IN JAPAN

Greyhound

Scenicruiser

SAN FRANCISCO CABLE CAR

This toy is made from fine pressed steel or tinplate and measures just less than 8½ inches. It is a non-motorized push along toy, with a bell on the roof, and sports eight wheels in a double bogie configuration. It is a delightful, fully lithographed version of the often-modeled cable car found on the hilly streets of San Francisco. This example was made by Verona and is marked "US Patent Pending, Made in Japan."

The toy shows car 514 to Powel and Mason Streets in San Francisco, with a full load of particularly happy passengers—soldiers and sailors as well as members of the general public.

Right: The lithographed people on this toy give it a true sense of realism as they travel happily in Car 514 to Powell Street and Mason Street in San Francisco.

ERTL GREYHOUND SILVERSIDER AND SCHOOL BUS

Fred Ertl Senior began making cast metal toys in 1945 in Dubuque, Iowa, and was best known for making toy tractors and other farm machinery. These two toy buses are great representations of the General Motors Corporation PD 3751/4151 "Silversides," which was a common sight on US highways throughout the late 1940s and into the 1950s and can often be spotted in classic movies of the period. The toy was made from cast aluminum in a simple three-part construction, the two sides held together by one bolt and the front end held in place by another. The top toy is in traditional Greyhound livery, with dog logo and Greyhound Lines on each side.

Less often seen today is the school bus version in all yellow with the dog logo covered over by a rectangular piece of metal—this would have saved the costs of a new casting. These toys were, of course, on sale at Greyhound bus stations—in some cases well into the late 1950s. The Ertl Company is still producing toys in Dyersville Iowa.

ARCADE YELLOW COACHES

Another of the many bus toys produced by Arcade is this very prototypical representation of a General Motors' Yellow Coach 743. The real bus was made between 1937 and 1939 and was known as the "Super Coach" because of its luxury standard. It included a high floor to the passenger deck, which prevented the discomfort of protruding wheel arches and also allowed more luggage space underneath. It also sported electric drinking fountains. However, this Arcade toy is made with the usual simple two-half construction, but with a separate polished metal

front and rear. The toy coaches shown here are in the blue and red Coast to Coast versions. The red example is extremely hard to find—the more common livery is the standard Greyhound version with a white roof.

Two of the three color schemes to be found on
this toy. A Greyhound version with the dog logo
and a white roof is the most common.

REALISTIC FLXIBLE CLIPPERS

The Realistic Toy Company was based in Freeport, Illinois, and is sometimes known as The Freeport Manufacturing Company. Illinois was a popular location for toy making, as evidenced by Tootsietoy in Springfield and Arcade in Freeport. In fact Realistic seem to have used some of the original Arcade molds for some of their toys—however unlike Arcade they did not make cast iron models but instead used

Right: Three different liveries on the Clipper. Badger Bus Lines of Wisconsin is one of the most pleasing, advertising Madison to Milwaukee in 1 hour 55 minutes.

Above Simple cast metal toys with a "realistic" look!

aluminum. They produced many excellent bus toys that were sold in bus stations across the U.S.A.

The Flxible Clipper was one of several prototypical bus models that were made by Realistic. The Flxible Company originally built motorcycle sidecars with a flexible connection to the motorcycle, and their name was deliberately misspelled so that it could be copyrighted in 1919. The real bus on which the toy was based was built between 1937 and 1950 and featured a streamlined body. From 1940 most Clippers featured the classic air scoop on the rear of the roof, and the sloping back.

REALISTIC ACF TRAILWAYS

Realistic also produced some good representations of an ACF BRILL IC41. Two versions are shown here: the regular, and more commonly found version with the smooth sides; and the much scarcer silver-sided version. It should be noted that the more common version can be found with either rounded corners to the windows, as is shown here, or with the larger rectangular windows. ACF stood for the American Car and Foundry Company of Philadelphia. In Canada the

IC 41 was made by CCF or Canadian Car and Foundry. The real buses were built between 1945 and 1953, first using gasoline engines by Hall-Scott and then the Cummins under-floor diesel engines. The toys were made at around the same time and were sold in bus station gift shops to enthusiastic young travelers of the day. Play worn examples are sought after today by eager—but usually much older—collectors of toys and model buses.

Above: This model can be found with rounded or rectangular windows.

Above: The Realistic silversides version is very rare.

ARCADE SILVERSIDES

Arcade made their version of the Silversides bus in 1941. The design of the real bus was new then, with its fluted aluminum sides that were to give the style its name. The buses were modeled as toys in the 1940s and early 1950s by Arcade, Ertl and Realistic in the simple cast metal, bolt together style that proved to be both practical to make and durable. In this Arcade example, the use of cast iron makes it much heavier than the light aluminum of the Ertl toy. Other toy manufacturers also copied the Silversides, in pressed steel and in plastic. Arcade made this toy in Greyhound Lines silver/blue with a white roof, but also in the silver and blue version shown here with "Coast to Coast

GMC" on the roof. General Motors Corporation made the real buses with various PD designations, the most famous being the PD-3751 (37 passengers) and PD-4151 (41 passengers) of 1947 and 1948.

Right: A sticker that shows this is "An Arcade Toy" is just discernable on the underside of the bus.

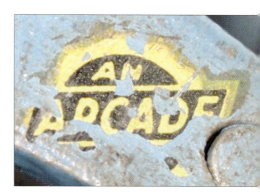

Below: This is the blue-roofed "Coast to Coast" version of the silversides.

GREYHOUND SILVERSIDES BUSES

Here are two more examples of toys modeled on the famous Greyhound Silversides of the immediate post World War II era. The bus shown in the upper photograph was not produced as a child's toy, instead it was intended for the collectors' market. It was made by Streamline and was copied from the Realistic example in the early 1990s. It is made of cast aluminum and was made in extremely small numbers, on a cottage industry scale.

The lower toy is Realistic's attempt at the model. The company probably used the old Arcade mold but the finished product lacks the much finer lines of the Arcade example on page 61, or indeed the superb lines of the Ertl example on page 55.

DUBUQUE TOYS TRAILWAYS BUS

The Dubuque Toy Company, later to be known as Ertl, made this toy in their factory in Dubuque, Iowa. It follows a whole line of toy buses, made by various manufacturers to this size of around 9 inches long. For the present-day collector of toy and model buses, this provides an opportunity to make a great shelf display featuring buses from the 1930s to the 1950s.

This toy probably represents the GMC PD-4103 of 1951. It has fluted silversides, which were becoming a regular feature in bus styling. Over 1,500 of the real buses were made for Greyhound, Trailways and other operators. This toy example was made in at least four liveries, for Trailways, Jefferson Lines, American and Greyhound, and was sold in the operators' gift outlets.

Above: Note the more sloping front end on this bus, compared to the Silversides on page 62.

Right: The words "National Trailways Bus System" are featured within an outline map of the U.S.A.. The paintwork on this model is quite play worn.

TRAILWAYS BUSES

This page features two fine toy buses in the National Trailways livery of red and cream. Both buses are meant to represent prototypes of the American Car and Foundry Company (ACF). The first bus is an Arcade toy with the trademark map of the U.S.A. on the sides. It represents an ACF Brill H9P of 1937 and this model was also made by Arcade in the colors of Greyhound and Santa Fe Trailways. It is a highly sought after toy bus today, in any of the colors.

The second toy bus is by National Products, who generally produced promotional models of cars. It represents an ACF Brill IC41 and is similar to the Realistic toy on page 60, except this one is a money bank with filled in windows, a coin slot in the roof, and a removable stopper on the base to extract the money.

Below: Arcade ACF Brill H9P, in National Trailways livery. Both buses on this page are around 9 inches long, although Arcade also produced a smaller version around this time.

LONG HOOD BUSES

This page features three toy buses with distinctive long hoods. The first two photographs show the Arcade GMC Yellow Coach in Greyhound "Coast to Coast" colors of blue and white, and a second one in green and gold. Both buses have "Greyhound Lines" printed on the roof, but green livery for a Greyhound seems unusual. The real bus was also made in all blue and all red. The sloping back and slightly more rounded lines mark a departure from the rectangular styling of the early to mid 1920s.

The bottom photograph shows what is probably a Kenton Toys of Ohio generic 1920's bus in light blue.

Left: The rectangular styling on the bottom bus contrasts with the more rounded design of the other two, which dates from the late 1920s or early 1930s.

COMMEMORATIVE BUSES

Arcade produced several toy buses to commemorate special occasions and events, including the Chicago Fair in 1934, The Great Lakes Exposition in 1936 and The Texas Centennial 1836 to 1936, as well as the two buses shown here.

The 1933 fair in Chicago, to celebrate "A Century of Progress," is depicted on the lower tractor/trailer bus. Real vehicles like this were used to move visitors from car parks to fair exhibits, just like modern day "people movers" operate in theme parks such as Disneyland and Disneyworld. The toy was made in as many as five different sizes, ranging from 14½ to 5½ inches,

providing an affordable souvenir to fit the pocket money budget of most visiting children. All but the smallest size featured a detachable tractor unit. The example shown here is the second largest 12-inch toy. The large sales of this item probably saved Arcade from going bankrupt in the Depression of the early 1930s. Arcade also produced a bus that looked more like a trolley car to celebrate the 1939 New York World's Fair. Real buses like this have been reproduced today to operate Downtown City Tours in many parts of the U.S.A. The Arcade toy was offered in three sizes, ranging from 7 to 10½ inches—the smallest is shown.

Below: The 1939 New York World's Fair bus, with imitation trolley poles.

Above: The 1933 Chicago "A Century of Progress" people mover.

TWO CONTRASTING TOY BUSES

This page features a pair of very different toy buses, although they are similar in size and at first glance mainly because of the long hood. The red and cream bus is a French Citroën, as evidenced by the famous double chevron on the radiator grill. However, it was probably manufactured in Portugal by an unknown maker. It is made very crudely from tinplate and has several sharp edges and a rough, unsophisticated paint finish, although it does have a clockwork motor with a fixed key. The bus is 7½ inches long.

The blue bus is a model of a late 1920s/early 1930s streamlined bus, made by Metalmasters in the U.S.A. It is die-cast metal in a simple one-piece casting, without a base plate and with thin plastic wheels and two axles. This example is 7¼ inches long, but it was also made in a larger size and came in a choice of red, green or blue.

Below: The rather crudely made Portuguese tinplate toy bus.

Above: A Metalmasters, U.S.A., die-cast, streamlined bus.

WOLVERINE BUS

Wolverine was founded in 1903 in Pittsburgh, Pennsylvania, by B.F. Bain, who was from Wolverine, Michigan—hence the name. Wolverine patented a unique drive mechanism for some of their toys, the "Mystery Motor." It involved a spring, cog and double fly wheel operation, activated by pressing down on the back of the roof. This caused the back axle to move up about ¼ of an inch, activating the motor and moving the toy along a few feet. The space needed above the back axle can clearly be seen in the side of this bus. The toy is made of hollow, thin pressed steel or tinplate, without a base, with wooden wheels.

Above: The streamlined lithography is accentuated on the rear of the bus. The license plate suggests that the bus may have been made in 1950.

SPEEDAWAY BUS

Wolverine produced several different designs on their basic tin pressings incorporating the "Mystery Motor" system—this is the "Speedaway Bus." It says "Press Down Here" on the back of the roof. The lithography is in red, blue and white, depicting happy-looking passengers. Although the same toy as the one opposite, this looks somewhat different mainly because of the lithography.

The same pressing was produced as the Jackie Gleason "Aw-a-y We Go" "Honeymooners" special in blue, red and white, with Jackie at the wheel. This version is highly sought after by collectors of toy buses and collectors of film related ephemera. Another version is a military transport bus in cream, green and khaki with "U.S.A. Transport" on the sides. It also appears as a suburban bus in green, red and white.

Above: Note the space above the back axle for the motor to operate.

Below: This bus runs along Main Street, U.S.A.

RING-A-LONG BUS

This bus was also made by Wolverine, but is different from those featured earlier. It is a representation of a city bus of the 1930s or 1940s—or even earlier—and was clearly made before the "Mystery Motor," although it is again made of tin with wooden wheels and a pull cord. When pulled along a bell rings, so although the bus has no motor the bell motivates the child to pull it along to hear the ringing. A tin base conceals the bell. The toy, although simple in concept and construction, is charming and has tremendous appeal. The

lithography is smart in red, black and white, with period passengers that emphasize the importance of hats to both men and women in those days. The wooden wheels are concealed by the body, since the pressing does not have cutout wheel arches, but an impression of wheels is depicted in the lithography.

Right and far right: The No. 161 runs along Main Street. The rear shows "Wolverine made in U.S.A." with a diamond-shaped panel.

TUDOR ROSE SCENICRUISER

This is a model of the GMC PD-4501 Greyhound Scenicruiser of 1954. The Scenicruiser is evocative of classic American bus design and has been modeled by many toy and model manufactures over the years—some of these are scale models and others, like this one, are simple toys.

Tudor Rose, as the name implies, was an English company that manufactured simple and cheap molded plastic toys during the 1950s and early 1960s. They made a number of buses, as well as other vehicles such as a taxi and a jeep. This bus is one of the firm's largest items, since it is 20 inches long. It has a gyro motor powering the rear axle and consists of three pieces of plastic—bottom, top, and interior—plus the wheels, axles and a motor. The bus has a detachable top section, which enables a young operative to place toy passengers on the seats, and comes with a destination blind showing "San Francisco." The underneath of the bus carries two maker's marks. One shows a picture of the Tudor rose with "Tudor Rose Plastic Products" stamped around it, the other says, "This is a Tudor Rose design." While other Tudor Rose toys are not uncommon today, examples of this large Scenicruiser are difficult to find.

Below: The impressive one-and-a-half decker lines of the Scenicruiser look even more imposing on this large toy.

Above and right: *Note the double rear axle,*
allowing for extra length and weight.

CRAGSTAN BEEP BEEP GREYHOUND BUS

This toy is probably based on the GMC PD-4104 Highway Traveler, built by General Motors between 1953 and 1960. It has the same picture windows and the silversiding—which was by then almost a bus industry standard. This was one of the first buses to have the sloping window pillars, which became an industry standard for years to come. Over 5,000 of the real buses were made so it is not surprising that it was reproduced in toy form.

Made in Japan and marketed under the famous Cragstan name, this bus is 20¼ inches in length, and beautifully made in shining pressed steel with tasteful lithography. It is operated by battery, housed in a compartment in the base that has an on/off switch. The bus makes a "beep beep" noise as it moves.

Below left: *Note the etching to highlight the windows.*

Left: Happy passengers, and interesting packages on the rear window shelf. Note that the seating is arranged along the bus so that passengers face each other.

LINCOLN BUS AND STREETCAR

These are hard plastic toys with steel bases, made in the U.S.A. by Lincoln, and are generic in outline so they do not really represent any particular prototype. The same body molding was used for both the bus and the streetcar, but the wheel arches were cut out for the bus. The streetcar is missing its pole on this example and has metal wheels with rubber inserts. The bus has all rubber wheels with metal hubs. The bus is operated by remote control from a handset containing the battery, while the streetcar is push-along and not remote control. The streetcar carries advertisements for Curtiss Baby Ruth candy and Wrigley's spearmint gum. Both toys are 14 inches long. They were probably made in the late 1940s/early 1950s and are difficult to find today on the collectors' market.

Below: The same body molding is used for both streetcar and bus.

The remote control handset contains the battery that operates the bus.

Above: This view of the remote control handset clearly shows the main control knob.

Below: The bus has cut out wheel arches and is battery-operated via a remote control handset.

TIPPCO BUSES

The firm of Tipp and Company, also known as Tippco or TCO, was founded in Germany by Philip Ullman. The company produced a range of automotive toys in fine tinplate, with smart lithography and the typical lining out detail of the period. Ullman fled the Nazis in the 1930s and set up the Mettoy Company in England and in the 1950s Mettoy took on the famous Corgi name. Tippco continued after the departure of Ullman and continued producing fine toys well into the 1950s, including a wide range of buses.

The buses featured here are from the 1920s and are generic representations of typical hooded buses of the period, with their familiar angular appearance. They both measure 10¼ inches long and feature clockwork motors with a fixed key. The brown example has a sliding roof section and "spoked" wheels, with "Dunlop Cord 905 x 130" on the tin tires. The red and blue bus has thinner tin wheels, with "Balloon Tires 6 x 24" marked on them. Both buses carry finely detailed lithography, with beautiful lining out. It is also possible to pose the wheels on a lock, which enables the toy to move around in a circle or simply allows the modern-day collector to make a more realistic and interesting display on the shelf.

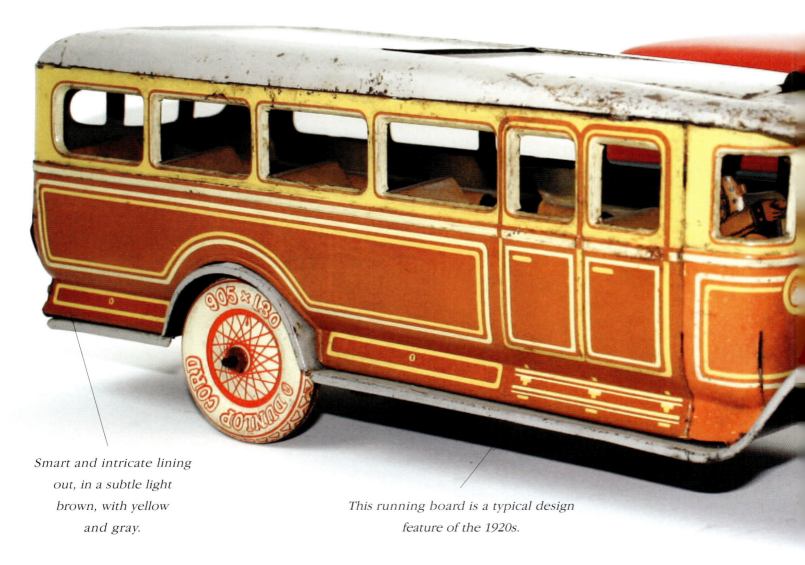

Smart and intricate lining out, in a subtle light brown, with yellow and gray.

This running board is a typical design feature of the 1920s.

Above: Note the "spoked wheels" and tire detail showing "Dunlop Cord 905 x 130."

Above and left: Spot the differences on the same basic toy: different wheels and a roof that is either plain or has a sliding section.

GUNTHERMANN LONDON BUS

This toy was made circa 1930 by the renowned German toy company, S.G. Gunthermann of Nuremburg. They produced a wide range of quality automotive toys and this bus was made in several sizes and modifications. The example pictured here is the largest and most imposing at 19½ inches long, and features a strong clockwork motor with a fixed key and electric front headlamps. Made essentially for the British market, it is finished in authentic pre-1933 London General livery of red and cream, with intricate black lining and represents the LS type of three-axle double deckers that were operating at the time. This would have been an expensive toy then, with most children having to be content with a smaller version.

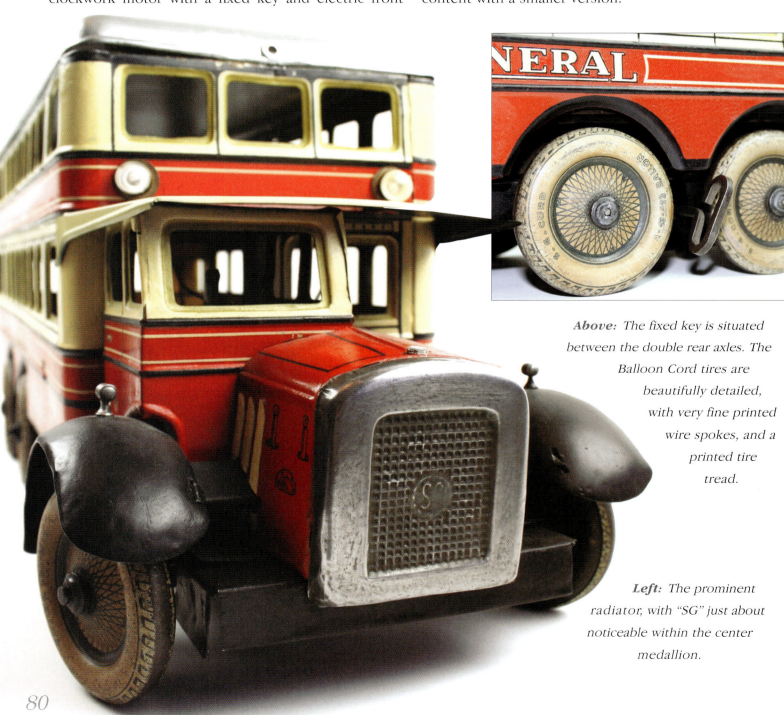

Above: The fixed key is situated between the double rear axles. The Balloon Cord tires are beautifully detailed, with very fine printed wire spokes, and a printed tire tread.

Left: The prominent radiator, with "SG" just about noticeable within the center medallion.

This is the control lever to operate the electric front lights.

Above: Note the distinctive lined out General livery of the period.

BISCUIT TIN BUSES

These toys were made by the Chad Valley Company of Harborne, Birmingham, England. They made a wide range of toys and games and the name is still going today, having been bought by Woolworth's several years ago. These buses are made from pressed metal—the green one is steel and the red one a much lighter alloy. The red tin was a promotional tool for Carr's Biscuits of Carlisle, England, and was sold full of water biscuits, which are crackers to eat with cheese. Both have lift off lids and after the crackers were finished the tin could be used as a toy, since it came complete with clockwork motor. Both are an excellent representation of an AEC STL type bus, as operated from the 1930s through to the early 1950s on the streets of London. The red bus is in London Transport colors and the green one in Greenline colors of the time. Both are 10 inches long and carry much detail for an item that was made firstly as a tin and secondly as a toy.

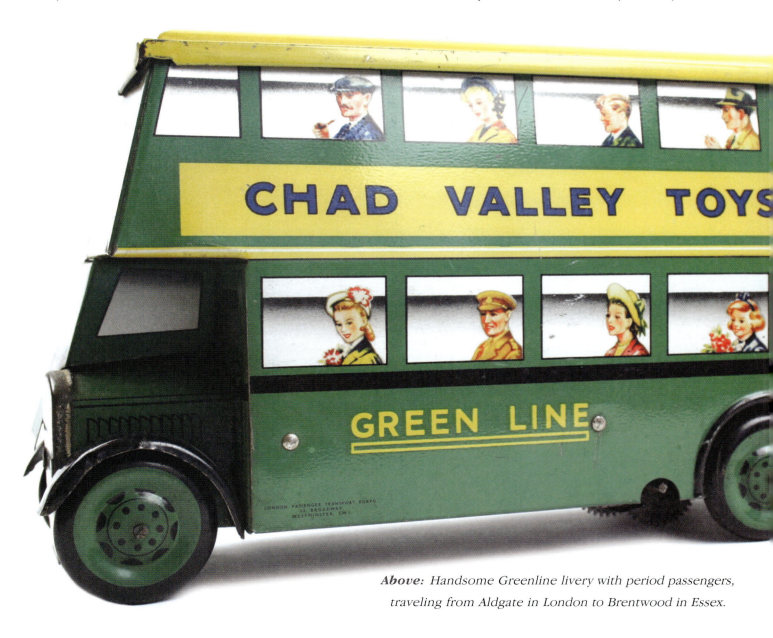

Above: *Handsome Greenline livery with period passengers, traveling from Aldgate in London to Brentwood in Essex.*

Right: The "Queen" is the Queen Consort of George VI; the toy pre-dates the coronation of Elizabeth II.

MG PARIS BUS

This is a fine model of a typical Paris service bus, made by MG of France in tinplate and with a clockwork motor. The open back was a feature on buses in the French capital, right up until the early 1970s—passengers entered and exited the main saloon via the rear. Numerous toy versions of these prototypes have been produced by firms such as CR, JEP and CIJ, in a wide range of sizes. This MG example was probably made as late as the early 1950s, and unlike most Paris bus toys features lithographed windows. It is 10½ inches long and shows route detail for Etoile, Concorde, Opera and Bastille. It is a good representation of a Renault TN4 and came in a fairly plain but smart fawn box, with the route lined out on the side. On the collectors' market, the existence of an original box greatly enhances the value of a toy, but it must be remembered that many of the early toys, especially the much cheaper die-cast models, were sold direct out of a tray and therefore never had a box.

Left: The destination blind shows that this bus is traveling route 115 to Etoile.

Above: Note the open rear boarding platform, which typifies Paris buses of the period.

Above: *The characteristic Paris colors of green and cream.*

Above: *The long hood of a Renault TN4 and the open sided driver's cab.*

STRAUSS INTERSTATE BUS

Ferdinand Strauss began making toys around the time of World War I, and his factory was located in East Rutherford, New Jersey. He was known as the "Toy King" and was a key entrepreneur in promoting the manufacture of mechanical toys in the U.S.A. Louis Marx worked for him in the early days, before breaking away to form his own company. Strauss probably encountered financial difficulties in the late 1920s as he seems to have disappeared from the scene for a time, but he then came back to the industry until the early 1940s.

This open top bus was made in the 1920s and is a generic representation of a New York double decker of the time. It measures 10½ inches in length, has a clockwork motor and the steering can be altered to make it go in a circle or turn a corner. It is called an "Interstate Bus," which was its trademark, although it is hard to imagine a real bus like this traveling between states. The toy has a fairly large-looking tin driver in a smart brown uniform. Most of these buses are found in this attractive green color, probably representing New York, but a hard-to-find variation exists in light brown.

Above: The side markings stress that "Interstate Bus" is a trademark.

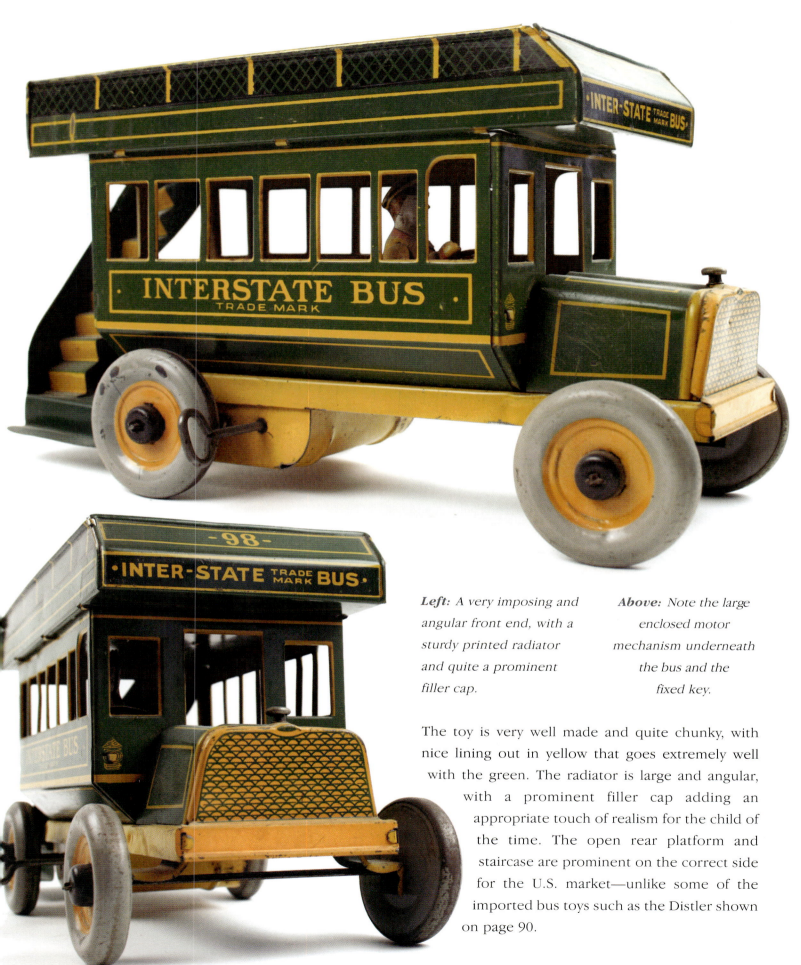

Left: *A very imposing and angular front end, with a sturdy printed radiator and quite a prominent filler cap.*

Above: *Note the large enclosed motor mechanism underneath the bus and the fixed key.*

The toy is very well made and quite chunky, with nice lining out in yellow that goes extremely well with the green. The radiator is large and angular, with a prominent filler cap adding an appropriate touch of realism for the child of the time. The open rear platform and staircase are prominent on the correct side for the U.S. market—unlike some of the imported bus toys such as the Distler shown on page 90.

STRAUSS BUS DELUXE

This is another fine toy bus made by the Ferdinand Strauss Company. It is 12½ inches long with the same type of clockwork motor as the "Interstate Bus," as well as other similar features such as the radiator, filler cap and driver. This model is called a "Bus Deluxe" and has curtains to shade passengers from the sun featured as an integral part of the tin pressing. One of the most attractive parts of this bus is the rear, with its twin oval windows and the Strauss globe trademark. It was made in 1927 in this very American Greyhound-style blue livery and has the hood and angular appearance of the period. As with the "Interstate Bus" on the previous pages, the steering on this model can be adjusted to make it go around a circle.

Above: *The familiar Strauss large radiator with filler cap. The inset (above left) shows the Strauss trademark.*

Above: Note the curtains to keep the passengers shaded from the sun.

Right: Stylish twin oval windows at the rear of the bus, with the Strauss brand name and trademark on the bodywork below.

BICO "FARES PLEASE" BUS

This colorful open topper was made by Johan Distler of Germany and marketed in the U.S.A. as a Bico toy; the same toy was marketed in Great Britain by Distler in red. It was probably made around 1920, but may have pre-dated World War I. This is a well proportioned toy, made of fine tinplate and measuring 8⅓ inches long. It represents a typical open topper of the period, except of course that in the U.S.A. the staircase and entrance would have been on the other side. At that time, even in countries driving on the right, buses were sometimes right-hand drive so that the driver could make sure that the passengers were safely loaded before driving off. The selling point for this toy was the conductor, who fits in a groove on the upper deck floor and moves up and down

collecting the "fares please." He works off the clockwork motor, so as the bus moves along, so does the conductor. Sadly, on this well played-with example he has gone missing (or is having a well earned rest on the lower deck). A few of the tin passengers on the upper deck also appear to be missing—you can see the empty slots in the seats. The wheels are set on a left hand lock making the bus move around in a circle.

Above: *Seated tin passengers and the groove in which the conductor would have moved up and down collecting the fares.*

Right: *There should be a small canopy over the driver's cab.*

Fixed-position wheels make the bus move in a circle.

Note the protruding fixed key. The large tin wheels are red with white tires.

The destination is shown on both sides and the front!

Above: A smart green and yellow color scheme, with black and green lining.

JOUSTRA TROLLEY BUSES

The electric trolley bus is a clean and cheap form of urban transport. It became popular across the world from the 1920s to the 1960s and is still found in parts of North America, Europe and Asia. It is therefore not surprising that toy makers decided to produce their own versions. Joustra of France made a range of colorful tinplate toy trolley buses in various sizes and two of them are featured here. The 3-axle, or 6-wheeler, was made in a number of variations from the early 1950s. It measures 11½ inches long and has opening doors and a clockwork motor. Early versions were plain with pressed headlights and unlined color schemes, such as blue and red, red and yellow, blue and yellow, or green and cream. Later ones, such as those pictured here, have electric headlights, roof boards, modified poles and a smarter, lined out finish. The 2-axle bus is late 1950s and models a Vetra trolley bus of the period in Paris colors of green and cream. It measures 14½ inches and is the rare "Beaumont" version. This model was also made without advertising, and in red and cream—Lyon colors—proclaiming "Mon Jouet Favori."

Below: A green 3-axle trolley bus with electric lights.

Right: This model was also made in green and cream without advertising, and red and cream.

Above: *Note the later front on this example, although the bulbs are missing from the headlights.*

CR TROLLEY BUSES

These buses were made by CR (Charles Rossignol) of France, who made a wide range of toy Paris buses from the 1920s to the early 1960s, as well as other toys dating back to the late 1800s. These tinplate trolley buses measure 10½ inches in length. The lower picture shows an early version, with tin wheels and clockwork motor. The upper picture is the later version, with rubber tires, modified radiator and electric lights.

Below: This later version has electric lights.

Above: An earlier version with tin wheels.

MINIC SINGLE DECKERS

Tri-ang Minic toys were made in England by Lines Brothers at the Tri-ang Works, Merton, South London, from 1935 to the early 1960s. The company offered a wide range of vehicles in strong pressed steel or plastic and die-cast ships. These buses represent a range that ran from 1935 to the late 1950s/early 1960s, varying only in color, single or double deck and radiator grill. The toys were dipped in paint and baked at high temperature for a durable finish. These examples look similar at first sight, but are very different. The maroon and stone version is pre-World War II and features

large hubbed tin wheels. The two-tone green one is a post-war New Zealand production with cast wheels fitted the wrong way round. In the 1950s parts were shipped to New Zealand CKD (Completely Knocked Down) and assembled there—this was a practice also employed by the makers of real cars.

Right: A pre-war maroon and stone single decker to Dorking.

Above: New Zealand-made toys appeared in different colors to the English versions.

MINIC DOUBLE DECKERS

These double deckers appeared in a range of colors over the years. Pre-war they were either maroon and stone or two-tone green, but post-war bright red buses tended to mirror current changes in real London transport buses. Early advertisements were for real drinks products, Bovril and Ovaltine, later ones were for "in house" Tri-ang products. In later years the clockwork motor was superseded by a friction motor, and a blue and cream and a red/cream/gray double decker appeared as well as a red Routemaster version.

Right: The destinations shown were real places in London

Above: This early 1950's version has cream around the upper windows.

Above: Pre-war green version of the No. 177 to Mitcham The Cricketers public house.

Below: The pre-war maroon and stone version.

MOTORIZED TROLLEY BUSES

All these trolley buses are to a scale of 1:87, or HO scale, and are compatible with electric trains of the same scale. The buses are fitted with electric motors within their bodies and take power from overhead wires, just like the real thing. The wires are set up and connected by vertical poles standing on the floor, and the current is passed through the wires and picked up by the poles or booms on the roof of the bus. The system is operated via a controller just like a train set. The buses illustrated were made by Rivarossi of Italy, Eheim (later Brawa) of Germany and Silvine of Japan. The last two were also marketed in the U.S.A. by Aristocraft. The 3-axle Rivarossi is a good model of an Alfa Romeo trolley bus as seen in various Italian cities in the 1950s. The 3-axle Eheim is a model of a Henschel, complete with luggage trailer. The 2-axle Ehiem in blue is a Bussing and also came with a color-matching trailer. Both Eheims were also made in red, green or yellow with cream. The articulated bus is also made by Eheim/Brawa, and is a Henschel in the hard-to-find blue and orange of the German city of Kaiserslauten. This "bendy bus" also comes in red, green, blue or yellow with cream. The Japanese Silvine is a generic bus, for the American market.

Above: This Italian 3-axle bus also comes in red/silver, green/silver and yellow/brown.

Left: There are also some other rarer color versions of this Eheim, such as gray/white and all white with a red band.

Above: *The 3-axle Eheim trolley bus has a luggage trailer. The articulated bus below is also an Eheim.*

Right: *Note the connection of the poles to the body.*

Left: *The Japanese Silvine with its heavily riveted sides is a generic bus, for the American market. The Ehiem to the right also comes with a matching trailer.*

SOUTH STREET

2133

TOM FIELDS LTD. BUBBLE BUS

This is an example of clever marketing by Tom Fields, since the packaging for the product is attractive to the consumer and also has a secondary use as a toy. In this case the product is a bubble bath made to attract the young consumer not only to bathe using special bubble crystals, but also to play with the box. The bus is a generic 1950's bus in an attractive blue and white color scheme, measuring 10 inches in length. It is made of cardboard and has red wooden wheels to give the whole thing some rigidity and more lasting play value. The top lifts off, initially to reveal a package of bubble bath salts, but when these are all used up the young person can load the bus full of anything from miniature people to sweets—or it could even be used as a pencil case. Imagination is at the heart of young people's play!

The Tom Fields company name is prominent.

Left: *A generic front-end appearance to the bus and a driver with an extremely determined expression: "Get me to the bath on time!"*

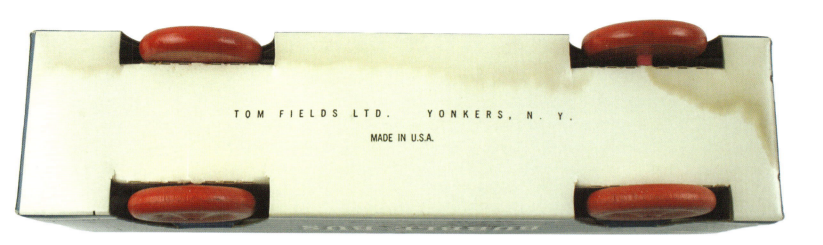

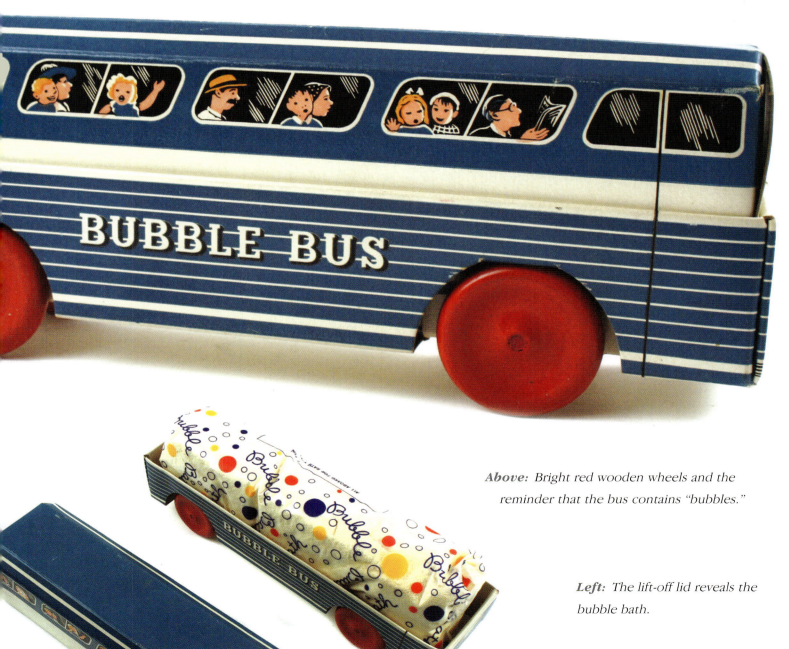

TOM FIELDS LTD.   YONKERS, N. Y.

MADE IN U.S.A.

BUBBLE BUS

Above: Bright red wooden wheels and the reminder that the bus contains "bubbles."

Left: The lift-off lid reveals the bubble bath.

MARX BUS TERMINAL

This charming tinplate bus station is by Louis Marx and was made in the late 1930s. It measures 12 inches in length and features fine lithographed detail, showing phone booths, restaurant, clock and many destinations across the U.S.A. This example is missing some gas pumps, but is still evocative of the period and brimming with charm and has tremendous play value. Marx also made a larger bus terminal in 1938, which measured 16 inches long. Both terminals carried the Greyhound logo and as such must have been good advertising for that operator. These terminals are not easy to find on the collectors' market, but would make a good display center for any toy or model bus collection. They now provide stimulation for the imagination of the collector, just as they did for the young people of their time.

The buses also featured did not come with the terminal, but suit it quite well. The red bus is a Tootsietoy Fageol from 1927, the blue one is a more recent copy of the same bus by Accucast, and the green one is an Overland bus by Tootsietoy from the late 1920s/early 1930s.

Below: This tin bus station has plenty of room for several toy buses, but Marx also made a larger version 4 inches longer. Both types are difficult to find these days.

Above: *The trademark of Louis Marx, with "Made in U.S.A."*

Right: *The bus station features good details, with phone booths, restaurant, clock and destinations across the U.S.A.*

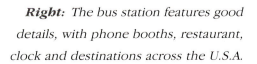

TIPPCO "DEL MONTE" BUS

This beautiful toy was made in Germany by Tipp and Company around 1934. It is constructed in fine tinplate with a clockwork motor and a fixed key, and the lithography is superb with many advertisements for real products. The near side features DEL MONTE Quality Canned Fruits—interestingly, the same logo and advert continue to this day, with the fruit company still emphasizing the excellent quality of their product. The off side encourages the drinking of Wincarnis Tonic Wine, with the "get fit, keep fit" adage. However, perhaps the most impressive use of advertising is at the back where, just like on the real buses of the time, the rear staircase carries a sweeping ad for Dunlop

tires. Also promoted are BP Petrol with a colorful Union Jack, the *Sporting Life*—a British newspaper predominantly about horse racing—and the *Daily Mirror*, a British national newspaper. The bus is a very good model of a real London NS type of the 1920s, and it carries the license number YN 1141 and bus number NS 2126.

Below: The advertisement for "DEL MONTE Quality Canned Fruits" on one side of the bus. The toy measures 10 inches in length overall.

The other side features Wincarnis Tonic Wine.

Superb advertising
on the rear for
Dunlop, BP, and
the Sporting Life
and the
Daily Mirror
newspapers.

DAIYA SCHOOL BUS

Buses taking children to school can be found in many countries of the world. In some countries the buses are regular service buses on a school contract only at the beginning and end of the school day, or older buses or coaches that take tourists for the main part of the day and children at school times. In the United Kingdom double deckers are often seen transporting masses of

Below: The Daiya trademark, with the maker's name inside a diamond shape.

children to and from school. In the U.S.A. and Canada the special yellow school bus is part of the culture, and as such a host of toy school buses have been churned out over the years to mirror real life. These buses are often owned or leased by the school district and are kept and maintained in the district depot.

This particular toy does not represent any particular bus model, but is very typical of the traditional school bus as seen on American streets over the years. It is made in Japan by Daiya from pressed steel, and

This generic toy typifies the classic American school bus.

Left: *A timely reminder on the rear of the vehicle that it is unlawful to pass a stopped school bus. The on/off switch can just be seen, under the center of the rear bumper.*

measures 13½ inches in length. The toy is battery driven via a compartment in the base, and operated from an on/off switch that is concealed under the rear bumper. The front wheels can be manually turned to enable the toy to move in a circle, which also allows it to be posed attractively in a display.

TIN SCHOOL BUS TOYS

These three simple school bus toys would have been very inexpensive when on sale in the 1970s/early 1980s and they are at the lower end of the market when it comes to play value and authentic representation. The 3-axle toy is probably the most authentic, looking like a Crown school bus as often seen in California in both 2- and 3-axle form in the 1970s and 1980s. The Crown company was founded in 1904 and produced an integral school bus in 1932. They enjoyed a reputation for quality and longevity of product. This toy measures 7 inches long and has friction drive, rubber tires and chrome hubs.

The one-and-a-half deck toy looks least like a school bus. It is just over 7 inches long and has charming lithography showing happy children and a rather too contented-looking driver! The creatures on the sides suggest the toy was meant for younger children. It also has friction drive, rubber tires and chrome hubs.

The third toy is a generic full front bus, measuring just over 6½ inches long with friction drive and basic plastic wheels. All three toys were made in Japan by unknown manufacturers and are made of tin plate.

Above: An interesting school bus toy, with creatures on the sides.

Above left: *La rge rear lights and a firm reminder that this is a "School Bus."*

Above right: *A contented driver—indicating well-behaved children on this school journey!*

SIKU SCHOOL BUS

This is a current school bus toy made in Germany by Siku. It is just less than 8 inches long and is made of die-cast metal, with a plastic base and other parts. Siku have been in business since the 1920s and became famous for a range of plastic toys in the 1950s. The company turned to die-cast metal in 1963 and currently manufacture a fine range of toy vehicles, including this very traditional yellow school bus.

The hood lifts forward to reveal the engine compartment and the octagonal "Stop" sign on the side can be rotated out when the bus is stationary. The wheel hubs are nicely detailed and the tires are made from rubber; the bus features double rear wheels. The only real flaw is on the rear of the vehicle, where a sign reads "STOP WHEN LIGHT FLASH"—which does not sound quite right!

This is a traditional hooded school bus design, with good rear view mirrors and windshield wipers.

SCALE MODELS SCHOOL BUS

This is a simple and chunky school bus toy made by Scale Models in Dyersville, Iowa. The company was founded by one of the Ertl brothers as an independent company making toys—and of course, in particular, farm toys. This bus is made from die-cast metal with a steel base, and is similar to the Hubley Gabriel "Mighty Metal" school bus from the 1970s. It is quite crude and lacking in detail, but is certainly tough and capable of handling some rough play down on the farm or on the city streets.

Scale Models tended to make promotional toys and models and this bus could easily be decorated with the local school district's name for use as a shelf piece, or even for a sales person to give out when taking orders for the real thing. This bus carries the name of the Decorah Community School District in North East Iowa.

Below: *Another toy of traditional school bus design, made for the Decorah Community School District.*

TIN SCHOOL BUS

Left: These children must be homeward bound, as they look far too happy to be heading to school. One is even dressed as a cowboy!

This is another tinplate school bus made in Japan by an unknown manufacturer. It is 11¼ inches long and has friction drive to the rear wheels. On the rear is marked the usual safety warning, but in a somewhat strange wording: "DO NOT PASS WHEN SCHOOL BUS IS DISCHARGING CHILDREN." It reads rather as if a surgical plaster is needed to stem the flow!

KEYSTONE PLASTIC BUS

This hard plastic bus was made by Keystone of Boston, Massachusetts, in the 1950s. Keystone had been making pressed steel toys, before going over to plastic after 1945. This bus is just over 7¼ inches long with opening passenger and rear compartment doors and a revolving destination blind. These buses were made in blue/white, white/blue, red/white and white/red, and two different-sized composite board bus terminals were also available with them. The plastic is prone to warping, giving the toy a curved banana shape.

Above: Much of the charm of this toy is in the driver and passengers, who are printed on a strip of cellophane placed across the windows.

Right: The simple revolving destination blind shows many major U.S. cities. Both the passenger door and the rear compartment door can be opened.

HARD PLASTIC TOY BUSES

Hard plastic toys were very popular through the late 1940s/1950s—they were cheap, simple and made in bright, appealing colors. A vast range of toy vehicles was available from many different U.S.A. manufacturers and these toy buses represent products from some major firms. The small photograph shows six buses, from left to right: a "Marx Inter-City Bus Lines" in red, measuring just over 5½ inches, with a friction motor, two large rubber rear wheels and two small plastic

Above: The Hollywood Bus Lines toy in red and green.
It came in a range of color combinations.

Below: The Hollywood Bus Lines toy in blue and yellow. Collectors try to obtain all the variations.

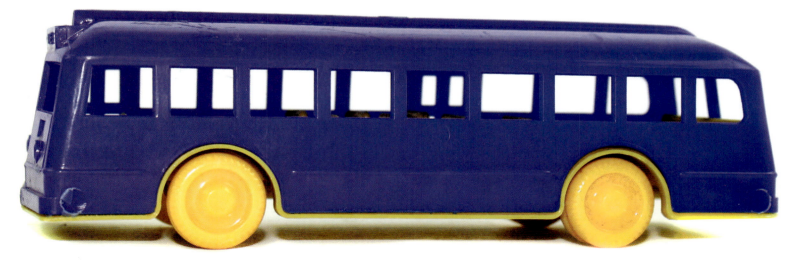

Above: *The Nosco bus has a plastic clockwork motor.*

Below: *The Reliable bus features rubber tires and a clockwork motor.*

front ones; a blue push along airport bus made by Superior, measuring 4¾ inches; a yellow Nosco Plastics bus measuring 4 inches, with a wind-up motor; a push along Renwall "Citybus" measuring 4½ inches; a push along Renwall school bus the same size; and a push along Wannatoy city bus in green and yellow, at 5½ inches. All were available in a range of colors, and the Marx and Renwall City Bus were previously made in metal. The Hollywood Toy Company made their bus 6 inches long and in a mix of two colors. The red and silver bus is by Reliable of Canada and is 6¼ inches long; it has a clockwork motor and rubber tires.

Y TOYS AVENUE BUSES

Y Toys is another name for Yonezawa of Japan, who made a wide range of toy vehicles in tinplate and in die-cast metal. They made numerous toy buses, as did most Japanese toy manufactures. In fact the Japanese still produce many toy and model buses today, to mirror the real buses on the city streets of the twenty-first century. As with most toy production, these toys are now usually made in China under the name of the commissioning company.

These "Avenue Buses" were made in the late 1950s or early 1960s, from tinplate. They carry the Y Toys symbol on the front and have the Y trademark stamped on the rear, with "Made in Japan." Both buses are the same, but in different colors, and are 9¼ inches long with friction motors powering the rear wheels. They have rubber tires and plated metal hubs and carry the number NS5420 on the rear. These are attractive and simple toy buses, but are spoilt by poor metal pressing on the curve of the rear roofline, where

Below: A prominent Y Toys symbol on the front, and a Broadway destination. The roof features two opening ventilators, one at the front and one at the rear.

the metal has crumpled during the manufacturing process. This is very unusual for Japanese-made products, which are normally associated with excellent quality. However, it is quite a minor defect and is

Below: This version goes to 57th Street. Both buses are made of tinplate and have rubber tires.

compensated for by the presence of two opening ventilators on the roof. The green bus featured here has a Broadway destination and the red one is going to 57th Street. It is not at all uncommon for Japanese interpretations of U.S.-style buses to be called "Avenue Bus" and several others were also produced during the 1960s.

CHAD VALLEY SINGLE DECK BUS

The Chad Valley Company of Harborne, Birmingham, England, made a wide range of toys and games in a variety of materials: tinplate and die-cast metal for vehicles; cloth for teddy bears and dolls; card for board games; wood for baby toys. This bus is tinplate and is 12 inches long, with a clockwork motor and fixed key. It is in the colors of Greenline, which operated long distance coach services across London—many bus toys have been produced in these colors over the years. A pleasing feature of this toy is the lithographed passengers and driver; it depicts the trends of the time, with all the adults wearing hats—even the little girl has her hair dressed with a ribbon. This pressing was inherited by Chad Valley from Burnett, who made a similar bus pre-1939 but with punched out windows. Chad Valley also made an open window version in heavier pressed steel and in red/white and blue/cream, before making this lithographed toy in an authentic livery. It was also made in the red and cream of Midland Red, and blue and cream with Chad Valley on the sides.

Above: Period lithography nearly always shows at least one person smoking, making the habit legitimate for the children of the time.

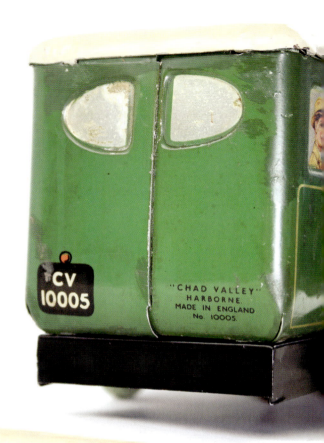

Right: *A split oval rear window, the Chad Valley brand name, and the CV license plate with the toy number. The rear also has a rather over-prominent join in the pressing.*

TINPLATE TROLLEY BUSES

The trolley bus, powered by electric current picked up by poles or booms from an overhead wire network, was popular in Britain from the 1930s to the 1960s. In other parts of the world such quiet and pollution-free transport can still be found. Toy trolley buses have been made around the world, but these two examples are evocative of Britain with their bright red color.

The smaller bus was made by Wells-Brimtoy of London. The company produced trolley buses in three sizes; this is the largest at 8¼ inches. Some were made in the late 1930s, but most were produced in the late 1940s and 1950s. This toy is clockwork with a fixed key and asks the public to "Buy British." The rear of the bus says, "Brimtoy Trains are the Best," encouraging the purchase of other Wells toys. The lithographed passengers mostly wear hats, and a man in a check suit has his golf clubs on board.

The other bus was made by Betal and is the larger of two made by this company. It is slightly bigger than the Wells at 8¾ inches long and better looking, except for the out-of-scale conductor. This toy is clockwork with a separate key. Both buses are meant to represent London Transport buses, who only had one 2-axle trolley bus, the rest being 3-axle. However, these were only toys, and many other British cities operated 2-axle trolley buses.

Left: *A rather out-of-scale conductor smiles from the rear entrance platform.*

The trolley poles, or booms, which on the real buses picked up the electric current from overhead wires.

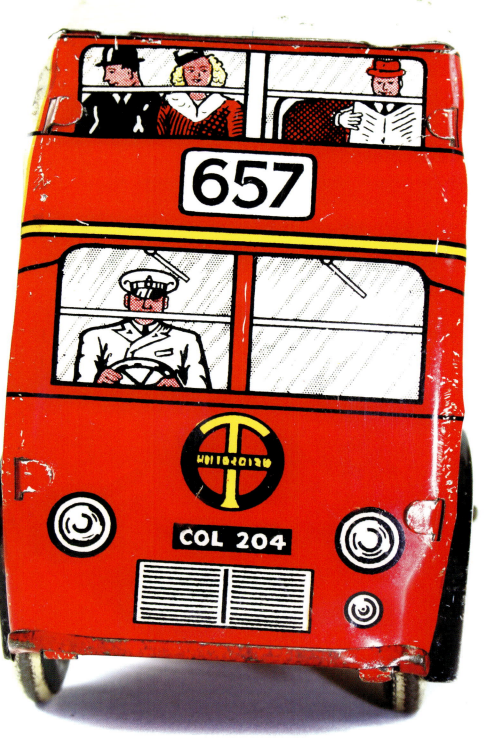

TRICKY TAXIS

The Marx toy company made these cute taxis between 1935 and 1940. They are wind-up toys with a keyhole set in the back left side fender and are 4¾ inches long. The bodies are stamped out of thin sheet metal with fairly rough edges, the windows are unglazed and the dummy front wheels are part of the body stamping, although the grill is a separate stamping. Underneath the front is a convex bump and a transverse rubber-edged wheel, and at the rear a rubber-covered drive and dummy wheel. When wound up and set on a table top the car travels until it reached the edge, at which point the convex bump drops to allow the transverse wheel to pivot the car sideways back onto the table. It then travels along until it hits the edge again, and the process repeats itself until the toy runs down. The key to successful operation is to wind the toy only halfway; otherwise the motor is so powerful the car flies over the edge onto the floor! The finish on the cars pictured is remarkable, considering the number of falls from tabletop height they must have sustained.

Also shown is a promotional toy from 1939 promoting Roi-Tan Cigars, a brand advertised with the slogan: "Man to man smoke Roi-tan." At the time, Roi-Tan was giving away a new car every day. Although not strictly a toy, this type of item is also very collectable.

Three color variants of the taxis: red over cream, green over cream and cream over red.

THREE JAPANESE AUTOS

The two older jalopies are both famous "Lever Cars" tagged: "A-1620." Marketed as "Lever Action Old-timers," they are wind-up toys activated by a lever on the right side of the cab. Once the motor was wound the lever was pulled backward in the direction of the arrow that says "Lever Action" and the car is off! The cars were sold in an era when vintage cars were popular, being perceived half as valuable collector's items and half as "fun" things, which helped sell the toy. These cars were made in Japan by the Modern Toy Company and have the TM trademark—the patent number is #27579. The red car with blue seats was a very popular color combination, while the more somber blue and gray car has red seats and hang-on, carriage-style lamps. Both are around 7 inches long.

The "Dog Chasing the Car" toy was also made in Japan and it says, "Taking a day off for a Sunday drive." The driver is wearing a fashionable driving cap and the dog is fixed onto a spindle attached to the car's front fender. The car is luxuriously appointed with chrome bumpers, lithographed plaid seats and fender skirts covering the rear wheels. It dates from the late 1940s.

Below: A close-up of the TM trademark of the Modern Toy Company of Japan.

Below: The trendy driver with sports coat and cap looks somewhat askance at the rumbustiuous dog bounding by his side.

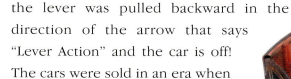

TRADE MARK
TM
MODERN TOYS

MADE IN JAPAN
PATENT NO. 27579

TWO BATTERY OPERATED CARS

These tin lithographed toys were made in Japan in the early 1950s, modeled in the style of automobiles from the early 1900s since vintage cars were popular at the time. Both cars are 10 inches long. They are battery operated and have working headlights in one case, carriage style lamps in the other. The lithographic decoration of the seats, radiator grills and dashboards is finely detailed and the paint finishes are red and black respectively, with coach stripes. The on/off switches for the battery-powered motor are located by the front seat on the black car and at the bottom of the radiator on the red car.

The windshield is glazed with a piece of clear plastic, which is quite advanced for the 1950s.

Right: A close-up of the fine detail of the black car. The on/off switch is positioned by the front seat and the coachwork has extensive lining out.

CAP CARS

Obviously the result of a toy company creative meeting, when some bright spark thought of combining the two most popular toys of the early 1950s—cars and cap guns—this toy must have driven all parents crazy! Both cars are made of self-colored red and black plastic, with very distinctive gold grilles and lights: red convertible, black sedan. The cap-firing mechanism is located right underneath the car and connected to a hand-held trigger by a long metal cable, which is also used to pull the car along. As soon as the trigger was squeezed, these old jalopies would emit an extremely realistic backfiring sound.

The cars themselves are modeled on the vintage style of those of the early 1900s, which was a very popular era with toy-makers half a century later in the 1950s. The fact that cars of this period did often backfire—and as a result are usually affectionately referred to today as "old bangers"—made the sound effect doubly appropriate. These particular toys are rare and very collectible mainly because, being only made of plastic, very few have survived the rough play of small boys over the years—not to mention the clumsy feet of any nearby adults.

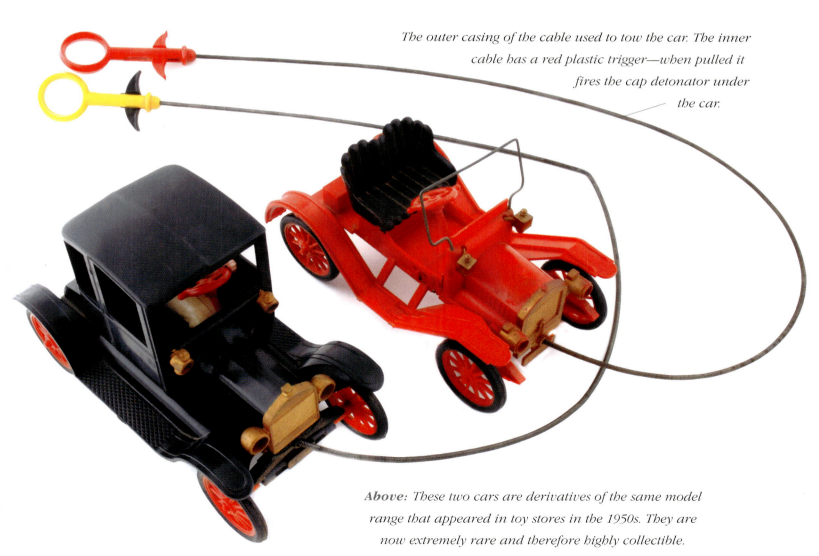

The outer casing of the cable used to tow the car. The inner cable has a red plastic trigger—when pulled it fires the cap detonator under the car.

Above: *These two cars are derivatives of the same model range that appeared in toy stores in the 1950s. They are now extremely rare and therefore highly collectible.*

ASSORTED POLICE CARS

Police cars are an ever-popular toy and here we have eight classic die-cast models, ranging from the 1940s to the 1990s. The line up features a variety of panel trucks and hardtops. The large, late-1940s Ford Mercury is a recent Chinese-manufactured version of this earlier classic and depicts a Florida Highway Patrol Vehicle from the period; the late 1940s Chevy Panel van is also a modern Chinese-made toy. The Buick on the end of the line is made by Ertl and we also have an Ertl '57 Chevy Bel Air, with an opening hood and rubber tires. Finally there is a brace of Ford Crown Victorias from the 1990s and an Ertl signature model: the 1974 Dodge Monaco, which appeared in different livery including Blues Brothers and Dukes of Hazzard police vehicles. Makes of police car are fairly standardized, so the fun of collecting police cruisers is having them in all the different PD colors and variations. Toy manufacturers have recognized this and have used the same basic mold to offer a whole range of different toys.

Below: The Chinese-made police car has no markings but is similar in style to the Maisto range, with plenty of detail and opening doors and hood.

Left: This Buick could almost be real, which shows how well designed and detailed these models are.

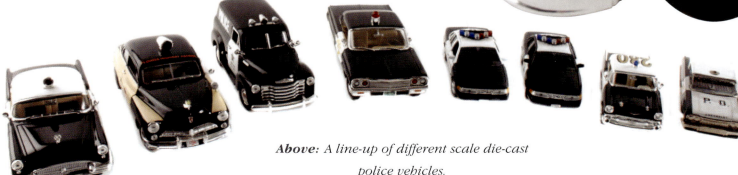

Above: A line-up of different scale die-cast police vehicles.

Below: *This large, late 1940s Ford Mercury is a recent Chinese-manufactured version of this earlier classic*

Right: *The two-color paintwork is in great condition.*

TN POLICE JEEP

This neat police vehicle with two cops is a tin toy dating from the 1960s and is battery operated. The passenger cop's hat is not original to the piece but came with it, so this is how it was played with and somehow it works in the context of the toy. It is marked TN, Japan, which is the Nomura Company, and is thought to have been distributed by Bernye & Co. The overall style is very similar to the Tonka jeep on page 196 but this has more detail, such as a better windshield, police department sign, riveted front bumper, working lights, more interior fittings—yellow seats, a parking brake, mesh behind the grille—and

This red flashing police light actually works.

Finely detailed headlights have chrome surrounds and working lenses.

Left: This view reveals even more detail: Police Dept shield and grab handles on the hood, fire extinguisher, radio in back seat, and spare tire bolted to the tailgate.

The front bumper is made from a U-section pressing riveted to the chassis just like the real thing.

***Below left:** The two life-like cops look perfectly at ease but ready for anything!*

better finished wheel trims. The #3 patrol officer has his tool kit, his first aid kit, his radio and antenna on the back seat, and his fire extinguisher. The uniforms of both policemen are lithographed and nicely detailed, including collar and ties, badges, pockets, brown leather gauntlets, and stripes down the side of the pants. The expressions of both cops are very lifelike and their arms swivel at the shoulder.

MATCHBOX TOYS

Although Matchbox has been owned by Mattel, its longtime competitor since 1997, it has been allowed to maintain its separate identity as a producer of small toy cars that pack in maximum reality. Originally founded in Homerton, East London, England, in 1953, the concept was designed for co-owner Jack Odell's daughter—her school had a rule that you could only take a toy to school if it would fit in a matchbox. The company duly designed a small scale car that would do just that and it was packaged in a matchbox-style pack just to prove it! The original models (the 1-75 series) averaged just 2½ inches long (the white MGA pictured is only 2½ inches) and were one-piece metal moldings with metal wheels. As time went by they gained plastic windshields, interiors, tires and gradually increased in size to 3 inches by the late 1960s. By the 1970s they had graduated to cardboard and clear plastic blister packs like their competitors,

but in recent years they have relaunched the Collectors' series, which again has Matchbox style packaging. The model range was mostly British vehicles at first, but by the late 1950s many American models had also been added. Another series— called the Yesteryear— was added, which specialized in vintage models like the Ford Model T. The model dies were based on detailed photos of the actual vehicle, giving a high level of accuracy and realism that was never attempted by chief competitor Hot Wheels. Like everything else, Matchbox has its staunch followers who prefer realism to the fantasy approach of Hot Wheels.

ORIGINAL HOT WHEELS

Breakthrough products like Hot Wheels have made Mattel the world's largest toy company. Before these dynamite little cars were introduced in 1968, die-cast models were aimed at adults rather than children and were for display, not play. The first sixteen castings of Hot Wheels changed all that. They were just over 2 inches long (1:64 scale) and designed to run on unique orange track. Their motive power came from gravity alone and die-cast models became fun at last! The designs were way out and proved immediately popular with both children and collectors, many of whom regard the first four years of production as a golden era. One hundred and eighteen castings were produced in this period, and some totally innovative features like "Specterflame" paint finishes and redline tires were introduced. Mattel continued to develop the brand for over 35 years. The line up has included "Formula Fuelers," "AcceleRacers," and "Sizzlers," with tiny battery-powered motors. The average child owns 41 Hot Wheels; the average collector 1,155!

Above: *The first Hot Wheels were promoted with pressed tin badges like these, in the shape of a tire with the car's name inside. These are collectible in their own right.*

A sample of six of the earliest cars, released in what collectors regard as a golden era.

Unique free-rolling wheels meant that these cars rolled faster than their competitors.

HOT WHEELS GARAGE

In order to make their cars more fun and to give them more "playability" Mattel cleverly introduced a number of concept play sets. From the word go Hot Wheels had a head start with their unique track system, which allowed children to shoot the cars round in loops. This idea is exemplified in classics like the "Mongoose and Snake Drag Race" set in 1970, and reaching a peak, in the author's opinion, with the "Gorilla Attack Track" set, where the track spirals down around a seriously vicious-looking King Kong-type character. Other concept play sets were developed to allow children to create their own play scenarios, like the "Robo Wheels Crash Coasters," the "Highway 25 Performance Track" and the "Backpack Beach Toy Set." In 1979 the garage shown here was added the to line up. A little less zany than most Hot Wheels ideas, toy garages had been available since the 1920s, but this is still a very cool toy. It gave the opportunity to take your favorite redlines to the "Dynamometer Test Center," "George's Radiator Shop," "A1's Service and Tire," "Mike's Transmission," "Brakes and Mufflers," the café, and carwash. It came in a box and folded neatly in half for transportation.

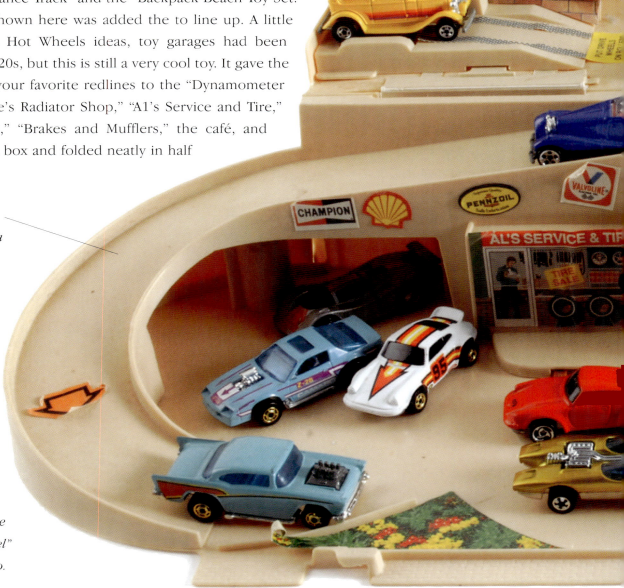

The down ramp to the ground floor observes a strict "one way" rule.

Right: *The garage has all kinds of interesting nooks and crannies for the imaginative child to explore. Seems like some pretty groovy "Hot Wheel" cars have turned up too.*

SPEED 35 LIMIT

RAMP

MIKE'S **TRANSMISSIONS** BRAKES · MUFFLERS

Best BRAND BRAKE SHOES

George's **RADIATOR** BOIL·OUTS·REPAIRS

CAR WASH

CASHIER

HOT WAX

The elevator bottom left transports cars to the roof to descend by this ramp.

VINTAGE AMBULANCES

These three ambulances with friction motors date from the 1930s, 1940s and 1950s respectively and are made of plastic, tin and pressed steel. The 1930's model with the distinctive flared fenders is a Wyandotte. All Metal Products of Wyandotte, Michigan, were situated close to the hub of the motor industry, as their concept was to use scrap metal from the car plants to keep their costs down. They also used mass production techniques and skilled labor from the car industry to found their reputation for high quality toys at cheap prices. This ambulance has a separate grille and rear opening door. The average length of these toys is 11 inches.

The 1950's toy (top left) is Japanese-made with good detailing; the 1940's model (left) is a plastic molding in the style of a Renwall.

CHEVROLET CORVETTE

This 1:18-scale, die-cast model of a 1957 Chevrolet Corvette is an example of the high quality toys recently made in China. Brand marked "Road Signature" its level of detail is extremely high. Finished in signature Corvette colors—red over cream—it has an opening hood (with engine) and trunk (with spare tire). The cockpit has wraparound windshield, speedometer and switches, gearshift lever, chrome ashtray, steering wheel operating the front wheels, rear view mirror and door interiors with window winder and lock release levers. Underneath the car has twin mufflers, a drive train and a fully-detailed chassis and suspension. Many parts are chrome plated, such as the engine, bumpers, and wheel trims. The length is 9½ inches.

Above: So realistic it really does look like the real thing.

Right: The view under the hood reveals in great detail the 283 V-8 power plant and Ramjet fuel injection—both new for 1957.

MAISTO 1948 WOODY

Marketed by California-based Maisto and produced in Thailand, this die-cast model of a 1948 Chevrolet Fleetmaster is a magnificent specimen. Maisto, like many U.S. toy manufacturers today, rely on production in the Far East—originally the decision was doubtless made for cost reasons, but these days the standard of workmanship could not be higher. The 1:18 scale of this model was popularized in the late 1980s, when there was a renewed interest in collectible classics; manufacturers like Ertl and Revell also marketed 1:18 models. This toy has opening front doors and hood, a die-cast body and a plastic roof. The wooden door framing and paneling is also in plastic. The interior is extremely detailed, with dashboard and full seating including chrome guardrails. The steering wheel turns the front wheels through a linkage and underneath the chassis is detailed in plastic, with a chrome-plated muffler. The overall length is 11½ inches.

Chrome radio antenna completes the detail.

Opposite page: *With the hood up you can see how accurately this model captures the Stovebolt-six engine and single barrel carburetor.*

With a magnifying glass it is even possible to read "Firestone Deluxe Champion" on the tires!

1948
WOODY

MINIC SUNSHINE SALOON

This toy was made in 1938 by Minic toys, part of the Lines Brothers company started just after World War I. The original factory was at Merton in South London, England, but by World War II they had moved to factories in Margate and Canterbury in Kent, England. During World War II they suffered the same fate as many toy manufacturers; war production took priority over toys so the factories made Sten MkII Submachine guns. After the war, the company returned to toy production and by the 1960s Lines Brothers owned 40 companies worldwide and had added Meccano (which included Hornby Railways and Dinky Toys) to its portfolio. However, they ran into financial trouble in the early 1970s and were broken up and sold off. The "Sunshine Saloon" shown here dates from happier times—in the warm glow of the late 1930s it was still possible to enjoy the finer things of life. Our model is based on a 1936 Bentley Derby Sports Sedan, but the "sunshine" roof hatch gives the model its name. It was part of the Minic "Quality Car" range, which included Rolls Royce and Daimler toys, open tourers and sedanca models. There were electric and non-electric versions—the electric one had a small battery in the trunk to powered the lights.

This red and beige "Sunshine Saloon" is the non-electric version, with a clockwork motor.

Above: *The two-tone color scheme of red and beige denotes pre-war production. Later cars were red and black.*

All Minic toys had finely
detailed wheels with
hubcaps and rubber tires.

Above: A detail of the rear panel
shows no sign of wear—this toy is
in mint condition.

DAYTON FRICTION AUTOS

The Boyer patent that had led to toy manufacturers being centered on Dayton, Ohio, in the last few years of the nineteenth century continued to influence toy production in the first few years of the twentieth. The friction mechanism, which was charged up by running the toy along the floor and then releasing it, was a big breakthrough in powering toys. Dayton was also the center of sheet steel toy cars. Because sheet steel expertise in America had developed late—in the 1860s, accelerated by the Civil War—traditionally many toys had been imported from Europe: Germany, France and England. As skilled immigrants from those countries peopled much of Ohio, it is not surprising that American-made metal toys sprang from the area. The cars featured here are fairly current copies of 1900-type cars, which although

they are pretty crude in their design have stood the test of time extremely well because of their very robust construction.

The wheels are early spoked type, made of steel castings with single rod spindles.

Above and left: *Many early cars had cast figures representing drivers. As was the custom of the times they would often be dressed as chauffeurs, rather than owner-drivers.*

DAYTON COUPE

A later product of the Dayton toy industries, this stylish streamlined coupe dates from the early 1920s. The design has evolved quite a bit from the cruder-looking toys on the facing page—the body stampings, like the radiator grille, the door panels and the hood louvers, are more detailed and defined. The black front and rear fenders also have more complex profiles, instead of being flat strips of sheet steel as on the earlier toys.

The spoked wheels are pressed steel, painted dull yellow to give some representation of wheels and tires. The paintwork is distressed in a few places but this only enhances the toy's value, as most collectors would feel that it proves its authenticity—there is nothing worse than a restored piece in many people's opinion. This example is powered by friction, which remained a popular motive force right up until World War II. Toys of this kind were cheaply priced, and for this reason their manufacturers survived the depression well.

This toy reflects the car styling of the 1920s, possibly a Studebaker Light Six?

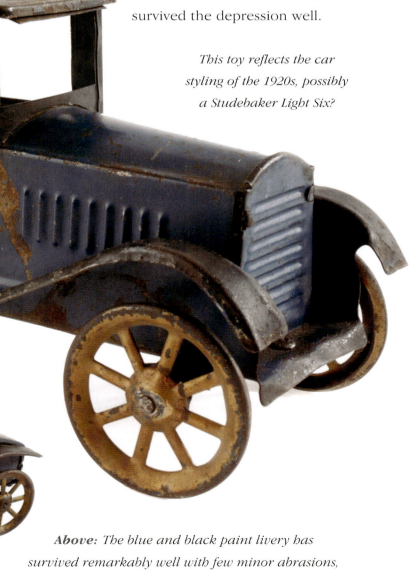

Above: *The blue and black paint livery has survived remarkably well with few minor abrasions, which only add to the sense of authenticity.*

WYANDOTTE COUPES

In its proximity to the hub of American car manufacture in Michigan, All Metal Products of Wyandotte is situated just a stone's throw from the major plants. Is it not possible then, that the company got a "thumbs-up" from car industry giants to copy the latest designs? What finer compliment for your new model than to have a child's toy echoing it—indeed, as we shall see later, major manufacturers like Ford produced promotional toys for that very purpose. So here we have two coupes in pressed steel with lithographed detailing, which are strongly reminiscent of Pontiac styling of the late 1940s. The silver streak side details, as fitted to Torpedo models by designer Frank Hershey, are quite evident in this toy and the "woody" effect on one car was also a great favorite in this period. The two cars shown both have retractable roofs, but the one with square headlights has suffered some damage since it has lost its windshield. Both cars also have opening trunks. Red, brown, and yellow were popular colors for toy automobiles at this time. The coupes are 12 inches in length and both vehicles would be sought after by collectors today.

Below: Two late 1940's Wyandotte Coupes, with different paint jobs.

This retractable roof is in perfect working order.

The Woody look was definitely "all the rage" at this time.

KINGSBURY AIRFLOWS

The Kingsbury Toy Company of Keene, New Hampshire, had a long history of keeping pace with young consumer's tastes, from H.T Kingsbury's takeover of the company in 1894 to the sale of the toy division, forty-five years later, to Keystone at the outbreak of World War II. During that time they specialized in high quality detailed cast-metal toys, which were so accurately made that they were advertised as "so life-like they seemed turned small by magic." During the 1930s, when the toys featured were made, Kingsbury were the only toy manufacturer licensed to display the emblem "Body by Fisher," which appeared on the Chrysler Airflows.

Chrysler deemed the models so accurate that the Kingsbury were also allowed to reproduce each of the company's models, year by year. These toys have electric headlights and rubber tires—and the tires have Kingsbury logos. The yellow car is an example of an Airflow proper; the green car is of the same era but possibly a Ford. Both examples have a lot of damage to the paintwork and they have obviously been played with very consistently in their time. They are both 14 inches long.

Above right: The yellow car is a proper Chrysler Airflow, with working headlights, but the grille detail is missing.

Above left: The green car is a generic "airflow-type" from the 1930s, when the style was strongly in vogue.

MARX AMBULANCE

This rare surviving example of the Marx tinplate ambulance dates from the 1930s. It is a civilian version, but this model was also produced in green war dept livery with MD decals on the doors in place of the "Ambulance" sign seen on our example. A wind-up toy—with a very loud siren, which made it totally irresistible to young boys—the key to the motor is located on the right side of the body, in the base of the door. It has extra realistic features, including rubber tires and an opening back door, just waiting for a John Doe to load! The red and cream paint finish typical of the pre-war period is nicely contrasting on the body, running boards and fenders. The toy itself has a pleasing shape and is 14 inches long, a size that a child could really get to grips with. It is also weighty and solid, in the way that many newer plastic toys are not—what pressed steel toys often lack in detail, they usually make up for in sheer "playability."

Totally realistic ventilated wheels and rubber tires.

The Marx ambulance has
the look and feel of a
substantial toy. Despite
its age, it just cries out
to be played with.

Marx graphics are
always great and
stand the test of time.

Above: The hinged back door adds a further dimension to
the toy's "playability" factor. It is quite unusual to find one
in such good condition, as many have missing doors.

WOLVERINE AIRFLOW

This cute pressed steel Airflow dates from 1936 when Chrysler's outrageous design was at the height of its short-lived popularity. Like all cutting edge design fads, the Airflow itself was quickly celebrated in toy form and the Wolverine company of Pittsburgh, Pennsylvania, must have acted rapidly to add this particular toy to their range. The company was founded by Benjamin F. Bain and his wife in 1903 and specialized in metal toys, particularly sandbox toys like pails, spades and sifters. Their toys were cheap and enjoyed a long sales life—toys designed in the 1900s were still selling in the 1950s. Wolverine survived the depression with no ill effects because their toys remained affordable.

Our example dates from the 1930s, when things were tough for industry generally, but here is Wolverine creating a new toy based on a novelty car design. Far from designing a straightforward replica, the Wolverine version is also a stunt toy, a bold decision indeed. It has a friction motor,

Above: The rear panel of the car has a decal that advises "Press down here to operate mystery car."

These rear wheels are connected to the friction motor.

Above: *Symmetry of rounded fenders and built-in running boards is a recurring theme in 1930's Wolverine car design.*

which stored up the energy to flip the car when you pressed down on the rear: a printed decal on the roof says "Press down here to operate mystery car." The original blue paintwork has suffered much damage because of the tendency of the toy to fly through the air! The one-piece pressing of the body is fairly rudimentary, with holes punched for windows and few details. The wheel spindles are fixed through the outer rim of the fenders. The headlights, front bumper and grille are separate stampings.

DOEPKE MGTC

After the end of World War II many U.S. servicemen returned home after being based in England, where they had seen and fallen in love with the MG sports car. As a result MG had a ready-made market for their cars from 1945 onward—and toy manufacturers also seized the opportunity to model the small sports cars. One such company was the Doepke Toy Company, based in Rossmoyne, Ohio, founded by Charles W. Doepke and

Left: A close-up of the printed graphics on the dashboard, which faithfully represent the gauges and switches of the real thing.

his brother Fredrick in 1947. At first their toys reflected a war theme but, encouraged by their mother, they began to model popular autos of the day, including foreign cars like the Jaguar XK120 and the MGTC. From the start Doepke were renowned for their realism—mobile crane salesmen carried Doepke toy versions of their cranes to show how the real thing operated. Both founders had worked in the steel industry and knew how to achieve realistic results—in one case, a model by Doepke is said to have solved a design flaw in its larger relative. The company prospered whilst metal toys reigned supreme, but failed to make the transition to plastics and closed down in 1960. Their legacy is the large number of dedicated collectors of their excellent toys. The MG dates from 1954 and is 15½ inches long.

Doepke toys were fitted with rubber tires made by Goodyear.

Replacement parts for Doepke toys are now available, including headlights, steering wheels, windshields, and bumpers.

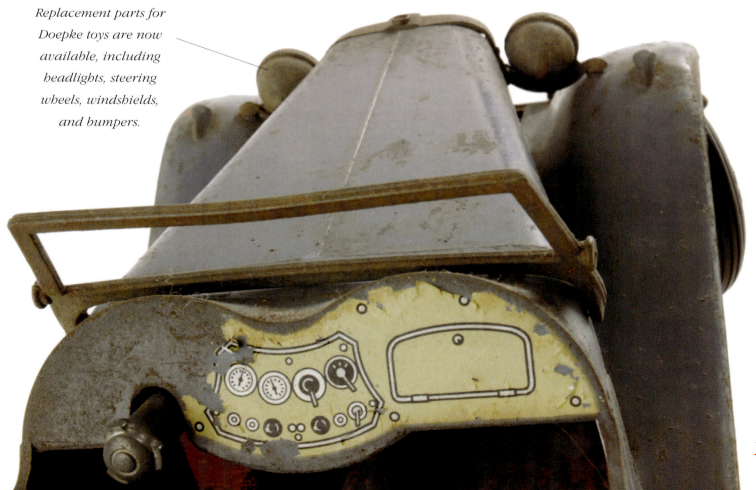

WYANDOTTE CORD AND LASALLE

Two magnificent toy cars from Wyandotte, a company founded in 1920 that grew up in the heart of "Motor City" and benefited from cheaper materials such as recycled steel. They also had their finger on the pulse regarding new designs, and the pick of which to model as toys. Wyandotte versions followed closely upon the heels of the real thing: in this case the LaSalle is a 1936 four-door sedan, and the toy dates from the same year. The Cord toy is based on a 1937 Cord 812 Cabriolet, and again the toy dates from the same year. Perhaps

to wind the motor, release, and watch it go! The red pressed-steel LaSalle is an exaggerated depiction of the 1937 sedan; the Wyandotte interpretation has more bulging fenders, a longer hood and a more steeply raking windshield. The heyday of Wyandotte toys was probably in the 1930s, when many of the company's more familiar signature toys were produced. In an attempt to keep costs low they moved to Ohio in the early 1950s, but the move failed to save them enough money and they went out of business in 1956.

they had a peek at the design studio's sketchbook, or perhaps they tooled up very quickly when the new models were announced? The green and cream Cord 812 is 13⅜ inches long and the toy faithfully replicates the real car's great lines, such as the coffin nose hood, chrome horizontal louvers and pontoon fenders. It also has an inertia motor—pull the car back

Right: This toy has seen action! The paintwork is chipped and the cabriolet top is bent.

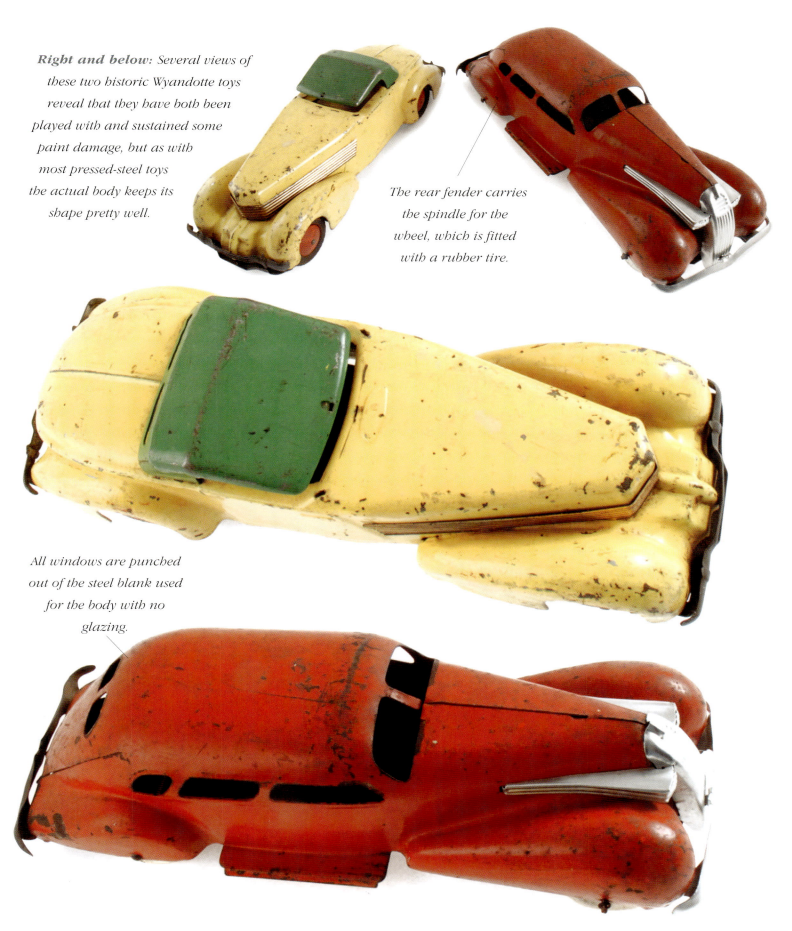

Right and below: Several views of these two historic Wyandotte toys reveal that they have both been played with and sustained some paint damage, but as with most pressed-steel toys the actual body keeps its shape pretty well.

The rear fender carries the spindle for the wheel, which is fitted with a rubber tire.

All windows are punched out of the steel blank used for the body with no glazing.

MARX FIRE CHIEF AND POLICE CHIEF CARS

Made by Marx in the 1930s the "Siren Fire Chief" and "Siren Police Chief" are two versions of the same body tooling. Both models are extremely well detailed, with fittings like bumpers, grille, wheels and hubcaps, and grooved running boards, as well as details of the doors and hood frames incorporated in the panel stamping. This is not entirely typical of Marx toys at the time; many models in the range had lithographed detail,

rather than separate fittings and complex stamping. Groundbreaking, too, are the battery-operated headlights and sirens driven by wind-up motors—the key aperture is on the right side above the running board, at the rear of the door. An on/off lever is situated at the base of the front right hand door. Made in sheet steel and 15 inches long, the toys are pretty weighty, but very robust. Many fire and police toys suffered rough handling—children liked riding on them—so they were often constructed to last.

Both below: Two examples in excellent condition. The police car even has its original headlight bulbs that would have been powered by a battery..

Opposite page: A close-up showing the detail in the body panel pressings, which include door hinges and handles, window framing, access hatch, and roof frame. It is also unusual to see such clean original graphics.

1ST
BATT.

SIREN
FIRE
CHIEF

1

TIN TAXI AND COUPE

By the early 1930s Louis Marx was rising in his profession to become known as the "Henry Ford of the toy industry." At the same time Wolverine were extending their product range beyond sandbox toys with the "Sunny Andy" and "Sunny Suzy" toy ranges, which included airplanes, boats, buses and cars for boys and stoves, fridges and grocery stores for girls. Sexism was not even a concept in those days! Both companies cruised through the Depression virtually unscathed, largely because they both offered good value for money—even in times of hardship parents strive to give toys to their children. It is also true that often children of working-class people are better served for toys than those from poorer middle-class homes. The two toys featured here are prime examples of good value playthings. The Marx coupe uses the same body as the toy featured on the previous page, but is

Below: The Wolverine taxi and the Marx coupe share a popular red and cream color scheme and were both competitively priced to ensure a successful sale, despite the tough times. One dates from the early 1930s the other from the 1940s.

The Wolverine is quite a simple one-piece stamping that relies on its lithographed graphics for detail.

Above: The Marx toy has both graphics and extra detail such as running boards, grille bumpers, and working headlights.

Right: The Wolverine taxi has one extra feature up its sleeve however—it is a stunt toy. Press down on the back and it will streak off at high speed!

in a "civilian" livery. Marx could offer it at a competitive price because the development costs had been covered—the more derivative models they were able to make the better. By smartening the design up with a two-tone red and cream color scheme and extra lithographed details, and keeping its working lights, they guaranteed a new sale for basically the same toy.

Taxis are always a popular toy—the Wolverine one dates from the early 1940s and is made of lithographed tin. This would have been relatively cheap to make because it is a one piece pressing with no separate detailing; the windows are printed on, rather than stamped out like those of the Marx coupe. This model is 13 inches long.

TWO TONKA PICKUPS

Just after World War II six cash-strapped Minnesota teachers set up the Mound Metalcraft Company and began producing hand tools for gardeners in the basement of the local schoolhouse. In 1947 they acquired a toy company owned by Edward C. Streater and went into steel toy production. Named after local Lake Minnetonka, the new toy company was called Tonka, the Sioux word for "great," and soon gained a reputation for durability, realism and keeping up with changes in real life vehicles. Pickups were added to the range in 1955, and were popular because they can be loaded up with all kinds of things! The trucks here date from the early 1980s and appear to be loosely based on the Chevrolet K10 of 1979.

Both above: These black and red Tonka pickups show signs of lots of play! The tough construction means the bodies are still in good shape, but both tailgates are missing.

Tonka added graphics as a stick-on plastic decal, which has stood the test of time.

TWO TONKA PACERS

Here is proof that toys reflect cultural changes in society. In the mid 1970s the fuel crisis made people reconsider their attachment to big, fun cars and the American motor industry started to build cars like the Pacer instead. This turtle-shaped car was made by the American Motors Corporation, and masqueraded as "Eco-friendly"—when apart from looking different, it retained many conventional features. Tonka dutifully modeled the car—but the toy, like the real-life version, was short-lived. The real car appeared in the 1992 movie *Wayne's World* and now Pacers are collectible.

This paint finish is "Mellow Yellow" after the Donovan song.

Above: *From this angle the metallic red Tonka toy captures the avant-garde styling of the 1975 Pacer extremely effectively.*

Right: *The Tonka has a complicated body pressing, with considerable detail of the Pacer's styling—such as door and roofline, the wraparound front light clusters, and raised headlight fairings.*

The front lights, grille and bumper are on a separate fitting.

TWO PICKUPS

Here are two of America's leading metal toy manufacturers head to head: a green Buddy L and red Tonka model of the same Ford late-1950's pickup. Buddy L toy production started in 1921 after Fred Lundahl of the Moline Pressed Steel Co. took some samples of a toy he had made for his son Arthur—who preferred to be known as Buddy—to the New York Toy Fair. The reaction from toy buyers was fairly lukewarm, but the large size and the quality of the toys won through and by 1925 Lundahl had a range of 20 toys. The unique thing about them was that right from the start they were made from the same materials that real cars and trucks were made of—Lundahl used the scrap steel from his manufacturing business at first—and their design closely followed that of the real thing. Because of the quality of the production the older vehicles have held up well and still look good today, so this is a popular brand for collectors.

Similarly Tonka started as a company making garden tools and ended up specializing in toys when that market proved stronger.

The Buddy L has a glazed windshield and side windows.

Above right: The Buddy L paintwork is in better condition, the grille and bumper are brighter and the model's tailgate is still intact.

The red and white Tonka has fared a little less well than its counterpart. The grille and bumper fitment has tarnished, and the tailgate is missing.

Above: Head to head the two cars still look great, with their company decals proudly displayed on the doors.

TWO TONKA PICKUPS

Two great pressed-steel toys, which mark the evolution of the pickup in the years immediately following World War II. Both are made by Tonka, who were just starting to establish their toy company in Mound, Minnesota, when the Gambles-signed truck on the opposite page was current. It is based on the Ford F-100, which was Ford's first all-new post-war truck—its styling ran for two years from 1948 to 1949. This toy truck, launched in 1958, would have been one of Tonka's very first pickups, since they were only part of the range from 1955 onward. It is a styleside and the graphics on both doors and tailgate feature "Gambles, The Friendly Store," a company who were based at St. Louis Park, Minnesota, which was not far away from the Tonka factory. Possibly the graphics on the truck were the result of some sort of licensing deal to promote both companies at the same time.

Above: *The decal of the graphic is original and despite a few cracks is in good shape.*

The front bumper is part of a separate fitting that includes the grille and headlights.

Below: *The "24 hr. service" decal that appears on the side of the truck is still in good condition. Replacement logo decals are available on the Internet.*

Gambles made their name in auto supplies and ended up being the fifteenth largest retailer in the U.S. Their first store was in St. Cloud, Minnesota, so, as ever, toys are a witness to history.

The second toy is based on the 1961 Ford F-100 pickup—Tonka seemed to model Ford trucks in preference to other manufacturers at this time. This toy has fared rather better, since its paintwork is brighter and less scratched. Its graphics herald the "Tonka AA Wrecker Truck" on the doors and offer "24 Hour service" on the side of the truck bed, both are applied as decals rather than printed on. The windows in the cab and the windshield are glazed with clear plastic that is still in very good shape. The white paintwork has evolved into a bright white that is typical of the 1960s, rather than the more muted cream seen on the 1950's truck. Both of the trucks shown here are 12½ inches long.

Above: The Gambles' logo is badly worn as the truck has really seen some play action.

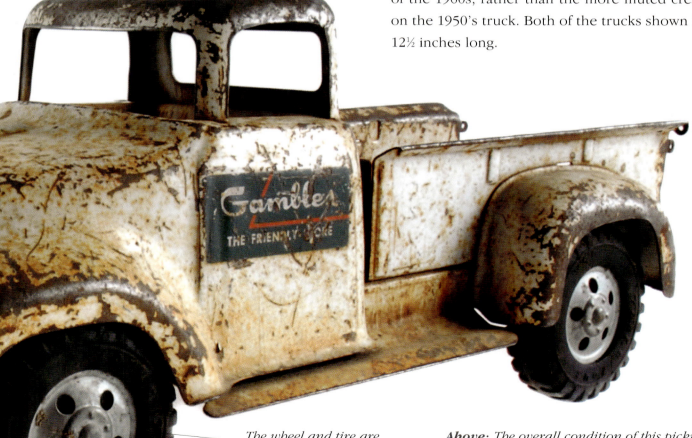

The wheel and tire are nicely detailed, even down to the "Tonka Toy" embossed on the rubber tire wall.

Above: The overall condition of this pickup would count against it in the money stakes, but it is still an interesting piece and worthy of collectors' interest.

STEER O

This neat red convertible dates from the 1950s. It is a generic car, reputedly based on the Nash Healey and Kaiser Darrin sport convertibles of the same period in a time when the American car industry was waking up to the call for sports cars. At the same time another popular car for toy manufacturers to copy was born—the Chevrolet Corvette. However, the toy featured here is unusual in that the sales of the original car that influenced it only ran into hundreds, so they are not at all well known and have faded into obscurity. Most toys are based on mass-market cars like the Corvette, which by 1957 was selling in the thousands—by which time the Nash Healey and Kaiser Darrin had both disappeared. The toy is made from self-colored red plastic; the body is extremely shiny and the molds used must have been of very high quality to achieve this level of finish. The plastic has also proved to be stable, unlike the roof of the Marx Suburban on page 183. The front has a magnificent plastic chrome grille, bumper, and chrome headlights. The wheels are rubber tires on metal rims, with plastic chrome hubcaps. The underside of the car also reveals a well-engineered

Below right: The interior of the car has smart black plastic seats and a chrome steering wheel. The plastic body has remained stable, unlike some other cars of the same era.

The red plastic body is in great shape after 50 years of play.

toy—the thickness of the plastic molding is quite apparent from this angle and this probably accounts for the stability of the body. It was clearly designed for strength, because the metal mechanical parts were bolted direct to the body and it needed to withstand the strain. There are two complex metal transaxles, the front comprising a series of complex linkages that allow the car to be steered by pressing down on either front corner; the resultant

down energy was converted into a corresponding movement of the front wheels and two coil springs return the car to a straight line when the pressure is released. This is of course what gives the car its name:- Steer O.

Above right: The all-metal back axle contains a friction motor that operates the car when the tail is depressed.

FAIRLANE AND THUNDERBIRD

The turquoise and white Ford Fairlane is based on the Ford model of 1958. It has the TN trademark of Nomura, one of the biggest and most prolific of all post-war Japanese toy makers, who specialized in mostly mechanical and wind-up toys featuring creative designs. The car is powered by a battery-operated mechanism controlled by a remote control box attached to the car by a cable. It is a nicely finished toy with bright paintwork and printed interior—the fancy chrome detailing gives it a special appeal.

The red and white Ford Thunderbird, based on the Ford model of 1956, was also made in Japan. Like its partner it is a pretty faithful copy of the full-size version, made in die-cast metal with clear plastic windows. Body detailing includes a rear wheel housing, Thunderbird chrome logo on the rear fender, bonnet airscoop, front fender cooling vents, and chrome bumpers. This toy dates from the late 1950s.

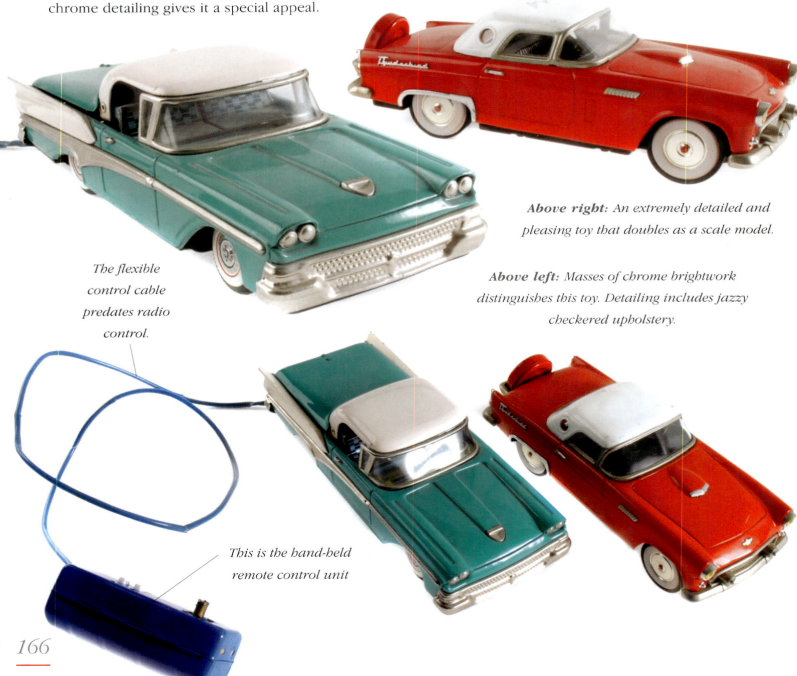

The flexible control cable predates radio control.

Above right: *An extremely detailed and pleasing toy that doubles as a scale model.*

Above left: *Masses of chrome brightwork distinguishes this toy. Detailing includes jazzy checkered upholstery.*

This is the hand-held remote control unit

BUICK AND PONTIAC

The brown toy is based on the 1949 Pontiac Chieftain Eight Deluxe drop top and is a pressed tin toy with separate components for grille, bumpers and extensive body brightwork. The seats and windshield are molded plastic and the car has detailed wheel trims and rubber whitewall tires. It dates from the early 1950s.

The Buick toy is based on the 1950 Deluxe-trim Special Touring Coupe in two-tone pink and white, colors that were popular in the 1950s. The body is nicely detailed, with the three decorative chrome Ventiports on the hood that distinguished the Pontiac range for some years. It is of Japanese manufacture, dating from circa 1952.

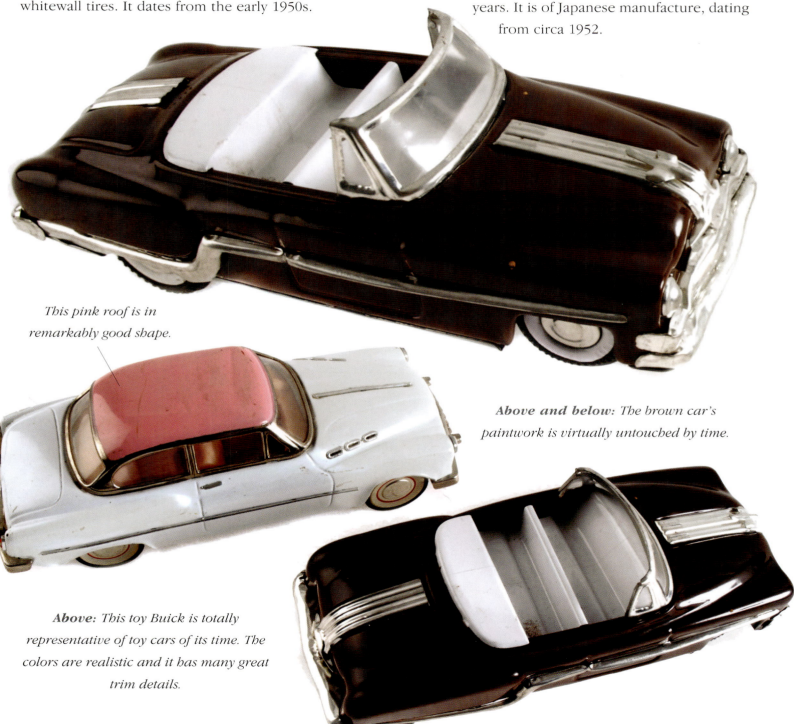

This pink roof is in remarkably good shape.

Above and below: *The brown car's paintwork is virtually untouched by time.*

Above: *This toy Buick is totally representative of toy cars of its time. The colors are realistic and it has many great trim details.*

TWO GERMAN CARS

After the end of World War II the German toy industry was reorganized under American control and toys were marked "U.S. Zone Germany" and were part of the "Uhrwerk" program. Many were constructed in pressed tin and they were extremely well made and detailed. The Mercedes Benz Cabriolet shown here was made by Distler and coded B-2727. It is wind-up toy with a clockwork motor—the key fits into a housing in the spare wheel. Keys often go missing and replacement keys, like some other parts, are available for this model. Distler was founded in 1895 by Johan Distler in Nuremburg's toy district. This model dates from 1954. The other light green convertible is probably based on a late 1940s Lincoln and is by an unknown German manufacturer—but it bears many similarities to the Distler Mercedes.

Both above: The toys are well detailed, with features such as chrome bumpers, radiator grilles, split-windshield frames, headlights, wheeltrims, and rubber tires.

The interior of the Distler is realistic, with steering wheel and 4-speed control on the dash. The bottom panel of the car (far right) is a single pressing with some details.

TOOTSIE TOYS 1930S & 1940S

The die-cast toy car started out with Samuel Dowst of the Dowst Manufacturing Company of Chicago, who bought a Linotype machine to print the *National Laundry Journal*, a trade paper he published. The machine cast the type as it went along and Dowst adapted this idea to produce the first metal die-cast cars from the same lead alloy as type. His first successful toy was a miniature Model T Ford, in 1906. In 1922 he was looking for a brand name and thought of his brother's granddaughter, whose name was Tootsie. The company was bought out by Nathan Shure in 1926 and in 1934 production switched to the new zinc-based alloy, Mazac. The toys in the front row of our picture are models of the "Graham Blue Streak Eights" designed by Amos Northup with body detailing by Raymond Dietrich, and the first to use full-skirted fenders—a trend soon adopted by the other auto

Above, left to right: Five beautifully preserved examples of the Tootsietoy "Graham Blue Streak" from 1932 show the variety of liveries and body styles.

The two fender-mounted spare wheels gave the Graham "six-wheeled" status.

*Body castings in Mazac
for the 1940's production were simple
one-piece moldings, painted one color.
These cars have all the signs of
well-played-with toys, which has
resulting in a lack of paint.*

manufacturers. The toys were more successful than the real cars, selling by the millions. They were produced as sedan, rumble seat roadster, coupe and sedanca body types, in a variety of colors. Tootsietoys survived the Depression but body shapes tended to be less detailed and more generic in the 1940s, as exemplified by the four cars at the top. Castings were also simpler, perhaps due to an overlap with war production.

*Tootsietoys had
steel axles and
wheels with
rubber tires.*

*Body details like the bumpers and
headlights were all part of the casting.*

DIE-CAST CARS FROM THE 1950s

In the years following World War II toy manufacturers started to recover from wartime shortages as metal and rubber became available to make toys again. Consumer expectation also seemed to have cranked up a notch and what might have passed muster during the war years—like toys crudely fashioned from off-cut wood blocks—would no longer do for the post-war generation. Toy cars were no exception to this rule and

we show here a selection of 1950's models from Tootsietoy, Dinky and Corgi.

The upper crescent of cars, representing (from left) Two Hudson Commodores, a Studebaker Land Cruiser and two Ford Fordoors, were made by Dinky Toys. This company started in December 1933 as "Modeled Miniatures," and was part of the Hornby Trains empire—Frank Hornby originally intended the cars to

Bright two-tone paintwork was common on 1950's Dinky Toys.

Above: A range of 1950's cars, from sports cars like the Cunningham to Cadillacs and Packards. There is even a small Chevy pickup.

Below center: The two-tone Studebaker Golden Hawk was one of the first Corgi Toys to feature plastic windows in 1956.

be accessories for the railroad toys. By April 1934 the range had been renamed Dinky Toys and had developed a life of its own. Although the toys were developed in England there were plenty of American cars in the range because they were popular with English children, being rather exotic. They would also sell in America alongside the company's other toys, like models of the MGA and Jaguar XK.

Realistic cast hubs and rubber tires were added to all post-war toys.

MORE AUTOS FROM THE 1950S

Dinky Toys were part of Meccano Ltd., famous for its construction sets. During the 1950s Dinky continued to develop their range of die-cast cars, either at the Liverpool, England, or the Bobigny, France, factories. From 1956 onward Corgi had stiff competition from Corgi, owned by Mettoy Playcraft Ltd., whose range of toy cars was known as, "the ones with windows." This improvement helped Corgi sell 2.75 million toy cars in 1956, their first year of operation. By 1959 they were producing cars like this 1959 Chevrolet Impala Taxi.

Also shown is the Tekno Ford Thunderbird. Tekno were, at this time, a Danish Manufacturer still recovering from German occupation in World War II, but they were well known for their toy trucks.

Above: The handsome Packard Caribbean with figure at the wheel was made by Dinky Toys.

Above: The Chevrolet Impala by Corgi came in different models.

DINKY TOYS

After World War II had ended Dinky Toys put all their pre-war stock on the market for the Christmas season of 1945, in an attempt to catch some sales. In fact no new production took place until 1946—when the first model was appropriately a jeep. At this time a number of improvements began: wheel hubs were cast in more detail and rubber tires were added, and in 1947 tire treads were introduced. Pre-war dies for the toy bodies were still being used through the remainder of the 1940s, but by the beginning of the 1950s many new models were introduced. Here are some models based on English cars of the day. From the top we have a two-tone Vauxhall Velox, a red Jaguar XK120, a convertible Austin Atlantic, and green Morris Oxford. With the exception of the Austin, the cars are devoid of any internal detail or windows—these features were to follow at the end of the decade after competition from other manufacturers like Corgi.

Left: Although of English manufacture, the Vauxhall Velox styling is heavily influenced by owners Gamete.

Above and right: The Austin Atlantic and Morris Oxford are examples of toys based on early 1950's English cars. Many English children preferred more stylish American cars.

PRESSED STEEL CARS AND BUS

A selection of pre-war pressed steel toys mostly attributed to All Metal Products of Wyandotte, Michigan. The company began production in 1920, deliberately located close to the hub of America's motor industry to take advantage of scrap steel and rubber and so hit the budget end of the toy market: the nickel and dime stores. The other benefit was in being on the inside track regarding auto development, enabling them to get new models out first—it is likely that car manufacturers may have encouraged All Metal to copy their latest models. The toys became known as Wyandotte and after a while this became their brand name. The company's heyday was in the 1930s, when their characteristic flowing, full-fendered models were at their height of popularity. Many of the bodies shared tooling in order to make sedans, coupes and convertibles from the same basic die stamp, and this can be seen in the examples shown here.

Separate pressings of streamlined body features and grilles were added to the basic pressed-steel shell.

This bus shows how the pressing stamped out the hood in two parts.

The car directly above is the same body stamping as the one above left. It has seen a tougher life so some details—like the grille—are homemade replacements. Cars left and right share tooling elements.

TURNER PACKARD

Toys have traditionally been part of Ohio's industry since the Boyer-patented, friction mechanism for driving toys was invented, in the last few years of the nineteenth century. The John C. Turner Company of Wapakoneta, Ohio, was one manufacturer who used the Boyer mechanism. Originally employed as a shop worker by the D.P. Clarke Company in Dayton, Ohio,

Turner set up his own company in nearby Wapakoneta in the early 1920s. It is believed Clark used Turner's innovative ideas in his toys and, unsurprisingly, Turner soon decided to use his ideas to make his own fortune. This Packard toy is based on a 1922 Single Six Roadster, so it must have been one of Turner's original models to be produced in Wapakoneta. It is 26 inches long.

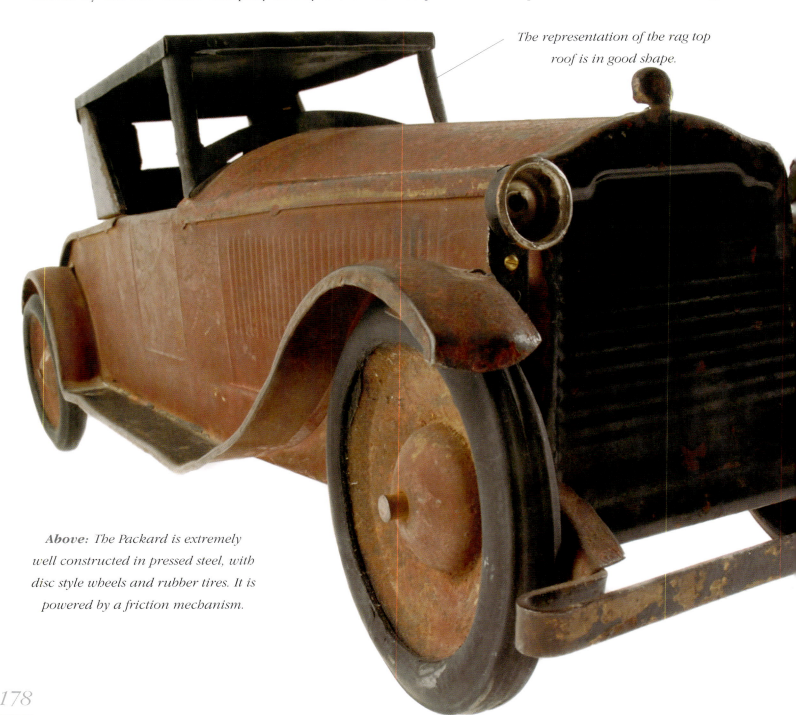

The representation of the rag top roof is in good shape.

Above: The Packard is extremely well constructed in pressed steel, with disc style wheels and rubber tires. It is powered by a friction mechanism.

The distinctive Packard hood mascot is only one of many fine details on this toy.

Below: *Although the bulbs are missing, this toy had battery-powered headlights—a very advanced feature for the 1920s.*

DISTLER

Prior to World War II the German toy industry was centered on the city of Nuremburg. Johan Distler founded his toy works here in 1895 to produce high quality steel toys. This fine large four-door sedan was made for the English-speaking market—presumably England itself, as the marking on the tires is spelt "Tyres." The word "Stop" also appears on the rear. Made in the late 1920s, the toy would have been a prestige one in its day. It had advanced features for the time, such as a clockwork motor, battery-operated headlights, and an illuminated rear number plate. The tinplate body is lithographed in brown, maroon and cream with orange lining. Strangely the license plates don't match—on the front is JD (Johan Distler) 5681,

but 7673 appears on the back. Perhaps it was based on Distler's personal limousine. Other markings include "Made in Germany" on the rear and the letters "JDN" (Johan Distler Nuremburg) inside a globe trademark. The red steel disc wheels have the words, "Balloon Tires" with the size "775 x145" printed on. Both rear doors open and there is a uniformed chauffeur in blue with red trim on the side pockets of his coat. Its length is 12 inches.

Above: The entry point for the clockwork key can be seen above the running board, above which is the operating lever.

Left: *A close-up of the [b]operated headlights, wh[ich] still have the bulbs inta[ct] reveals how sophisticat[e] toy is for the late 1920s.*

An illuminated rear license plate and above it the manufacturer's trade mark and the words "Made In Germany."

Right: *The wheels are stamped out of one piece of tin and beautifully detailed, and there is a side-mounted spare on the offside. This was a rich child's toy!*

THREE TIN CARS

These three toys from the late 1940s are first class examples of tin lithographed toys at their finest. The "Safe Driving School Car" has the slogan "Learn to drive" emblazoned on the hood and "Dual Control" on the trunk lid. It is made by Marx and is a wind-up toy with a key in the left side rear fender. Underneath, is lithographed detail of engine, muffler and transmission in red and black. This model comes in different colors, the author has seen a yellow-roofed version.

The bakery delivery van is made by Courtland of Philadelphia, Pennsylvania. It proclaims "Fresh Bread" on the doors and a lithographed delivery driver appears in the side window and on windshield, while the "Model Bakery" logo is repeated on the trunk lid. The van is finished in dark red and cream, which was very popular on toy cars in the 1940s, and is often seen on Courtland toys. This model is 7¼ inches long.

This page: Although the three cars are made by totally different manufacturers, they are very similar in size, styling, and method of assembly.

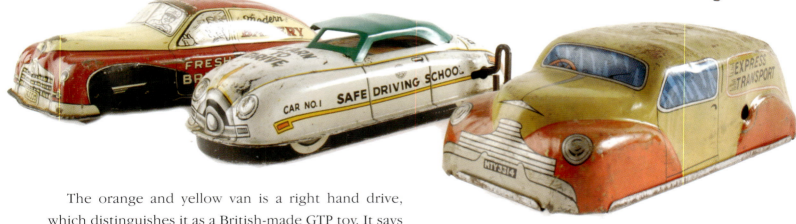

The orange and yellow van is a right hand drive, which distinguishes it as a British-made GTP toy. It says "Express Transport" on the side panels and the steering wheel is printed on the windshield on the right hand side. It is a wind-up toy and there is a hole for the key to the clockwork motor in the left hand side above the rear fender. Underneath the full-fendered body are pressed metal wheels and tires. This example has quite a few dings in the roof that will lessen its value on the collectors' market.

MARX SUBURBAN

Based on Chevrolet's famous people mover from the late 1940s, this fine Marx toy measures 20 inches in length and has the Marx logo on the side and on the front. It is two-tone blue and light blue trimmed with chrome, with lithographed detailing and is in good shape except for the molded roof. It was made in 1950–1951 when Marx first began using plastic and the first toys were horribly unstable—the styrene type of plastic was not yet perfected and it warped into shapes that bore no resemblance to how it was molded. The roof on this car is one example and another is a toy truck made by Marx called the "Auto-Mac." It originally had a flat dump bed but by now there are no examples that have not warped so badly that they will still function. Plastic obviously made the cars cheaper to produce and this was important to Marx, who always targeted their toys at the value market. This toy's roof and windows, which cleverly came as one piece, was molded in the Marx plant at Erie, Pennsylvania. The body is in metal and was probably made at the West Virginia plant in Glen Dale, where most Marx cars were made. The graphics are beautifully detailed and in great condition, so despite the roof, this item is still very collectible.

Above: A close up of the grille, bumper and headlight shows the Marx Suburban's finely-detailed features at their best.

Above: The toy has survived beautifully in terms of its paintwork and lithography. Shame about the roof though!

MARX SPORTSTERS

Louis Marx liked to offer value for money—give the customer more toy for less money was one of the company's founding policies. Well no toy more successfully demonstrates that ethic than the late 1940s sportster. The car is a generic design, with accents of great 1940s cars like the Cadillac Series 62 convertible, the Hudson Commodore Convertible and the Lincoln Series 9EL. The model is a stunning 20½ inches long, making it a

Left: The cars came in various colors, including red and the rarer light green.

Realistic door handles are part of the extensive body lithography.

really substantial toy to play with. It has a friction motor that drives the two back wheels and all the wheels have metal hubs with rubber tires. Originally the cars had clear plastic windshields, but these would have been vulnerable in play situations and all but a few mint examples have lost this part. Illustrated are two examples in red and light green. All body detailing is lithographed including grille and bumpers, door handles, chrome side stripes and front and back lights. Inside the car the upholstery and the dashboard are also detailed in lithography.

Below: *The sleek lines of the sportster are extenuated by the loss of its windshield.*

Above: *The grille and bumper lithography is a true work of art.*

TWO RED COUPES

These two cars are from the late 1920s or early 1930s and represent a slightly crude style of toy. The roadster has no markings but it has the look of something from Dayton, Ohio, about it—it is 18¼ inches long and seems to be emulating the lines of a Duesenberg. It has one-piece, stamped metal, ventilated-style wheels and a spare mounted on the trunk lid. Some detail is stamped into the pressed steel body, such as a louvered hood, door outlines, and radiator grille. The one-piece roof is missing a windshield and the toy is dented quite regularly over its entire surface, and has possibly been repainted at some point.

The second car is also from Dayton, but is identifiable as a Dayton coupe with a friction motor. Made at David P. Clark's Dayton Friction Toy Works around 1927, this toy is pressed tin. It has separate pressings for the grille and headlights, running boards, the roof and the windshield. Body details include hood louvers and top hinge, doors and ventilation flap on the front scuttle and the toy is 17 inches long.

Left: From this angle the amount of damage to the roadster is apparent. Only the fact that it is made of substantial sheet steel has allowed it to survive.

The wheels are a one-piece stamping and are hollow on the inside.

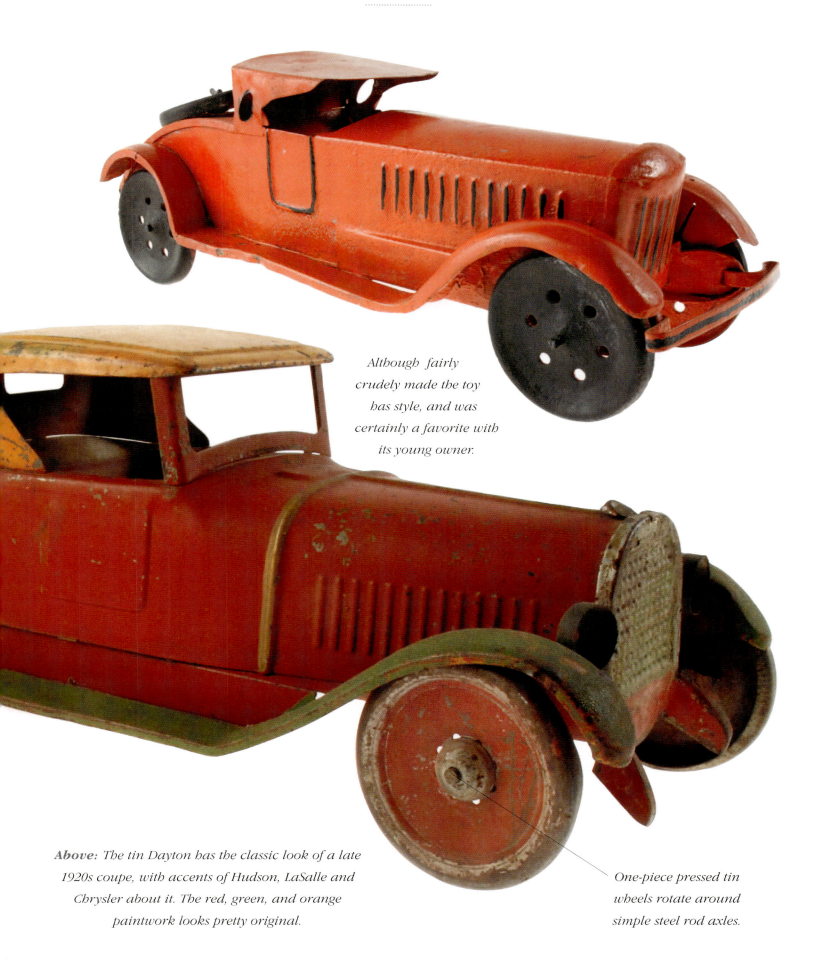

Although fairly crudely made the toy has style, and was certainly a favorite with its young owner.

Above: *The tin Dayton has the classic look of a late 1920s coupe, with accents of Hudson, LaSalle and Chrysler about it. The red, green, and orange paintwork looks pretty original.*

One-piece pressed tin wheels rotate around simple steel rod axles.

TWO BUICKS

The blue and white Buick convertible has a wind-up mechanism and the key is located in the right front fender. This was made in Japan by Marx in the late 1940s, when America was helping to get the Japanese toy industry back on its feet after World War II. It has the classic Marx look and quality about it nonetheless, with its lithographed detailing—such as Buick-style ventiports, lots of chrome, lining out, a dashboard,

grille, headlights and a license plate. The detail is further defined by the addition of several plastic molded parts, such as the white plastic driver and the clear windshield, neither of which—rather unusually for Marx toys from this period—have warped. It has snow-grip rubber tires imprinted "Buick" and there is a Marx logo on each of the side doors. The license plate reads "D6581."

Above: A front view of the Japanese Buick shows the imposing detail of the grille, bumpers, badge, and headlights.

Right: The rear of the Marx Buick is a simple stamping, with lithography for the detail of rear lights, license and trunk outline. The tab bottom center is where the upper and lower halves join.

The key is a fixed item that cannot be lost. This is a practical feature, which was based on experience of how children and toys interact!

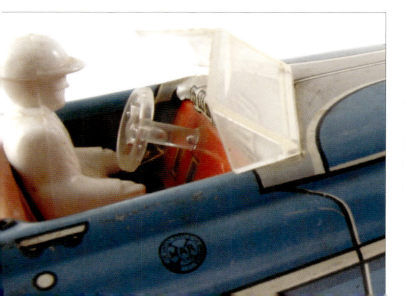

The second car was also made in Japan by an unknown manufacturer in the early 1950s, and is based on a Buick Roadmaster of the late 1940s. It has more surface detailing than the Marx, with separate pressings for the grille, bumpers, headlights, badge and hood mascot. This toy has clearly seen a lot of play and the paintwork is virtually extinct! It is powered by a friction mechanism, rather than a wind-up motor.

TWO FUTURISTIC AUTOS

Futuristic cars were extremely popular in the 1950s but after the austere years of World War II car design really took off, so these two are not as whacky as they might originally have been intended. The pressed steel blue car with gold trim, heavy bumpers and the Plymouth-look front was made by Mattel, the company who also created "Hot Wheels." The company was founded in 1945 by Matt Matson and Elliot Handler—hence Mattel. The second car has no maker's name and has lost some body detailing, such as the rear light clusters. The aerodynamic styling, central cockpit, headlights and low door sills put it ahead of its time in design terms.

The brass-plated body detail casing on the rear fender of the toy has ventiports, which were popular in the 1950s.

Above: This car shares the design influences of the Batmobile.

Left: The original paint can be seen where the decals have preserved it.

KARMANN GHIA AND ISETTA

The model of the Volkswagen late 1950s sports car is not marked, but its similarity to the second toy shown here leads one to assume that it is of identical manufacture. It shares its two-tone color scheme of cherry red and gray with the pressed tin Isetta three-wheeler "bubble car"—the full size version was made during the same period by BMW in Germany. This toy version was made in Japan by Bandai, the world's third largest toy manufacturer, which was founded in 1950. It is powered by a friction motor and has a lot of body detailing, including chrome air intakes and bumpers, side lights on the front, chrome hub caps, and an opening front door. The inside of the toy features a front seat lithographed with a checkered pattern. This would also date from the late 1950s.

Above: Model cars made by Bandai in the 1950s are now extremely collectible.

These air intakes serve the cooling and heating needs of the original and are part of the toy's charm.

Above: A neat and collectible model by any standards. The 1950s was the finest hour of tin toys.

BATTERY-OPERATED FERRARI

This red and cream toy car was made by Bandai in Japan. The Bandai company was founded in 1950, when the Japanese toy manufacturing industry was getting back on its feet after World War II, helped by American toy manufacturers. Ironically, Bandai is now the world's third largest toy manufacturer.

Like all things Ferrari, toys featuring classic models of the marque like the one shown here are extremely collectible and hold their prices particularly well. This toy, which dates from the 1960s, is accurately based on a 1957 Ferrari Superamerica model, which was designed by Pinin Farina. A battery-operated motor drives the rear wheels and also provides power for the working headlights and taillights. The fine body details include plastic headlights, red taillights, a hood scoop, chrome bumpers, chrome grille and door handles, and a blue tinted plastic windshield with a separate chrome surround. Unfortunately, the printed wire wheels are not particularly convincing! However, there is a proper replica of the Ferrari logo on the hood and Ferrari license tags. The fully-detachable hard top is nicely finished in a rich Rosso red, giving an overall two-tone effect, and the die-cast body has a molded sideline, louvers set in the front fender and hood, trunk and

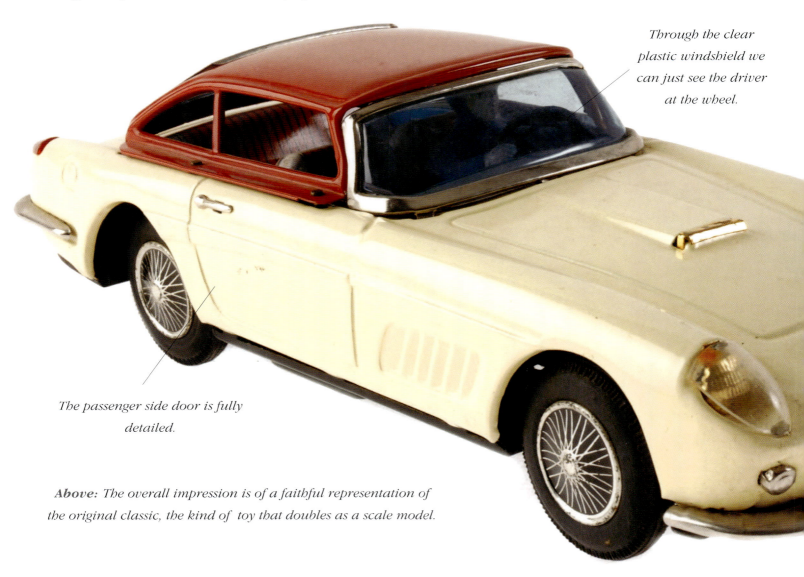

Through the clear plastic windshield we can just see the driver at the wheel.

The passenger side door is fully detailed.

Above: *The overall impression is of a faithful representation of the original classic, the kind of toy that doubles as a scale model.*

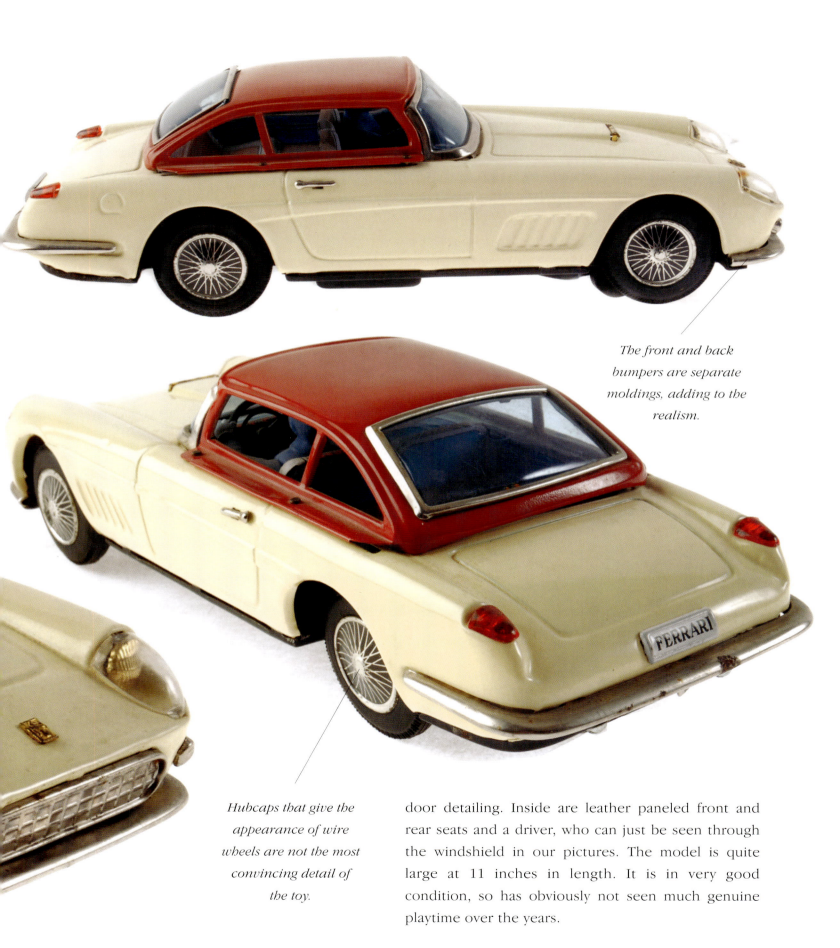

The front and back bumpers are separate moldings, adding to the realism.

Hubcaps that give the appearance of wire wheels are not the most convincing detail of the toy.

door detailing. Inside are leather paneled front and rear seats and a driver, who can just be seen through the windshield in our pictures. The model is quite large at 11 inches in length. It is in very good condition, so has obviously not seen much genuine playtime over the years.

SCARAB

This charming 1930's two-seater roadster built by Buddy L around 1936 is named for the Egyptian dung beetle, whose distinctive shape gave inspiration to a whole series of car designs in this period. The "Stout Scarab"—a sedan version—was another popular Buddy L model. Moline Pressed Steel began making models using the same gauge of metal used to make car parts; this eventually became the company's main activity and owner Fred Lundahl named his toy brand after his son Buddy. All Buddy L toys are robust and long lasting and were advanced mechanically—the scarab range featured cam-operated steering mechanisms activated by a spur gear linked to the rear axle. They were powered by clockwork motors, wound up by a key that was inserted into the left side of the body. The key is missing from our example but you can just see the entry port in the left hand side body trim. The body is a fairly simple, single sheet, steel pressing, with extra separate fixings such as the radiator grille and headlights, side embellishments, windshield frame and the 1920's-style lovers in the cockpit. The toy is 10½ inches long.

Below: The overall impression is of a wonderfully patinated toy in good condition after over 70 years of use.

A red upper body is fixed to the bottom plate by the flange that runs around the edge.

The windshield frame is secured by lugs that slot into the upper body.

Above: The ornate side embellishments add dash to the toy's appearance.

The two tin plate lovers' heads lean romantically close in a pose that is captured forever.

TWO JEEPS

The top jeep is made by Marx in pressed steel and dates from the early 1950s. Later models had plastic wheels, but this one has pressed tin wheels and tires, lithograph printed. The model is red with a yellow tinplate interior and a fold-down windshield, and has battery-operated working lights although the bulbs are missing. The guy leaning on the windshield is an 8-inch tall Tonka action figure, made of hard plastic, with a blue non-removable hat that has "Tonka" molded into it.

The bottom jeep is by Tonka. Made of pressed steel, it has plastic wheel and tires and a white plastic tray forming the upholstery inside the car.

Above: The Tonka action figure is wearing sunglasses and has red hair and a mustache. His arms, legs and head move.

Below: The Tonka jeep has battery-powered headlights and a red flashing light on the hood.

The wheels and tires are much more detailed on the Tonka than the Marx.

PICKUP AND TRAILER

Children love toy trucks that tow a trailer—in fact all of us like to pack up our stuff and transport it, even in play. Here we have a Tonka pickup truck dating from the mid 1960s paired with a similar vintage Nylint trailer. Tonka, a Minnesota company, was named for the Sioux word "Tonka," meaning "great" or "big." As befits their name, the toys were solidly constructed of metal, all-American playthings that could be handed down through generations. They have become valuable, just like the old vehicles they copy. This steel Stepside pickup farm truck is finished in the standard Tonka red of the period. The grille and headlight assembly is tarnished, but still present—many young fingers have

levered such accessories off over the years! The tailgate is missing, as are the plastic glazed windows, but the Tonka decals on the doors are still just visible. The hubcaps and whitewall tire trim plates appear to be missing from the plastic wheels, perhaps removed by a young customizer. The truck is 12½ inches long.

Like Tonka, Ny-lint (later Nylint) prided itself on sturdy construction and stylistic accuracy. The Nylint Tool and Manufacturing Company of Rockford, Illinois, specialized in toy construction items, trucks and cars, and many fans regarded the toys as better styled and built than their real life counterparts. Our trailer is a horse cart from the company's popular farm set.

Above: Two rival pieces of machinery with the same intent: to please generations of children. Both are now very collectible.

Right: A close-up of the Tonka front wheel, which has had the hubcap and whitewall cover plate removed exposing the cleverly-designed strut bracing in the casting of the plastic wheel that gives extra rigidity.

FORD BRONCO AND BARBIE JEEP

Two toys from companies at the top of their game signify a rivalry between Tonka and Nylint, and also between Ford and Jeep who were locked in a struggle for the real life SUV market in 1966. The jeep was based on the World War II all-purpose vehicle, which appealed to off-road drivers. It had also gained appeal in the posing market and this example in Barbie-pink, dating from around 1965, was in the latter camp. Designed by Tonka to appeal to a feminine audience, it was ideal transport for dolls.

Ford's answer to the Jeep was the Bronco, launched in 1966, a small rugged SUV that brought modern styling to the off-road market. This faithful copy by Nylint was launched a couple of years later.

Above: The glowing pink paint job with Surrey top in pink plaid just screams Barbie.

Right: The Nylint blue Bronco exudes masculinity.

The Ford-badged grille and headlight/bumper unit is a separate pressing.

TWO DUNE BUGGIES

Toys are good at recreating the past for all of us and these two toys bring back long-forgotten memories of a craze popular during the author's youth for tearing around sandy beaches in VW beetle-based buggies. Dating from the 1960s, when the craze was at the pinnacle of its height, these two excellent toys by Tonka have certainly caught the true spirit of the dune buggy. Most children would have played with them in the sandbox at home or on the beach anyhow, so it was all rather fitting. Finished in either red or blue, the bodies were simple one-piece pressings with plastic inserts for the seats, steering wheel, and roll bar. The wide wheels and detailed tires in black plastic complete the effect.

Right: A realistic pair of 1960's-style bucket seats and roll bar in black plastic.

Tonka captured the mood for wide wheels and tires in all their toys.

Above: The blue toy is a slightly higher-spec model with a decal on the hood and Tonka script on the tires. The wheels simulate magnesium alloys, which were popular then.

VW CAMPER AND BUG

This great VW camper van brings back the long summer days of the 1960s, when you could take off in your camper and cruise the beachfront with surfboards on the roof. Like the toy itself, surviving examples of the real thing are increasingly valuable these days. Made of tin in the 1960s in Japan, the camper has two-tone dark gray silver and bright red paintwork. Detailing is very good, with full interior equipment such as seats and an accurate steering wheel, and on the outside the front badge, headlights and bumpers all give the impression of a accurately modeled toy.

Likewise the heyday of the VW Bug, made famous in movies like Herbie, just has to be celebrated in toy form. The tin Bug is cherry red and was also made in the 1960s in Japan.

Below: This VW camper van looks all ready to be packed up for the next trip.

Below right: Two great period models of fun cars from the 1960s. The substantial-looking roof rack-good for surfboards is particularly appealing!

TWO MUSTANGS

There is an old adage in the car industry that if you can hook children onto car toys you have a ready-made future buying audience. Children also have a say in what cars their dads buy. To most people the decision on what car to drive is second only to where they live and it is a significant day when they visit the showroom to make such an important purchase. Ford were one of the first manufacturers to make promotional give-away toys of cars available to their dealer network. Whether they were only given to the children of actual purchasers or to prospective purchasers is not known, but it must have been a powerful lever to have the

child on the side of the salesman! The red model here represents the original 1964½ Mustang 260, which some consider the classic design. Recognized by the Tiffany Award for Excellence in American design (the only car to achieve this honor), the car sold over half a million copies in the first year of production. Little wonder that Ford produced promotional models of the updated design, which appeared in 1967. The blue car is the updated version, which was Ford's response to Chevrolet's "Pony car"—the Camaro with its fastback design. Both models are extremely well detailed and in demand from both toy and Mustang collectors.

Left: *The fine detailing in this model means that you could be looking at a close up of the real thing.*

Below: *Both models are so accurate that Ford could be confident they would show off the car's features to prospective buyers. The wheel trims are particularly appealing.*

TWO HUBLEYS

The Hubley manufacturing company of Lancaster, Pennsylvania, stared out making cast iron toys, but by World War II they had switched to die-cast zinc alloy. Acquired by Gabriel Industries in 1965, the company continued to make high quality metal cars—including some in kit form that the enthusiast could assemble himself. The two examples here are the yellow 1960s Hubley Phaeton and the 1950s MG TC. The phaeton has lost the upper part of its windshield and headlights. The interior is red and it has metal wheels with rubber tires. The red MG has also lost its windshield and its paintwork is in poor condition. It too has metal wheels and rubber tires.

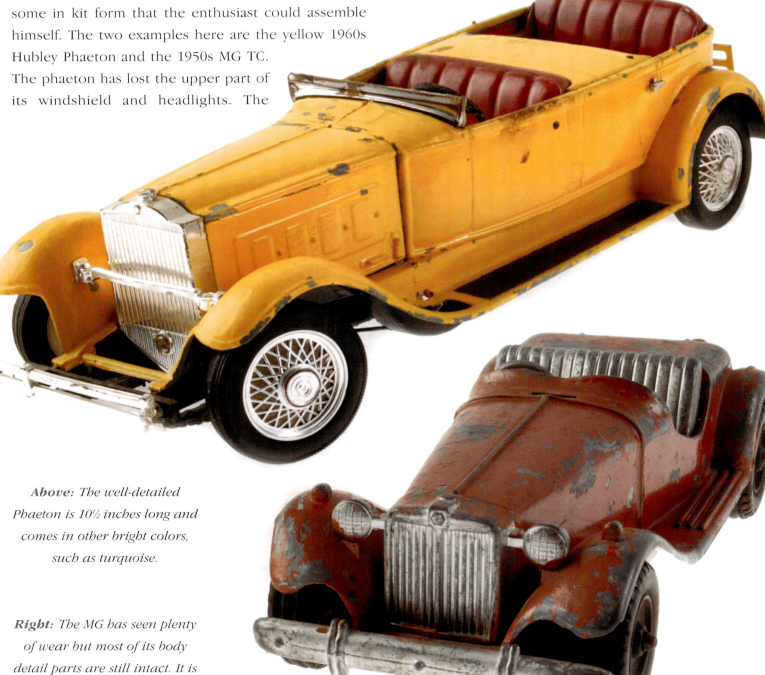

Above: The well-detailed Phaeton is 10½ inches long and comes in other bright colors, such as turquoise.

Right: The MG has seen plenty of wear but most of its body detail parts are still intact. It is 9 inches long.

TWO JAPANESE TIN CARS

These two cars date from the early 1950s when the Japanese toy industry was re-establishing itself after World War II and the U.S. represented a large potential export market. Japanese manufacturers like The Modern Toy company (TM Trademark), Nomura Toy (TN trademark), Bandai and SSS carefully researched what kind of cars American and European children liked to play with. These two examples are generic

Below: Inside the red car the cream seats are a separate metal tray.

Both toys have excellent details.

cabriolets with a strong European look to them, possibly Mercedes. American buyers started to import cars from Europe in the 1950s and the toy market began to reflect this. The cars are made of tin and the light green one has lithographed upholstery, while the red car uses a cream metal tray to represent the seats. The folded rag top of both cars is made of plastic, as are the wheels, and bumpers, grilles and headlight assemblies are separate metal moldings. The green car has twin horns on the front fenders but its windshield is missing. The red car has its windshield. The bodies of both cars have nice details in the pressings, such as running board strips, hood louvers, doors and handles, and ridged upholstery. Both toys are 8 inches long.

AMISH BUGGY AND BELL TOY

The heyday of cast iron toys was at the end of the 1800s—by World War II most metal toy makers had switched to die-cast zinc alloy, which was lighter and required a lower casting temperature. Early toys like this Amish buggy would have appealed to nineteenth century children. Made by A.C. Williams of Ravenna, Ohio, in the late 1890s, it was originally painted—it shows signs of red paint on the wheels. It is drawn by a single horse and travels on 8-spoke wheels. John

Williams founded his company in 1886 in Ohio and specialized in cast iron horse-drawn rigs, autos, airplanes and tractors. What more obvious model to include in his range than an Amish Buggy? The detailing on this toy is quite exceptional, since they can often be quite crude. It is 5 inches long.

The pull toy is a cast iron horse harnessed to a chiming gong on wheels, made by the Gong Bell Manufacturing Company who specialized in making

Below: A faint glowing hue is all that is left of the once-bright paint on this toy. The wheels and carriage interior appear to have been red and the horse brown or black.

Fine details in the casting, like this step, distinguish this toy from many cruder cast iron productions.

The ornate cast iron wheels house the two halves of the chiming mechanism.

The front wheel keeps the horse's feet clear of the ground.

bells and toys. The company was founded in 1866 by H.H. Abbe, E.C. Barton, E.G. Cone and A.H. Conklin in East Hampton, Connecticut. In 1872 Barton patented the "Revolving Chimes," which consisted of a pair of brass bell halves mounted between two cast iron wheels. This was the first Gong Bell toy, but in the 1880s the company pioneered the "Chestnut Bell" which became a craze all over America. It was attached to a coat lapel and rung to warn someone that their story was a repeat. The company was incorporated in April, 1899 and made foot bells for automobiles but in the 1920s made one of the most successful toys ever— the "Playphone 600," a toy telephone with a bell, earpiece and moving receiver hook. Gong Bell later made toys under license to Disney but foundered in the 1960s due to its failure to get into plastic toys, which took over from metal at that time.

STAGECOACH

Cast iron toys persisted into the 1930s, but suffered due to the war effort when many toys were handed in for melting down to make arms, tanks, aero engines and the like. This has greatly increased the collectibility of surviving examples of original cast iron toys from companies such as Kenton and Arcade. This fine stagecoach dates from the late 1930s when Western toys were still popular. The coach body is cast in two halves and held together with a screw and nut fixing, which can be plainly seen on the side of the door. The cast iron wheels rotate around steel spindles, with axles swaged (or formed) over at the ends to locate the wheels on the shafts. The body has detailed framing, which is picked out in gold paint. The two charging horses are mounted on either side of the shafts on two

screws fixed with nuts and there is a trailing wheel underneath the animals to allow the toy to be pulled along. The driver is cast and painted in great detail in what looks like a full "Forty-niner" rig of 10-gallon hat, blue collarless vest with the sleeves rolled up, and gray pants stuffed into knee-length riding boots. The paint scheme overall is in a good old smooth finish enamel that has some minor chipping. The coach body is in red with gold framing, the wheels bright yellow with gray hubs, and the horses white with gray reins and hooves, and manes and tails in a gray streaked effect. The item does not have a manufacturer's mark but the standard of finish would suggest Kenton, who did not mark their pieces in the later years of production. The stagecoach is 11 inches in overall length.

__Below:__ A beautifully crafted cast iron toy that has great lines, which exude a sense of speed and flowing movement.

Left: The driver is unusually lifelike for a cast iron toy. You can even see the bulges in his arms where he has rolled up his sleeves.

The parking brake is part of the body casting.

Wheels are fully functioning on steel axles.

TWO AIRFLOW AUTOS

The same toy in two sizes: one is 4½ inches long and the other 8 inches. Presumably the same mold scaled down provided the Hubley Manufacturing Company with two differently–priced toys for the price of one tooling. Hubley was launched in 1894 in Lancaster, Pennsylvania, by John E. Hubley and specialized in cast iron toys such as horse-drawn vehicles, toy guns, electric toy train equipment and parts, and household products like door stops and bookends. The company's toys were marketed as "Lancaster Brand Iron Toys" along with the slogan "They're different."

These two cute autos date from the late 1930s, when the airflow car craze was at its height. Although generic rather than exact copies, the design seems to slightly lean more to the Desoto than the Chrysler. They have one-piece castings for the bodies and separate castings to detail the headlights, radiator grille, bumpers, and running boards. The moving wheels have rubber tires on metal hubs.

Left: The beige car is smaller and the tires have perished.

Below: The red car is larger and in much better condition.

CAST IRON CARS

In the early years of car toys, cast iron was the most popular material. Dent of Fullerton, Pennsylvania, were one manufacturer who started producing in 1898 and were renown for the fine detail of their castings. This yellow cab, which dates from the 1920s, was a staple in their range. It was 7¾ inches long and the body is cast in two halves. The disc-type wheels are solid castings, attached by two steel rods as axles.

The black car is an Arcade Ford touring car, dating from 1923, which is also a money bank—many of the early cast iron cars doubled as banks. This toy is 6½ inches long.

HILLCLIMBER AUTO

When the D.P Clark partnership broke up in 1909 the Schiebel Toy Company launched a heavy lawsuit to protect the name "Hillclimber," which applied to toys with a weighted flywheel mechanism that could store energy from being pushed and move forward with enough power to climb a slope. D.P. Clark was one of several toy companies established in Dayton, Ohio, at the end of the 1800s to exploit Israel Donald Boyer's patented "Locomotive Toy mechanism," the power behind the "Hillclimber." The motor was used in a variety of toys, including boats, trains, trucks and cars. Despite the lawsuit, D.P. Clark, then trading as the Dayton

Friction works, continued to use the name—it was by then a type of toy rather than a specific brand, in the same way that a "Hoover" was any brand of vacuum cleaner. Our example is an extremely early one, judging by the construction and the style of car, which is definitely pre-1900. The driver and passenger's clothes are totally nineteenth century: the lady has a long skirt, waisted coat and trilby hat tied on with a muslin scarf, the little girl a "Buster Brown" cap. The toy is made of pressed steel stretched over wooden side panels and the driver's bench is made of wood. The lady driver is cast in two parts riveted together and the child in one piece; the wheels are cast iron also. The toy was originally painted in bright colors—much of the enamel used is still in evidence.

The cast iron wheels have stood the test of time structurally but have lost most of their beige paint.

The sheet steel is stretched over wooden side panels, which act as formers.

Above: *This is what all the fuss is about: the patented "Hillclimber" mechanism.*

The back of the bench seat is made from sheet steel.

The lady driver shows traces of a pink and blue outfit.

The little girl passenger, uncomfortably perched on the edge of her seat, has great detail: lace-up boots and a "Buster Brown"-style hat.

RACING CAR AND MOTORCYCLE

Two really early cast iron toys, which celebrate the dawn of motoring. The boat-tail speedster has the appearance of an early A.C. Williams, in the days before Adam Clark Williams retired in 1919. Small cast iron toys were Williams' specialty—particularly banks, cars and aircraft. A car of the same design appears in the 1932 catalog, but with the characteristic turned steel hubs and starred axle peens indicating a later model.

The unmarked motorcycle has the look of a Kilgore or Arcade casting, but it is pretty crude even by the standards of the time. The cast iron wheels are totally enclosed—we only know that they are there by the two peened-over axles in the body sides. This makes an interesting comparison with the Maisto motorcycle on the facing page.

Above: Cast iron is virtually back to its natural state here, with very few traces of remaining paint.

The only decorative detail redeeming this crude casting is the lightning bolt motif along the side.

HARLEY-DAVIDSON

Motorcycle toys have always been popular and this modern bike is based on the 1986 Harley-Davidson FLST in 1:18 scale—a classic motorcycle that uses design cues from the 1940s through the 1960s. It was made by Maisto, a Californian toy company who currently produce everything in Thailand or China. Maisto's success is in offering toys of popular models, cars or bikes, at really good prices. This toy is made from plastic with metal parts and is 5 inches long.

This model shows just how finely detailed the Maisto range is—even close up you could be looking at the real thing.

U.S. AIRMAIL MOTORCYCLE

This classic toy dates from the 1930s and is an Indian motorcycle with a side cart for carrying the U.S. Mail. It was made by the Hubley Manufacturing Company of Lancaster, Pennsylvania, whose toys were marketed with the slogan "They're different." The company, founded by John E. Hubley in 1894, specialized in its early years in cast iron toys like this one, but later it moved to die-cast alloy toys instead. The original toys were branded as "Lancaster Brand Iron Toys," but because cast iron was a valuable resource many Hubley toys were handed in at the start of World War II to be melted down to provide tanks and armaments—which has made surviving models like the one shown here even more valuable. It would appeal especially to both collectors of U.S. Mail items and those more interested in Indian motorcycle memorabilia—as well as general toy collectors.

As is usual with Hubley toys, our example is extremely detailed: the bike itself has moving handlebars with rubber grips, accurate engine casting, speedo, fuel cap and tank, saddle, footrests and lights. The metal wheels are spoked and have rubber tires. The toy is made in three parts and is held together with screws, which can be clearly seen on both the crankcase and sidecart. Both the bike and the sidecar are finished in red enamel paint work and has Indian decals on the gas tank, a red, white, and blue U.S. Air Mail flag on the side cart, and the cylinder heads, finned piston barrels, and handlebars painted gold. There is some rust on the spokes of the wheels, some paint chips, and the rubber tires are a little bit perished, but for a toy approaching 80 years old it is in a remarkable condition. It is 9½ inches long and there is no rider.

Below: The "U.S. Air Mail" and "Indian" decals are still intact after 80 years!

The side cart is
cast in two parts.

Rubber tires are slightly perished but
still present. Many toys lose their
tires and this affects the value.

Above left: From this angle the impression is of an
extremely pleasing toy that accurately represents the Indian
motorcycle on which it is based.

THREE MOTORCYCLISTS

If ever there were a toy that could be described as pure Americana, this is it. The Champion Hardware Company of Geneva, Ohio, was in business from 1883 to 1954, making novelty household products in cast iron: things like bookends and doorstops. A finely-cast pair of bookends, a conestoga wagon pulled by oxen, was offered for sale quite recently—the company's items are now highly collectible. During the Depression, however, the company was experiencing hard times because the sale of all but essential household goods was pretty much ruled out—those people who still had homes didn't have much to spend on them. The company therefore turned to toy production; it is a strange phenomenon that during hard times toy sales seem to stay

quite constant—most people try to treat their children to offset the tough time they are having. Champion produced toys only between the years of 1930–1936, under the management of C.I. Chamberlin, and during that period they produced a range of cast iron items that included cars like the Chrysler Airflow, a Plymouth-type coupe with opening rumble seat, an REO coupe, a race car and a sedan. A

series of trucks was also produced, such as the "Gas & Motor Oil Truck," a "Mack Dump," "Mack Express," "Mack Stake Bed Truck," and two wrecking trucks. One of the company's strategies was to produce the same toy in different sizes, for example the Mack Stake Bed Truck was 4½ inches or 7½ inches long.

Above: A close-up of the Champion CM 3 reveals what a delightfully detailed toy it is.

The CM 1 is only 5 inches long.

Possibly the most familiar toy made was their series of motorcycles and riders. Unlike some toy manufacturers who made the rider as a separate item, so it gets lost, Champion cast the motorcycle and rider as one piece. The motorcycle cop rider was painted blue with a flesh tone to the face and hands, the tires were white rubber and nickel spoked wheels were an option. Here we show two of the sizes: the CM 1 (5 inches) and the CM 3 (7¼ inches).

The third motorcycle is a Hubley HM32, on which the rider's head swivels. It is 6½ inches long.

1930'S CAST TOYS

An interesting assortment of cast metal toys from the 1930s. The light green car in the foreground has the appearance of a cast iron toy from Arcade and looks as if it is loosely based on a Ford coupe roadster. Ford was one of Arcade's favorite makes to copy. The white rubber tires on metal hubs are also a trademark of Arcade at this time. This toy is 4¾ inches long.

The small wrecker and the car it has rescued are most likely to be Barclay toys. During the 1930s and 1940s, New Jersey-based Barclay was the largest producer of lead alloy vehicles in the United States. Its fastest seller was the "No. 53 Racer," an early slush mold lead toy that was just 2 inches long.

This 1930's die-cast stake bed truck has a nicely authentic worn but original paint finish.

Below: Cast iron versus die-cast: the coupe roadster has much heavier moldings and less body detail.

AUBURN RUBBER MOTORCYCLES

Many toy manufacturers arrived at that happy state by way of making other products, like Tonka who started out making garden tools and Arcade who made coffee grinders. The Double Fabric Tire Company, founded in 1913 in Auburn, Indiana, started out making tires for the Auburn Automobile Company. That company, founded in 1893, was making a single-cylinder, chain-drive runabout, which became one of America's first cars. The fortunes of the tire company followed that of the car maker and by 1919 Auburn had lost its way—in 1924 production was down to 10 cars per day. At this time the Auburn Rubber Company was born out of the ashes of the old tire manufacturer, and the decision was taken to phase out production of tires and make other rubber products. In 1935 Auburn started making rubber toys, including motorcycles, buses, cars, trucks, tractors, figures and animals. The company made soles for combat boots and gaskets for "jerry cans" in World War II, returning to toy manufacture after the war. In 1959 the company was sold and moved to Deming, New Mexico, finally going out of business in 1969.

Here we have three examples of Auburn Rubber toys from the 1930s: a standing traffic cop in light blue rubber blows his whistle; a smaller motorcycle cop (under 5 inches) in light blue rubber with yellow wheels speeds past; and a larger cop (9 inches) in blue rubber, with yellow wheels and silver engine, eases back in the saddle.

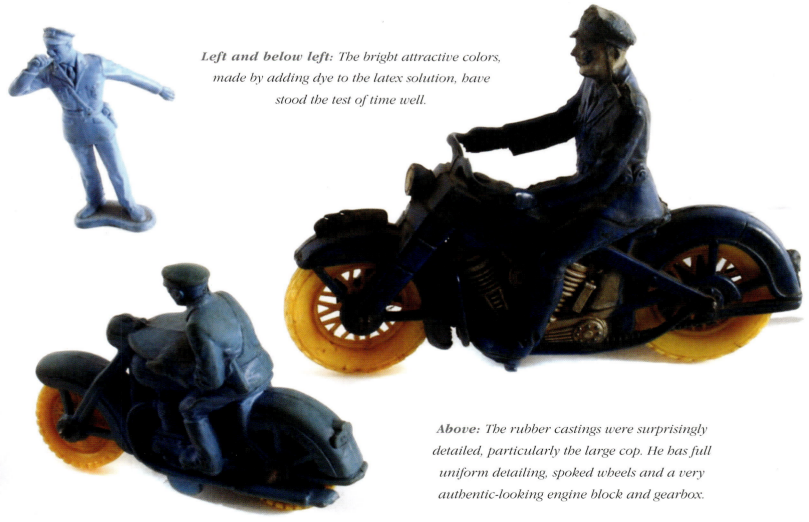

Left and below left: The bright attractive colors, made by adding dye to the latex solution, have stood the test of time well.

Above: The rubber castings were surprisingly detailed, particularly the large cop. He has full uniform detailing, spoked wheels and a very authentic-looking engine block and gearbox.

DICK TRACY CAR

When Chester Gould wrote his first Dick Tracy strip in *The Detroit Mirror* in 1931, it is unlikely that he conceived for a moment the amount of spin-off merchandising it would spawn. The rock-jawed, eagle-nosed detective's profile would grace a thousand toy products, and some key examples, like this green Marx toy car, are featured in this book. This magnificent tin lithographed car dates from the late 1940s and is clockwork powered with a battery for the roof-mounted spotlight and siren. The body lettering features "Squad Car No. 1" on the rear fender, "Dick Tracy" both sides of the hood, and "Police" and the small word "Tracy" on both sides of the front fenders. On both doors there is a shield with Dick Tracy's unmistakable features in profile. Other lithographed details are the full compliment of passengers, with Tracy at the wheel, Sam Catchem at his side and Police Chief Brandon in the back. The car has a lever at the left hand side rear that engages the clockwork motor. It is 11 inches long.

Lithographed characters inside the car include Dick Tracy himself at the wheel.

Left: *The police shield with Dick Tracy profile and copyright notice underneath.*

Above: A detail showing the entry port for the key to the clockwork motor. The squared shaft inside that winds the motor is just visible.

This tarnished grille and bumper assembly is a separate tin pressing over the lithography on the front of the car.

DICK TRACY COPMOBILE

Made by the Ideal Toy Company, this magnificent plastic car dates from 1963. Ideal was one of America's oldest toy companies, founded in New York in 1907 by Morris and Rose Michtom after they invented the Teddy Bear in 1903. The company traded successfully for many years during the founders' lifetimes and beyond, specializing in novelty and character toys like Howdy Doody, Batman and the Dukes of Hazzard.

The car is two-tone blue and cream with whitewall tires and, rather like Dick Tracy himself, it is full to the brim with gadgets. It has a battery-operated microphone, speakers and an amplifier, to enable the child to use it as a PA system and, also powered by battery, it has spotlights and

a siren, controlled by a switch in the trunk. A nice feature is the chrome plated grille and bumper in true 1960s style, which accents the front of the car. The car has decals on the side with the familiar "Dick Tracy and watch" copyrighted image, plus the words "Dick Tracy Copmobile," perhaps a play on "Batmobile"—another popular toy produced by Ideal.

Above: The car bristles with great electronic gadgetry like the antenna, the roof mounted loudspeaker and the spotlights. Imagine pulling this out of the box on your birthday!

One-piece plastic hubcaps and whitewall trim finish off the wheels nicely.

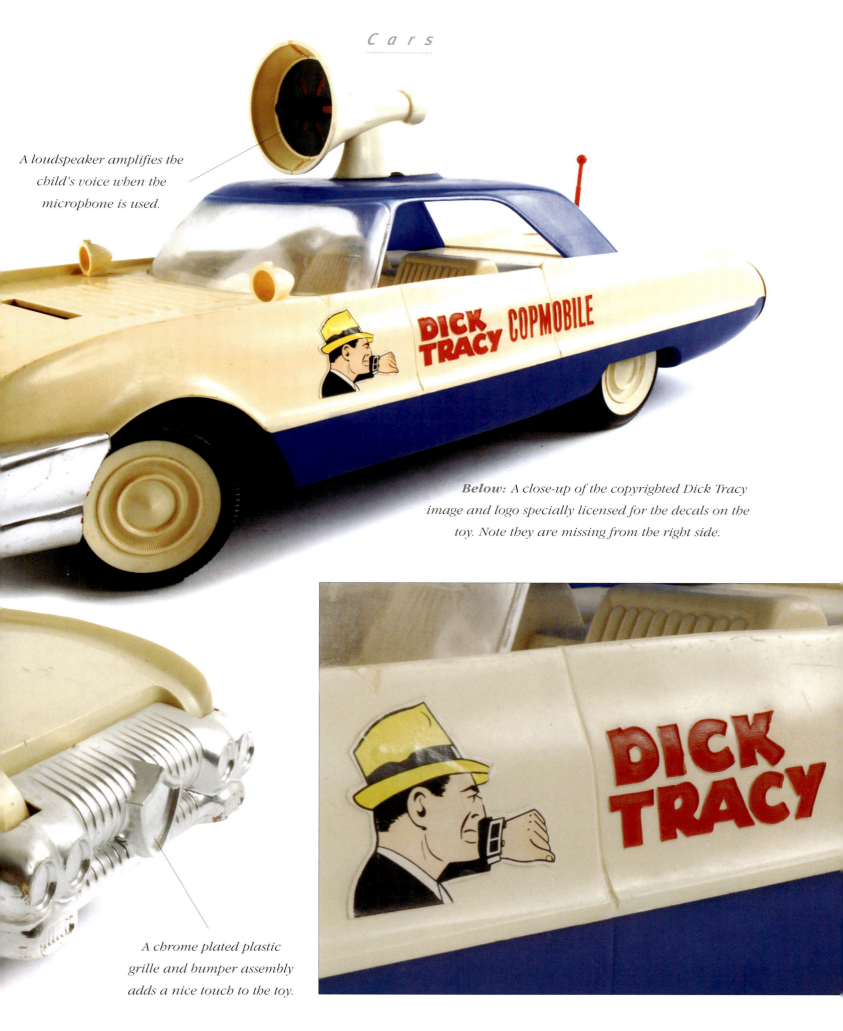

A loudspeaker amplifies the child's voice when the microphone is used.

Below: *A close-up of the copyrighted Dick Tracy image and logo specially licensed for the decals on the toy. Note they are missing from the right side.*

DICK TRACY COPMOBILE

A chrome plated plastic grille and bumper assembly adds a nice touch to the toy.

DICK TRACY

COWBOY BOOTS

In the 1950s every child wanted to dress up to play. After the austerity of the war years, when few people could spoil their children, the 1950s came as welcome relief. New-found prosperity meant that more people had better jobs, and seemed able to afford homes and new cars—things were generally on the up, so once again it was possible to indulge your children. Television in every home featured action shows about the Wild West, and shows like *The Cisco Kid* and the *Lone Ranger* inspired children to don western garb. Cowboy hats, simulated cowhide waistcoats and chaps were on sale in most toy stores, but these were mainly cheap interpretations of the real thing. Some children yearned for something more realistic—like these perfectly scaled down cowboy boots, which must have cost some doting 1950's parent a small fortune. The cowboy boot is specifically made for riding: the pointed toe and slick sole allow the boot to be easily inserted and removed from the stirrup. The high heel is designed to prevent the foot sliding forward in the stirrup, as well as giving a height advantage. Most boots were originally made from cowhide, but later other more exotic hides, such as rattlesnake, alligator, elk, moose, and buffalo, were employed.

Below right: These classic children's boots are based on the "roper" style with more rounded toes and heels. They are plain black cowhide.

Left: These western-style boots employ ornate stitching and have exaggerated pointed toes. This was a design conceit from the 1940s.

It is hard to tell if these children's boots were used in play or everyday life but they have certainly seen some wear.

ROY ROGERS JACKET

Roy Rogers, "King of the Cowboys," was born Leonard Franklin Slye in Ohio in 1911. His parents worked hard and were adventurous, traveling all over until the family finally settled in California. Roy found work in movies and got his big break when Gene Autry walked off a movie that Roy was also acting in. Roy could play guitar and sing, as well as act, and he became the embodiment to many of the all-American hero. He featured with his wife Dale Evans, his smart horse Trigger, and his German shepherd dog, Bullet, in over one hundred movies. The *Roy Rogers Show* ran on radio and subsequently on television for a total of fifteen years. Children all wanted to be Roy and this beautifully-made buckskin jacket would have been a cool thing to wear.

Above top: *The detail of the label shows Roy Rogers with his trusty steed Trigger and the title "The King of the Cowboys." Its owner, Mike, wisely wrote his name on the label.*

The western fringe was one of Roy's trademarks; even his shirts were heavily fringed.

TWIN HOLSTER SET

This toy would have been every boy's dream back in the 1950s, when it was made. Hubley of Lancaster, Pennsylvania, specialized in really realistic western toy guns that were virtually full size—these guns are basic Hubley Cowboys and are full 12 inches long. They are based on the Colt 45 single-action, and were one of the most popular toy guns of their day. The Cowboy model is available in a variety of finishes, including a gold plated "Classic" that has black grips. Our guns are finished in a realistic gray cast finish, which goes very well with the ivory-colored plastic grips. The name "Cowboy" is cast into the frame and the grips have

Above: The whole set with the guns stowed in the holsters.

Left: A close-up of the belt shield, showing a pioneering scene of a wagon train passing through the mountains.

Above opposite page: A detail of the "Cowboy" name cast into the frame and the fine handgrips with steer's heads.

Left: The whole set with the guns out, ready for action!

embossed steer's heads and the Lone Star of Texas. The cylinder on these guns rotated when the trigger was pulled, just like the real thing, and they fired reel caps like the Star Brand ones on page 231.

Supplied with the guns was a pair of all-leather holsters with the trademark H rivets for Hubley, fancy edges with extensive studding and three pressed steel wheel motifs on each holster. The belt has wheels on each side of an embossed shield showing a wagon train scene, and also has a silver-colored western-style buckle and tip. The belt is 33 inches from tip to tip and the holsters are 11½ inches from the top of the belt to their bottoms. This is a very collectible piece.

G MAN GUN

Toys reflect society's interests and concerns and in the 1930s the spotlight was on organized crime. A popular weapon on both sides of the battle was the Thompson sub-machine gun, which was developed by Colonel J.T. Thompson during World War I, but arrived too late for

out in 1935, starring James Cagney, and the term became fashionable and therefore of potential interest to toy manufacturers. Marx Toys were always pretty quick off the mark with toys at the cutting edge of public interest, so this G-Man automatic gun was

action. Peacetime sales were stimulated by the arrival of bootleggers and organized crime, brought about by Prohibition. The Division of Investigation of the United States Government (DOI) affected the arrest of gangster Machine Gun Kelly in 1933 and legend has it that Kelly shouted "Don't shoot G-Men," giving birth to the slang expression for government men. The DOI morphed into the FBI and a popular radio program called *G-Men* was launched, developed in part by J. Edgar Hoover himself. This program was also known as *Gangbusters*—the other term associated with the activities of the FBI at the time. The movie *G-Men* came

Above: The lithography shows two G-men packing the gun. It was also marketed as a "Gangbusters" model, with the magazine horizontally mounted in the frame.

launched in the late 1930s. Made of tin with heavy lithography showing two agents packing the guns, the toy was loosely based on the .45 caliber Thompson with the 50-round drum magazine. It had a wooden stock and a wind-up mechanism—the fixed key is in the right side of the frame at the rear. When wound, pulling the trigger caused the gun to emit a raucous, machine-gun sound. The gun is 24 inches long.

A solid wooden stock just like the real thing.

Like all Marx toys, the G-Man gun is colorful and eye-catching, helping sales considerably.

HUBLEY DAVY CROCKETT

A classic toy gun from Hubley of Lancaster, Pennsylvania. Davy Crockett, a real life backwoodsman from Tennessee, was turned into a screen legend by actor Fess Parker when Walt Disney Productions launched the television show on December 15, 1954. The movie *King of the Wild Frontier* premièred the following May. "The Ballad of Davy Crockett," sung by the Sandpipers, and the movie music, by the Mitch Miller Orchestra, hit the charts. Children went wild for coonskin hats and Davy Crockett muzzleloaders—and this "Davy Crockett Buffalo Rifle."

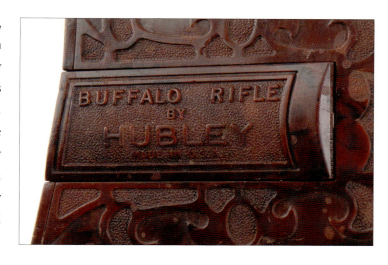

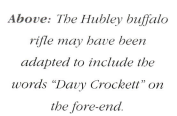

Above: The Hubley buffalo rifle may have been adapted to include the words "Davy Crockett" on the fore-end.

Top right: A close-up of the patchbox lid with the words "Buffalo Rifle by Hubley, Made in the U.S.A."

Right: A close-up of the cast metal flintlock action with an engraving of a buffalo. Hubley are famous for this level of detail.

WESTERN ACCESSORIES

To the serious juvenile western fan in the 1950s and 1960s, having the right accessories was very important. A cool Marshal's badge, a pair of handcuffs hanging from your belt to apprehend rustlers, and a pair of spurs jingling from beneath your chaps, were absolute essentials. These extras were things that your Auntie could buy you for your birthday—they didn't cost the earth. The attached assortment of accessories are all items from this time. In the photo below, the spurs are from the 1950s (left) and 1960s (right), the handcuffs 1950s (left) and 1960s (right). The selection of lawman stars are in die-cast metal or plastic and one is even in the original packaging. But when was Billy the Kid ever a Sheriff?

Above: *This Marshal's badge looks extremely realistic.*

SELECTION OF CAPS

The real thrill of playing Cowboys and Indians was in hearing the satisfying crack of the cap exploding and seeing a puff of smoke as you pulled the trigger—and smelling the enticing aroma of cordite. The trouble was that not every cap detonated: the blue rolls with bigger blobs exploded better than the cheaper red rolls with hardly any explosive. In the heat of a battle rolls were changed in a hurry, so torn off cap roll littered the ground. The manufacturers strived to make their products explode every time—like the "Shootin' Shell"

range by Mattel, where a "Greenie Stik'M'Cap" (center of display) was stuck on the end of the shell case like a real primer. The "Bang Caps" made by Kilgore are for repeating pistols, 50 rolls and 2500-shot packages. The Mammoth Company of New York proudly states on the box "Guaranteed Sure Fire" and "Where American workers are paid American Standard wages." Also shown are the Halco "Jet" roll caps, 20 rolls with 100 shots, originally sold for a dime! A "Daisy Red Ryder Treasure Chest" has 23 packs, with 3500 BBs.

Rare Wales Brand "Giant Caps," with 72 shots.

Above: *Caps by Kilgore, Marx, Kent, Star, Stevens, Hubley, and others. The "Shootin' Shells" are for the Fanner 50.*

Kilgore "Lubricated Caps" are disc type caps: "Extra loud, safe and harmless."

FRONTIER SCOUT RIFLES

The two Hubley rifles shown here can be regarded as his 'n' hers. The "Scout Rifle" (bottom) was specifically marketed for cowgirls back in the 1950s, with its white fancy stock. It has two short barrels with a band based on the Winchester 1866, and the lever action pulls down to load the reel caps into a tray. The words "Scout Rifle" are engraved into the sideplate and is 33 inches long. The "Frontier" with the single barrel has "Frontier" engraved on the sideplate and "Hubley MFG" cast into the buttplate. It also has a tray for loading the caps, which drops down from under the mainframe, and it is 35 inches long.

BUFFALO BILL RIFLE

Daisy and Heddon combined for a while to produce the magnificent BB gun shown below. It dates from the late 1960s and has "Buffalo Bill Scout" engraved on the side of the polished steel action. There is a sling ring at the front of the fore-end and an engraved medallion inset in the right side of the plastic stock celebrating "Buffalo Bill Chief of Scouts." The Model number is 3030 and the gun is based quite closely on the 1866 Winchester "Yellow Boy" Carbine. It was made in Rogers, Arkansas.

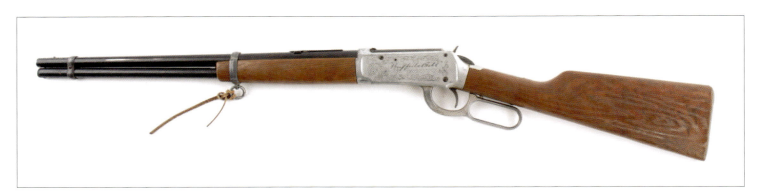

THE RIFLEMAN

The television show featuring former Brooklyn Dodgers' star Chuck Connors aired in 1958 and was reckoned to be the most violent show of the time. Lucas McCain (Connors) had invented the world's fastest-loading rifle and the plots revolved around his awesome firepower in the face of bad guys. Hubley won the contract to produce this toy gun based on the very special rifle in the series. It was available with a brown (as here) or black stock.

MAVERICK PISTOL

When ABC launched their original comedy-western series back in 1957 starring James Garner, they created a new genre in western entertainment. Nobody could ever quite take Bret Maverick seriously—until he reached for his gun and turned out to be unexpectedly good with it. This merchandised gunslinger-style pistol and holster, copied from the one used on the show, was made by Esquire Novelty/Leslie-Henry. It is a bronze long-hammer revolving cylinder pistol, with white stag grips and a very fancy leather holster.

A pretty fancy holster, for a gambling man!

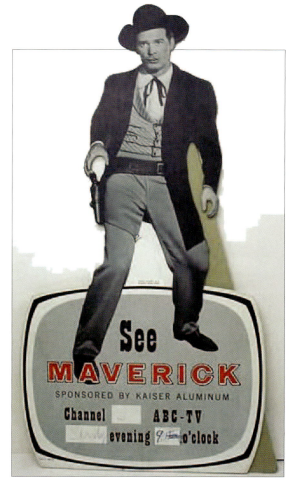

See
MAVERICK
SPONSORED BY KAISER ALUMINUM
Channel   ABC-TV
evening 9 o'clock

FOUR TOY PISTOLS

To real western fans the later 1950s- and 1960s-type pistols and rifles, like the Hubleys and Fanners where realism mattered, are the ones that people collected. Earlier, much cheaper, pressed steel and tin toys seem so much less interesting. But then much of the enjoyment of a toy is in the imagination of the child, and perhaps a small boy in the Depression would have been delighted to receive one of the guns pictured here. Let us start with the gun at the bottom right from Wyandotte, the manufacturer from Detroit who set up in close proximity to the auto industry to take advantage of cheap off-cuts of pressed steel. This gun

is a 5-star dart gun, which had a strong spring inside to shoot darts from the barrel, and is 8½ inches long and 4 inches high. Wyandotte also did pop guns branded "Red Ranger" in similar body pressings. The two guns on the left are Marx "clicker" pistols—when the trigger was pulled they made a loud clicking noise. The gun at the top right is a Japanese lithographed tin toy from the early 1950s, the kind of gun that would be offered for sale in dime stores. It has "Cowboy" lithographed on the grips and fired darts or corks. At best, these guns could be described as novelty lines but they are still part of the western toy story.

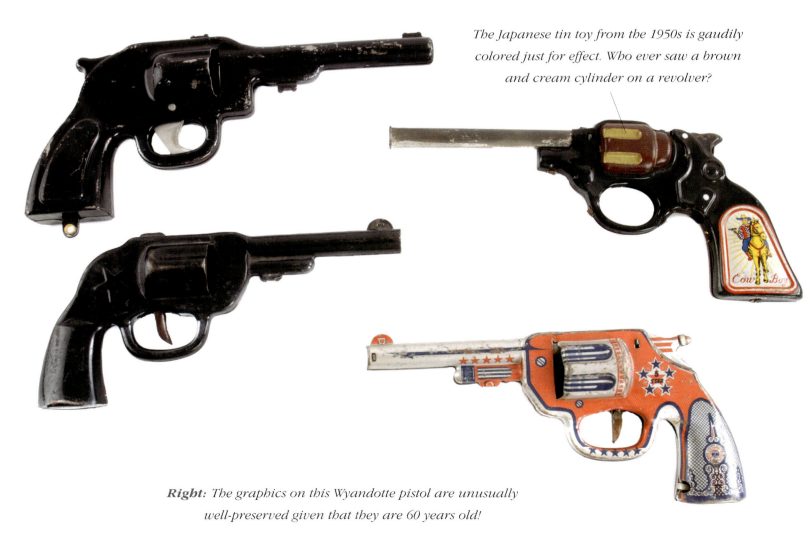

The Japanese tin toy from the 1950s is gaudily colored just for effect. Who ever saw a brown and cream cylinder on a revolver?

Right: *The graphics on this Wyandotte pistol are unusually well-preserved given that they are 60 years old!*

THREE CAST IRON PISTOLS

These are some of the oldest examples of toy guns in our western section, dating right back to the beginning of the twentieth century.

The bottom gun is a Kilgore, manufactured when the company was operating out of Westerville, Ohio, in the 1930s and is marked "Made in the U.S.A." and "Patented." All of these guns have a real quality to them, despite their lack of detail. They have the weight of a real gun because they are made of cast iron and this definitely puts them ahead of the pressed tin types. The fact is that there was little call for any realism in toy guns until after the advent of the movies, when guns were shown in much more detail on the big screen, which rekindled interest in the frontier and its weapons.

Guns were cast in two halves and bolted together; the heads of the nuts were then ground off.

This Federal-Kilgore is the oldest gun on the page.

The Dixie pistol at the top of the page dates from the 1920s, but the original cap pistols made by the company were patented as early as 1894. This gun has rather the look of Smith and Wesson about it.

The middle gun is a Federal-Kilgore and was made by the Federal-Buster Corporation of Homestead and Pittsburgh before World War I. It is a single shot cap gun. These guns were numbered #1 up—ours is a #7 which you can see cast into the top of the grip.

HUBLEY DETECTIVE SPECIALS

Handguns on the frontier were carried openly in holsters as part of the western rig. However, as times progressed and guns were not carried so openly, there came a need for concealed weapons—for detectives particularly. Alan Pinkerton and his agents achieved a lot by using undercover methods and were responsible for bringing in several notable criminals by these means. The type of gun that could be carried comfortable under a coat and also drawn quickly needed to be of short-barreled design, lightweight construction and a compact action—but still carry a punch. Children now played Cops and Robbers as well as Cowboys and Indians and thus the toy market needed to address this need; toy gun specialists Hubley of Lancaster, Pennsylvania, were one of the first manufacturers to design a range of detective specials.

The top left gun dates from the 1950s and is based on a cut-down Colt single-action—it may well even have been an adaptation of another casting for a full-sized gun.

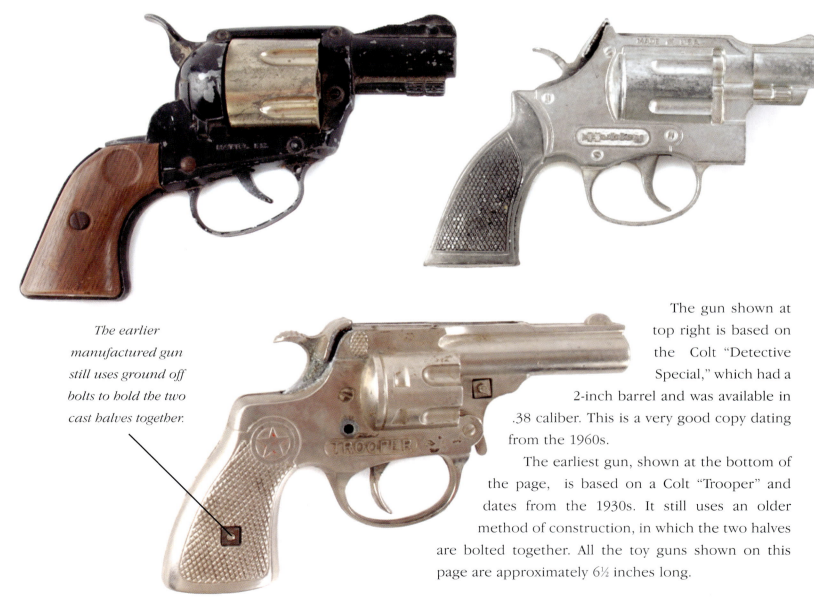

The earlier manufactured gun still uses ground off bolts to hold the two cast halves together.

The gun shown at top right is based on the Colt "Detective Special," which had a 2-inch barrel and was available in .38 caliber. This is a very good copy dating from the 1960s.

The earliest gun, shown at the bottom of the page, is based on a Colt "Trooper" and dates from the 1930s. It still uses an older method of construction, in which the two halves are bolted together. All the toy guns shown on this page are approximately 6½ inches long.

KENTON CAP PISTOLS

The Kenton Lock Manufacturing Company was founded by F.M. Perkins and incorporated in May, 1890 in Kenton, Ohio. In November of 1894 it became the Kenton Hardware Manufacturing Company, and soon started making toys as well as household novelty items like bookends and doorstops. The company specialized in cast iron products, so cast iron toy pistols were an obvious line to pursue. To start with castings were pretty crude and the guns were stylized approximations of guns, rather than any real model. They had names like "DOC," "PUP," and "BAT" rather than any kind of western branding, which came later when the western

toy audience became more sophisticated due to the influence of movies. The guns were titled revolvers, but they didn't actually work this way since they were just single piece castings. Instead they fired caps—the

Pins hold the two halves of the gun together.

Left and above: These guns have "K" for Kenton cast into their handgrips.

big Mammoth round, single shot type. The three examples here are from the 1920s and have big, clumsy firing hammers for the caps, while the bodies are held together with exposed steel pins. The top one is marked "Oh Boy," and there is a "K" for Kenton cast into the upper grip of the middle gun. Similar guns were made by Denton and Stevens.

THREE CAST IRON CAP PISTOLS

The Kilgore Company of Westerville, Ohio, is responsible for the cast iron cap pistol shown at the top of the page. It is in the style of the Colt "Trooper" launched in 1935 and dates from just a couple of years later—Kilgore had a patent on this type of heavy detective gun. It is finished in natural black cast iron and appears to have been repaired, because the bolt acting as a pivot for the barrel and chamber has a non-standard hexagonal nut on it.

The middle gun is a Hubley "Flash" from around 1934 and has a revolving cylinder, which is an advance on the solid casting of the Kilgore. This gun was originally nickel plated.

The third gun, at the bottom of the page, is a 1937 Hubley "Dandy" model, which still has traces of its nickel plating. This has a revolving cylinder, which turns as you pull the trigger—just like the real thing. All three guns shown here are approximately 5¾ inches long.

Above and right: *The two Hubleys have the names of the model cast into the upper part of the handgrips, "Flash" and "Dandy."*

The cast iron guns are beginning to look more modern than the ones on the previous pages and are evolving towards the later guns on the facing page.

THREE DIE-CAST CAP GUNS

During the late 1930s cap gun manufacturers turned away from cast iron and began using die-cast alloys instead. This was easier to work with, was much lighter and finer detail in the casting was possible.

The gun at the top of the page is a "Bronco" made by Kilgore, and dates from the early 1950s. This is a short-barreled version with a low sight, engraved with a bucking horse on the frame and a mountain lion on the barrel. The white plastic grips have a molding of a saddle and boots and it has revolving cylinder that opens and closes. Black grips were also available for this model.

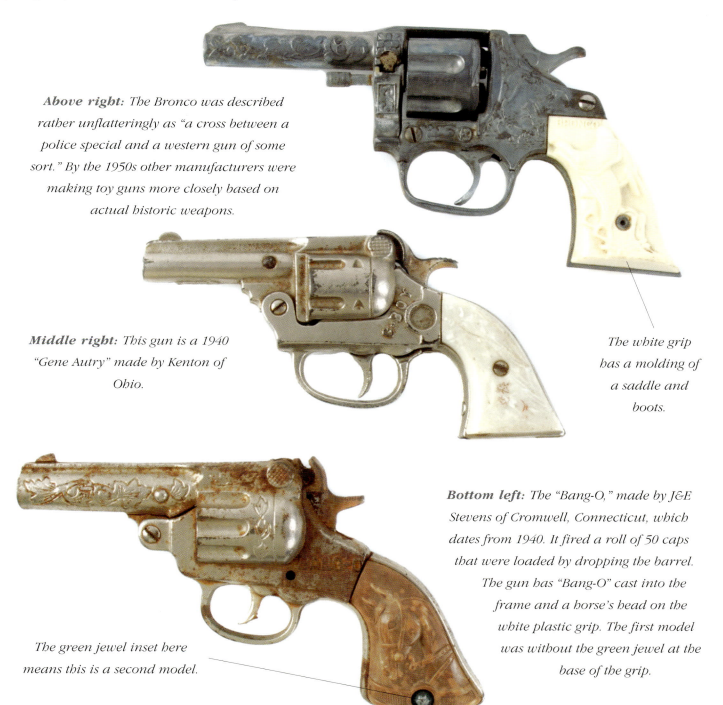

Above right: The Bronco was described rather unflatteringly as "a cross between a police special and a western gun of some sort." By the 1950s other manufacturers were making toy guns more closely based on actual historic weapons.

Middle right: This gun is a 1940 "Gene Autry" made by Kenton of Ohio.

The white grip has a molding of a saddle and boots.

Bottom left: The "Bang-O," made by J&E Stevens of Cromwell, Connecticut, which dates from 1940. It fired a roll of 50 caps that were loaded by dropping the barrel. The gun has "Bang-O" cast into the frame and a horse's head on the white plastic grip. The first model was without the green jewel at the base of the grip.

The green jewel inset here means this is a second model.

239

SHOOTIN' SHELL FANNER

By the 1960s realism was very important and this gun was at the head of the field. The "Shootin' Shell" system developed by Mattel Inc. for their Fanner range allowed the owner to put caps into the actual cartridge and load the cartridges into the revolving cylinder—just like the real thing! The "greenie" caps and spare bullets for the gun are shown on page 231. The gun is high quality die-cast and nickel plated, with plastic stag grips that were based closely on the Colt 45 Peacemaker, and was produced between 1959 and 1965. It is 11 inches long.

Right: *The gun is shown here with a Paladin-style holster (see page 242).*

"WANTED DEAD OR ALIVE"

Back in the 1950s there was nothing like a television series to get toy sales going! When Steve McQueen starred as Josh Randall, the bounty hunter with the sawn off rifle which he used as holstered weapon, it was an ideal opportunity to roll out some new merchandise. The series ran from 1958 to 1961 and during that time both these rifles were on the market. The packaged cap-shooting gun on the left is from Marx and was billed as the official version of the "Mare's Laig"—the gun's name in the series. It comes with a fairly basic holster and two bullets and the packaging material virtually tells the story of the television series.

The Esquire-made version on the right is a little more extensive, with a gold hammer, trigger and guard. It fires caps and comes with a full-length holster, complete with clip and thong.

Below: A rather unflattering picture of Steve McQueen on the highly informative packaging of the Marx toy.

PALADIN HOLSTERS AND PISTOLS

"Have gun, will travel" was the motto of Paladin, the gentleman-scholar turned gunslinger. Craggy-faced Richard Boone (inset below) starred as the man in black clothes who righted wrongs for a fee of $1000. When off-duty he lived in a fancy San Francisco hotel, the Hotel Carlton, dressed in fine clothes and quoted poetry, but when on a case he was a ruthless killer. If the person who had hired him turned out to be the villain, he would switch sides. His name is from the most versatile piece on the chessboard—the white knight, or Paladin; perfect inspiration for some toys. This handsome holster and belt in black leather has pressed metal, white knight chess pieces on each holster, tie-downs and a silver buckle. The belt has "Paladin" printed on it and loops for 14 spare bullets. The guns were made by Leslie-Henry of Wilkes-Barre, Pennsylvania, for Halco Distributors (J. Helpern Company of Pittsburgh, Pennsylvania).

Above and opposite: *Paladin's card and one of the Leslie-Henry cap guns. They have similar grips to the Marshal model; the trigger guards resemble the Maverick.*

FANNER 50 IN BLACK

This black-finished "Fanner 50" comes with its original holster. Made by Mattel Inc., this particular model is not the "Shootin' Shell" type (see page 240) but the ordinary Fanner. It works by fanning the hammer, which feeds the caps through firing them as you go. This particular version is quite rare—it was made in 1962 to tie-in with a new Chuck Connor's *(The Rifleman)* television show, *The Cowboy in Africa*. The white pearl grips have impala's heads on them.

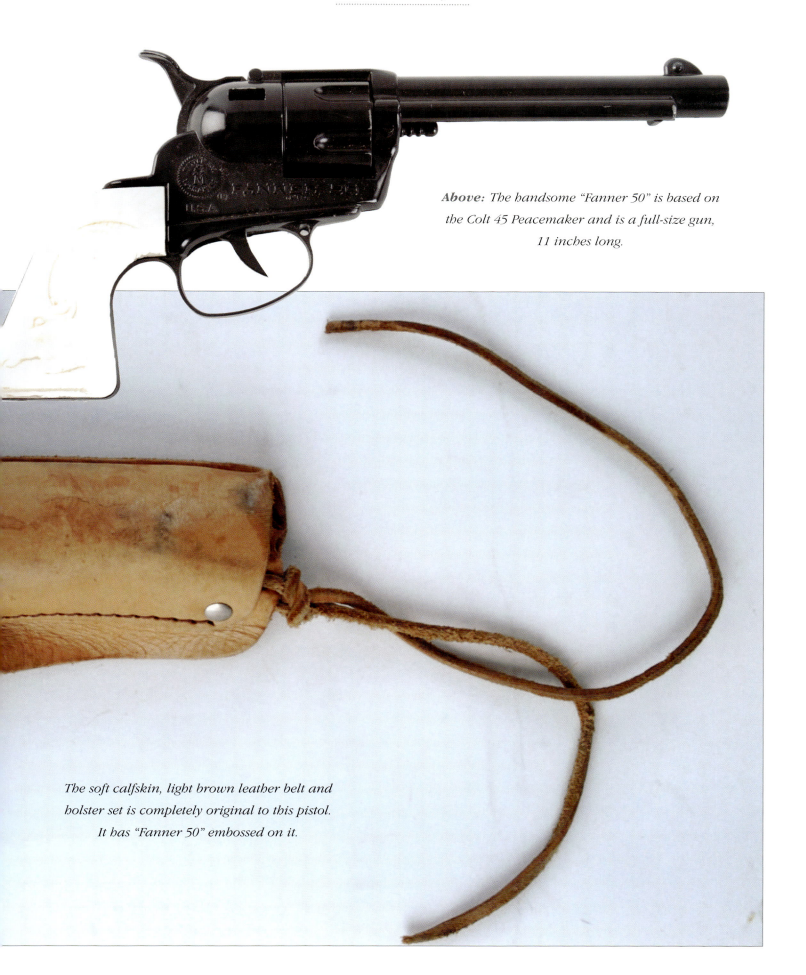

Above: *The handsome "Fanner 50" is based on the Colt 45 Peacemaker and is a full-size gun, 11 inches long.*

The soft calfskin, light brown leather belt and holster set is completely original to this pistol. It has "Fanner 50" embossed on it.

NICHOLS DERRINGERS

Two brothers, Talley and Lewis Nichols, founded Nichols Industries in Pasadena, Texas, around 1945. The company concentrated on cap guns of all sorts. Their guns were extremely realistic, like the two Derringers shown here. The guns break like the Remington single-shot Derringer that they so strongly resemble and a 3-piece bullet comprising of a case, shell and red plastic pellet is primed with a Stallion round cap. Fit it into the breech, pull the trigger and wham—the pellet is fired.

Above: Replacement packs of firing shells and plastic pellets were available for Nichols guns.

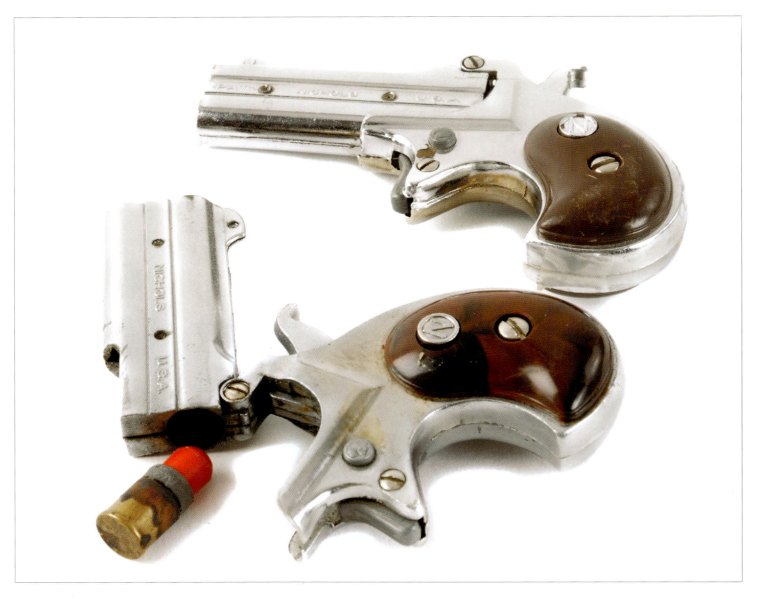

DERRINGERS AND BELT BUCKLE

In the mid 1950s a new breed of hero emerged. 1930's and 1940's movies had shoot outs, fist fights and chases on horseback, but heroes like Maverick and Paladin were subtler and more refined. They carried concealed guns like Derringers in the sleeve of dandified clothes, leading to a demand for small cap toys. The Nichols company was pre-eminent in this field; after being taken over by Kusan in the mid 1960s they also made cheaper versions of their quality Derringers, marketed as "Dyna-mite" like top gun here. Earlier Nicols had screws to fix the two halves of the gun together, later ones were riveted like this gun.

The two lower guns are made by Hubley. The white-handled one takes a bullet (shown) rather like the Nichols system (see facing page), but the red-handled one is a "dummy" meaning that it does not.

The "Buckle Gun" is by Mattel Inc.—push out your belly and the Derringer pops out! It is labeled "Remington Derringer 1865."

PAPER SHOOTERS

Described by the manufacturer as "absolutely harmless" these three "Paper-buster" guns date from 1940. They sold for 25 cents in those days, but are now extremely collectible. The Langson Manufacturing Company began in Chicago in 1923, where they made industrial tools, dies and stampings. It was founded by Otto A. Langos, who arrived in America from Hungary in 1904, and was an inventor with at least 19 successful patents to his name. One of his inventions was a range of "Nu Matic" toy guns that produced a loud bang without the need for caps and these were marketed as a sideline to the core business. The guns used strips of scrap paper that were fed into the top; as the trigger was pulled the paper was stretched tightly against a rubber grommet that created a tight seal, simultaneously air was compressed in a chamber inside the gun and released, exploding through the paper and causing a loud bang. The company produced toy torpedoes and a cannon that worked along the same lines.

Three different models of "Nu Matic" paper busters.

The toys are stamped with the address of the Langson Manufacturing Co. at West Huron Street, Chicago, Illinois.

DIE-CAST AUTOMATICS

Toy automatic pistols really took off in the late 1930s and early 1940s—perhaps seeing your dad go off to war took the interest out of the Wild West for a while. All the major toy gun manufacturers added automatics to their ranges, although a lot of the guns were generic copies using different characteristics from various types of gun. Some were pretty crude, but others were accurate copies. Our top gun here is a Hubley "Forty Five" and is a fancy looking gun with green engraved hand grips and nickel silver finish. It was probably based on the Browning or Colt service 45. The name "Hubley" is stamped on one side and the words "Forty Five" on the other. When the lever in front of the trigger guard is depressed, the top flips up so that the caps can be loaded. The gun is 7¼ inches long and 4¼ inches high.

The other two guns are both made by Kilgore of Westerville, Ohio. The middle gun is a Kilgore "Presto" from 1940, the name is cast into the side of the frame. The bottom gun is a Kilgore "Captain" from the 1930s.

Top right: The Hubley "Forty Five" has a lot of intricate filigree-style detailing, both on the frame and the handgrips.

Bottom left: The Kilgore "Captain" is the oldest of the three toys.

AUTOMATIC PISTOLS

Three more classic automatics made in American in the late 1950s and 1960s. In 1965 Nichols Industries sold out to Kusan of Nashville, Tennessee. Some of the guns produced after that time were a little more mass-market and perhaps they looked to reduce costs. The Colt 45-inspired automatic at the top is a Nichols-Kusan from the late 1960s and has a top-loading hatch for loading the caps. The nickel silver finish is worn at the muzzle-end of the gun, but this is quite usual in this model. It is 7 inches long.

The middle guns is probably the most valuable—it is a Hubley "Hawk" dating from 1958. It has very good nickel finish and the entire frame is covered with elaborate scrollwork. It has white plastic pearl grips and is 5¾ inches long.

The lower gun is the Hubley "Dick" a 1950's detective special that was very much a budget line for Hubley. Sold on a card (rather than in a box) it was a 50-shot cap repeater—the grip pivoted forward to allow access to the cap bay. It is 4 inches long.

THREE LONG TOMS

Cast iron was the material that made the Kenton Lock Manufacturing Company of Kenton, Ohio, famous. The company made hardware products—particularly locks and keys—from its incorporation in May 1890, but in 1903 it brought out its first toy lines. These were cars that were called "Red Devils," since most cars in those days were painted red, but cast iron cap guns very soon followed and by the 1920s these were one of the company's most popular toys. The three examples here are all long-barreled revolvers that are known as "Long Toms."

The top gun dates from 1928 and is in a natural cast iron finish. It has "K" for Kenton and the words "Trooper Safety" cast into the handgrips.

The middle gun is earlier and has the words "The Scout" cast into the frame just above the handgrips.

Top right: *The barrel breaks down to allow the caps to be loaded.*

Center above: *This gun is a single-shot, taking the old round caps. It has a fixed barrel.*

The hammer on this gun still works fine.

Bottom right: *This gun is the same model as the top one but has a much brighter nickel finish.*

TWO HUBLEY WESTERNS

The Hubley Manufacturing Company of Lancaster, Pennsylvania, was long renowned for its well-made and attractive cast iron toys. By 1940, however, the cost of producing cast iron toys was becoming prohibitive and Huble—then the largest producer of cast iron toys and cap pistols in the world—began to change over to die-cast zinc alloy toys. A very popular die-cast line was the western range shown here. Although they have been described as "rather simple guns," they are perhaps only simple by Hubley's very high standard of accuracy.

The range was nickel plated, which has mostly worn off these two guns, and the name "Western" was cast in the sideplate just above the trigger. The handgrips came in a choice of colors—here blue and white, but brown and green were also available. A steer's head was molded into the plastic grip and a cast star motif held the grip at the top. The barrel broke downwards on this model to access to the cap compartment. The guns were repeaters and took roll caps, like the box of Star Brand caps shown. The gun is 8½ inches long.

THREE HUBLEY TEXANS

Three examples of Hubley's celebrated "Texan" range dating from the 1950s, shown in three different finishes; silver, gold, and pewter. These are some of the most popular cap guns ever made—at least, some of them are cap guns. Since some American states didn't allow guns that fired caps, Hubley also produced some special guns with dummy hammers to get round the legislation, and the top gun is an example. All three have the Hubley trademark white plastic grips with steer's heads.

In 1952 the company manufactured 11,184,878 die-cast cap pistols—many would have been Texans.

TWO COLTS

The top gun is a Hubley Colt 45 based on the Civil War Colt Army Model 1861. The only markings on it are the words "Colt 45," and it has plain pearl plastic grips and a working loading lever under the barrel—these are often missing in examples of this particular model. Nichols also do a Model 61 in the "Stallion" range that resembles this gun. Another interesting feature of the Hubley is the cylinder, which is different color nickel plate than the barrel and frame. This huge gun is a massive 14 inches long.

The lower gun is a Nichols "Stallion 45 MkII" in bright nickel finish with black handgrips, based on the Colt Peacemaker. Nichols, in their heyday, prided themselves on the fact that their guns were designed to take apart—it was their belief that children loved to take things apart so their guns were designed to do just that.

Above: *The distinctive "N" for Nichols shown here on the handgrip meant quality in the 1950s and 1960s.*

THREE PIRATE GUNS

When children weren't playing Cowboys and Indians they often liked to play pirates. The author used to dress up with a bandanna, a patch over one eye and an old plaid scarf over one shoulder. A favorite part was to heft a Hubley double-barreled flintlock "Pirate" gun. This was remarkably accurate for the times, with scrolled trigger guard, engraving on the barrels, lock and hammers—it even had its own ramrod.

The second gun is a "Hubley Flintlock," a name cast in heavy capital letters into the barrel; again it is a double-barreled weapon with twin hammers and filigree engraving on the lock and barrels, and it has a very authentic wood-effect butt.

The third gun at the bottom is a "Frontier Automatic Cork Pop Gun," perhaps a bit more Davy Crockett than Davy Jones!

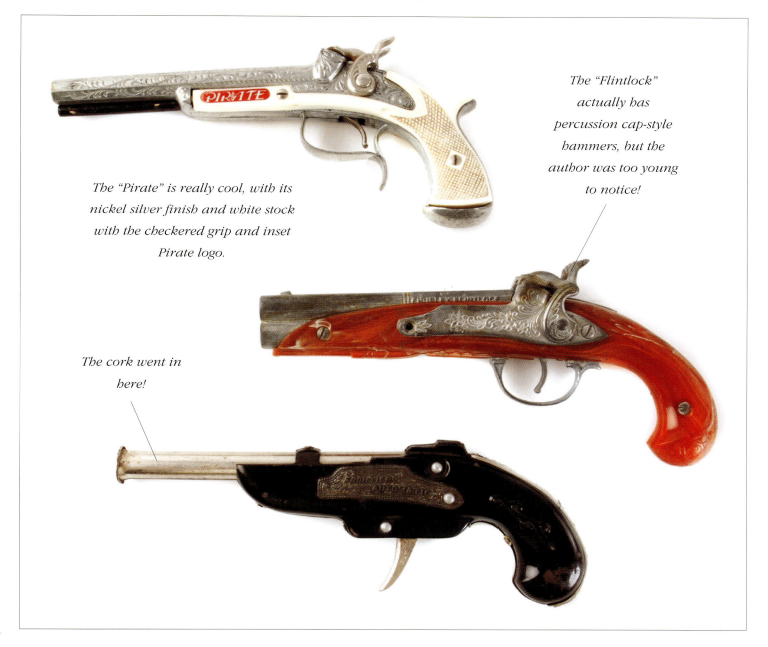

The "Flintlock" actually has percussion cap-style hammers, but the author was too young to notice!

The "Pirate" is really cool, with its nickel silver finish and white stock with the checkered grip and inset Pirate logo.

The cork went in here!

DAISY RED RYDERS

"Boy, that's a daisy!" was the reaction of the General Manager of the Plymouth Iron Company when he fired designer Clarence Hamilton's new gun. This was 1886, and the company, which produced farm windmills, was looking to diversify its manufacturing base. The market was uncertain, with the arrival of electric or gas-driven machinery, and the gun which started as an incentive (farmers were given a free one with the purchase of a new windmill) ended up saving the company.

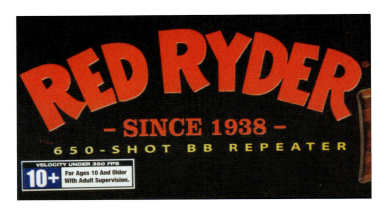

Three generations of Daisy. The bottom gun is a "Model 39 Carbine," the forerunner of the "Red Ryder."

BUZZ BARTON SPECIAL

Way back in 1932 Daisy made history when they were the first manufacturer to name one of their guns for a personality. Buzz Barton was a circus performer and Hollywood actor. Born William Andrew Lamoreaux in Galatin, Missouri, he was known by various aliases, including Billy LaMar and Red Lennox, before becoming "Buzz Barton—the Boy Wonder of Westerns," as he was known in Hollywood. He endorsed the Daisy model 195 as the "Buzz Barton Special." This particular gun had a walnut stock, blued metal, and a working scope sight. The first models had a paper label but afterwards the name was branded into the stock in a star-shaped—or later an oval—logo. In the later models, stocks were made of light maple and dark mahogany. The example shown here is a later gun, originals are hard to find!

DAISY CORK GUN

As a committed toy company, Daisy always triedvery hard to emulate interesting real guns in their model range—most children like the idea of toy guns that look just like the "real thing." Their "spittin' image" range of the 1960s set out to emulate classic models like the Winchester 1894—the first in the range and their best seller! Other models offered were the "Model 26 Remington Fieldmaster" and the "Colt .45 Frontier Revolver." The cork gun shown here was for younger children and is based on a Stevens or Remington trench/riot carbine-style shotgun. It has the traditional Daisy quality about it, with a wooden stock, authentic pressed metal barrel, and slide action painted black. The spring that ejects the cork from the barrel is tensioned by the lever under the barrel and activated by pulling the trigger.

BENJAMIN PUMP RIFLE

The motto of the St Louis and Benjamin Air Rifle Company was "The Gun that Shoots." Before about 1925 in America air guns were just for children, but with the advent of guns like the Benjamin, which had plenty of power and were also very quiet, adults started to take an interest in them as well. This gun is bronze colored with some blueing on the barrel—earlier guns were made of brass—and has a walnut stock. It dates from 1937–1938. It is a Model 300 (if BB Cal.)—but this was almost identical to the later Model 310 except for the pump. The Benjamin was considered one of the best BB guns around at the time, since it was not only very powerful but also properly engineered out of the finest materials.

HAHN BB GUN

The Hahn "Super Repeater BB" rifles dates from the 1950s and has a black finish over steel. The gun's name is cast into the left hand side plate and in its day it was a more powerful BB gun than a lot of the competition. P.Y. Hahn had been the chairman of Crosman when their first BB guns were produced and he went on to run the Hahn Company under his own name. The Crosman Company made guns for the O.S.S. during World War II, to be used in special operations when silence and stealth were important. Special agents had to live off the land and an air gun was ideal for this purpose, thus there was a demand for more powerful air guns by the time the war finished. The Hahn BB gun looked extremely good too, with accents of the Winchester model 1903 to really sell it to the children. It is 34 inches long.

ANTIQUE CORK GUN

This vintage cork gun was made by Chad Valley toys of Harborn, Birmingham, England. The company was founded by Anthony Bunn Johnson in the early 1800s—a small stream called the Chad flowed by the factory and the company was named after it. This gun dates from 1939, a year after the company was granted the Royal Warrant of Appointment as Toy Makers to Her Majesty the Queen. It is made of pressed steel painted black, with a wood stock and underbarrel slider to pump it up. It is 20 inches long.

THREE PISTOLS

The design of these pistols is influenced by automatics like the Browning and Walther. They are all heavy, long-barreled guns by good quality manufacturers; Daisy, Harrington, and Crossman. The top gun is a Daisy "Targeteer," produced between 1936 and 1953. As with all Daisy guns it certainly looks the part, and could be played with in an imaginative sense as well as on a practical level.

The middle gun is a Harrington "Gat Model" that fires .177 caliber lead pellets. It is a single-shot gun and is loaded by pushing the barrel against a wall.

The lower gun is a Crosman pistol from the 1930s; Crosman were founded in 1923 in Rochester, New York. This gun is rather clumsy looking, but it is without doubt the most powerful of the three. It works by pumping up a chamber under the barrel with the lever—you can give it as many pumps as you like, depending how long you have before you need to fire. This one is .22 caliber and fires lead pellets, which are fed into a breech on the top of the gun.

The lever used to charge the gun's reservoir of air.

PUMP ACTION DAISY

The Daisy Model 25 was the most ubiquitous air gun ever. Designed by Fred Le Fever, it ran from 1913 to 1986 and in that time over 20 million were produced. The gun is cocked by a breaking slide beneath the barrel, which greatly increases its power. The BB magazine is unscrewed from the barrel to load and holds approximately 50 pellets.

Two examples are shown here: top, a gun with a plastic stock and scrolling; below, a gun with a more traditional wooden stock. lighter and stronger than wood and with die cast methods they could achieve much greater detail.

DAISY POWERLINE

"Danger: not a Toy" it says clearly on the advertising literature for this gun, and that is certainly true—although only .177 caliber, it still has plenty of punch. Powerline is Daisy's range of more serious airguns:

"When shooting skills demand a higher level of performance move up to a Powerline." The Model 880 was launched in the 1970s as Daisy's first pneumatic system gun.

DAISY MODEL 1894

The Daisy Model 1894 BB gun was an exact copy of the Winchester 1894.

DAISY DOUBLE BARREL

This double barrel gun was a cork shooter, made by Daisy between 1955 and 1960.

DAISY SPACE GUN

This is the "Lunar Jet Space" air rifle made in Rogers, Arkansas in the early 1960s.

KEYSTONE RIDE-ON STREAMLINER

This robust pressed steel ride-on was manufactured by Keystone in the 1930s. The metal handle, mounted at the front, steers the front wheels. The blue and yellow paint is quite wrong, but the toy is in good working order. Keystone was founded in 1911 as a partnership between two brothers, Ben and Isidore Marks. The company started out by supplying human hair wigs to American doll manufacturers, and branched out into making their famous "pictograph" in 1919. They started to manufacture toy autos in 1925, but did not start to make ride-ons until 1934, with the "Siren Riding Toy". This was overwhelmingly popular, and Keystone ride-ons began to rival those of Buddy L, the market leader.

Below: The child sat on the roof of the toy, and steered with the handlebars.

The blue and yellow paintwork is quite worn in many places.

Below: This small set of handlebars steers the front wheels. Keystone was particularly proud of their robust toys. They boasted that a 200-pound man could stand on the toy.

KEYSTONE RIDE-ON STEAM TRAIN

This Keystone steam train dates from the company's years of ride-on manufacture, probably from the early 1930s. The company's highly successful ride-on toys helped Keystone to survive the Depression. Although they produced fewer toys, they remained solvent, as at this time of economic hardship, people valued their high quality but competitively priced models. The black and red paintjob on this model has survived very well. Unlike the ride-on "Streamliner," this Keystone model has a specially constructed seat mounted on the cab, and a pair of handlebars mounted on the locomotive itself. The pressed steel train is equipped with a charming cowcatcher and the child could use the empty steam box to stow his possessions while he rode. Keystone launched several ride-on toys during the 1930s, all of which were successful. These included the "Ride 'Em Mail Plane" in 1936 and a ride-on fire engine. This toy was 25 inches in length, as were most of their ride-on models. The Keystone Manufacturing Company finally went out of business in 1957.

The locomotive has a ringing bell.

Left: The red-painted wheel hubs have the Keystone "K" logo. The wheels have rubber tires.

Above: The ride-on steam train's lucky owner could use the empty steam box to carry his or her treasures.

The train is fitted with a charming pressed steel cowcatcher.

KEYSTONE RIDE 'EM TRACTOR

This "Ride 'Em Tractor" is from Keystone's successful series of "Ride 'Em" toys, which date from the 1930s. They were a pivotal product for Keystone, and helped them to survive the financial difficulties of the Depression. The "Ride 'Em" line include a steamroller, mail plane, fire engine, truck, and steam engine. The tractor's light red paintwork has survived very well, as

has the company logo. It has a steering handle mounted on the front of the tractor and a pair of large wheels at the rear, with painted yellow hubcaps. The tractor has a pair of small wheels at the front; all four wheels have rubber tires. The Keystone Manufacturing Company was located in Boston, Massachusetts, from 1925 until 1957. The company first made doll wigs, rag dolls, jack-in-the-boxes, and doll voice boxes. Motion pictures helped launch their first toy line—in 1919, Keystone made a moving picture machine featuring Tom Mix and Charlie Chaplin. Soon after the company went into making automobile toys and made toy trucks under license from Packard.

Above: The company logo refers to Keystone's famous "Ride 'Em" line of toys.

The tractor has a steering handle that is mounted at the front.

AMERICAN RIDE-ON TRAIN

This maroon and black ride-on train, which has been repainted, was probably made by the American National Company. This company was established in Toledo, Ohio, in the early 1900s by three brothers, Walter, Harry, and William Diemer. They used the Giant trademark and the company slogan referred to their many ride-on toys: "Raise the Kids on Wheels." American also made quality scooters, pedal bicycles, and sidewalk toys—including several pressed steel trucks—and trains like this one. They briefly competed with manufacturers like Keystone and Buddy L.

Marx also produced many ride-on toys throughout its many decades of toy production. Starting with simple ride-on trains and fire engines (like this American National example), they moved towards battery-operated cars in the 1950s. The "Stutz Bearcat" was one of their most successful models in the early 1960s, but the "Marx Big Wheel" was perhaps their most memorable ride-on toy, many variations of which were produced.

Buddy L ride-ons were manufactured by the Moline Pressed steel Company in East Moline, Illinois. They made several similar models to this American National train, which was a popular ride-on form at this time. All of these companies survived the Depression, except for American National.

This maroon and black ride-on train has been repainted.

Above: *The American National Company of Toledo, Ohio competed with several other ride-on manufacturers, including Keystone, Buddy L, and Marx.*

MOBO ROCKING HORSE

This metal rocking horse, with its metal riding frame, is from the product line of an English toy manufacturer, Mobo. Mobo was a division of D. Sebel and Company, and based in Erith, Kent, in England. Founded in 1921 by David Sebel, a Russian émigré, the company first made wheels. David's son, Harry Sebel looked for a new product line in the 1940s, and decided to go into toys, which the company made between 1947 and 1972. His first product was a rocking horse—he had taken out a patent for the mechanism in 1942, but toy manufacture did not actually begin until 1947. "Mobo" came from a brain-storming session, and was a contraction of "Mobile Toys." The company's most well known rocking horse is the "Bronco" ride-on horse, which moves along when the rider pushes down on the stirrups, and then releases them. They also made the "Spring Horse," "Night Rider," "Prairie Price," and "Range Rider."

Mobo toys were very popular in America.

The company had a showroom on London's Oxford Street.

Local schoolchildren chose the horse's colors.

Above: The company was taken over by Chad Valley in 1970, but Mobo toy production ceased in 1972, and the Erith factory was closed.

Above: The fire hose is missing, but the reel still has a working crank handle.

Keystone's "Ride 'Em" models were made from robust pressed steel.

Left: This "Ride 'Em" fire truck retains its working siren and ringing fire bell.

RIDE-ON KEYSTONE FIRE TRUCK

This Keystone ride-on fire truck would have been a highly desirable toy for a young child in the 1920s. Made by the Keystone Manufacturing Company of Boston, the truck is loosely based on real fire trucks of this period. This sturdy pressed steel toy is steered via the wooden handle, which extends through the cab to the truck's front axle. The truck is missing its original hose and ladders, but the cab-mounted siren and radiator-mounted bell still work. The hose reel has a turning crank handle, which also still works. The truck has a molded steel seat to the rear of the toy, on which the driver sits. Its steel wheels are equipped with rubber tires for a smoother ride. As well as having working headlights, the toy also has a cab-mounted emergency light, but the bulb is missing. The pressed metal radiator grille is decorated with a faint pattern. During the 1920s and 1930s, Keystone made a whole range of their famous "Ride Em" toys, which consisted of a variety of robust vehicles. These included a dump truck, jet fighter plane, train, steam shovel, emergency truck, and power shovel.

Keystone's "Ride 'Em" models generally measure between 23 and 25 inches in length.

***Below:** The worn paint finish bears witness to rigorous outdoor play.*

AMF MUSTANG PEDAL CAR

This AMF pedal car was launched in 1965, and first originated in 1964. Originals like this one are rare and highly collectible, but new versions are now on sale, made with the original AMF tooling. The original car was offered in blue and red. Pedal cars and ride-ons were extremely popular in the 1920s and 1930s, but experienced a great resurgence in the 1950s and 1960s. These models were mostly chain-driven. Pedal cars produced in the post-war period tended to reflect the styling cues of the full-size models of the time, which included working lights, working horns, moveable windshields, ragtops, chrome detailing and hood ornaments, white wall tires, and custom paint jobs. The hot 1960's models were also reproduced in pedal car versions, like this Mustang. America's increased affluence in the 1950s meant that families had more money to spend on luxuries like toys.

This ride-on model is 39 inches long, 16 inches wide, and 18 inches high, and it reflects a good deal of skilled workmanship. The pedals are adjustable so that a child of between 2 and 5 years old could use the toy and it has solid rubber tires.

Below left: AMF first launched this car onto the market in 1965. The car has now been reissued, produced with the original tooling.

Right: The rev counter and speedometer is also painted onto the dashboard.

The car shown here originally retailed for $25.

Above and below: The AMF Mustang was issued in both blue and red paint. The chrome detailing is reminiscent of the 1960s.

AMF FIRE TRUCK PEDAL CAR

AMF made this hook and ladder pedal car, model number 508. One of AMF's main competitors in the pedal car field was Murray, who also produced a pedal car fire truck. AMF made several versions of their fire truck pedal car, which included the "503 Fire Chief," "505 Fire Fighter," "Jet Sweep," "Tote-All," "508 Fire Truck," and "519 Fire Truck." The fire truck was one of AMF's final pedal car models, and was very popular—many have survived.

When the automobile made its appearance, the pedal car followed soon afterwards—this type of toy dates right back to the 1890s, and most were modeled from the real cars on the road. But such toys were comparatively expensive, and only lucky children's parents could afford them—home made ride-ons were played on by less fortunate children. No pedal cars were produced during the steel shortages of World War II.

The narrow wheels have rubber tires. The truck also has a ringing bell.

Left: The fire truck chassis is based on a pedal car, with quite minimal modifications.

The steering wheel turns the front wheels.

Right: *The shiny chrome bell is attached to the car/fire truck's hood.*

GARTON FORD PEDAL CAR

This Garton-made Ford pedal car was first offered in 1937. It is a red and crème pedal car, complete with the original hubcaps, lights, bumpers, and hood ornament, and the paintwork is in good condition. The Garton Toy Company had its headquarters in Sheboygan, Wisconsin. It was founded in 1878, but the company was originally known as both Garton and Logan, and Garton and Griffith, and they concentrated on making wagons, sleds, and wheeled toys. The first toy catalogue issued with the Garton Toy Company name was published in 1887. The company became hugely successful, manufacturing millions of toys—their factory became known as the largest juvenile vehicle plant in the world. They were a significant employer in Wisconsin, with thousands of workers. Their toys were so ubiquitous that a shade of red used on their pedal cars, wagons, tricycles, and trucks became known as Garton Red. They had showrooms in New York, Chicago, Dallas, and Los Angeles, and also sold their toys internationally. Garton also made useful items, such as wagons, small tables and chairs, but they were most famous for the luxury toys, including the Kidillac.

Below: This Ford pedal car was produced at the biggest juvenile vehicle plant in the world.

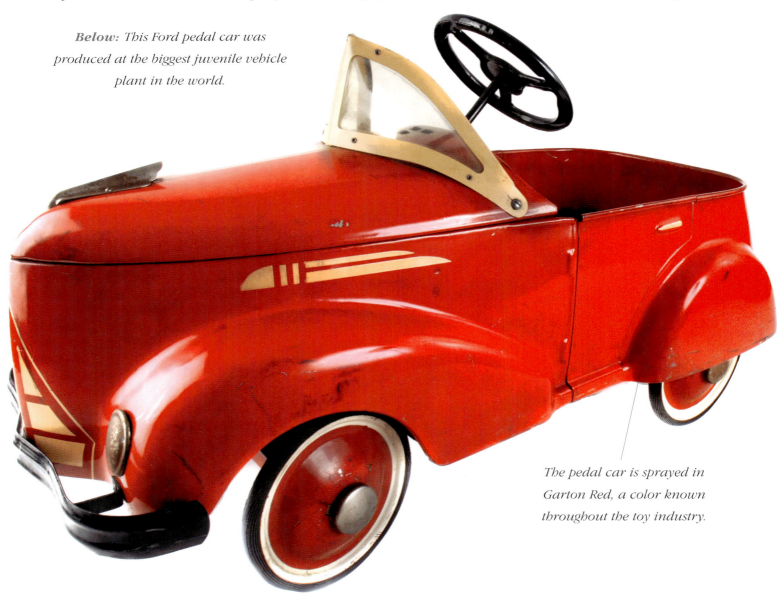

The pedal car is sprayed in Garton Red, a color known throughout the toy industry.

Below left: *The car has an unusual triangular windshield.*

This is the original hood ornament.

Ford endorsed several pedal cars in the 1930s, and sold some through their petrol stations.

277

KEYSTONE RIDE 'EM STEAMROLLER

This Keystone steamroller comes from its popular line of "Ride 'Em" ride-on toys, first introduced in the 1920s. A pressed steel toy, it was made in the U.S.A., at Keystone's Boston plant. The graphics on the toy read "Oil Axels Frequently." Keystone made several versions of its ride-on steamroller, which varied in length between 20 and 23 inches—this is a 1920s model, measuring 20 inches. The child sits on the curved, corrugated roof of the toy, and can steer using a handle mounted on the front of the vehicle. Unlike other steamroller models produced by Keystone, this toy does not have a separate, molded seat, but is equipped with a ringing bell, and an ornamental steam chimney. The roller and two rear wheels are all made from pressed tin.

Above: The decal shows this is one of the Ride 'Em series.

Real steamrollers are heavy construction machines designed to level surfaces on engineering projects such as roads and airfields. They were originally powered by steam engines, but later diesel took over. Steamrollers always have smooth rear wheels and a roller at the front, while traction engines have spoked wheels. Steamrollers were used in Britain until the 1970s. The character George the Steamroller appears in the Rev. W. Awdry's *Thomas the Tank Engine* stories.

The child sits on the corrugated roof.

Right: The steamroller is equipped with a ringing bell to warn people out of the way.

Above: This durable toy has been constructed from heavy gauge pressed steel.

CHAMPION WAGON

This Champion wagon dates from the 1930s. It has a sturdy pull-handle, and spoked red and yellow wheels with four grooves etched into the hubcaps. The Champion Hardware Company of Geneva, Ohio was in business between 1883 and 1954, and made toys between 1930 and 1936. It was founded by John and Ezra Hasenpflug and specialized in cast iron transportation toys, as well as making components for other toy manufacturers.

Toy wagons were a popular toy in the 1930s—they are four-wheeled toys that consist of a main body section and a steering handle. Wooden wagons were first introduced onto the American market in the 1880s, and the basic design has hardly changed since.

The wagon has a sturdy hauling section, strong wheels, and a steering handle.

Left: By the 1930s, the wooden construction of the first toy wagons had been replaced by pressed steel.

RADIO FLYER WAGON

Sixteen year-old Antonio Pasin emigrated from Italy with his parents in 1917. Arriving in Chicago, he struggled to find work, even though he was a skilled cabinetmaker, and ended up working for a sewer digging crew. But he never lost sight of his American dream, and invested in some used woodworking equipment. He used this to make wagons by night, which he sold by day. Pasin's first wagons were named Liberty Coasters, in honor of the statue that had welcomed his family to their new country. The business grew, and by 1923, he had several employees. Pasin was later inspired by the mass-production techniques of the automotive industry to make a new metal wagon from pressed steel. He called this the Radio Flyer in honor of two great products of the 1930s: Marconi's radio, and the airplane. Even during the Depression, Americans tried to buy toys for their children, and the company continued to grow. Wagon production was suspended between 1942-45, while the company manufactured steel cans for the armed services, but production resumed after the war. Baby boomers loved the Radio Flyer, which was by now an American classic. In the 1950s, Radio Flyer built a special blue wagon exclusively for members of Disney's Mickey Mouse Club, and also a yellow wagon to celebrate the release of *Davy Crockett*. Over the years, the company has continued to add to its toy range, and has also brought out several products for adults, such as garden carts and "Ski Sleds." The Radio Flyer itself has continued to develop, and the all-terrain "Quad-Shock Wagon," complete with Monroe shock absorbers, is its latest incarnation. The company is still family-run—now by Antonio Pasin's grandsons, Robert and Paul Pasin.

The Radio Flyer was originally retailed for $2.79.

Radio Flyer now make both steel and wood wagons.

Above: *The Radio Flyer is still manufactured by the Pasin family in its original home of Chicago, Illinois.*

COLUMBIA BOY'S TRICYCLE

This Columbia child's tricycle, a model designed for boys, dates from the 1890s but still has its original paint. It was made by the Pope Manufacturing Company, which is now known as Columbia, a business that began as bicycle makers and importers and was located at 45 High Street, Boston, Massachusetts. Since its foundation by Colonel Albert Pope in 1877, the company has been credited with many firsts in the bicycle production, and many consider it to be the father of the American bicycle industry. Pope's first self-manufactured model was the 60-inch "Hi Wheeler," which sold for a very considerable $125 when it was introduced in 1878. The "Standard" Columbia model followed in 1879, and several other Columbia models followed. The 1882 "Expert" Columbia was the first bicycle to be ridden across America, covering a total of 3,700 miles. This "Three-track Tricycle" was introduced in 1883.

Columbia recently introduced the "Custom Deluxe Cruiser" to celebrate their 125th anniversary.

VICTORIAN GIRL'S TRICYCLE

This Victorian tricycle for girls was probably made in the late 1800s or early 1900s. The tricycle became very popular with women in the 1880s; models like this, with a seat rather than a saddle, were made specifically for women. Women were particularly strong adherents of cycling in the early years of the sport—they greatly appreciated the mobility it gave them, with healthy exercise in the open air. Many saw cycling as a step towards emancipation. Several women's cycling clubs were formed, and cycling costumes were designed for the fashionable woman about town. In London, the Knightsbridge Cycling School was established to teach women to cycle. Many women campaigned for the right to wear so-called "rational clothing" in which to cycle. According to *Woman's Life* magazine, this consisted of Dr. Jaeger's hygienic woolen underwear, a divided petticoat, or skirt, or knickerbockers worn under a skirt. But "wheelwomen," as lady cyclists were known, were slow to adopt "rational" cycle wear, and continued to wear the voluminous skirts of the period.

Below: *This early tricycle looks like a small three-wheeled carriage. Early cycles had no tires, and were known as "boneshakers."*

STRAWBERRY SHORTCAKE BIKE

Hedstrom made this Strawberry Shortcake bicycle in the early 1980s. Its sweet decals and red, white, and pink color scheme make it essentially a girls' model. It has a 16-inch frame, and a banana seat—the seat was originally covered with a strawberry-printed plastic. The bike has a large chain guard, and useful front basket. Although it was a short-lived first edition model, it has now been re-released and become even more popular. Hedstrom also made a smaller version of the bike for younger children, with a conventionally shaped saddle and Strawberry Shortcake decals. The Strawberry Shortcake character, and her cat Custard, were first drawn by Muriel Fahrion in 1977, during her time as a greeting card illustrator at American Greetings' Juvenile and Humorous card department.

Fahrion subsequently designed 32 Strawberry Shortcake characters for the company's licensing design division. The characters became hugely popular in the 1980s, and endorsed many products.

Above: *Strawberry Shortcake herself was given the Berry Tricycle to ride around on.*

Left: Strawberry Shortcake was first drawn by Muriel Fabrion in 1977. She became a hugely successful 1980s franchise.

Below: The Strawberry Shortcake bicycle has a large red metal chain cover, complete with Strawberry Shortcake decal.

ORANGE KRATE SCHWINN BICYCLE

The Schwinn "Orange Krate" bicycle, which dates from around 1968, is now highly collectible. It has a stick shift for its five speeds, and the wheels are equipped with unusual sprockets. The bike has a redline rear slick and a fenderless front wheel, as well as generous chrome trim. Ignaz Schwinn founded Schwinn in October 1895; the company was first located in Chicago, Illinois, and its products have been American cultural icons for over a century, famous for quality. Back in the 1940s, the Schwinn "Cruiser" set the standard for Hollywood's portrayal of cycling chic, with its cantilever frame, swooping handlebars, and absence of any brake levers. The Schwinn "Sting-Ray" was a classic model from the company's 1960s output—it was a cook street bike, which was often modified for BMX-ing. Like the "Cruiser," this bike has also been relaunched, with the slogan: "The rebirth of cool." Schwinn remained a family-owned company until 1993, when it was bought out and moved to its current location at Madison, Wisconsin. It has been part of Dorel Industries since 2004. The company still claims to provide "World class performance on an economy class budget," although its most expensive model actually retails for over $40,000.

This long saddle became very popular in the 1970s.

Left: The "Orange Krate" has a stick shift for its five gear speeds.

Far left: Moving the stick shift up and down the slot changes gear.

Right: Schwinn has always had a reputation for quality construction.

HAWTHORNE BICYCLE

This gray and blue Hawthorne bicycle dates from around the 1940s, and was made for girls by H. P. Snyder and Company. It has a 26-inch frame, and Springer forks—the fork design is unusual in that it also incorporates the standard truss-rods found on lesser models. It is also equipped with wide handlebars and sensible safety features, including a full chain guard and a rear tire guard. It has attractive whitewall tires, a sprung saddle for riding comfort, and a useful bag platform over the rear tire.

Snyder also made a Hawthorne bicycle for boys. Offered in a similar color scheme, the most obvious difference from the girls' model is the lack of the bag carrier at the back. The company also made Rollfast bicycles. Snyder was originally a general hardware company that also made bikes, but in 1917 the company decided to restrict production just to bicycles, wagons, and tricycles. Hard hit by the effects of the Depression, Snyder formed an exclusive retail partnership with the Montgomery Ward chain of department stores.

The saddle is sprung for a very comfortable ride.

Above: *Hawthorne is a brand of the Snyder Company, well known for their extensive Rollfast range.*

Right: The Hawthorne has Springer forks. Unusually, these also incorporate standard truss-rods.

The handlebar assembly is wide and high.

The bike has attractive whitewall tires.

AMF JUNIOR ROADMASTER BICYCLE

The American Machine and Foundry Company made the 1950's AMF "Junior" Roadmaster bicycle shown here, which is in a restored condition having been repainted and fitted with stabilizers. It is equipped with hard tires.

Roadmaster Industries were the first to use the Roadmaster brand. Founded in 1925, the company quickly became a reputable toy and bicycle manufacturer. It became Junior Toy in 1929, and continued to make a wide range of metal-framed bicycles and tricycles under the Roadmaster name. After two decades of consistent growth, the AMF Wheel Goods Division bought Junior in 1951. The company lost much of its reputation for quality in the 1970s and 1980s, but has come back strongly to become one of America's strongest bicycle brands.

This AMF Junior Roadmaster bike has been repainted and fitted with a pair of stabilizers.

Right: *The Roadmaster brand name dates back to 1929.*

A useful piece of equipment is this metal parcel rack, attached to the forks.

Below right: *The bike's decal shows its heritage, Roadmaster, Junior, AMF.*

J.C. HIGGINS COLOR-FLOW BICYCLE

Murray Ohio manufactured this J.C. Higgins boy's "Color-Flow" bicycle in 1950. J. C. Higgins was Sears' own bicycle brand, which had been known as Elgin before World War II. They retailed this up-scale model for $59.99, but it is now worth well over a thousand dollars. The 26-inch frame has wide handlebars, and Springer forks. It is also equipped with a large comfort seat, and stylish whitewall ties. The tanks are flanked with highly unusual Buick-style "ventiports," which pick up on the styling of the 1950's Buick automobile range. It also has several other styling cues taken from the automobiles of the 1950s, for instance the extensive chrome trim and a jeweled tank. The bike is equipped with a full chain guard and has a useful rear package tray. Murray continued to make bicycles for several decades, but unfortunately they filed for bankruptcy in 2004.

Top right: *The sides of the "Color-Flow" are decorated with Buick-style chrome-trimmed ventiports, a feature on the 1950's models.*

Lower right: *This bicycle was made by Murray Ohio for Sears.*

Left: *This highly stylish bike retailed for a substantial $59.99 in 1950.*

GHOSTBUSTERS

This neat toy dates from between 1986 and 1991 when Ghostbusters fever was at its height. Made by Kenner, the car is ECTO 1 and the "Real Ghostbusters" figures are Egon Spengler, Ray Stantz, Peter Venkman, Winston Zeddmore, and Janine Melnitz. The figures came originally in two character modes: "Normal" and "Fright Features"—the second went into fright mode when you touched a body part. Kenner Products was founded in 1947 by Albert, Phillip, and Joseph L. Steiner, in Cincinnati, Ohio. The company was named after the street where the offices were located. During the 1950s and 60s they were responsible for some household name toys like the "Give a Show" projector and the Spirograph and were one of the first toy companies to advertise their products on television. The

company was bought by General Mills in 1967 who merged their Rainbow Crafts Division into Kenner, bringing Play-Doh, another household name into the Kenner fold. The company specialized in action figures and play sets licensed from movies and television starting with *Star Wars* in 1977.

Egon Spengler accesses Ghostbusting equipment from the back of ECTO 1.

Below right: Egon Spengler in normal mode at the wheel of ECTO 1. Both front doors open as well as the tailgate.

Below left and right: Ray Stantz appears in both "Normal" and "Fright" modes. His fright character is in a blue and yellow suit alongside the car and his normal one in the passenger seat, leaning casually out of the window.

GUMBY'S JEEP

Starting life as a humble pile of modeling clay in 1953, Gumby went on to have his own television show. His inventor, Art Clokey, introduced him on *The Howdy Doody Show* (see page 327) in 1956, where he had a regular spot until he got his own program *The Gumby Show*. During the 1960s his popularity continued to grow and Lakeside Toys of Minneapolis, Minnesota produced a range of Gumby merchandise, including windup toys and an electric drawing toy. However, as far as collectors go these two bendy action figures of Gumby, and Pokey, his loyal horse that can be posed with "Gumby's Jeep" are about as cool as you can get. Lakeside even produced costumes for the figures to wear. The Jeep has chrome bumpers, fold down windshield, and mudgrip tires. Although the show ended in 1967 Gumby's popularity remained strong and *Gumby: The Movie* came out in 1995 introducing the little green guy to a whole new generation of fans.

The smiling face of a character that has earned millions.

Above: Whilst Gumby seems perfectly comfortable, Pokey looks a little stressed with his feet sticking through the windshield.

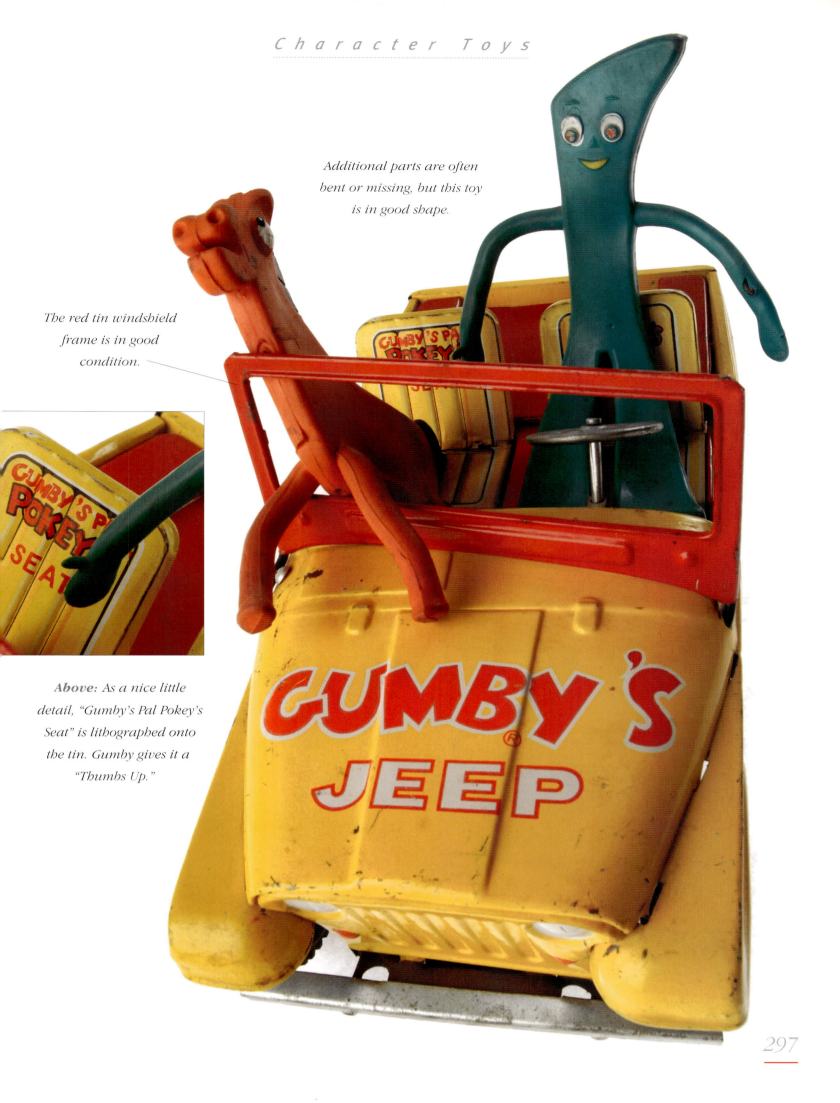

Additional parts are often bent or missing, but this toy is in good shape.

The red tin windshield frame is in good condition.

Above: *As a nice little detail, "Gumby's Pal Pokey's Seat" is lithographed onto the tin. Gumby gives it a "Thumbs Up."*

PEZ

Its strange to think that something as fun as PEZ was originally conceived in Austria as a breath freshening aid for smokers. The striped mint candies were initially sold in a small tin, but a new dispenser designed to look like a cigarette lighter was introduced in 1947, and the product became more as we would recognize it today. The name PEZ comes from the German *pfefferminz* for peppermint. The company moved to the U.S.A. in 1952, and immediately realized that children are the biggest candy consumers. They introduced a range of fruit flavors to appeal to a younger audience and added character heads to the dispensers, including Popeye, Mickey Mouse, Santa and Dino, even the Flintstones' dinosaur. There is a thriving collectors' market (of so-called "PEZ heads") for this American pop-art classic—a record of $6,575 was paid for a PEZ dispenser in 2002. We show a selection of characters here, from left to right: Bugs Bunny, Spiderman, Sylvester, Speedy Gonzales, Wonderwoman, Yosemite Sam, Leprechaun, Tweety-Pie, Pebbles, Pluto, and at the front two PEZ trucks.

RAISIN GUYS

When Marvin Gaye sang "I heard it through the grapevine" in 1968, he could not have dreamed that twenty years later a group of the Dancin', Singin' California Raisins, molded in clay, would do the same! A generic promotion for Californian raisins, the raisin guys were the invention of Will Vinton, the Walt Disney of clay animation, who started his prestigious career in the early 1970s in his home state of Oregon. Setting up his studios in Portland, his first notable success was his trilogy of fairy tales shot in 16mm film: *Martin the Cobbler* (1977), *Rip Van Winkle* (1978), and *The Little Prince* (1979). A seventeen-minute film showing behind the scenes of the animation processes entitled *Claymation* entered a new word in the dictionary, which thereafter stood for clay animation in general.

In 1987 he was asked by the California Raisin Advisory Board (Calrab) to devise some characters to encourage people to eat more raisins, and he duly created probably the biggest claymation phenomena since Gumby hit the TV screens in the 1950s. Within no time there was a Raisins Christmas special, two primetime programs on C.B.S. *Meet the Raisins* and *The Raisins Sold Out*. A video game was devised called The Grape Escape. To mass-produce the characters as toys required a more durable medium than clay, so our group of examples is made of PVC. They were originally given away as a premium gift by fast food chain Hardees against a purchase of Cinnamon Raisin Biscuits. Each toy is dated underneath—usually 1987–1989 when Raisin fever was at its height.

DICK TRACY

When the great detective first came on the scene in October 1932 he gave birth to a whole merchandising industry of toys and collectibles. Dick Tracy was a detective with grit and determination; he was a good shot but his real claim to fame were the hi-tech gadgets he employed. He used microphones to record criminal's conversations before real-life wire taps even existed, he used spy cameras to record criminal activity before the police had ever dreamed of them. Little wonder, then, that the toys based on his character reflected this element. We show some great examples here from the 1930s through the 1950s. "The Big Little Book" is part of a series of 26 Dick Tracy adventures, which ran from 1932. *Dick Tracy and the Stolen Bonds*

Below and right: The camera was acquired with the original mailing carton which shows it was sent to a Master Curtis Vaughan.

The G-Man gun is a tin wind-up toy with authentic sound.

Colorful Dick Tracy belt marketed by Disney.

Below: *Remco Industries of Harrison, New Jersey, made this 2-way radio toy in the 1950s. The radio was worn on the wrist, just like Dick Tracy! The company specialized in licensing deals for their range of popular toys.*

was published in 1934. The working plastic camera from 1950 was made and distributed by Seymour Sales in Chicago. It took pictures on 127 film in a 2 x 3 inch format, had a 50mm Graf lens. The 2-way radio dates from the late 1950s and was made by Remco whose slogan was "Every boy wants a Remco toy." The 1940's G-Man gun is not strictly a Dick Tracy item but it fits in with the theme. The Dick Tracy belt is by Disney.

MICKEY MOUSE

Walt Disney (1901-1966) enjoyed early cartoon success with Oswald the Lucky Rabbit. "Who?" I hear you say. Well, Oswald didn't last long because Walt lost the rights to him in a business dispute and went on to create another character—Mickey (Mortimer) Mouse instead. Mickey and his leading lady, Minnie, made their movie debut in *Steamboat Willie* (1928) and the little rodent, whom Disney once described as "a little personality assigned to the purposes of laughter," swiftly became the most recognized and popular of all cartoon characters. He has gone on to appear in over 120 movies and featured in a digitally animated Walt Disney video, *Twice upon a Christmas* in 2004. The Mickey Mouse Club was formed in 1929 and it had more than a million members by 1932. It is hardly surprising, therefore, that a host of products quickly grew up around the Mickey Mouse legend. We show two examples of dolls: the first a plush doll from the 1930s, shortly after Mickey's appearance in *Steamboat Willie*. This charming, early-style Mickey has the characteristic "Pie-eyes." It is not sure whether the cap and scarf are original or if some enthusiastic seamstress has added them—people in the past would often customize a favorite toy. The Mickey on the right is the more modern version that most people would recognize.

Right and far right: *1930's Mickey has all the right features but the scarf, cap, and bows around his shoes and wrists give him a certain style.*

PINOCCHIO AND DOPEY

Walt Disney began a series of "Animated Features" in 1937 when *Snow White* was released by R.K.O. Radio Pictures; the second was *Pinocchio* released on February 7, 1940. Both movies were in Technicolor. The toys featured here date from the same time and are characters from those movies: Dopey is one of Snow White's dwarfs and Pinocchio is the star of the movie of the same name. These two charming tin toys were made by Marx, who licensed the characters from Disney. They are wind-up toys that actually walk, while at the same time their eyes flutter up and down.

Right: The fixed key in Dopey's back winds his motor.

Below: The Marx "crossing" logo and the Disney copyright from 1939 on Pinocchio's back.

PORKY PIG AND FRIENDS

Warner Brother's answer to Disney was the Looney Tunes and Merry Melodies series of cartoons, featuring Porky Pig who ended each short with the words "Th-Th-Th-That's all Folks." The lovable stuttering pig began his career as a slightly different version in a short cartoon in 1935 entitled *I haven't got a Hat* directed by Friz Freling. His animator at Warner Bros

was Bob Clampett. Our cool Marx tin wind-up toy is based on Clampett's version of Porky—slimmer, cuter and smarter with possibly less of a stutter. The toy's hand is raised as originally he was holding an umbrella. The body is made in two halves fixed together with

Below: A close-up of the Linemar toy shows the on/off lever, its wind-up key and the Walt Disney copyright stamp.

Both arms swing up and down ringing the bell in Pluto's left paw.

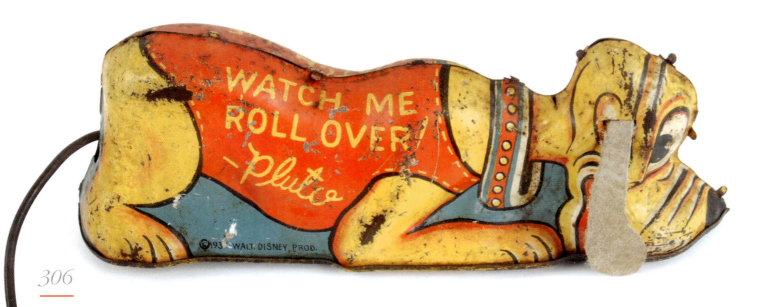

Below: *The copyright information on Porky's shoulders reads "Copyright 1939 Leon Schlesinger" (head of Warner Brother's Studios). The Marx logo can be seen to the left of the copyright notice.*

metal tabs. On the facing page we have two versions of Pluto, Mickey Mouse's faithful hound. The "Watch Me Roll Over" Pluto is again by Marx and is a tin wind up toy dating from 1939. It literally turns over, flipped by its tail. The upright Pluto with the hat, trumpet, bell and whip, dates from the late 1940s. It is a tin Linemar toy, made in Japan for Marx. Both arms move, it walks forward and the top of its head also nods back and forth.

POPEYE

Popeye is a grizzled one-eyed sailor who gets into difficult situations and turns to a can of spinach, usually conveniently secreted about his person, to give him super-strength. Then he knocks the opposition, usually his archenemy Bluto, into next week. Originally appearing in the King Features comic strip *Thimble Theater* in 1929, Elzie Crislar Segar's creation was morphed into cartoon form by Max Fleischer and by 1938 Popeye had replaced Mickey Mouse as America's favorite. Popeye and Bluto were duly enlisted in the U.S. navy to aid the war effort. The sight of Popeye's pipe spinning in his mouth enabling him to take off like a fighter plane (after a dose of spinach) in pursuit

of Japanese battleships is a wonder to contemplate. The toys we show are all from the 1940s, when Popeye merchandising was at its peak. The Popeye Transit Co. truck is a pressed steel Structo, made in the Freeport, Illinois works. The copyrighted truck has images of Popeye and Sweetpea (Olive Oyl's child), and is sign written with the words "Local or long distance Moving." Popeye smoking his yellow pipe, wearing a blue and white cap, is a Cameo doll. His body is cloth and his head and arms are rubber. The tin toy is called "Popeye with Parrot Cages" and was made by Chein. This is a wind up toy that walks forward with the cages rolling at his sides.

Below: This 14-wheeler rig has a red cab and blue white and cream trailer with chrome grille and headlights and a black fuel tank.

Above: The trailer has King Features copyright images all over it, even on the roof.

The Cameo doll has rubber arms and a cloth body.

Right: This Popeye toy is of similar construction to the Marx G.I. Joe on page 642.

309

CAT IN THE HAT

Sometimes toys are fun, sometimes they are educational, the trick is to do both if you can! In the 1950s there was concern about the staidness of school primers—it was felt that the nation faced an epidemic of illiteracy and that schoolbooks were to blame. In both text and illustrations, many books of the time portrayed children living idealistic lives, abnormally courteous, unnaturally clean boys and girls who never misbehaved. Clearly this was enough to turn off many young would-be readers. Illustrator Dr Seuss (Theodore Seuss Geisel), who specialized in children's books with rhyming text and outlandish titles and characters, was interested in children's education and responded to concerns by creating his famous character. He set out to write a story, limiting it to a basic vocabulary of 223 words, and choosing the title *The Cat in the Hat* because "cat" and "hat" were the first two occurring in the basic vocabulary that rhymed.

The first book appeared in 1957, featuring the Cat who brings a cheerful yet slightly disturbing form of entertainment to two children one day when their mother is out—the stuff of future children's entertainment like *Home Alone*. The Cat arrives with his two creatures, Thing One and Thing Two, performing all manner of wacky tricks to amuse the children and causing chaos. The book has remained a children's classic ever since and not surprisingly merchandising has followed. This plush Cat in the Hat has a white and blue body. He is wearing a red neckerchief, the familiar bow tie, and his red and white striped top hat. The doll dates from 1983, when the Cat was enjoying one of several rises in popularity. The toy was made for the Cole Company (CNC), who—by acquisition in 1981 of Child World Inc.— were positioned as major toy supermarket retailers. They had 100 stores in 21 states making them second only to Toys R Us. A toy, which had educational properties and is based on a book is always a reassuring purchase for parents.

Left: The wacky Cat in the Hat has a plush body and a rubber head and hat.

SNOOPY

Created by Charles M. Schulz, Snoopy is Charlie Brown's pet beagle in the long-running comic strip *Peanuts*. He first appeared on October 4, 1950, as an unnamed dog but soon emerged as the star. Based on Charles Schulz's childhood dogs, Snooky and Spike, Snoopy was a silent character to begin with, but eventually his thoughts were expressed in a balloon. His ability to convey what he was thinking to the reader gave him a sort of superior intelligence, and made him seem smarter than the humans in the story. He also has a dream world existence, which humorously belies his role as a dog. In the animated films and television specials Snoopy's thoughts are not verbalized but communicated with more dog-like growls, sobs, grunts and facial expressions. Part of the charm of the character is his facial cuteness and the fact that we can all recognize dogs we have known in him. The plush toy wearing goggles and a scarf shown here is a older version of Snoopy—the goggles refer to Snoopy's alter ego as a World War I fighter ace, in which he climbs on top of his doghouse to engage in a dogfight with his archenemy the Red Baron, clad in leather flying helmet and scarf. Many toys depict him thus. The slick "Joe Cool Snoopy" is a rather later toy made of plastic.

THE FLINTSTONES

Two great plastic toys from the 1960s when *The Flintstones* was on television. Set in Bedrock during the Stone Age, *The Flintstones* was the first prime time animated cartoon to be geared for adults (a lot of the jokes were quite sophisticated) but children loved it too. It ran from 1960–1966 and was the first ABC cartoon show to go out in color. The show's creators, Joseph Hanna and William Barbera, were also responsible for other 1960's hit characters like Huckleberry Hound and Yogi Bear.

Fred Flintstone works at the rock quarry but likes to wear a collar and tie to keep up appearances.

Barney Rubble in skin costume and bowling ball conveys the comparison between the stone age and mid twentieth-century America.

Above: *Both toys are licensed from Hanna-Barbera.*

THE DUKES OF HAZZARD

Originally aired on CBS from 1979–1985 this television series achieved cult status even in this short time, with its story of the Duke family and their struggles with Boss Hogg, the corrupt Commissioner of Hazzard County. Most plot lines involve Boss Hogg finding ways to incriminate Bo and Luke Duke, so he can get his hands on their land. This involves lots of outrageous car chases where Bo and Luke's car—The General Lee, a 1969 Dodge Charger—never fails to outrun the police cars of Boss's incompetent accomplice, Sheriff Rosco P. Coltrane. The reason for the show's popularity may lie in its rekindling of a retained Civil War sentiment about the honorable South (the Dukes) being persecuted by official corrupt forces (Hogg and his men). Confederate flags and country music abound in the show and it was therefore a natural for merchandising products of all kinds including toys. Both of the Dodge Chargers shown here are made by Ertl. The larger car is the famous 1:18 model of the General Lee, while on the left is a smaller scale hopped-up example, with bigger wheels. In the background is an 8-inch action figure of Bo Duke by Mego, and beside him is the original carrying case for the Charger.

The Confederate Flag was an important symbol in the television show. The General Lee's horn played several bars of "Dixie."

Above: *Ertl Scale models of the General Lee in carrying cases are still widely available on the market and popular with collectors.*

BATMAN

The Mego Corporation was a toy company that was originally famous for its dime store range selling at 88c, mostly in bargain basements. Founded by David Abrams and his wife Madeline in 1954, the company concentrated on budget toys until David's son Marty graduated from business school. At around this time the company launched into action figures and began to specialize in licensed toys from motion pictures, television shows, and comic strips. Superheroes, like this selection of Batman characters, were typical of Mego's output at this time. These toys date from 1974 when the *Batman* television series was going great guns and characters like Batman and Robin (seated in the car) and (left to right) arch criminals The Joker and The Penguin were household names. The figures are 8 inches high and, like most Mego figures, they have interchangeable heads. The Batmobile is plastic and fits the figures perfectly. The company faltered when it failed to secure the *Star Wars* licensed range of toys (see pages 748–751), which were snapped up by rivals Kenner Products. The enormous success of the *Star Wars* phenomenon and the accompanying products drowned Mego's attempts at fighting back with lesser-known licenses, and they eventually filed for bankruptcy in 1982. Mego toys are now highly collectible.

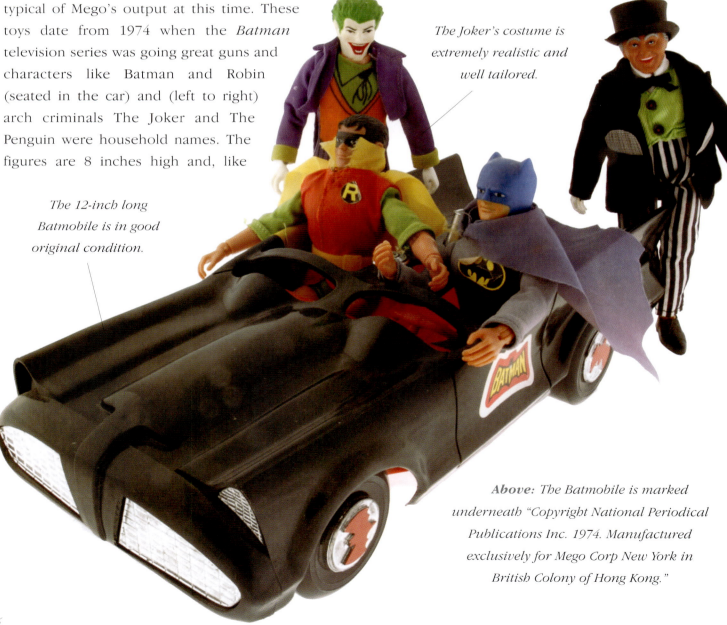

The Joker's costume is extremely realistic and well tailored.

The 12-inch long Batmobile is in good original condition.

Above: The Batmobile is marked underneath "Copyright National Periodical Publications Inc. 1974. Manufactured exclusively for Mego Corp New York in British Colony of Hong Kong."

SPIDERMAN

Fictional superhero Peter Parker first appeared in print in a Marvel Comic strip in 1962. Created by Stan Lee and Steve Ditko, Parker was never quite as comfortably predictable as Clark Kent. The toys came soon afterward and here are (from left) the Mego 8-inch toy with movable joints and the Toy Biz 10-inch wall hanging figure.

This Mego figure is very collectible.

Right: The Toy Biz Spidey hangs on the wall courtesy of its two suction pads on the wrists. This is a 10-inch figure made in self-colored hard plastic. It is currently available.

Left: Production variations occurred in the clothes during Mego's extended production of Spiderman. This pattern with the exaggerated hourglass style tunic and the larger spider chest motif indicate an early toy.

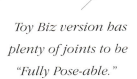

Toy Biz version has plenty of joints to be "Fully Pose-able."

315

SPIDERMAN MOTORCYCLE GAME

"The Amazing Spiderman Stunt Cycle" #713 is a battery-operated toy that makes an authentic motorcycle sound and simulates speeds of up to 160 miles per hour. It looks really exciting—an ideal holiday gift, and most children love interactive toys that simulate driving. The realistic handlebars, brake lever with black rubber twist grips and working speedometer on a stable red base give it a hands-on appeal. Spiderman's stunt bike is extremely well detailed in red and blue plastic with chrome plated engine and twin muffler pipes, front mudguard, headlight and wheel spokes. The whole set-up looks pretty much ready for Spiderman to roar into battle on the streets of New York against his arch foe Venom. The toy is copyrighted 1979 to the Marvel Comics Group and was made by AMICO Inc. of Philadelphia Pennsylvania, a subsidiary of Walter Kidde and Company, who made fire safety products. No trace of this subsidiary manufacturer can now be found, although the toy isn't all that old—it probably dates from the early 1980s.

Above: The realistic speedometer records speeds of up to 160mph!

Solid-looking handlebars bolted to the red plastic base give the toy a purposeful look.

Right: Fully detailed model of a superhero on his superbike, ready to take on archenemy Venom. Venom bikes are also available.

TEENAGE NINJA TURTLES

"Turtles Forever" was the cry as the teenage mutant ninja turtles leap from their hiding places in the sewers of Manhattan—a bunch of guys outside society who fight petty crime, alien invaders and criminal masterminds. Mirage Studios presented the turtles back in 1984, when they premiered them in comic book format. In December 1987 the first cartoon series was launched as a 5-part mini series; this was followed by a series of feature films in the 1990s. In 1987 Playmates Toys released a range of action figures along with vehicles, play sets and other accessories.

Playmates were originally founded in Hong Kong in 1966 by San Chan as a doll making company, but by 1981 they were moving into the big league licensing Disney items and were incorporated in California in the U.S.A. in 1982. The acquisition of the rights to the Turtles was one of their cannier decisions and by 1990, three years after the launch of the action figure range, they reported group sales in excess of $500 million. The figures had fully flexible joints and heads and came in scores of different poses and colors. They are pictured here with an ATV, also part of the Playmates range.

The Ninja BO or staff accurately reflects real Ninja equipment. Although a child's toy the designers paid attention to detail.

SUPERMAN

Without doubt Superman is the pre-eminent superhero. Although known rather disrespectfully by his fellow superheroes as "the big blue boy scout," this is probably not repeated to his face! From his first appearance, in Action Comics in 1938, he has constantly been relaunched in movies, books, comic strips, radio serials, and television series. We have examined just about every angle of his life: his infancy on his home planet Krypton before he is rocketed to earth by his scientist father minutes before the planet's annihilation; his juvenile years spent on the Kansas

farm where he grows up with Jonathan and Martha Kent; his college years in Smallville; life at the *Daily Planet* where he meets his girl, Lois Lane. It has been suggested that we know more about him than we do about some of our relatives. He was first devised by illustrator Joe Shuster and writer Jerry Siegel in 1932, who eventually sold the rights to Detective Comics in 1938. In view of the subsequent value of the property, legal issues are still evident to this day. Superman

Left: Great retro graphics on this modern tin toy made in 2004.

This unknown Superman statue is made of plastic and probably a promotional toy.
It is mounted on a solid base, which makes more of a collector piece than an action toy.

Cool Superman clock abounds with copyright images.

became an instant success and a part of popular western culture—the comic book was regarded as essential wartime supplies to the marine base at Midway Island.

As early as 1939 the excellent wooden toy shown right was available. It is made of laminated wooden strips, and is intricately jointed at the shoulder, elbow, waist, thighs, knees and ankles. It has a (now faded) red cloth cape. The whole style of the doll is true to the original image of Superman.

Because Superman has been with us for seventy years his appearance has been constantly but subtlety updated. The two toys left and center opposite are made by Schylling, a company that specializes in classic toys. The Superman clock has a face loaded with graphics of the "man of steel." On top of the blue clock case is a flying Superman figure that circles round on a wire.

To its left is the obligatory phone booth where mild-mannered Clark Kent transforms himself into Superman with the cry (beginning in Clark Kent's tenor voice) "This is a job for…. Superman" (ending in Superman's rather deeper baritone). The kiosk is made of lithographed tin and uses retro style graphics that show each step of the transformation, from Kent entering the booth to Superman flying out. It is a money bank toy.

Below: Original Superman logo from the 1939 figure.

The cape has faded from its original bright red to a dusky brown but this toy is still a valuable one.

TRANSFORMERS

Transformers was based on a mid-1980's animated series produced by Sunbow Productions, which was in turn inspired by the Marvel Comics strip. It was the animated show that really hooked children, creating a big opening for action toys based around the format. More easily said than done, however, because the changes that the robots underwent were complex and difficult to turn into reality. Japanese company Takara had already tried something similar with its Diaclone and Micro Change toys and at a meeting with American toy giant Hasbro at the 1983 Tokyo Toy Show it was decided the two companies would combine efforts to relaunch the toys as "Transformers." The exploits of Optimus Prime, Megatron and their associates in the rival factions—the heroic Autobots and the evil Decepticons—were transferred into plastic. The robot's ability to transform themselves into cars, jets, helicopters and motorcycles must have been a challenge the designers at Hasbro, who do the majority of the concept work, while Takara controls the manufacture.

This page: A selection of 1980's Transformers in various sizes.

Where would we be without a rocket-powered canine-type robot?

Bright contrasting colors make the robots more interesting.

WOODY

Our book cannot be complete without mention of *Toy Story*, a movie that features the toys themselves and their antics when the people aren't looking. The plot is a struggle between Woody, a traditional 1950's-style cowboy toy (our featured toy) and Buzz Lightyear, a fancy state-of-the-art space toy, loaded with gadgets. The simple charm of Woody wins through—which applies to a lot of the toys featured in this book. Woody is a cowboy doll suitable attired in a check shirt, black and white cowhide waistcoat, blue jeans, belt and holster, 10-gallon hat, Sheriff's star, boots and spurs. His head, with its clean-cut brown hair, and the hat, belt, and boots are made of soft plastic. Press his middle shirt button and he emits a series of witty epithets such as "Wanna go to a round up?" "Howdy Partner, my name is Woody," "Yee-haa cowboy," "Glad to see you deputy," and so on. The batteries that power this toy are amazing—the voice is still loud and clear after 10 years. Copyright notices appear on the sole of each plastic boot and on the back of the neck saying, "Copyright Disney, Thinkway Thinking Toys TM, Made in China." Thinkway, whose slogan on the pack is "I'm a thinking toy" also manufacture Jessie, Woody's female counterpart.

CHARLIE'S ANGELS

When the action show *Charlie's Angels* was launched in 1976, it quickly gained a huge fanbase. Merchandising appeared very soon afterwards in 1977—Hasbro cleverly recycled some body molds for the Miss Matchbox Disco doll of 1972 and restyled the faces to provide us with dolls of the three original Angels. They were all 8½ inches tall with a "twist and turn waist" and rooted hair that you could style. The dolls came as standard with jump suits, but a full range of evening wear (the Angels liked to live it up after a

case) tote bags and other accessories was available. Mego also produced a range of 12-inch dolls. The three original Angels were Jill Monroe, played by Farrah Fawcett Majors, Sabrina Duncan, played by Kate Jackson, and Kelly Garrett, played by Jaclyn Smith. After a year Farrah left and was replaced by Cheryl Ladd, who played Kris Monroe, Jill's younger sister.

Below: Dolls of Sabrina Duncan and Kelly Garrett flank Kris Monroe in the center.

BETTY BOOP

Miss Boop started life as a human-like dog in animator Grim Natwick's original cartoon in 1930. She featured alongside her dog "boyfriend" Bimbo. Gradually her dog ears morphed into round earrings and a garter appeared on her leg under Max Fleischer's pen and she emerged as the star, leaving poor old Bimbo in dogland! In 1934 she regularly appeared in cartoon strips drawn by Bud Counihan but signed by Max Fleischer. Her voice and phrase "Boop-oop-a-doop" reputedly came from singer Helen Kane and was the subject of a legal dispute later on when Boop's career outstripped Kane's. Originally short-skirted, her gowns were a little more modest by 1935, when the tide had turned against the frivolity of the 1920s. The character has remained perennially fresh and young and is still a popular subject for merchandising and collecting.

The toy featured here is by Applause and is a modern doll. Applause started out in 1979 as a division of The Knickerbocker Toy Company, which was founded in New York in 1925 by Leo L. Weiss and sold to Hasbro in 1983. The company was well known for its character dolls of Walt Disney cartoons like Snow White, Raggedy Ann and Andy, and Holly Hobbie. Applause was acquired by Wallace Berrie in 1982 and is now based in California.

Right: Betty Boop steps out with her long red evening dress, feather boa, and her faithful dog Pudgy.

LITTLE ORPHAN ANNIE

Created by Harold Gray, Annie first appeared in the *Chicago Tribune* syndicate cartoon strip in August 1924. The story features Annie, an orphan, who escapes from a Dickensian orphanage accompanied by her only friends—her doll Emily Marie and her dog Sandy. She is taken in by Oliver Warbucks, a philanthropic capitalist who insists she calls him "Daddy." Annie is distinguished by her mop of red curly hair and vacant circles for her eyes, while her catch phrases are "Leaping Lizards" and "Gee whiskers." The story at first appealed to children but took on a more serious social aspect as time passed and the Broadway show and movie brought Annie to a much wider audience. The appeal to children manifested itself in a lot of toy products from the 1930s to the present day.

Right: The doll certainly looks like Annie, who is described as having a mop of curly red hair and vacant eyes.

Bottom left: *The Ovaltine beaker was a promotional gift which reads "For extra pep and flavor keen, drink choc'late flavored Ovaltine." Sandy replies "Arf!"*

This early Marx tin toy has "Little Orphan Annie" printed around its waist.

The earliest of our toys are the two Marx tin toys from the early 1930s, which are wind-up toys of Annie herself and Sandy her dog. Annie jumps her skipping rope and Sandy shuffles along when wound. The large rag doll dates from 1972 and was made by the Knickerbocker Toy company—it is 24 inches high. The doll originally had a small puppy in the pocket on the front of her dress but this is missing.

LITTLE RED RIDING HOOD

The Grimm's Fairy tale adaptation of a older, darker folk tale tells of a little girl who sets off to visit her grandmother but keeps a rendezvous with the wolf who has already arrived and eaten the old lady. When Red Riding Hood arrives she is greeted by the wolf disguised as the grandmother. The wolf eats her too, but is interrupted by a hunter who chops the wolf open and releases the two women alive. The tale is a clear allegory, warning children of the dangers of straying from home into the dark and dangerous forest.

Our charming Red Riding Hood doll dates from the 1930s and is a Vogue "Toddles" doll made of composition material. Because this series of dolls is the precursor to the Vogue "Ginny" range it is sometimes referred to as "pre-Ginny, compo Ginny or #1 Ginny." The "Toddles" range are usually little girl subjects—themed dolls based on nursery rhyme or fairy tale characters as in this case, or just simply defined by their outfit, such as "Ice Skater" or "Southern Belle." The dolls have their facial features painted direct onto the composition heads and this leads to damage as seen in the left eye on our doll. The eyes tend to look to the right and the dolls have molded hair underneath their mohair wigs. The wigs tend to become matted and messy in time because the mohair is difficult to style or comb, but the hair on our example is in very good condition. She is 8 inches tall.

Left: The "Toddles" doll is in good order with all of her original clothing and accessories.

HOWDY DOODY

In 1947 *The Howdy Doody Show* began on television on NBC, featuring the marionette and Buffalo Bob Smith, his human companion, as residents of Doodyville, an imaginary Western town. The entertainment was a combination of slapstick comedy and amusing observations about life in the West. The show ran for over 2,000 episodes until 1960. Howdy had blue eyes and freckles painted onto his composition head, red molded hair, and a mouth that moved up and down to simulate speech. His Western-style clothing consisted of blue jeans, plaid shirt, red bandanna and cowboy boots. The show used three versions of Howdy: the main puppet; a duplicate for prolonged camera shots named Double Doody; and a doll without strings used for still photographs called Photo Doody. Rufus Rose, the puppeteer, donated one of the original puppets to the Smithsonian in 1980. Naturally children wanted puppets to play with and our example is one of the commercially available toys from the 1950s, which is 16 inches tall.

BARBIE

Ruth Handler, co-founder of Mattel, took inspiration for Barbie from her daughter, Barbara, who made paper dolls and imagined them in the "grown-up" world. Ruth devised a unique concept for a teenage fashion model doll, and Barbie debuted in 1959 at the New York Toy Fair. The first Barbie was dressed in a black-and-white striped swimsuit with a signature ponytail. She stood 11½ inches tall, and retailed for $3.00—these original dolls are now worth thousands of dollars. Initially, toy buyers found Barbie excessively small and sophisticated, but a "buzz" soon grew up around her, and she became the world's favorite doll.

Through the years, Barbie has reflected a keen interest in fashion, and her outfits had wonderfully evocative names, such as Enchanted Evening, Portrait in Taffeta, and Silken Flame. Several famous designers have created outfits, including Yves St. Laurent, Christian

This is an early blonde Barbie doll.

***Right:** Barbie's outfits have always reflected contemporary trends, and have been influenced by fashion icons like Madonna.*

Barbie has always retained her demure feminine charm.

Above left: Barbie's outfits are coordinated with accessories.

Above right: In the 2000s, Barbie has become a princess.

Right: An early brunette Barbie doll.

Dior, Versace, and Jean-Paul Gaultier. Fashion icons, such as Jackie Kennedy and Madonna, have also inspired Barbie's clothes and hairstyles. Different Barbies were introduced to reflect sociological and beauty trends: "Malibu Barbie," a tanned Californian, was introduced in the 1970s; black and Hispanic Barbies appeared in 1980; a range of "Movie Star Collection" Barbies was announced in the early 2000s. Barbie met her boyfriend, Ken, in 1961, named after Ruth Handler's son, and now has a network of friends and family. She stared in her first movie, *The Nutcracker* in 2001. From urban teen to fantasy queen, Barbie has been fulfilling dreams for nearly fifty years.

329

BARBIE CAMPER

Barbie has always loved pink, since her first introduction to the toy world in 1959—she even has a shade of the color named in her honor, Barbie Pink. She has also always been interested in transport and over the years, she has owned and used several campers, Winnebagos, and automobiles. Among these were the Barbie "Holiday Camper," and the Barbie "Country Camper" of 1970. This was a three-wheeled vehicle, which came complete with two sleeping bags, two campstools, and a checkered awning. Barbie has also had a pink Volkswagen "Camper Van," with a split windshield and complete with a surfboard. Barbie's cars have usually been pink convertibles, including a Corvette, Porsche, Mustang, and a Ferrari. She has also

Barbie's camper opens out to make a spacious holiday home.

Pink is Barbie's favorite color, and she has a special shade, Barbie Pink, named in her honor.

The camper has a surprisingly well-equipped kitchen.

Above: *Barbie is modeled in 1:16 ("playscale"). Her body mold was redesigned in 1997 to give her a wider waist.*

had several pink bicycles, and a Harley-Davidson motorbike (introduced in 1997). Barbie was the first toy whose marketing toy was substantially based on television advertising, and it seems appropriate that she has endorsed many other products over the decades. Mattel estimates that there are now over 100,000 avid Barbie collectors, collecting both the doll and her accessories. The average profile of a Barbie collector is a forty-year-old woman and 45% of collectors spend over $1,000 a year on their hobby. Mattel now manufactures a range of collectors' edition Barbies for her most loyal followers.

SMOKEY THE BEAR

This Smokey the Bear teddy was made by Ideal. He wears his "Prevent Forest Fires" badge proudly—his character has been the focus of America's longest running public service campaign, which began in 1944. His famous message, "Only you can prevent forest fires" is one of the best-known slogans in history. Jackson Weaver provided his voice for the campaign. Ideal launched their Smokey Bear teddy in 1952, and the character also appeared in stories and coloring books. Smokey was also celebrated in the "Ballad of Smokey the Bear."

Above: Ideal's Smokey the Bear wears a "Prevent Forest Fires" badge and commemorative belt buckle.

TEDDY RUXPIN

Teddy Ruxpin is shown with his original box, reading "The World of Teddy Ruxpin" and "Kid's First Animated Talking Toy." Teddy Ruxpin is an animated bear who moves his mouth and eyes as he reads various stories—he originally had a standard audiotape deck built into his back. As well as many different costumes, extra Teddy Ruxpin cassette tapes and books were also available. Ruxpin also had a companion bear, Grubby, who could be connected to him via a cable, which facilitated some limited interaction. Teddy Ruxpin was invented by Ken Forsse, Larry Larsen, and John Davies, and The Worlds of Wonder toy company launched the first version of the toy in 1985. The company filed for bankruptcy in 1988, but this did not signal the end of Teddy Ruxpin. The bear has undergone three further reincarnations: he was revived by Playskool in the late 1980s; by Yes! Entertainment in 1998; and by Backpack Toys in 2005. In this fourth version of the toy (which is still available), the original tape deck was replaced with digital cartridges.

This bear was the first version of the Teddy Ruxpin toy.

STEIFF TEDDY BEAR

The year 2002 marked the hundredth birthday of the teddy bear, which was invented almost simultaneously in both America and Germany. Steiff had been in the soft toy business since 1880, and had a factory in Giengen, Germany. Margarete Steiff, a disabled seamstress, owned the company and she based her first bear on her nephew Richard's drawings of performing bears from a traveling American circus. This Steiff teddy was the first jointed bear. It stood on its back legs (just like a performing bear), and had a humped back, elongated arms, curved paws, and a long snout. It was introduced to the Steiff catalog in 1903, and launched at that year's Leipzig Trade Fair. Three thousand of these early bears were immediately shipped to America and by the outbreak of World War I, millions had been sold. They were immediately recognizable by the small brass button that Steiff placed in the left ear of all of their toys.

Above: This later Steiff bear is made from a longer ply of mohair plush.

The Steiff bear became the generic shape of many teddy bears.

Steiff bears all have a small brass button and label in the left ear.

The teddy bear was immortalized in W. J. Bratton's song "The Teddy Bears' Picnic."

MERRYTHOUGHT BEAR

For many toy collectors, Merrythought Toys Limited is the spiritual home of the British teddy bear. A former employee of rival British toy company Chad Valley founded the company in 1930 and it was located in Ironbridge in Shropshire, in a former iron foundry. As well as teddy bears they also had a range of soft toy hippopotamuses in a sludge green color, which were extremely popular and came in a wide range of sizes, from 11 inches to 45 inches, excluding the tail!

Although Merrythought had an extremely high reputation for all its toy products, and especially teddy bears, the company unfortunately ceased manufacturing toys in November 2006. Despite this, the grandson of the founder created a very small line of toys for 2007.

Right: Merrythought manufactured British teddy bears for nearly three-quarters of a century. They are premium bears made from the finest materials.

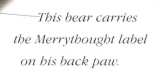

This bear carries the Merrythought label on his back paw.

RAGGEDY ANNE DOLL

This Raggedy Anne doll is dressed in her original outfit and striped leggings, and has several original accessories, including a plate, and several books. Raggedy Anne is the creation of John Barton Gruelle, a political cartoonist. He drew a face on an old rag dog, and gave the toy to his daughter, Marcella Delight. Marcella was delighted with the doll, which very soon became her best friend. Johnny Barton was so amazed by the doll's wonderful effect on his daughter that he submitted a hand-drawn illustration of the doll to the U.S.A. Patent Office, and he was awarded Patent #47789 in 1915. Tragically, this almost exactly corresponded with the untimely death of Marcella, aged just 13, in November 1915.

Johnny drew the Raggedy Anne Stories in his time of grief, and P. F. Volland published them in 1918. They became hugely popular, and Johnny later invented a companion for Anne, Raggedy Andy in the 1920s. Together, they enjoyed adventures in the Dark, Deep Wood. Members of the Gruelle family made the first Raggedy Anne dolls in 1918, in a loft in Norwalk, Connecticut. These first dolls had candy hearts, and were sold mainly to promote the stories that were being published by P. F. Volland. Raggedy Anne and Raggedy Andy dolls are still now available, marketed by Hasbro, and their stories are still in print, published by Simon & Schuster. Johnny Gruelle himself died in 1938.

This Raggedy Anne doll wears her original "homespun-looking" clothes, including her striped leggings.

P. F. Volland first published the Raggedy Anne stories in 1918.

BLACK DOLL WITH STOVE

This black folk-art doll poses with a cast iron stove, wearing a traditional outfit of a red and white striped dress, together with a rick-rack trimmed apron, and scarves around her head and neck. She carries a pink mop. This doll is based on a black "Mammy" character, and is part of a long tradition of black American dolls, dating back to pre-Civil War days. Many of these early toys were made from cloth, but this is a later china doll. There has been a great tradition of black dolls in America and Europe, many earlier examples of which were homemade from various kinds of cloth. These early cloth dolls also included male and female golliwogs. In the 1930s, celluloid baby dolls became very popular; some of them were in miniature sizes, as small as 3½ inches high. German china doll manufacturers also made black dolls, including Schoenau & Hoffman's 1909 black doll, which has a bisque head. Heuback Koppeldorf made their black

Below center: Several toy manufacturers made cast iron stoves like this one in the early 1970s, including Keystone.

Above: This doll is part of a tradition of black mammy dolls that dates back to pre-Civil War times.

bisque model #399 in the early 1900s. Several manufacturers, including Reliable, also made black rubber dolls in the 1940s and 1950s. The 1960s was a fertile time for black dolls, including a black Thumbelina, the black Babyland rag doll, various black Sasha dolls (male and female), and Ideal's "Black Velvet" doll, which was part of the "Christy Family." Mattel has also offered several black Barbie dolls during the past years.

Kenton, Eagle, and Crescent also made toy stoves.

HORSEMAN DOLL

This Horseman doll dates from the 1930s or 1940s, but it is not dressed in its original clothing. Horseman dolls were very well made, and many have survived in good condition. Established in 1865, Horseman is the oldest doll name in America. For its first forty years, the company imported German dolls, toys, novelties, and sporting goods, but they began to make dolls in the early twentieth century, when the founder's son, Edward Horseman Jr. joined the company. The company specialized in American composition dolls. However, both Horsemans died early, and their company almost went bankrupt—Regal Dolls bought it in 1933. Harry Freedman and Lawrence Lipson managed the Regal, but realizing the great value of the Horseman brand, they adopted the earlier company name. The 1930s and 1940s were decades of success for Horseman dolls—they did not use any gimmicks or clever marketing schemes; they simply made well-dressed baby dolls for little girls to love.

Above: Horseman made composition dolls until wartime material shortages. During this era, kapok, mohair, and metal were all difficult to source.

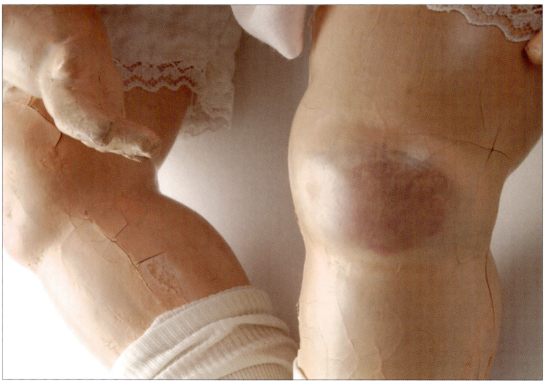

Right: Horseman made soft vinyl prostheses during the war, and started to make plastic dolls in 1947.

*Horseman termed their
product the "People's Doll:"
a fine product at a
modest price.*

BONNIE BRAIDS

Bonnie Braids is the daughter of comic strip character Dick Tracey, and his wife Tess Truehart. The doll's official birthday is May 4, 1951—according to legend, she was born on the backseat of a taxicab, on the way to the hospital. Bonnie (sometimes also spelt Bonny) had a vinyl head, and hard plastic walker body. Toy company Ideal manufactured the doll in two different heights, 11½ inches, and 14 inches. She is shown here wearing a charming lace dress and with a carry case.

She has jointed arms and came with several outfits, but her signature feature was her special molded hair, styled into yellow braids. This doll dates from 1951, but the model stayed in production until 1953.

The Ideal Novelty and Toy Company was founded in 1903 and originally made teddy bears, but soon diversified into dolls and became the first company to manufacture plastic dolls. In the 1930s, the company produced three iconic models, Shirley Temple, Judy

Bonnie Braids was part of Ideal's successful doll range for the 1950s.

Left: Bonnie Braids' traveling trunk has a luggage label from Frisco Lines.

Garland, and Deanna Durbin, which are now highly sought after. They used various materials (including wood, cloth, composition, hard plastic, vinyl, and magic skin) to make a wide range of high quality dolls. As well as Bonny Braids, Ideal's 1950's product line included "Judy Splinters," "Tickle Toes," "Tiny Girl," "Sara Ann," "Miss Revlon Pink Fairy," and "Baby Mine."

PAPER DOLLS

Paper doll Sandy is shown here with a range of paper outfits. This set was printed in America, and dates from World War II years. A paper doll is a two-dimensional object, drawn or printed on paper, which comes with a set of paper clothing. Although home-made paper dolls have been around for centuries, the first manufactured paper doll, Little Fanny, was produced by S. & J. Fuller of London, England in 1810. The first American paper doll appeared two years later, made by J. Belcher of Boston in 1812. Celebrity paper dolls soon appeared, based on renowned ballerinas Marie Taglioni and Fanny Elssler, and Queen Victoria. In the early twentieth century, McLoughlin Brothers, founded in 1828, became the largest manufacturer of paper dolls in the United States. Raphael Tuck was another notable producer. However, Betsy McCall is probably the most famous American paper doll—she appeared in McCall's

Left: Paper dolls like Sandy were very popular during the war, when a materials shortage led to a dearth of more sophisticated toys.

Above: *Costume historians use paper dolls as a major source of information. They often show every layer of clothing.*

catalog from 1904 to the 1990s, drawn by a succession of different artists. The decades of the 1930s, 1940s, and 1950s were the golden era of the paper doll, when their cheapness accounted for much of their popularity. The highly regarded artist, Queen Holden, produced many different types at this time—some of her best-loved dolls included Baby Patsy, Judy Garland, and Snow White. Her work is also believed to have inspired Barbie.

BLONDE AND BRUNETTE DOLLS

These dolls, a brunette and a blonde, are dressed in traditional dolly gingham and are both plastic dolls, with painted eyes and features. Early dolls were mostly made from easily-breakable materials, like bisque, porcelain, wax, and composition, so vinyl dolls were a great leap forward in playability, as they didn't chip, smash, craze, or crack. Two kinds of vinyl, or plastic, evolved for use in doll making: hard and soft, each with their advantages and disadvantages. One of the great pluses for vinyl dolls was their hair—they could have rooted hair, rather than the glued on wigs of their predecessors. However, hard vinyl tended to lose its color, and soft vinyl often became an unattractive brown or orange with age. Fashion dolls, toddler dolls, and baby dolls were all made in vinyl.

Cellulose acetate, or "hard plastic" was introduced in the 1940s, and was soon recognized as an excellent material for doll making. Many dolls were made with soft vinyl heads, thus retaining the benefits of "rooted" hair, and hard plastic bodies. Baby dolls, on the other hand, tended to have hard plastic heads, and soft vinyl bodies—vinyl made realistic baby skin, and was more huggable. Later baby dolls tended to be all vinyl; many modern dolls are still made from soft, durable vinyl.

MRS. BEASLEY

Mattel made the very much-loved Mrs. Beasley doll shown here—the model was produced from 1967. The doll was constructed with a vinyl head, which had yellow rooted hair, and a blue with white dotted body with yellow boots. She wore a blue and white dotted dress and a neat matching apron, trimmed with yellow rick-rack braid. The doll shown here stands 16 inches tall, but she is not wearing her original (removable) glasses. Mrs. Beasley paper dolls were also very popular.

The original Mrs. Beasley doll appeared in the successful 1960s television sitcom, *Family Affair*. The doll was owned by one of the show's main characters, Buffy Patterson-Davies, who was Jody Patterson-Davies's twin sister. The show first aired in 1966, and a total of 138 episodes were filmed before it was cancelled in 1971. At the height of its popularity, *Family Affair* was number one in the ratings. While the series was on television, Mrs. Beasley was the best-selling doll in America. The doll had a voice box, and said several catch phrases, familiar from the show.

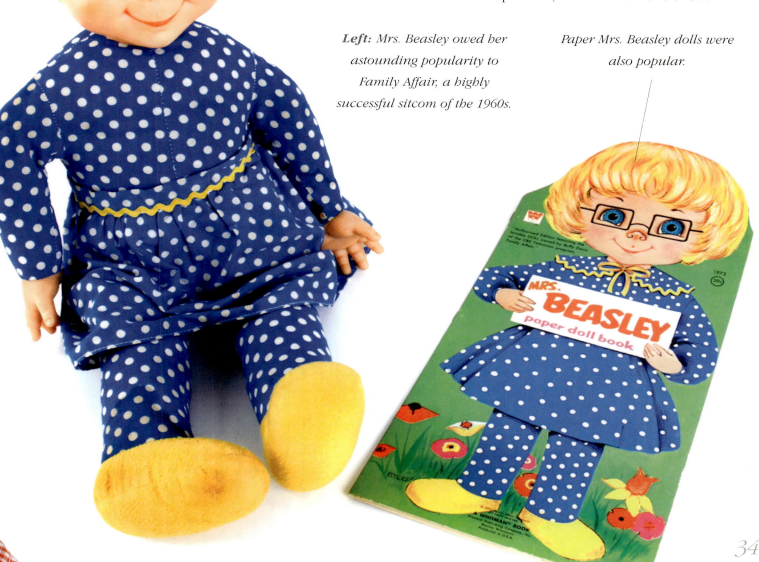

Left: *Mrs. Beasley owed her astounding popularity to Family Affair, a highly successful sitcom of the 1960s.*

Paper Mrs. Beasley dolls were also popular.

CHATTY CATHY AND CHATTY PATTY

Chatty Cathy, shown far right, is wearing a satin sleeveless blouse with yellow ribbon trim and dates from the 1960s. The Chatty Patty black doll shown below is wearing a pink outfit with lace trim, which has its original tag. Chatty Cathy was made by Mattel and went on sale in 1960. The doll was a revolutionary concept for this time, as it spoke eleven random phrases when the string in her back was pulled. Mattel added seven more phrases in 1963. Chatty Cathy became the second most popular doll in America, behind fellow Mattel product Barbie, and Mattel went on to launch several other dolls in the Chatty series. All of the dolls were restyled in 1970, when actress Maureen McCormick (Marcia Brady of *The Brady Bunch*) became the new voice of Cathy. Chatty Patty was launched in 1984.

Mattel is America's largest toy manufacturer by revenue (having earned $5.179 billion in 2005), and has 26,000 employees. Harold Matt Matson and Elliot Handler founded the company in 1945. Elliot Handler's wife, Ruth, was the originator of Barbie and Mattel's classic product line up also includes Hot Wheels, Matchbox cars, Scrabble, and Monopoly. Barbie is currently responsible for over 80 per cent of Mattel's corporate profit.

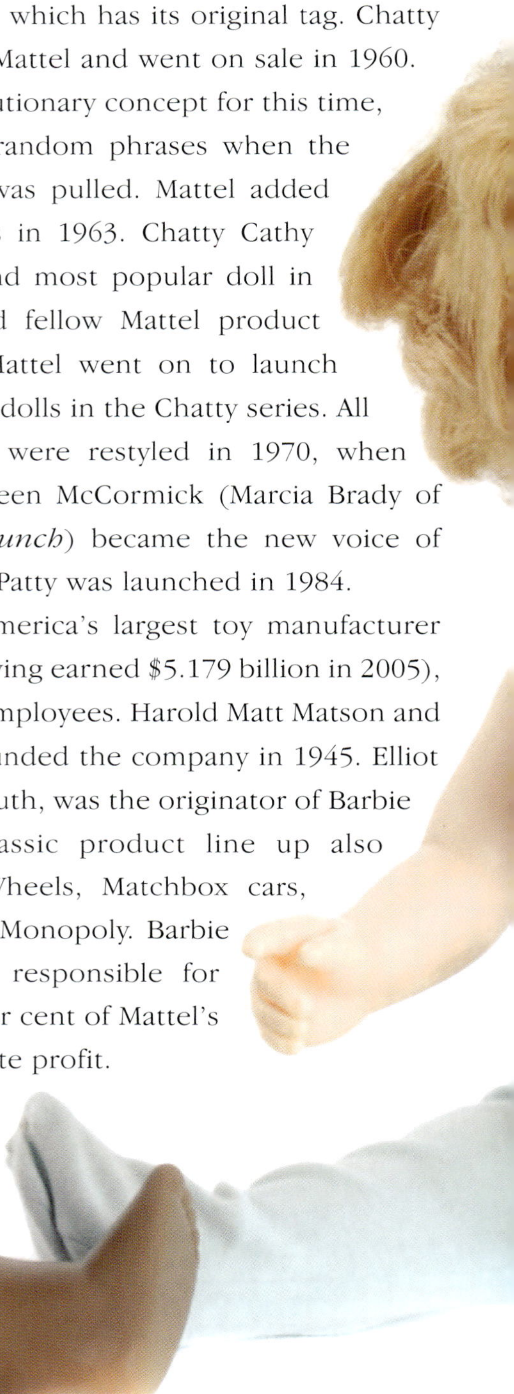

Mattel introduced the Chatty Patty doll in 1984.

The Chatty Patty doll retains her original tag.

Chatty Cathy is an earlier doll, dating from the 1960s.

Above: Chatty Patty was introduced later in 1984. Chatty Cathy was America's second most popular doll in the1960s. Another Mattel product, Barbie was number one.

BABY DOLL

This classic baby doll is marked "1961" and is the product of an unknown maker. The first sitting up baby doll was introduced in Europe, around 1860. The baby doll then went through several evolutionary stages, including the introduction of celluloid heads in 1862. Horseman initiated the American doll-making industry in 1865, and made many early baby dolls. By the end of the century, the market was showing an overwhelming preference for baby dolls over the earlier "lady" dolls. Ten American doll manufacturers were active by this time, while Reliable of Canada made many high quality baby dolls in the 1930s. Baby dolls retained their pre-eminence in the toy market until Barbie was launched in 1959. Early baby dolls were styled to look like human babies, and most were made from bisque or composition materials, but all kinds of baby doll currently remain in production. Some are still aimed at children, but many are now by premium manufacturers, and are aimed at the adult collectors' market. Many of these dolls are offered at high prices, and are made from fine materials, including bisque.

The first sitting up baby doll was introduced around 1860.

Left: The baby doll went through several evolutionary stages, including the introduction of celluloid heads in 1862. They were pre-eminent in the toy market by the end of the nineteenth century.

MATTEL SISTER BELLE DOLLS

Mattel introduced their "Sister Belle" dolls in 1961. The dolls were 16 inches tall, and made from stuffed cloth and hard plastic, with yarn hair. The two sisters shown here are blonde and red haired and also have painted facial features. Our dolls are wearing a simple red costume, and a blue and white-checkered dress, while both have black cloth shoes. The dolls are from Mattel's line of talking dolls, which the company had initiated with the introduction of Chatty Cathy in 1960. The "Sister Belles" are part of the Chatty series and are equipped with a battery operated pull talker, which was programmed with eleven phrases. These included "It's time to eat," "I think you're nice," and "I love you." Mattel also introduced a male doll in the series, "Matty Mattel The Talking Boy," in 1961, and "Casper the Talking Ghost."

The blonde "Sister Belle" doll has yarn hair, and big blue eyes.

The "Sister Belles" were part of Mattel's Chatty series. They also produced "Matty" and "Casper" dolls.

GLAMOROUS DOLL IN FUR COAT

This glamorous doll in her luxurious fur coat is part of a modern phenomenon, premium dolls made specifically for adult collectors, rather than as playthings for children. Many, like this one, are made from bisque, and are known as porcelain dolls. Millions of bisque dolls were made in America between 1865 and the 1930s, but the majority were broken during play. Most modern collectors' dolls are offered at prices between $20 and $500. Collectors are often split between those collecting bisque and those with vinyl dolls. Himstedt, Tonner, and Alexander use high quality vinyl, while Marie Osmond use bisque.

Below: A detail of the doll's beautifully modeled face

The doll's black coat is trimmed with fake leopard fur.

Collectors' dolls have been valued as highly as $200,000.

MODERN PORCELAIN DOLL

Like the glamorous doll in the fur coat, this tall brown-haired doll was produced with adult collectors in mind, rather than as a plaything for young children. Whereas dolls' clothing is often a reflection of contemporary fashion trends, this doll wears a ruffled blue and white dress and bonnet that is reminiscent of late nineteenth century women's apparel. Sewing dolls' outfits is now a growing hobby, and many of the books and patterns on offer concentrate on historic outfits. "Off the peg" doll wear is also available for many popular dolls. Porcelain (or bisque) has been considered a good material for doll making for many years. Dolls whose faces have been glazed are usually referred to as being made from china, whereas unglazed dolls are usually referred to as bisque. The technique of making these dolls originated in Germany, Denmark, and France in the early 1800s, but china dolls were not mass-produced until the late nineteenth century. The French manufacturer Emil-Louis Jumeau introduced the very first baby doll in the mid nineteenth century, but "lady dolls" like this brown haired doll remained popular until the early twentieth century.

Many of today's reintroduced china dolls are considered artistic pieces in their own right.

They are often numbered and have a registration certificate.

Early china dolls had painted shoes.

KEWPIE DOLLS

The Kewpie doll was based on Rose O'Neill's illustrations of cherubic babies, which appeared in 1909 in the *Ladies' Home Journal*. Her illustrated stories are considered to be the first examples of the comic strip. The word "Kewpie" is derived from "Cupid," the Roman god of the erotic, and equivalent of the Greek god Eros. The first Kewpie dolls were made from bisque, and are now worth thousands of dollars, but a celluloid version was introduced in 1913. This version became hugely popular, and a celluloid Kewpie was included in the 1939 New York World's Fair time capsule. Toy company Effanbee launched the first hard plastic Kewpie in 1949. Kewpies also endorsed many other products with their image, including cups, plates, and coloring books—this was the first example of merchandising based on a comic character. The image of Kewpies became ubiquitous, and Rose O'Neill became rich and famous—even a hamburger chain was named for the dolls: Samuel V. Blair founded Kewpee Hotel Hamburgs in 1923. "Kewpie" has also passed into the language, being used to describe the appearance of children with a growth hormone deficiency.

Above: *Rose O'Neill wanted to design a character that would be loved by everyone.*

Right: *Kewpie dolls come in many different sizes, from miniature to over 18 inches tall. Early dolls were bisque, but later a celluloid version was introduced.*

Below: Original Kewpie dolls bear red and gold hearts on their chests. Several different companies manufactured them.

This is one of the larger Kewpie dolls manufactured. It has a red plush body.

Early Kewpies also had Rose O'Neill's name on their feet.

KEWPIE
REG U S
PAT OFF

Left: Kestner and Jesco made some early Kewpies. The Effanbee dolls are still in production.

355

CABBAGE PATCH DOLL

Xavier Roberts invented the first Cabbage Patch doll in 1976—they were also known as "Little People Originals" dolls. An art student, Roberts re-discovered the early nineteenth-century German technique of fabric sculpture and he combined this with his mother's quilting skills to "soft sculpt" the dolls. Having won a firm following at local craft fairs, Roberts was still a teenager when he started the Babyland General Hospital in Cleveland, Georgia. Customers went to Babyland to "adopt" a doll, which came complete with full adoption papers. Roberts then started the Original Appalachian Artworks company to produce the dolls. The Coleco Toy Company, who really liked Roberts's original ideas, began to mass-market the dolls in 1983 under their new brand name, the Cabbage Patch Kids.

The first mass-produced Cabbage Patch Kids were made in 1982.

Above: *The "Kids" were honored with a stamp in January 2000.*

Three millions "Kids" were sold in their first year on sale.

KISSIN' THUMBELINA

Ideal made a series of Thumbelina dolls between 1961 and 1972—they came in a range of different versions, "Newborn," "Tiny," and "Toddler." The dolls were issued in various sizes at 9, 14, 16, and 20 inches in height. The original baby Thumbelina squirmed when a knob was turned on its back. Thumbelina underwent a complete redesign in 1968, and was reissued as a 9-inch tall "Newborn" doll, which moved by means of a pull string mechanism. This version of the doll remained in production until 1972. Another doll in the series, "Toddler Thumbelina" was launched in 1969—this doll came complete with an accessory rocking horse, car, or walker.

The "Kissin' Thumbelina" shown here was issued in 1970, and came with her very own blue plastic baby carriage. She is 9 inches tall, and squirms by means of a pull string—she also has a mechanism that makes her arm swing, so that it looks as though she is throwing kisses, when you put her hand to her mouth. The doll has a vinyl head with kissing lips, cloth body, soft limbs, painted "sleep" eyes, and rooted hair. She is dressed in her original outfit.

Morris and Rose Michtom founded Ideal in New York City in 1907.

Above: As well as throwing kisses and squirming, later Thumbelina dolls also had criers to make them even more realistic.

BEANIE BABIES

Ty Warner launched the first "Original 9" Beanie Babies in 1994. The line-up included "Chocolate the Moose," "Pinchers the Lobster," "Spot the Dog," and "Squealer the Pig." Warner had conceived the idea of an inexpensive toy aimed directly at children's pocket money. The real appeal was that each toy had its own name and birth date and Ty sustained the interest by constantly retiring Beanies and introducing new ones —there are now over 250 Babies to collect. The slightly larger Beanie Buddies (the Babies are usually between 8 and 10 inches long) were introduced in 1998, followed by Beanie Kids. The large number of retired toys means that there is a very active collectors' market—country-specific Babies like "Britannia," "Liberty," "Germania," and "Maple" are particularly desirable. McDonald's has offered "Teenie Beanie Babies" as premium gifts, and Teenies were a major part of the 2004 twenty-fifth anniversary celebrations for the Happy Meal. Beanie Babies have been so successful that they have even spawned a thriving counterfeit industry, but several prosecutions have been mounted successfully to counter this.

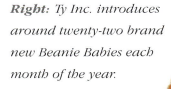

Right: Ty Inc. introduces around twenty-two brand new Beanie Babies each month of the year.

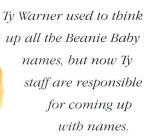

Ty Warner used to think up all the Beanie Baby names, but now Ty staff are responsible for coming up with names.

Below: *The tie-dyed "Peace Bears" were introduced in 1997. Each one is unique.*

Below: *Beanie Baby "Teddy" is stuffed with plastic beans to make him more buggable.*

A pristine ear tag can double the value of a Beanie Baby.

G.I. JOE

Toy merchandiser Stan Weston brought the G.I. Joe concept, "a rugged-looking scale doll for boys" to Don Levine, Hasbro's creative director. Weston had been inspired by the television series *The Lieutenant* and Levine quickly realized the potential of a toy aimed at boys, which could have limitless accessories. He decided to go ahead with G.I. Joe and from the beginning, Hasbro was careful to market the toy as an action figure, rather than a doll. The granddaddy of all action figures was launched in 1964, with a range of 75 figures, vehicles, uniforms, and accessories. The line-up included the "G.I. Nurse," who is now worth in excess of $6,000. The toy has been re-incarnated more than a dozen times. Sales declined in the post-Viet Nam era, and Hasbro re-launched the model as an adventurer to reflect the change in world politics. G.I. Joe has been offered in several different sizes, including 3¾, 4½, 6, 8, and 12 inches tall.

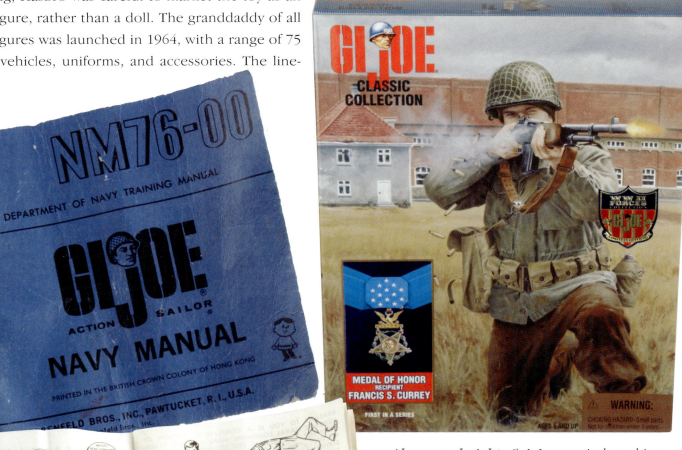

Above and right: G. I. Joe was inducted into the National Toy Hall of Fame in November 2004.

Left: "America's Movable Fighting Man" starred in the movie Valor vs. Venom.

547233.00

NOTE: Adult should remove and discard plastic fasteners.

TWO TOY REFRIGERATORS

These two toy refrigerators are examples of girls' toys popular in the 1940s and 1950s. Walt Disney's "Snow White Refrigerator" is 15 inches high, 8 inches wide, and 7 inches deep. The single door (complete with Snow White monogram) opens to reveal a shelf and two compartments. This is an early Snow White-endorsed product. The Wolverine double-door refrigerator, also with freezing compartment, measures 13 inches high, 8 inches wide, and 6 inches deep. Wolverine Supply and Manufacturing, founded by Benjamin F. Bain and his wife, was based in Pittsburgh, Pennsylvania between 1903 and 1950. Wolverine began with a famous range of sandbox toys, but expanded their line to include toys for girls at the 1918 New York Toy Fair. The new lines were dubbed "Sunny Andy" and "Sunny Suzy," and included tea sets, sand pails, washtubs, glass washboards, ironing boards, and miniature grocery stores. 1929 saw the introduction of more boys' models to the Wolverine range; airplanes, boats, and buses. Wolverine continued to add new products, even during the Depression. These included a wide variety of kitchen play sets, which consisted of various appliances and accessories, including refrigerators, washing machines, wringers, stoves, canister sets, washday sets, toy groceries, and kitchen cupboards.

The Wolverine refrigerator has special ice-making trays, and cherry colored handles.

Above: *The "Snow White Refrigerator" was shown in the 1950 Spiegel catalog.* Snow White and the Seven Dwarves *was released in 1937.*

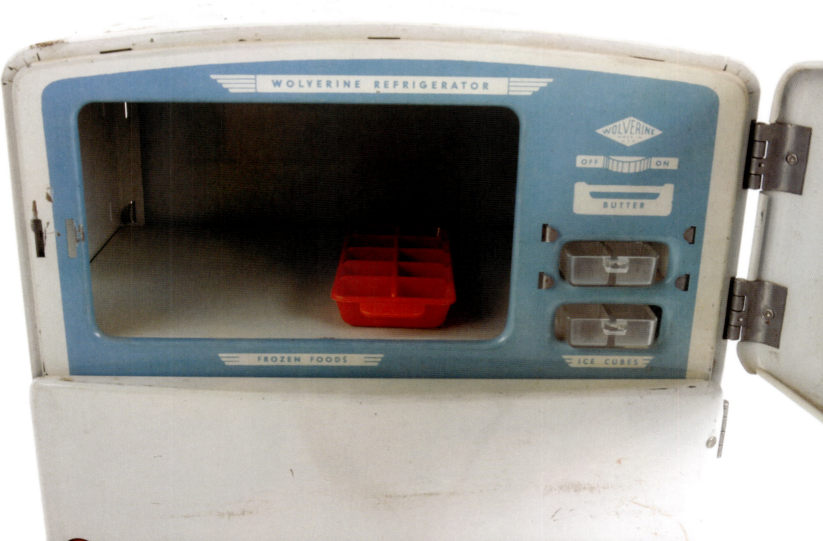

THREE TOY IRONS

These three toys irons date from the 1940s to the 1960s and range from cast iron models to modern steel ones. Wolverine made the red iron—it was one of their "Sunny Suzy" miniature kitchenware models. Many had electrical cords, and actually heated—they were teaching toys, designed to help girls understand their domestic duties. Mass-produced kitchen toys were a popular product for girls from the mid-1800s, and are still available from many different manufacturers today. One of the most successful kitchen toys ever was the "Easy-Bake Oven," introduced in 1963—half a million were sold in the first year. Every kind of kitchen equipment, both accessories and appliances, were miniaturized for children to play with.

In real life, the first smoothing appliances were heated stones, used right back in the eighth century. These were later replaced by the cast iron "smoother," which was heated at the fireplace—some skill was required to get the correct temperature. Henry W. Seely of New York City patented the electric iron on June 6, 1882; he was awarded patent number 259,054 and the appliance was first known as the electric flatiron and weighed 15 pounds. Early models used a carbon arc to create heat, but this proved unsafe. Irons heated by electrical resistance were introduced by Compton and Company, and steam irons were launched in the 1950s.

The earliest flatiron toys were made, like the grown up versions, from cast iron.

Later toys were powered by electricity, and really heated.

WICKER DOLL CARRIAGE

This blue wicker doll carriage has spoked wheels, hubcaps and a wooden handle, and dates from between the 1940s and 1960s.

The baby carriage was invented in 1933 by the English architect William Kent, who designed the first for the Duke of Devonshire's children. It was shaped like a shell, and designed to be pulled by either a dog or a Shetland pony. American William H. Richardson patented an improvement to the "child's carriage" in 1889 (U.S. patent number 405,600). In Victorian times, baby carriages were often constructed from light and durable wicker (and reproductions of these early models are available to this day). They became very popular, and even Queen Victoria pushed one. One of the early baby carriage manufacturers was Heywood Brothers & Company. Sears Roebuck and Marshall field sold many wicker carriages through their catalogs.

This baby carriage is fitted with a wooden handle.

Wicker is an excellent material, light and durable.

The carriage is equipped with lightweight steel wheels.

TOY PHONES

Toy telephones have been around almost as long as the telephone itself, and have reflected changing models. The candlestick model here has the telephone number Kiddie 5432 and was made in the 1930s, while the vintage style payphone dates from the 1940s. Many American toy manufacturers have traced the history of telecommunication equipment through the twentieth century to today, including Remco, Tootsietoy, Fisher-Price, Ideal, Mattel, and Chatty Baby. German manufacturer Putz was also active in the early years.

Alexander Graham Bell introduced his first commercial telephone in 1877. The first telephone exchange was established in New Haven in 1878, and by 1880, there were 47,900 telephones in America. The first telephones were simple wooden boxes, but the first desk model was introduced in the 1880s. The electric dial telephone was launched in the 1920s, and the 1950s saw the introduction of "colorized" models. The classic Trimline model dates from the 1960s, and the 1970s saw an explosion of wild designer styles. By the 1980s, style had given way to sheer practicality, and cordless phones were all the rage. This decade also saw the widespread introduction of cellular phones, which have now become ubiquitous.

This is an early toy candlestick phone.

This vintage style payphone dates from the 1940s.

The toy's phone number is Kiddie 5432.

STOVE AND TEA SET

This pink enamel kitchen toy dates from the late 1940s/early 1950s—the stove/washbasin combination is unusual. Several toy manufacturers made kitchen appliances in pink enamel, including Little Lady and Wolverine. The Little Lady pink enamel stove is electric; the inside of the oven and burners heat up.

The aluminum tea set comes from around the same era. Children's tea services have been made for over a hundred years, often constructed in the same materials as full-size versions. The first tea sets were made in porcelain and faience, then aluminum, and finally plastic, while china tea sets were made in occupied Japan. They are still popular today; manufacturers include Wolverine, Ohio Art, Irwin, Marie Osmond. Many tea sets featured fairy tale and Disney characters, including Pinocchio, Red Riding Hood, Cinderella, Hansel and Gretel, and Alice and Wonderland. Tea drinking is now becoming more popular than ever. Not only is tea drinking considered stylish (and a beautiful tea service is essential for this), but healthy, too.

The stove burner heats up.

This stove is enameled in girl-pleasing pink.

Above: *The aluminum tea service dates from the 1950s.*

KOKOMO LITTLE LADY STOVE

This red and crème Kokomo Little Lady stove is shown with an aluminum kettle and two aluminum pans. The age of electric toys can often be determined by the style of their electric cord and plug, which is how this one has been dated to the early 1930s. Many toy stoves of this vintage also heated up.

Charles T. Byrne and James F. Ryan founded the Kingston Products Corporation in the 1890s in Kokomo, Indiana, and used the name of their town as a brand name. Kingston first produced brass castings for the plumbing industry, but soon diversified into several different product lines. Kokomo made toys, including fire engines, racers, and trucks. Several were equipped with electrical features, including the "Fastest Electric Toy Made." But expensive toys like this were cancelled in 1931, when the economic effects of the Depression began to bite. Successful during the 1920s and 1930s, Kingston is now part of the Scott & Fetzer Company, and manufactures parts for the automobile industry.

Above: The Kokomo stove has an opening door, and an electrically heated oven. It is finished in dark red enamel.

This substantial metal toy was constructed by Kokomo in the 1930s.

Above: The sales of Kokomo's electrical toys were affected by the Depression.

The electrical plug dates the stove to the 1930s.

The age of the electrical cord is also relevant.

WOLVERINE GENERAL STORE

This Wolverine General Store is a replica of a Wolverine model from the 1930s and 1940s and is completely charming with its miniature shelves filled with miniature packages and grocery products. The store measures 12 inches by 20¼ inches, plus the awning and was just one of several large scale lithographed tin toys that the company produced. These include dollhouses, the "Number 40" racing game, a ski jumper game, shooting gallery game, and Shell gas station. The Wolverine toy company was

Below: The shelves of the Wolverine General Store are filled with toy groceries.

The General Store is very attractively lithographed.

founded by Benjamin F. Bain and his wife in 1903 and began by offering a famous range of sand-powered novelty toys. It was located in Pittsburgh, Pennsylvania until it folded in 1950. Wolverine introduced a new line of toys, specifically aimed at girls, at the 1918 New York

Above: The store is equipped with a striped awning, in lithographed tin plate.

Toy Fair. Marketed under the brand name "Sunny Suzy," these toys included tea sets, sand pails, washtubs, glass washboards, ironing boards, and miniature grocery stores. Further boys' toys were added to Wolverine's line in 1929, including airplanes, boats, and buses. Even during the Depression, Wolverine continued to expand its range of toys. Kitchen play sets were one of their most successful lines; they included many appliances and accessories, as well as toy groceries.

FISHER-PRICE TOYS

The Fisher-Price sweeper on the left dates from around the 1950s and plays "Whistle While You Work" while it sweeps. The Fisher-Price teaching clock is a tin plate model from around 1968.

The Fisher-Price company was founded in 1930 by three partners; Henry Fisher, Irving Price, and Helen Schelle, and was located in East Aurora, New York. The founders took 16 new toys to the 1931 New York International Toy Fair, and launched their first product, "Dr. Doodle." Fisher-Price's most successful line in the 1960s was "The Little People" range, which were originally wooden, but are now plastic. In the 1970s, the line was expanded to include the Sesame Street characters. The company is still running—it is now a subsidiary of Mattel, and is the home of all their preschool products.

Below: The sweeper is one of 5,000 toys launched by the company.

Opposite page: Learning through play is a Fisher-Price tradition. This teaching clock is a tin plate toy.

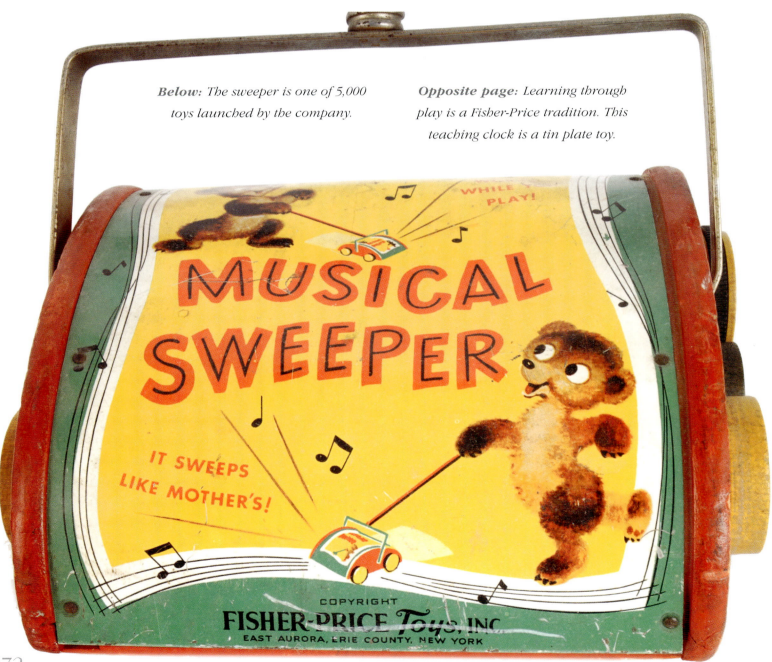

SCHOOL

FISHER · PRICE TOYS

373

KINGSBURY FIRE PUMPERS

These Kingsbury fire pumpers are equipped with steamer tanks and date from the late 1920s or early 1930s. They are highly collectible. The Kingsbury Manufacturing Company was established in Keene, New Hampshire, in 1919. Its founder, Harry T. Kingsbury, had bought the Wilkins Toy Company in 1895, and amalgamated it with the Clipper Machine Works. They started to make toy cars in the early 1900s and gradually, the Wilkins name was dropped in favor of Kingsburg.

Kingsbury specialized in making pressed steel ride-on wagons, model aircraft, cars, trucks, and buses. Fire engines were always a popular line. World War II led the company to switch to war contracts in 1942, and this was the end of toy production for Kingsbury—their toy manufacturing equipment was sold to Keystone in Boston. The company still exists as the Kingsbury Machine Tool Division, a subcontractor for industry giants like IBM and General Motors.

Below: Kingsbury made fire pumpers like this from around 1918.

Kingsbury patented the design for these fire pumpers.

The fire pumpers had a wind-up mechanism.

TEXACO FIRE CHIEF HELMET

Texaco Fire Chief helmets like these, complete with the company logo, were sold in gas stations in the 1950s. The hat is fitted with a microphone and speaker system powered by three AA batteries, so that the junior fire chief could yell out commands. The battery compartment is located in the top of the helmet, and the speaker in the crest at the front. The helmet has a plastic chinstrap, and a metal loop at the back so that it can be hung from the wall.

Underneath the helmet is a Brown & Bigelow logo. Brown & Bigelow of St. Paul, Minneapolis, is a promotional and advertising specialist who produce calendars and incentive gifts. In the 1940s and 1950s they were one of the biggest calendar manufacturers in the world—it is estimated they placed calendars in over fifty million American homes. They published the work of many major American artists, including Rolf Armstrong, Mabel Rollins Harris, Gil Elvgren, and Norman Rockwell.

The helmet was a promotional product designed for Texaco.

The engine is well equipped with a ringing bell, turning pump, detachable fire hoses, and turning wheels.

The quality of the printing on this model is superb.

Above: These buriki toys became increasingly sophisticated and sought after, as Japanese toy manufacturers adapted their products for American children.

FIRE DEPARTMENT NO. 7

This extremely attractive fire engine, from Fire Department No. 7, was made in Japan. It is battery operated, and equipped with an on/off switch on the side of the truck. It is an excellent example of a high quality *buriki* (Japanese tin plate) toy and is beautifully printed in red, gold, and black.

Japanese manufacturers had imported the technique of printing on tin plate, and the use of clockwork mechanisms, from the German toy manufacturers and these innovations greatly assisted the success of the Japanese toy trade. The devastation of the German industry in World War I left the market open to the Japanese, and their products were widely exported to both America and Europe.

These Japanese toys are now highly collectible.

The wheel hubs are printed tin.

Right: *The model displays how Japanese toy manufacturers injected as much play value as possible into their attractive products.*

WYANDOTTE HOOK AND LADDER

This Wyandotte fire struck dates from the 1940s. Wyandotte Toys, also known as the All Metal Products Company, was founded in the fall of 1921 in Michigan. They based their production on the use of assembly line techniques and cheap raw materials, such as metal scrap from the automobile industry. Despite this, Wyandotte produced toys of exceptionally high quality. In the 1920s, the company mostly produced toy pistols and rifles, working under the slogan "Every boy wants a pop gun," and by 1929, they were the most prolific manufacturer of toy guns in the world. At this point, the company suspended its production of air rifles, but continued to make toy guns, but they knew that it was time to diversify, and added various new toys to their product line. These included doll buggies, musical toys, games, wagons, model cars, trucks, and planes. They also changed their slogan to the more ubiquitous "Wyandotte toys are good and safe." Their toys were

The fire engine is equipped with a folding ladder.

simply made, in heavy gauge steel, with a baked enamel finish and wooden wheels; many have survived in good condition. Tin toys, like this fire engine are rarer. Wyandotte moved into lithographed novelty toys in 1936 and in 1937 added spring-driven motors to propel some of their vehicles. They also made wind-up and lever-actions toys. During the shortages of World War II the company produced wooden models, and after the war they moved into clockwork trains, together with die cast and hard molded plastic toys for the dime store market.

Above: With the steel shortage during World War II, Wyandotte fitted wooden wheels onto its models.

Opposite page below: Wyandotte moved into lithographed tin toys in 1936. The printing on this model is extremely clear and attractive.

TURNER FIRE TRUCK

The Turner Company, based in Wapakoneta, Ohio, made this fire truck, which dates from the 1940s. The company was known for its colorful and realistic toys, which sold for modest prices of between 60 cents and $4. John Turner founded the company in 1915, and it became known for its line of "Victory is Won" flywheel toys, sold to the public through direct mail. This fire truck is decorated with several logos, including one of a fire helmet, and the Turner boy-in-a-cap logo. The truck's radiator grille is painted and stamped for greater realism, and it has two ladders and a winding mechanism.

Left: *The fire truck is decorated with several logos, including the boy-in-a-cap Turner decal.*

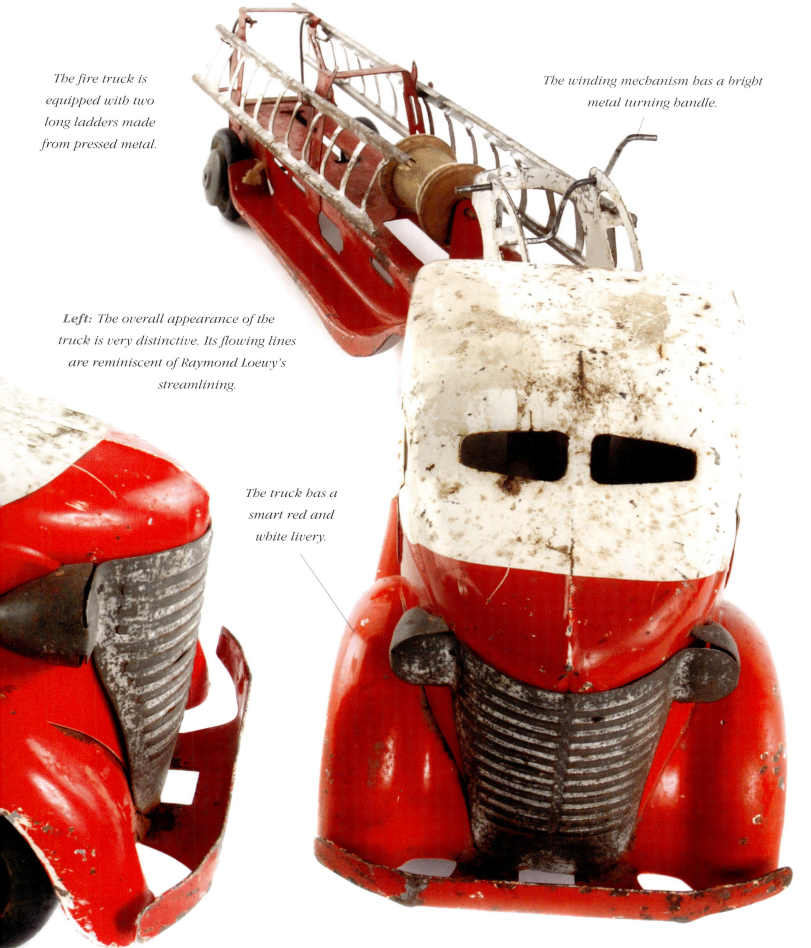

The fire truck is equipped with two long ladders made from pressed metal.

The winding mechanism has a bright metal turning handle.

Left: The overall appearance of the truck is very distinctive. Its flowing lines are reminiscent of Raymond Loewy's streamlining.

The truck has a smart red and white livery.

MARX FIRE TRUCK

Marx made this tin friction fire engine, with its fantastic graphics and an extendable ladder, in the1950s. Louis Marx founded his toy company in 1919. He was often described as a brilliant businessman with the mind of a child and he firmly believed that children enjoyed playing with models of the vehicles they would see in real life. These included dump trucks, garbage trucks, road graders, telephone trucks, tractor trailers, car haulers, army trucks—and of course fire engines. Marx also produced a wide range of service stations. Many of these toys are celebrated in the Official Marx Toy Museum of Glen Dale, West Virginia, which is located just one and a half miles from the Marx factory in Glen Dale, and which Louis Marx had opened during the Great Depression of the 1930s. Its displays cover over five decades of Marx playthings. This fire engine comes from the 1950s, which was the company's most successful decade.

Above: The decals show a fireman decked out in full fire-fighting gear and ready for action.

The fabulous decals have survived well over the years.

The fire engine's grille is a separate pressing.

Above: *This fire engine is equipped with a wraparound running board.*

TURNER RINGING BELL FIRE ENGINE

The Turner Company in Wapakoneta, Ohio, made this fire truck, circa 1937. John C. Turner founded the company in 1915 and he chose Wapakoneta as the location for his enterprise because it was situated on the active trade route between Cincinnati and Detroit. The company was known for the high quality of its product lines and this fire truck demonstrates the robust materials from which their toys were made. They were also colorful and realistic, but despite all this, the toys were offered at relatively modest prices of between 60 cents and $4.00. This was extremely important in the difficult economic times of the

This Turner fire engine is well equipped with two pressed steel ladders, a turning winch, and a ringing bell. Considering its age, it is in good condition—it appears to be complete, and has moderate wear to the paintwork.

The cab door has the remnants of a decal.

Depression, when toys were a luxury that many American families could not afford. Although Turner survived the Depression, and the shortage of raw materials during World War II, it folded in 1948 and ceased trading. Later Turner toys were often decorated with the company's cheerful boy-in-a-cap log. Most of their toys are also marked as having been produced in America, important to many consumers at this time. This toy fire truck is now worth several hundred dollars, and would be highly sought after at auction.

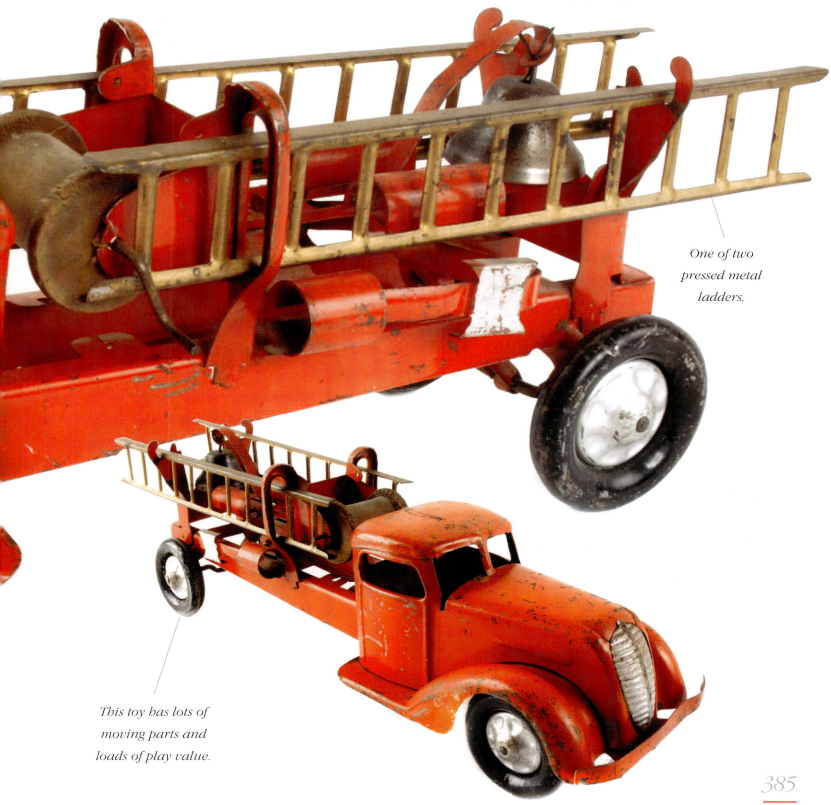

One of two pressed metal ladders.

This toy has lots of moving parts and loads of play value.

LINEMAR FIRE ENGINE

Linemar was established in the 1950s as an import subsidiary of successful American toy company Louis Marx. They manufactured mechanical and battery operated toys in low wage Japan, and sold them in America. Some of their most successful lines were toys based on Disney characters, such as Popeye. Linemar toys always offered the consumer plenty of play value and performed various interesting functions. Linemar went out of business in the 1960s.

Linemar always used attractive packing.

Below: This beautifully modeled fireman waves a red flag.

TURNER FIRE TRUCK

This Turner fire truck dates from the 1940s and is equipped with a ringing silver bell and two yellow ladders. It has a company logo on the truck door and a smart silver radiator grille, as well as rubber tires, and a bright red paint finish. The fire truck comes from the company's last decade of production.

The Turner Company was founded in 1915, and was located in Wapakoneta, Ohio. John C. Turner established the company in this town because of its auspicious position on the trade route between Cincinnati and Detroit. Despite surviving the Great Depression and the production difficulties of World

Left: *The fire truck dates from the company's last decade, the 1940s. It has a bright red paint finish.*

War II, Turner folded in 1948. In general, the American tin toy trade thrived until the late 1950s, and toys from all eras of production are now highly sought after by collectors. Ironically, these toys had survived during the Great Depression due to their affordability, but the affluent years of the late 1950s and 1960s prompted an influx of more sophisticated toys onto the market, which led to their demise.

Right: This Turner fire truck has two yellow ladders, but is equipped to take three. The third ladder rests on the two holders on top of the truck.

SMALL WYANDOTTE FIRE TRUCK

This small red fire truck has two pressed tin ladders, painted in yellow, and was made by Wyandotte in the 1940s. It is a high quality toy, and its printing and decals, which proclaim the engine to be from the "Wyandotte Fire Department," are in great condition. The Wyandotte Company, also known as the All Metal Products Company, was founded in Michigan in the fall of 1921. The company used modern assembly line techniques, and cheap raw materials, such as metal scrap from the automobile industry. Henry Ford first employed mass production techniques in the early twentieth century, in the manufacture of his Model T. His assembly line methods led to high productivity from a reduced workforce. These methods meant Wyandotte, like Ford, could offer well-made and attractive products at highly competitive prices, and like Louis Marx, the company culture was that the customer should be offered "more toy for less money." They launched their first pressed metal transport toys in the 1930s.

The truck's metal hubs are fitted with rubber tires.

Above: *Wyandotte employed the assembly line techniques of mass production to ensure that they could offer high quality toys at attractive prices.*

The cab is molded from one piece of tin, the grille from another.

The printing on this tin plate toy is good quality, and has survived well.

TWO MARX PLASTIC TRUCKS

Marx manufactured these two plastic trucks. The yellow one is the "Siren Emergency Wrecker," and the red example is a fire truck, equipped with a ladder turntable. Using plastic came from Louis Marx's desire to make his toy products truly mass market. When the company returned to toy production after World War II, he started to make much more use of the modern plastics that had been discovered in the earlier part of the century. Although it was thought that toy buyers would resist the change from tin plate toys, they actually responded very favorably to the cheapness and safety of plastic playthings. Whereas tin toys had inflicted endless cuts and scrapes, plastic was smooth and had no sharp edges. In fact, the company grew even stronger in this era of mass production and plastic toys and the 1950s proved to be a Golden Era. By 1955, Marx produced over twenty per cent of the all the toys sold in America; their sales were worth more than $30 million and their product line totaled more than 5000 items. The company opened factories in ten different countries, including Linemar in Japan. Marx also distributed the toys of Distler in Germany.

Above: These Marx plastic trucks are simply molded with turning wheels and steering.

The fire truck is made from red colored plastic.

Both trucks have turning wheels, with plastic tires.

SIREN EMERGENCY WRECKER

Left: *The yellow truck has retained a very clear decal, which details its model name: "Siren Emergency Wrecker."*

YOSHIYA/KO FIRE TRUCK

The fire truck had metal wheels and rubber tires.

Japanese toy manufacturer Yoshiya made this fire truck, complete with box. Their logo was KO, which was printed in a diamond shape. The company was also known as Kobe Yoko Ltd. and was a major Japanese toy manufacturer in the post war period—its years of operation were between 1950 and 1970. They specialized in mechanical or wind-up toys decorated with fanciful designs in litho printing. As well as several fire trucks, KO also manufactured toy trains, tin animals, and Robby the Robot toys. Japanese tin plate toys first appeared in the Meiji and Taisho era, but it was not until the late 1940s that the industry became internationally successful. The list of Japanese tin toy manufacturers from this time is very extensive, and some still survive today.

Above: Yoshiya's fire truck is equipped with a lifting, extendable ladder. The company specialized in litho printed toys like this.

The fire truck still has its original packaging, although it is now possible to buy replacement boxes.

KEYSTONE AND TURNER FIRE TRUCKS

This Keystone fire truck is 27½ inches long. Keystone first ventured into toy vehicles in 1925, with a truck based on a full-size Packard Motor Company model, which was so successful that Keystone's product line began to rival that of Buddy L. A major selling point of their playthings was their strength and reputation for durability that led to a growth in sales and an increased market share.

The Mack Fire Truck VFD #86 was made by Turner in the 1920s.

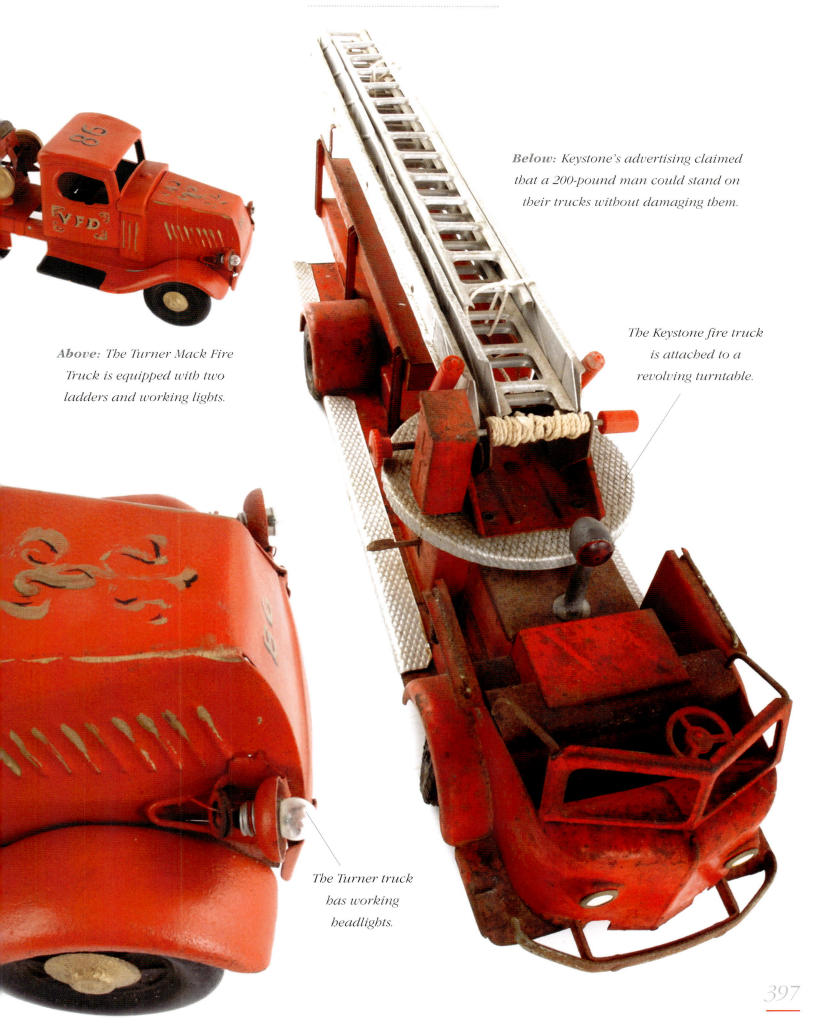

Above: *The Turner Mack Fire Truck is equipped with two ladders and working lights.*

Below: *Keystone's advertising claimed that a 200-pound man could stand on their trucks without damaging them.*

The Keystone fire truck is attached to a revolving turntable.

The Turner truck has working headlights.

DOEPKE FIRE TRUCK

This fire truck comes from Charles William Doepke Company, Inc., who were located in Rossmoyne, Ohio, and launched their first toys in 1946. Charles Doepke managed the manufacturing side of the business, while his brother Fred ("Fritz") handled the company's sales.

This red fire truck, complete with hook and ladder was one of their typically faithful replicas of full-size vehicles and dates from the 1950s. Toys of this type retailed for around $12, which was a very high price for the time. Doepke marketed their toys under the brand

This Model Toy fire truck is a clockwork toy, with a key located in the side below the turntable.

Left: *Model Toy concentrated on making large, up-market toys that would last.*

name "Model Toy." Like Keystone, they had an excellent reputation for making rugged, heavy-gauge steel toys, which also tended to be larger than most (1:16 scale). Doepke also concentrated on giving their toys moving features. Their model line included road graders, cranes, farm vehicles, automobiles, and fire trucks. The company slogan was that their toys would "outlast others by 3 to 1." This proved to be true and many Model Toys have survived.

Above: The winding mechanism on this high-quality Model Toy fire truck still works perfectly.

MARX PLASTIC FIRE ENGINE

Marx made this red and yellow plastic fire truck in the 1950s, during their post-war period of production. It bears the New York Fire Department logo, and is a wind-up toy.

During their Golden Era of production in the 1950s, Marx constructed many traditionally themed toys in plastic. These included plastic soldiers, cowboy equipment, animals, trains, trucks, and automobiles. The main reason for this switch of materials was price, and Marx became hugely successful by offering comparatively inexpensive playthings. This is in stark contrast to up-market toy manufacturers like Doepke, who went out of business.

Above: This Marx fire engine is simply molded in red, yellow, ad white plastic. It has a working light.

The yellow plastic ladder can be both raised and extended.

STURDITOY FIRE TRUCK

This rare model is the Water Pumper No. 9, from Sturdy, which measures 34 inches in length. It has several interesting decals, including "American La France" on the sides. Sturdy used the brand name Sturditoy, which is molded onto the rubber tires.

The Sturdy Corporation was founded in 1929. Their sales office was located in Providence, Rhode Island, and the manufacturing plant was at Pawtucket, Rhode Island. Two partners established the company, Victor C. Wetzel and Charles I. Bigney. The company made fifteen different models, which included an American Railways Express truck, an ambulance, and several dump trucks. They aimed to made models that were exactly the right size for children to play with. Their most direct competitors were Buddy L and Keystone, but although Sturdy made similarly stylish toys, their models tended to be generic, rather than replicas of specific full-sized models. Sturditoys were also made of lighter gauge steel, which meant that fewer examples have survived intact and undamaged. This has made good surviving examples particularly valuable, and this fire truck is worth several thousand dollars. The company folded in 1933, so our fire truck comes from this narrow period of production.

Pumper No. 9 has a second, rear steering platform.

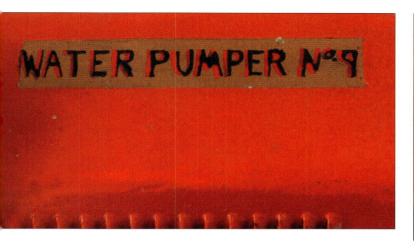

Above: This fire truck is one of only fifteen models manufactured by Sturdy during its short history.

Above: It looks this pressed steel truck may have been fitted with new fire hoses.

KEYSTONE FIRE TRUCK

This early Keystone fire truck comes from a long tradition of toy fire trucks that have been offered to America's children. The earliest toy fire trucks were based on horse drawn fire vehicles, before the motorized trucks of the twentieth century were introduced. Images of horse drawn fire trucks also appeared on building blocks, board games, and jigsaw puzzles. There was then a transitional phase when both horse drawn and motorized fire trucks were used in the real world, sometimes fighting the same fire. Toy manufacturers were quick to make representations of the new motorized vehicles, and the early "steam pumpers." Initially, many of these early models were made in cast iron. Manufacturers including Hubley, A. L

Williams, Kenton, and Keystone produced various fire truck toys in the 1920s and 1930s, most of which had moving parts and were supplied with freestanding firefighter figures—except those of A. L. Williams, which had no moving parts. Keystone's first model truck, a Packard, was launched in 1925.

The Keystone fire truck seen here has several play features and an interesting "Chicago Fire Department" logo on the ladder, which both raises and extends. The wheels, axles, and steering wheel all turn. The truck's red paintwork is in excellent condition and the radiator grille is painted in gold. An early Keystone fire truck of this type is now a highly sought after collectible, and it is worth several thousand dollars.

This fire truck was one of
Keystone's early vehicles.

Left: *The red paintwork on this early Keystone model has survived the years very well.*

Like most other toy fire trucks of this era, this Keystone model is equipped with several working features, including the ladder.

Below: *The wheel would have worked the ladder on the full-size original.*

The wheels still turn freely.

BUDDY L FIRE TRUCK

This Buddy L extension ladder fire truck is a pull toy, with the company logo featured on the cab door, and dates from around the 1930s. Since its foundation in 1910, Buddy L has produced many toy fire trucks, and continues to celebrate the fire services today. Early, cast iron, examples included the No. 205 Fire Pumper Truck, released in 1925, and an early hook and ladder fire truck. Some early models had working hydraulic cylinders, and there was also a ride-on version that measured 25 inches in length, and had a handle mounted on the cab, which was 14½ inches high. Endorsed fire trucks were also included in the Buddy L product line-up, for instance the "Backdraft" No. 7 fire truck celebrated the famous movie. This pressed steel model was particularly detailed, and was equipped with an emergency light, hose reels, front headlights, a plastic ladder (with skull saver on the end), a detailed dashboard, steering wheel, helmet rack, a working bell (with crank handle), and fire extinguishers. The Texaco "Fire Chief" fire engine was another milestone model. Buddy L currently offer a Pedal Fire Truck constructed from stamped steel, with two removable ladders, a working bell, and hose reel. It measures 42 inches long, 15 inches wide, and 21 inches high.

This truck has turning wheels and rubber tires.

This is a pull-along toy with a bright steel pull handle.

Above: The Buddy L "Extension Ladder Fire Truck" decals have survived intact.

Left: The Buddy L extension ladder fire truck was an early example of Buddy L's continuing fascination with the fire services. This perennially favorite theme has always been popular with children.

MACK-STYLE TURNER
FIRE TRUCK

This Mack-style Turner fire truck dates from the 1920s. It is equipped with two ladders and originally had working headlights although the bulbs have been lost. Turner made a range of high quality toys, constructed from heavy gauge automotive steel, finished in fine enamels in bright colors, and fitted with rubber tires as standard. Many Turner vehicles were also equipped with the famous Turner gear motor.

America's very first trucks were neglected vehicles, constructed from any surplus or obsolete car parts, but John ("Jack") Mack was destined to change all that. He ran away from his home hear Scranton, Ohio, in 1878, to work as a teamster. In 1893, Jack and his brother, Augustus, bought a small carriage and wagon building firm in Brooklyn. They launched their first hand-crafted Mack motor vehicle in 1900—and by 1911 Mack was America's premier manufacturer of quality heavy duty trucks.

Left: The truck is constructed from heavy gauge auto steel.

Two of the three ladders have survived.

Above: *Turner's fire truck follows the styling cues of early Mack trucks.*

TONKA FIRE TRUCK NO. 5

Tonka made this Fire Truck No. 5 in the late 1950s and it is complete with Tonka logos on the gauges, sides, and tires. It came equipped with working hoses and had fire extinguishers on the running boards, as well as a red light mounted on top of the cab. It has the 1956 front bumper and grille; although, like the 1955 front bumper, the 1956 version was still constructed from plated steel, it was held in place with a single, clear, smooth, headlight on each side. Like most Tonka trucks of this vintage (the first had appeared in 1955), this truck is manufactured in 1:18 scale. In the early and mid 1960s, Tonka began to add models in various other scales—their new series included the Tiny-Tonkas, Mini-Tonkas, and the Mighty Tonka series. The company also originated a distinctive series of logos, which were applicable to all model series.

Left: The fire truck hose is still in place. It came complete with this hand-operated winding mechanism.

The Number 5 logo is very well preserved.

Right: This Tonka truck comes from the late 1950s, and is fitted with the 1957 front bumper and grille assembly.

There are fire extinguishers mounted here on the running boards.

This truck is from Tonka's classic "Regular" series.

TURNER FIRE TRUCK

This Turner fire truck was made in the 1940s, the final decade of Turner production. It is equipped with a working bell, and fitted with wooden wheels. Originally, this Made in America toy was equipped to carry three ladders, but only one has survived. The styling recalls the streamlining popularized by Raymond Loewy.

Turner was well known for its high quality, robust toys. John C. Turner founded the company in Wapakoneta, Ohio in 1915, and used high quality, heavy-gauge automotive steel for toy construction. The models were finished in luxury enamel paints in various attractive colors and were often fitted with rubber tires. Many Turner vehicles were also equipped with the famous Turner gear motor. One of their earliest fire trucks was based on the Packard truck. Despite their high quality, Turner toys were retailed at modest prices during the Depression, ranging from 60 cents to $4.00. One of the company's most famous lines was their "Victory is Won" fly-wheel driven models, which were sold to the public by direct mail. Capable marketing enabled the company to survive these economically challenging times and they also managed to endure the shortages of raw materials during World War II. Despite this, the company folded in1948, and ceased trading.

Only one of the truck's three original ladders has survived from the 1940s.

Above: *Turner also equipped the fire truck with a ringing bell.*

BUDDY L FIRE TRUCK

This Buddy L fire truck was made in the 1930s. It has a gold Buddy L logo on the radiator grille, and golden ringing bell and is fitted with chrome wheels. It has been restored and now looks fantastic—despite not being in original condition, it is still worth several thousand dollars.

Fred A. Lundahl founded Buddy L in 1910. Lundahl's original company, Moline Pressed Steel, manufactured automobile fenders and other stamped auto parts and Fred made an all-steel miniature truck for his son, Arthur (known in the neighborhood as Buddy L),

which was based on an International Harvester model. It proved so popular with Buddy's friends that Lundahl decided to go into toy production and took his prototype to the 1922 New York Toy Fair. Surprisingly, his truck received a mixed reception—toy buyers thought it was too expensive. Despite this, the public soon recognized the play value of these large, high quality toy trucks. The toy business prospered, and Moline moved out of car parts. By 1925, Buddy L's toy line had expanded to twenty items, including their original fire truck.

Left: *This Buddy L fire truck dates from the 1930s, and has been restored to its original condition. It is now immaculate.*

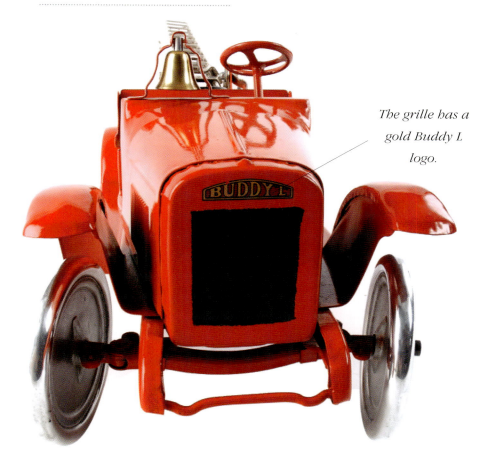

The grille has a gold Buddy L logo.

Above: The fire truck's bright gold bell still rings.

Despite the extensive work, the truck is still worth several thousand dollars.

Above: The gleaming red paintwork is set off neatly with bright chrome wheels.

NO. 56 KEYSTONE WATER PUMP TOWER

This is the No. 56 Keystone Water Pump Tower, a steam-pumper ladder truck manufactured by Keystone in the late 1920s or early 1930s. The model is made of pressed steel, and has brass railings along the side, with aluminum running boards on both sides. It is equipped with sold rubber tires, and a ringing bell made from brass. Although the paint finish is worn, the truck has most of its working parts. Originally, there was a gold, red, and black decal on each side of the water tank, which read "Keystone Water Pump with Real Pump," but these have worn away. The tank itself measures 4¼ inches in diameter, and 7 inches in length. It holds plenty of water and the hood lifts to reveal the "Real Pressure Pump," identified by its red, gold, and

This wheel still raises the ladder tower, to a height of 41 inches. The truck is 29 inches long.

Left: The truck has lost its "Siren" cricket noisemaker, which was originally fixed to the front of the cab. This was worked by a turning crank.

black decal, and operated by turning the front crank. The truck's ladders are missing, but the ladder tower still rises when the wheel at the back of the truck is turned. The nozzle levers were originally marked "Up and Down," and "Left and Right." The original hoses have also been lost—they often fell victim to dry rot. The truck has also lost its "Siren" cricket noisemaker, which was fixed to the front of the cab.

The No. 56's ringing bell is made from brass.

EARLY FIRE TRUCK

This fire truck comes from the 1920s, and may be a product of the American National Company of Toledo, Ohio. Three brothers, Walter, Harry, and William Diemer founded American National in the early years of the twentieth century. Trading under the brand name Giant, American's company slogan was "Raise the Kids on Wheels." This is particularly appropriate, since the company's 1935 catalog advertises a product line dominated by toys on wheels, described as "American Juvenile Vehicles." These include pedal cars, wagons, doll buggies, scooters, wheel chairs, sleds, tricycles, and bicycles. One of the company's most famous products was the Seagrave fire truck pedal car. This unusually styled fire truck is made in pressed steel and has a worn paint finish. It wheels are attached to fixed axles.

Left: This driver looks like he is original to the toy.

The truck's original ladder has survived.

Right: American National also produced sidewalk toys, including pressed steel trucks.

The American National company competed with Buddy L and Keystone during its brief existence.

The fire truck is made from pressed steel.

This toy has a fairly worn paint finish.

419

KEYSTONE FIRE TRUCK

This Keystone fire truck was manufactured in the 1920s or 1930s and is equipped with working electric lights (both headlight and emergency), and a ringing gold-colored bell. The maker's logo, "Keystone" is embossed into the tires. The truck was originally equipped to hold three ladders, but only two have survived the rigors of play.

The Keystone Manufacturing Company issued several different kinds of model fire truck over its long history of over four decades, which included a ride on fire truck, a working water pump tower, and a pair of plastic fire engines designed to fit the Keystone fire station. Early Keystone pressed metal toys like this fire truck had 22 gauge cold rolled steel bodies.

This truck was made with a cold rolled, 22 gauge, steel body.

Right: Keystone built its success on offering interesting extras, such as working lights.

This fire truck also has a working emergency light.

KEYSTONE FIRE TRUCK

The ride-on fire truck featured on these pages was made by Keystone. The company made several ride on toys, including trucks and fire engines, and this is the "Combination 49 Fire Department" model. It is equipped with a siren, electric lights, a bell mounted on the front radiator, as well as a roll up hose rack. The truck's two handles are mounted on the front of the cab—they turn the reinforced front axle. Even though the paintwork is not in great condition, it is now a highly collectible toy, worth several thousand dollars.

Above: The "Combination 49 Fire Department" is a sturdy ride-on toy from the company's early decades.

Below right: *This ride-on fire truck is equipped with a siren, roll up hose, a bell, and electric lights.*

The steel steering rack turns the truck's front axle.

The ladder tower can be raised.

The decals are worn, but are still readable.

The truck's wheels have rubber tires.

KEYSTONE PACKARD MODEL

This Packard model pumper was made by Keystone around 1928 and was retailed through the Butler Brothers Stores. Keystone's first model vehicles were pressed steel trucks modeled on full-size Packards. The models included the company's popular radiator device and logo. The truck made its debut in 1925. This fire truck shares several design features with other Keystone fire engines, including a ringing bell and lifting ladder tower. It is marked with a Butler Brothers' logo—Butlers made a huge impact on the American retail trade, when they opened their "cheap counter"

business in Boston, Massachusetts, in the 1870s, selling a variety of merchandise in a single outlet. This concept spawned a whole generation of department stores, including Macy's in New York, Wanamaker in Philadelphia, and Lehman in Chicago. By the 1880s, American department stores were retailing goods worth over $60 million per annum and this retail boom had a very positive effect on the U.S. economy, boosting employment and manufacturing. Butler Brothers ordered special products for their stores in New York and Chicago. They were bought out in 1974.

Left: The Butler Brothers logo appears in the cab of the Keystone Packard fire truck.

The ladder
tower rises
when a wheel
is turned.

Below: Turning this wheel on the rear
raises the ladder tower.

The model is based on a
full-sized Packard.

KINGSBURY FIRE TRUCK

This Kingsbury three-ladder fire truck has a red body and yellow ladders and is a wind-up toy dating from the 1920s. The Kingsbury Manufacturing Company operated in Keene, New Hampshire, between 1919 and 1942. In 1895, Harry Thayer Kingsbury had purchased the Wilkins Toy Company, with the financial backing of his grandfather. In 1910, Kingsbury diversified into the car business and during World War I he turned over production to the war effort, but the company returned to toy fabrication when hostilities ceased. Kingsbury also became the company trademark at this time. Kingsbury specialized in copying famous models of aircraft, trucks, and buses. Automobile-themed toys took off for the company in 1919 and Harry Kingsbury's sons joined the business in 1920—ultimately, they were responsible for selling the toy division to Keystone. Keystone went on to base much of its production on Kingsbury tooling.

Below: This Kingsbury fire truck dates from the 1920s. It has kept a good level of paint finish.

Below: Despite its age, this truck has retained all three of its ladders.

The truck is equipped with rubber tires.

Above: *Kingsbury was founded by Harry Thayer Kingsbury, and was located in Keen, New Hampshire, between 1919 and 1942.*

The three yellow painted ladders are detachable.

KINGSBURY FIREMAN'S LADDER TRUCK

This pressed steel wind up Kingsbury fireman's ladder truck is 23½ inches long. The wind up mechanism is on the bottom of the fire truck between the rear wheels and the ladder is hinged in two pieces. The truck is from the late 1920s, or early 1930s and is red painted with a silver radiator grille. Harry Thayer Kingsbury was awarded a patent from the United States Patent and Trademark Office for

"new and useful improvements in wheeled toy vehicles, and more particularly to a wheeled toy vehicle having a moveable object, such as a ladder, which can be moved or raised." He had started out in a modest bike shop located in Keene, New Hampshire, but his inventive spirit took him to the boardroom of one of the state's largest and most successful manufacturing companies. From the beginning, his toys were committed to detail and realism. In 1902, for example, he patented a clock-spring motor to propel toy cars. It was so efficient that it was used for the lifetime of the company.

This truck's ladder was the subject of a United States Patent. It is hinged in two pieces, and painted in yellow.

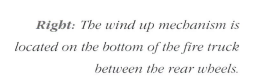

Right: The wind up mechanism is located on the bottom of the fire truck between the rear wheels.

Below: *From the beginning, Harry Thayer Kingsbury was committed to making his toys detailed and realistic.*

Right: *The tin plate ladder is hinged in the middle.*

The truck is equipped with rubber tires.

429

KEYSTONE FIRE TRUCK

This Keystone fire truck dates from around 1928 and has the Keystone logo on the balloon tires. The model originally retailed for $4.79, which was quite expensive at the time—it is now a valuable and highly collectible toy, worth several thousand dollars. Keystone issued many versions of the fire truck in its history of over four decades. These included a ride-on fire truck, and a working water pump tower, while a pair of plastic fire engines were added later. Early Keystone models like this were made from 22 gauge cold rolled steel, which made them extremely durable. At this time, the company's greatest competitors were Hubley, A. L. Williams, and Kenton—all of whom also manufactured fire trucks.

This truck was originally priced at $4.79.

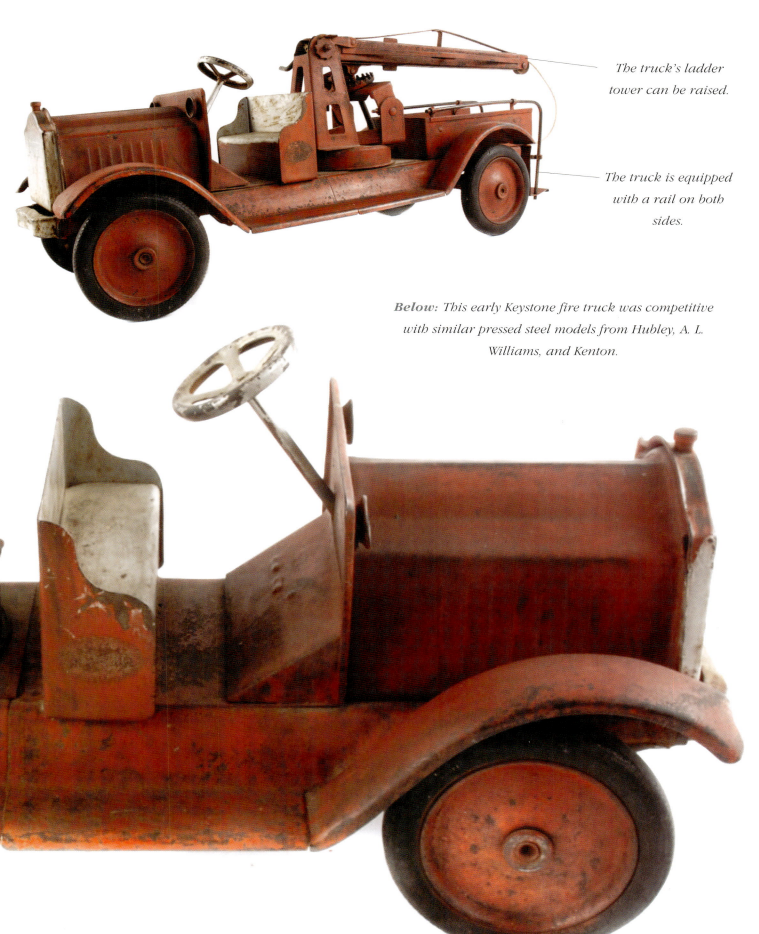

The truck's ladder tower can be raised.

The truck is equipped with a rail on both sides.

Below: *This early Keystone fire truck was competitive with similar pressed steel models from Hubley, A. L. Williams, and Kenton.*

KINGSBURY FIRE TRUCK

This Kingsbury fire truck dates from the 1920s. CFD No. 1 is an articulated, six-wheeler; its radiator grille and integral headlights are printed on a separate piece of rolled steel and the tires are embossed with "Kingsbury." It is now a sought after collectible.

In many ways, the history of Kingsbury reflects that of American industry itself in the early years of the modern Industrial Age. Harry Thayer Kingsbury was the driving force behind the company: adaptable and creative, he steered Kingsbury through the great challenges of the twentieth century, including two World Wars and the Great Depression. Harry became a toy manufacturer when he bought James Wilkins's company, with the financial backing of his grandfather, Edward Joslin. By 1900 he had expanded the company's toy line to include cast-iron carriages, farm machinery, and the first toy horseless carriage. But Kingsbury's skill was not limited to design—he was

also an expert in the process of manufacturing toys, particularly those with moving parts. The Kingsbury product line continued to increase as he added boats, cars, airplanes, trucks, submarines, and even blimps, reflecting America's fascination with motorized vehicles. Harry's eldest son Edward Kingsbury joined the company in 1916, having received a degree in Mechanical Engineering from the Maryland Institute of Technology. He made a substantial contribution to the company with his friction drive drilling machine, perfected in 1918. In the same year, the company became the Kingsbury Manufacturing Company.

The six-wheeled fire truck is articulated with a substantial rivet.

Above: The details on Kingsbury's toys reflected America's fascination with mobilized vehicles.

Right: The CFD No. 1's radiator grille and integral headlights are printed on a separate piece of rolled steel.

TEXACO FIRE CHIEF

Texaco commissioned two, almost exactly similar Texaco Fire Chief models from Wen Mac and Buddy L, which were sold through Texaco dealers in the 1950s. At the time, the company was keen to build up its profile, under the slogan, "Trust your car to the man who wears the star." Wen Mac, a subsidiary of The American Machine Foundry Company, based in Los Angeles, California, produced toys under the Imagination Products logo. Their version of the Texaco Fire Chief was model number 517. The fire truck itself is 25 inches long, and it came complete with a whole range of working equipment, like hoses, extension ladders, a red plastic light mounted on the cab, and a siren. On the Wen Mac model the siren was mounted on the left front running board but the Buddy L siren was positioned behind the bell. The toy was also supplied with an adaptor for the garden hose, so that real water could be shot through the truck's "deluge gun." The toy's box made it clear that this feature was "not designed for indoor use." The models were marketed in printed cardboard boxes, which specified that they were to be sold through Texaco dealers. They also proclaimed the Fire Chief to be an "Actual scale model. Made of heavy steel." The truck's paintwork,

Left: The truck's decals are in good condition. Replacements can be bought from Toydecals.

Above: This model has 12 ply tires imprinted with the Texaco logo.

Texaco decals, and clear plastic windshield are in good condition. Wen Max also constructed several other Texaco promotional toys, including models of a gas tanker truck, and the Texaco USS *North Dakota*. This model ship was battery powered.

Below: *The original decals used on the model were*
traditional "water decals."

S.F.D. PUMPER

This Structo Fire Department truck is complete with hoses and a fireplug and dates from the 1940s. The Structo Toys logo appears on both the tires, and the truck's front bumper. Over the years, Structo produced many different fire trucks for the Structo Fire Department, and all of their products tended to be large scale. This particular truck was sold as part of a set, which, according to the box, was the "No. 570 Fire Department 6 piece assortment. 2 coats individually baked metallic enamel. Structo maker of quality-price

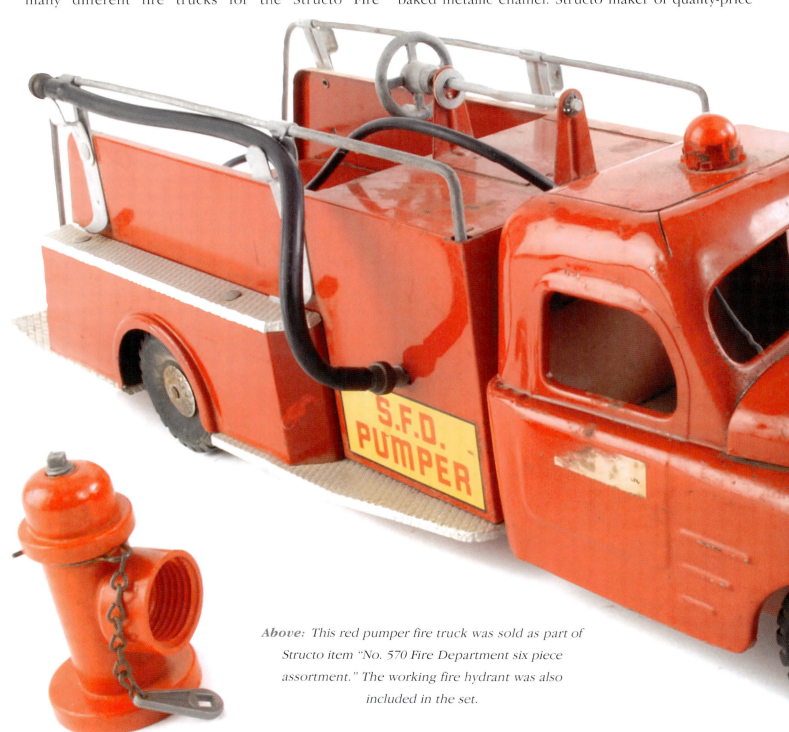

Above: This red pumper fire truck was sold as part of Structo item "No. 570 Fire Department six piece assortment." The working fire hydrant was also included in the set.

Above: The S.F.D. logo appeared on the hook and ladder and pumper fire trucks.

toys for more than 45 years." The set had three individual vehicles, including two fire trucks. The larger truck was a red painted hook and ladder fire truck with a raising ladder supplied with extension pieces. The smaller fire truck (the model shown here) was a red pumper fire truck, equipped with battery-operated lights, which could squirt real water through a specially-adapted hose that connected to the fire hydrant supplied as part of the set. The fire truck also had its own hose. This vehicle came with two ladders (now missing). Both fire trucks were decaled with the S.F.D. (Structo Fire Department) logo. The set also included a white emergency patrol truck, which had a decal on the side reading "Structo Fire Department Emergency Patrol." The back of the truck had double opening doors. The set also had a fire department road sign reading "Fire Station," and a red fire hydrant that squirted water from the pumper. As the box details, the set was a "Safe. Creative. Live Action" toy. The Structo Manufacturing Company was founded in 1908, in Freeport, Illinois.

PLASTIC TONKA FIRE TRUCK

According to the evidence of this fire truck's Tonka decal, it dates from between 1976 and 1977—these were the only two years when the company used the simple red oval logo with the white Tonka brand name. This was also the era when plastic trucks were taking over from the company's original robust metal products. The truck's tires were designed in 1974, when the entire three-

piece wheel cover-tire-sidewall assembly unit was replaced with a two-piece unit. This consisted of an ultra wide injection molded plastic tire, mounted on "mag" style wheels. This truck is also typical of this era of production in the heavy use of moldings and paint detail to suggest elements such as the radiator grille and

headlights—previously, these had been separate metal and plastic parts that were fixed to the basic chassis. The interior of this truck, including seats, is a single white plastic molding.

Left: The truck's red and white plastic ladder both rises and extends.

A Tonka logo is molded beneath the grille.

The ladder extends via a turning wheel.

The truck has a clear red and opaque white plastic light on top of the cab.

The clear plastic windshield is still present on this model and in reasonable condition.

Tonka

MODEL TOYS/DOEPKE FIRE TRUCK

Doepke made this Model Toys fire truck, around 1947. The Charles M. Doepke Manufacturing Company was based in Rossmoyne, Ohio, founded by two brothers, Charles and Fritz,who launched their first toy products in 1946. The Model Toys/Rossmoyne decal on the side of the truck reads "Authorized by American La France with Crest." The tires have the rating "Firestone 1100 X 26" embossed on them. The truck is approximately 34 inches long, and is constructed from heavy gauge pressed steel—Doepke prided themselves on the longevity of their toys. The front wheels steer and the truck originally had two ladders: the rising and extending ladder fixed to the turntable, and a second, removable ladder, laid on the back, which is missing here. The paint and decals are in good condition.

As well as the extendable ladder, the fire truck has retained its ringing bell.

TONKA FIRE DEPARTMENT TRUCK

This Tonka Fire Department truck has "Tonka" embossed on the grille and rubber tires. It is equipped with a chrome grille, two metal ladders, and a wind-up extension ladder for taller buildings. Judging by the distinctive red, white, and gold oval Tonka decal, the truck is from the 1970 to 1973 production period. This colored oval was used from 1962, but until 1969, "Mound, Minn." appeared on the gold half, and after 1970, this was changed to "U.S.A." The tires are also consistent with this vintage—iIn 1972, the narrow whitewall was replaced with what Tonka called their "billboard black sidewall;" In other words, the tire was a raised white letter sidewall on the same flotation tire already in use. These were changed again in 1974 when a two-piece assembly replaced the entire three-piece wheel cover-tire-sidewall assembly. The tire itself was changed to an ultra wide injection molded plastic tire mounted to "mag" style wheel. Mound Metalcraft was created in Mound, Minnesota in September, 1946. There were three partners in the enterprise, Lynn E. Baker, Avery F. Crounse, and Alvin F. Tesch. Founded to make garden implements, the company's first product was a metal tie rack. Erling Eklof coined the Tonka product name and logo and Mound Metalcraft changed its name to Tonka Toys Inc. in November 1955. In 1991, Hasbro of Pawtucket, Rhode Island bought the company. Although robust metal trucks were Tonka's signature toys, they also produced dolls, action figures, and computer games.

The T. F. D. logo is completely preserved.

Above: *This fire truck is from the 1970 to 1973 Tonka production period.*

*The extension ladder is
shown here unfolded.*

Below: *The truck's extension ladder was
for fighting fires in taller buildings!*

*The fire truck has an unconventional,
open cab, and clear headlight lenses.*

NYLINT AERIAL HOOK-N-LADDER

Nylint manufactured this Aerial Hook-N-Ladder fire truck in the 1960s. The main part of the truck is made from pressed metal, but the windshield, windows, and siren light bar on the cab are all made of plastic. This fire engine is 30 inches long, 6 inches wide, and 7 inches tall. The aerial ladder rises into the air when a wheel is turned.

The Nylint Tool and Manufacturing Company originally produced tools. They then decided to use their extensive knowledge of manufacturing processes and precision die-making to made toys, and they concentrated on making high quality toys at competitive prices. Nylint made their first toy in 1945, an automatic spring-wind car. It was introduced at the 1946 Toy Fair in New York City and over the time of the Fair, Nylint sold over 100,00 units.

Right: This turning wheel behind the cab raises the extension ladder.

Left: The fire truck has a distinctive silver Nylint logo on the front.

The white-painted extension ladder rises when a wheel is turned.

AERIAL HOOK-N-LADDER

Above: Originally, the truck had two pressed metal ladders, but these have been lost over time.

TONKA FIRE TRUCK

This 1970s Tonka fire truck has visible gauges on the side of the truck, for the operation of the vehicle. This fire truck comes from the later era of Tonka production, when plastic was more popular. It has a white extension ladder fixed to a turntable, which also has a fire-fighting platform—the ladder was raised by turning the metal wheel positioned behind the fire truck cab. The truck has an embossed grille, painted and embossed headlights.

Three partners formed Mound Metalcraft in September 1946; Lynn E. Baker, Avery F. Crounse, and Alvin F. Tesch. They planned to make garden tools, but the first product was actually a metal tie rack. Later Metalcraft decided to diversify into toys, and this soon became their primary business. Alvin Tesch designed the products, and Erling Eklof created the distinctive Tonka brand name and logo. The company changed its name from Mound Metalcraft to Tonka Toys Incorporated in November 1955. The Tonka truck soon became an iconic product, and the company released a large dump-truck toy to celebrate their sixtieth anniversary. Hasbro of Pawtucket, Rhode Island purchased Tonka in 1991. Although Tonka is closely associated with robust metal trucks (which have been inducted in the National Toy Hall of Fame), they have made a variety of different playthings over the years, including dolls and other girls' toys. They have also produced computer games, including Tonka Raceway.

This Tonka fire truck comes from the later era of Tonka production.

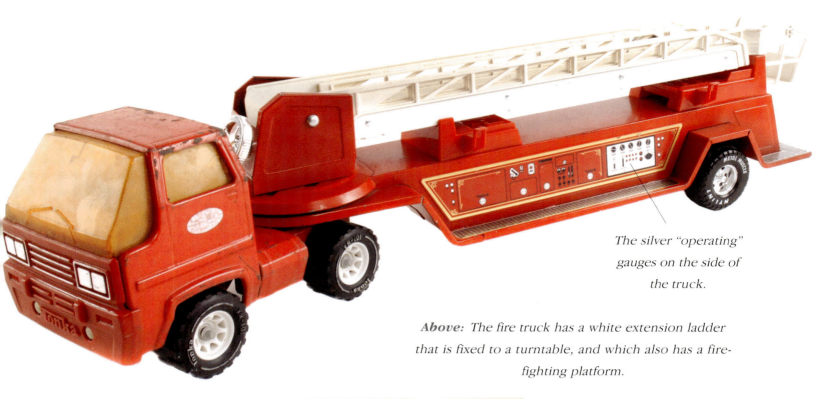

The silver "operating" gauges on the side of the truck.

Above: The fire truck has a white extension ladder that is fixed to a turntable, and which also has a fire-fighting platform.

Above: Tonka's earlier metal trucks have become synonymous with the company name. They have been inducted into the National Toy Hall of Fame.

This tire seems to have been cannibalized from a Nylint truck.

VARIOUS FIRE ENGINES

This composite photograph shows various fire engines from several different manufacturers; Buddy L, Corgi, Tootsie Toys, Tonka, and Dinky. Fire fighting toys have always been hugely popular with generations of children, attracted to the sheer heroism of real life firemen. These toys have also reflected the development of fire fighting strategies and equipment.

Early fire-fighting equipment was basic, and included hand-pulled pumpers, ladders, sledgehammers, and buckets. American cities began to establish paid fire departments in the mid-nineteenth century; Cincinnati in 1853, New York in 1865, and Philadelphia in 1871. This coincided with the development of more sophisticated fire fighting equipment, such as heavy

Below: *This selection of toy fire trucks demonstrates the perennial popularity of fire fighting toys. Both American and British toy makers manufactured these examples.*

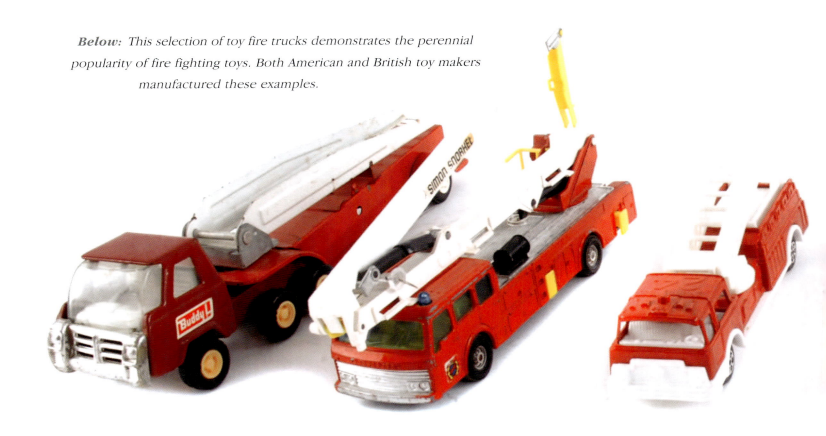

steam pumpers and large water towers, which were hauled to fires by teams of horses. Chicago was the first city to equip itself with horse-drawn equipment in the1870s. Toy companies produced miniature cast-iron versions of these new vehicles, including the Hubley Manufacturing Company in Lancaster, Pennsylvania, the Kenton Hardware Company in Kenton, Ohio, the Wilkins Toy Company in Keene, New Hampshire, and Francis W. Carpenter and Company in Harrison, New York. In their 1906 catalog, Hubley offered a whole range of fire fighting equipment, including a hook and ladder, a steam pumper, and a hose reel. In the twentieth century, motorized fire trucks came into use, and toy manufacturers, such as Keystone, Hubley, A. L. William, Ditzel, were quick to replicate these. Kenton also made free standing fire fighting figures.

An overview of a range of fire-fighting toys.

MATCHBOX FIRE ENGINE

This contemporary fire engine comes from Matchbox's "Best of British" series. There are twelve vehicles in the series, including the Land Rover Defender 90, the BMW Mini Cooper S, a 1961 Jaguar E-Type, and the classic London double decker bus. Matchbox is a die cast toy brand, currently owned by Mattel Inc. Their toys were originally packed in boxes that were similar in size and shape to a classic matchbox, and the toys themselves were around 2½ inches in length. Matchbox started in 1953 as a brand name of the now-defunct British toy company

called Lesney Products. The company's first toy was a 1948 model of a road roller, and heir 1953 model of Queen Elizabeth II's Coronation Coach sold over a million examples.

Matchbox was a brand name of Lesney Products, but is now owned by Mattel Inc.

FASTLANE FIRE ENGINE

Fastlane made the contemporary fire engine model shown below, which measures 6½ inches in length, and is 2 inches wide and 2 inches in height. The fire engine is a Man truck replica, and is constructed in metal alloy and plastic. It comes from a set of two fire trucks; the other is a fire rescue vehicle.

Fastlane is the brand name for toys made on behalf of Toys R Us, an extensive chain of toy stores, which has 587 outlets in the United States and a further 600 stores around the world. The company's flagship store is in New York's Times Square—it is the largest toy store in America, and features a working Ferris wheel. The post-war baby boom was the inspiration behind this huge enterprise. Charles Lazarus initially founded a baby furniture store in Washington DC, known as Children's Supermart, and later Children's Bargain Town U.S.A. Parents soon started to ask for toys in the stores, and so in 1948 the concept for the Toys R Us chain was born. The company is now the world's biggest toy retailer, with annual revenue of $11.1 billion, and has headquarters are located in Wayne in New Jersey.

CAST IRON PUMP AND FIRE BUGGY

Fire buggies like this model were used by America's first paid fire departments.

Kenton, Arcade, or A. C. Williams made the cast iron pump shown here, between 1911 and 1917. Heavy steam pumpers like this were first introduced in the middle of the nineteenth century—whereas earlier models were hand-pulled, these later versions were hauled to fires by teams of horses. Chicago was the first city to use horse-drawn pumpers in the 1870s. Miniature cast-iron versions of these toys were mass-produced by many toy companies, including Kenton,

The cast iron buggy has twelve spoke wheels.

The horse and rider were cast in two pieces.

Left: *Chicago was the first American city to use horse-drawn pumpers in the 1870s, like this cast iron toy version. Many companies manufactured cast iron miniature versions of these pumpers.*

This cast iron pumper is a finely modeled toy.

Above: *Pumpers like this one were among the first toys offered by several American toy manufacturers.*

Hubley, Wilkins, Dent Hardware, and Francis W. Carpenter. Images of such vehicles were also shown on puzzles and board games—and models made in wood.

The horse-drawn fire truck is also from this era. Toys like these were a speciality of A. C. Williams of Chagrin Falls, Ohio. Adam Clark Williams founded the company in 1886 and toy production started in 1893 after a fire forced them to move from Ravenna, Ohio. Williams was known for cast iron cars, trucks, and horse-drawn buggies, but also made tin vehicles, which are now very scarce. Their toy production ceased in 1938. Kenton Hardware was also known for cast iron horse drawn vehicles. F. M. Perkins founded the company in 1890 in Kenton, Ohio, and the first toys were produced in 1894, including banks and stoves. The company ceased production in 1952. The Dent Hardware Company was active between 1895 and 1937, founded by Henry H. Dent and based in Fullerton, Pennsylvania.

DENT HOOK AND LADDER

The Dent Hardware Company made this cast iron hook and ladder. A pair of horses draws the buggy, which also has two figures, a fireman driver, and another fireman at the back. It has four twelve spoke wheels, and is equipped with two ladders. Dent Hardware was based in Fullerton, Pennsylvania and was active between 1895 and 1937, but finally ceased production in 1952. A Dent catalog from the very early 1900s gives an interesting insight into the company's toy range, the "Iron Toys Manufactured by the

Dent Hardware Co., Fullerton, Pa." The catalog details many versions of their famous cast iron banks, including lion and elephant versions. Other toys included a single automobile, chariots, sleighs, trolley cars, coal wagons, steamboats, passenger trains, freight trains, locomotives, and the "Cruiser New York." In all, two hundred different products were illustrated and described. As the company evolved, replicas of "modern" phenomena were added to Dent's product line including the "Lucky Boy" Airplane and the Graf

The fire cart has four twelve-spoke wagon wheels.

Zeppelin airship. A later catalog from the 1920s shows that, as well as offering their signature cast iron banks, Dent was now concentrating on models of automobiles, trucks, planes, and guns. Professional fire departments started to use horse drawn fire fighting vehicles in the 1970s, and these paid fire-fighters gradually replaced volunteer fire companies. Volunteers had been forced to rely upon

The fire cart is drawn by a pair of horses.

The driver has lost his reins.

The cast iron firemen wear highly recognizable uniforms.

hand-operated equipment, including double-forcing pumps with central air chambers, ladders, and sledgehammers. The water was forced out when the handles, or brakes, were pushed up and down. Large pumps needed four men to carry, and two to operate them successfully. Smaller versions of the mammoth pumps were also sold to be used at home. A leather hose was attached to the nozzle extending from the pump barrel, the water could thus be directed straight onto the fire.

KENTON CAST IRON HOOK AND LADDER

This Kenton horse-drawn hook and ladder fire cart was made by Kenton between 1910 and 1915. It is pulled by three horses, and is fitted with four fourteen-spoke cartwheels. The horses are a mixed trio; two are black, and one is white, and they balance on two smaller, eight-spoke cartwheels. The cart has a single driver, but a second fire-fighter sits on a seat at the rear of the truck. The firemen wear recognizable helmets, and bright blue uniforms. The Kenton Hardware Company was particularly well known for its cast iron horse wagons, banks, and toy stoves. Kenton produced its first toys in 1894, but the company finally ceased production in 1952.

Right: The driver seated high up at the front seems to have lost his reins. A second fireman is seated at the rear.

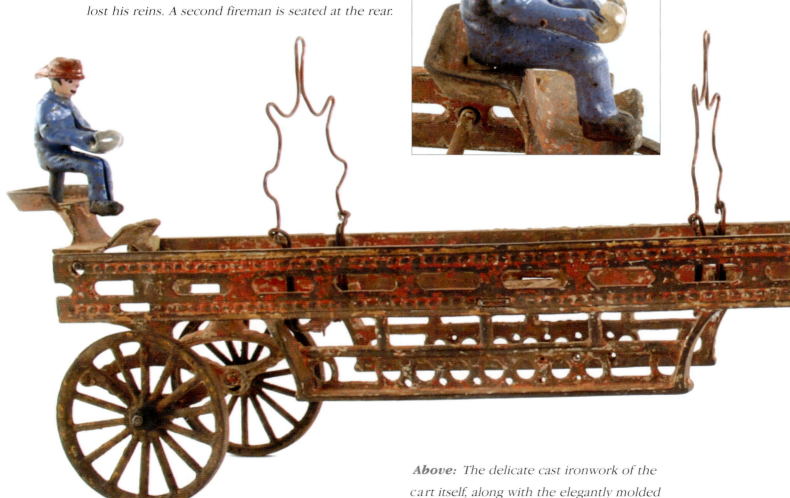

Above: The delicate cast ironwork of the cart itself, along with the elegantly molded horses, make this a very attractive plaything.

This hook and ladder dates from between 1910 and 1915.

ETCH A SKETCH

More than 100 million Etch A Sketch toys have been sold.

The world's favorite drawing toy was conceived by French auto mechanic Arthur Granjean. Its white knobs have been twiddled in over seventy countries, and Etch a Sketch is now available with zooper sounds and color. The Ohio Art Company first saw the Granjean's "L'Ecran Magique" at the 1959 Nuremburg International Toy Fair and decided to adopt it, paying $25,000 for the right to produce the newly renamed Etch A Sketch. The company began to market and advertise at once, and by Christmas 1960 this was one of the hottest toys in the US. Although there have been various versions of the Etch A Sketch over the decades, the internal workings of the "Magic Screen" are virtually unchanged. The back of the screen is coated with a a mixture of aluminum powder and plastic beads, which are scraped by the stylus.

Above: Etch a Sketch is in the National Toy Hall of Fame.

FRISBEE

During the 1870s, the Frisbee Baking Company of Bridgeport, Connecticut, began to use thin metal bases for their pies. These tins became playthings for college kids working at the factory, who enjoyed tossing them through the air. In 1948, a plastic disc based on the pie-plate shape and christened the "Flyin' Saucer" was developed by two Air Force veterans, Fred Morrison and Warren Franscioni. Their previous attempt at the toy was called the "Pluto Platter." Both names were an attempt to cash in on the UFO mania sweeping America in the 1940s and 1950s. They based their enterprise in San Luis Obispo, California. The famous toy company, Wham-O bought the concept in 1957, and re-named the toy as the Frisbee in 1958. At the time, Wham-O was based in San Gabriel, California. Wham-O sold over 100 million Frisbees, but sold the toy to Mattel in 1994 and the Frisbee's hometown is now Emeryville, California. Since Mattel bought the toy, world sales have topped 200 million. There are now at least nine variants of the flying disc on sale.

CHIA PET

Walter Houston first created the "Chia Pet" back in 1975, using small pottery animals made by Mexican villagers to grow the first ever chia fur. Still handmade, the "Chia Pet" is only offered for sale during the holiday season. Chia is the common name for *salvia columbariae*, a variety of sage, and is almost unique in that the seeds become sticky when they are wet, which makes them adhere to the terracotta body of the "Chia Pet." The plant is also fast growing—a "Chia Pet" can have a full head of hair (or fur) in two weeks. This speedy growth makes the "Chia Pet" ideal to teach children about germination. The toy was first marketed in 1982 and the concept is now owned by Joseph Enterprises of San Francisco.

HULA HOOP

The Hula Hoop is an ancient invention—Egyptian children were spinning large hoops of dried grapevine on their hips three thousand years ago. Hoops were also made from wood, metal, and stiff grasses. However, the inventors of the modern, plastic version are Richard Knerr and Arthur Melin, the co-founders of Wham-O Inc. The company was also behind the modern revival of the Frizbee. Back in the 1950s, Knerr and Melin heard from a visiting Australian that children in his country span hoops made from bamboo around their waist. Knerr and Melin immediately thought of how they could develop a

commercial, plastic version of the classic toy. They used a new material, Marlex, and launched the new hoop in a variety of hot colors. It was an instant success, and 25 million were sold in the first four months. The current interest in health and fitness has brought the Hula Hoop back into popularity, since it takes agility and practice to keep it spinning.

Right: First offered for sale in 1958, plastic Hula Hoops were originally priced at $1.98 each.

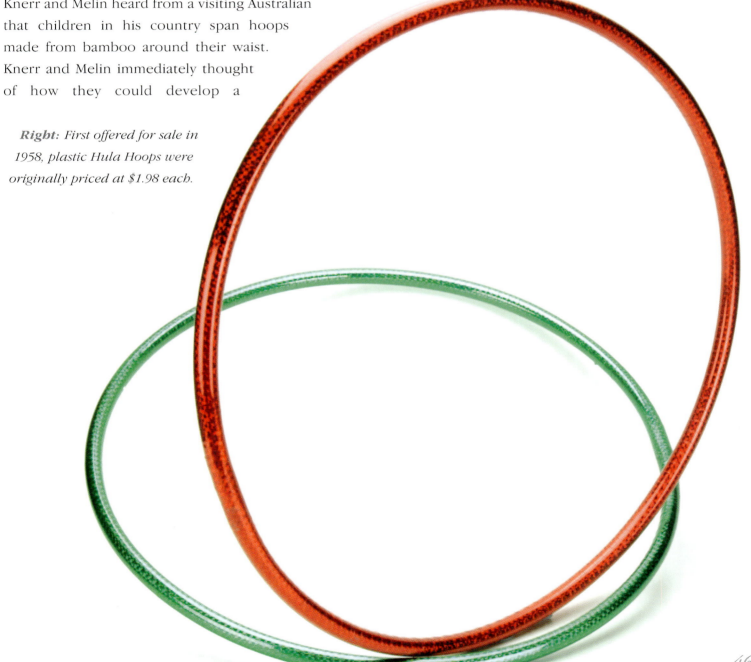

THE LOUISVILLE SLUGGER

The Louisville Slugger is the most famous baseball bat in the world, and the official bat of Major League Baseball. In fact, it is the "Lumber that Still Powers Our National Pastime" (according to Scott Oldham). The origins of the Hillerich & Bradsby stretch back to the mid-nineteenth century, when German immigrant J. Frederick Hillerich set up a woodturning shop in Louisville, Kentucky. The Hillerichs had left their native Baden-Baden in 1842. Their woodturning shop was soon making every kind of domestic woodwork, from balusters to bedposts, and the shop was employing around twenty workers by 1875. Hillerich's son John Andrew (who had been born in America, and was known as "Bud") was an amateur baseball player and an apprentice in the family business. Bud used his

company name was changed to J. F. Hillerich and Son. In 1905, the bat became the first sports product to be endorsed by a professional player, Homus "The Flying Dutchman" Wagner of the Pittsburgh Pirates. The Louisville Slugger is now used by over 60% of major Major League Baseball players and has been used by many of the game's most famous players, past and present, including Babe Ruth, Hank Aaron, Mickey Mantle, Tino Martinez, Roger Maris, Tony Gwynn, and Ken Griffey, Jr. The company now offers around 300 models, and sells 1.4 million wooden bats, and 1 million aluminum bats each year. The smallest bat on offer is Baby's First Louisville Slugger, which retails for around $5. The Hillerich and Bradsby Company award the Silver Bat trophy to the annual batting champions

father's equipment to turn up his own bats, and started making bats for several professional players of the day, including one from white ash for "The Old Gladiator," Pete Browning, in 1884. Browning played for the Eclipse, Louisville's professional team. With this kind of celebrity endorsement, the bat soon grew in popularity and became the signature product of the company. Originally known as the "Falls City Slugger," it was registered as the "Louisville Slugger" in 1894. In 1897, Bud became a partner in the business, and the

of the American and National Baseball Leagues. Hillerich and Bradsby are still in Louisville, Kentucky, as is the Louisville Slugger Museum. The museum is one of the most visited attractions in the State, and can be easily identified by the six-story, 120-feet long carbon steel bat that casually leans against the building.

***Above and below:** For over a century, the Louisville Slugger has been the baseball bat of choice for many of the world's greatest players.*

MONOPOLY

Ironically, the most Capitalist board game ever was a product of the Great Depression. The stock market crash had reduced inventor Charles Darrow to supporting his family with odd jobs. He remembered the enjoyable summers he had spent in Atlantic City and drew a map of the area on his kitchen tablecloth; he then constructed little wooden houses, hotels, and play money. His friends were soon sitting around his kitchen table nightly, selling real estate and spending stacks of play money. Parker Brothers bought the game concept in 1935, and were manufacturing 20,000 copies a week with a month of their agreement. The game originally sold for $4.

Below: Monopoly is now the world's most played board game. It is estimated that over 500 million people have played at least one game.

Hasbro now owns the Monopoly game.

MR. POTATO HEAD

George Lerner invented the original Mr. Potato Head, an all-plastic toy used as a cereal premium. Hasbro bought the concept, and launched their own version of the toy, with a Styrofoam body. A plastic body was added in 1960. Mr. Potato Head played a starring role in Disney's *Toy Story* (1995), and also in the follow-up, *Toy Story 2* (2000).

He also promoted Burger King's "Try the Fry" campaign in 1997. Hasbro celebrated the toy's fiftieth anniversary in 2002 by launching several special limited edition versions, including the "Patriotic Mr. Potato Head," while "Darth Tater" commemorated the 2005 *Star Wars* film, "The Revenge of the Sith."

Mr. Potato Head was the first toy to be advertised on television.

NERF BALL

Parker Brothers are an extraordinary games company, with such classics as Monopoly (1935), Sorry (1934), and Trivial Pursuit to their credit. George S. Parker of Salem, Massachusetts, founded the company, and launched the first Parker Brothers game onto the market in 1883. Since then, Parker has invented and marketed over 1,800 games and puzzles.

The Nerf Ball is probably the most famous toy (rather than board game) from Parker Brothers, self-proclaimed as "The world's first official indoor ball." Reyn Guyer, who also invented the classic party game Twister, also invented the Nerf ball concept. Parker

Brothers launched the toy in 1969, and sold over 4 million Nerf balls in this introductory year. The original Nerf ball was 4 inches across, and made from polyurethane foam, but a larger Super Nerf ball, Nerfoop, and Nerf Football very soon followed. This classic foam technology has now also been applied to the N-strike range of harmless, Nerf-loaded toy guns, "The Ultimate in Ball-Blastin' action" for children and adults, "loads of fun—classic Nerf stuff." It is estimated that to date over 31 million Nerf balls have now been sold around the world.

Below: Launched onto the American market in 1969, it is estimated that over 31 million Nerf Balls have now been sold.

SILLY PUTTY

General Electric Scientist James Wright was trying to develop synthetic rubber when he accidentally invented "bouncing rubber." Ruth Fallgatter (the owner of the New Haven Block toy shop) and marketing consultant Peter Hodgson adopted the product, and offered it at $2. It was an instant hit. Peter Hodgson began to manufacture the product in 1950, reducing the price to $1, launching the familiar egg packaging, and coining the instantly memorable product name, Silly Putty. A special metallic gold Silly Putty was introduced in 2000 to celebrate its golden anniversary.

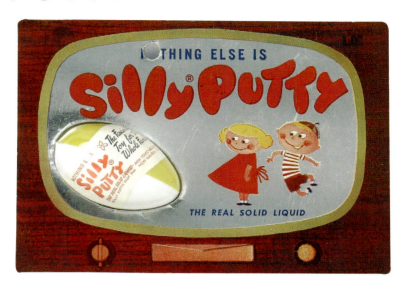

SLINKY

In 1943, mechanical engineer Richard James was aboard a U.S. Navy ship, testing spring-based devices that were intended to keep the vessel's instruments steady at sea. During the experiments, one of the coiled torsion springs he was working with fell from a shelf, and then kept moving across the deck! Back at home in Philadelphia, James demonstrated the phenomenon to his wife, Betty. By 1945, the couple had refined the "walking spring" into a toy that Mrs. James named "Slinky." They were unsure of its commercial potential, and so were surprised and delighted when they sold 400 Slinkys in just ninety minutes at Gimbels in Philadelphia that November. They were priced at $1, and unwound the toy measures 80 feet. Richard and Betty set up their own Philadelphia-based company to manufacture the unusual plaything, but when the James's marriage split up, Betty James took over the business and moved it to Hollidaysburg, Pennsylvania. Various Slinkys have been made there ever since, including a rainbow-colored plastic version. Their 1970s slogan was "It's fun for a girl and boy." It is estimated that over 300 million Slinkys have now been sold. During a sales downturn in 2001, Poof-Slinky Inc. CEO Bob Rollins wittily commented: "We'll bounce back no matter how far you stretch us." Slinky became the Official State Toy of Pennsylvania in 2002.

Slinky Dog appeared as one of the main characters in 1995's Toy Story.

MARX ROCK 'EM SOCK 'EM GAME

The "Rock 'Em Sock 'Em Robot" game was launched by Marx in the 1960s. It is a two-player game, devised by Marvin Glass and Associates. MGA devised many popular games since it was founded in 1941. Mattel acquired Marx in 1997, and now markets an updated version of the game. The two players take control of one or other of the robots (one red, one blue), which stand on a

boxing ring-like platform. The robots are controlled by joysticks and the game is particularly remembered for the phrase "Knock his block off!"

Marx and Co. was owned by Louis Marx, a leading player in the toy industry. He was born in Brooklyn, New York in 1896, the son of a tailor. As a young boy, Ferdinand Strauss hired Louis as an errand boy. He learned to work hard, and Strauss put him in charge of the company's East Rutherford factory in 1917. His dream was to make Strauss a

These plastic levers control the robot's movements.

The robots fling punches at each other.

Above: *The robots stand on a boxing ring-like platform.*

national brand, but Ferdinand was more interested in operating in the New York area. Louis started his own company with his brother, David, and started mass production. They also manufactured toys for other companies, including Girard, and Louis' old employer, Strauss. The 1950s were the company's Golden Era—by 1955, Marx produced over 20% of all American toys, with sales of more than $30 million and a product line of more than 5000 toys.

BOARD GAMES

Board games have been played by most societies, in all eras of history. Snet is the oldest board game known—it was depicted in a fresco found in Ancient Egyptian tombs from between 3000 and 2700 BC. Evidence of a board game from around 5870 BC was found in Jordan, and Go is an strategic board game from Ancient China. Board games became popular in the early 1900s, reflecting increased affluence of the middle classes. They were even more popular after World War II, and many classic board games date from then, including most of the games here. Many board games simulate aspects of real life, like Monopoly (real estate market), Cluedo (murder mystery), and Risk (warfare). Others, like chess and checkers, are more abstract.

Go To The Head of the Class is a question and answer board game. The questions are set at various levels of difficulty—some are appropriate for young players, others require more knowledge. When the student answers correctly, he or she advances to the front of the classroom. The first student to reach the "Head of the Class" and correctly answer the "Final Exam" questions wins the game.

Probe is a game of words introduced by Parker Brothers in the 1960s.

Pit is a fast-paced card game in which 3–7 players trade commodities. The concept is that a player should get rid of undesirable cards, and create a portfolio of desirable cards.

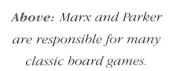

Above: *Marx and Parker are responsible for many classic board games.*

Left: *Mad has become America's longest surviving humor publication. It was originated by Bill Gaines in 1952.*

OUR GANG
TIPPLE-TOPPLE GAME

As a young man, Harman Fisher worked for the Alderman-Fairchild Company of Rochester, New York, who manufactured paper boxes and board games. When a separate company, All Fair Toys, was created to manufacture games, Fisher became vice president of the new company, holding the position for four years. He made an unsuccessful attempt to buy the company in 1930, after which he left to co-found Fisher-Price.

The "Our Gang Tipple-Topple Game" was one of more than a hundred games invented and marketed by All Fair, and dates from 1930. It was based on a famous series of short comedy movies, which featured a gang of kids from a poor neighborhood. The first of 220 *Our Gang* films was released in the silent era of 1922, and MGM launched the final movie in the series, "Dancing Romeo," in 1944.

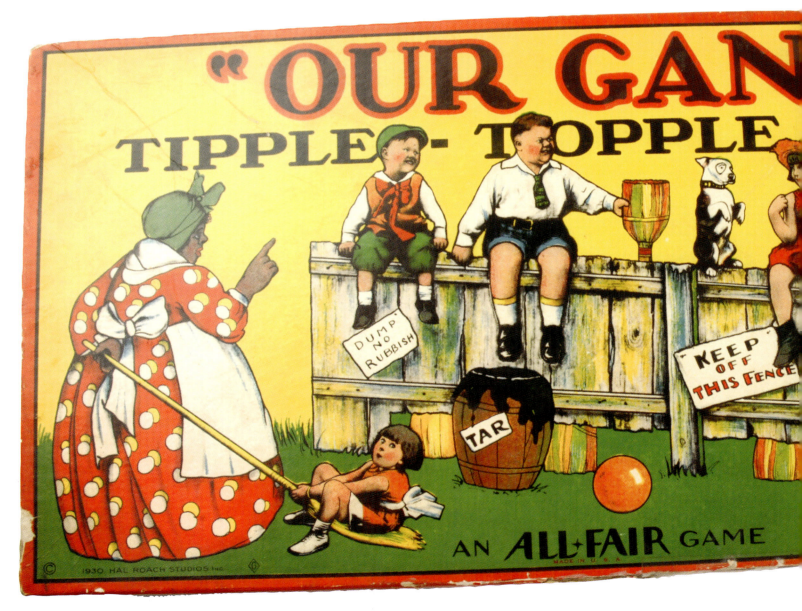

Above: The "Our Gang Tipple-Topple Game" was based on the famous comedy short films featuring neighborhood street urchins.

Left: Pete The Pup featured in the movies between 1927 and 1938. The films launched several famous characters, including George "Spanky" McFarland, Alfalfa, Buckwheat, Darla, and Froggy.

Far left: The game was invented by All Fair Toys, and released in 1930. It was one of many games invented by the New York company.

ERECTOR SET

A. C. Gilbert made this "Erector" set No. 8½, which builds a steam engine or Ferris wheel. The metal parts and electric motor are packed into a red metal box and sets like this were very desirable in the 1950s.

Company founder Alfred Carlton Gilbert entered Yale University in 1904, and supported himself by performing magic shows. By 1909, he and his partner John Petrie were manufacturing magic props. Gilbert bought out Petrie in 1911, and changed the company's product line to engineering and construction toys. His famous "Erector" sets were the first American construction toys to have moving parts and motors, and were an instant success. Their popularity reflected the massive American building boom of the early twentieth century. They were also well priced, starting at $1. By the mid 1950s, Gilbert had sold over 30 million sets. Gilbert took over American Flyer in 1938, and moved the company to New Haven, Connecticut.

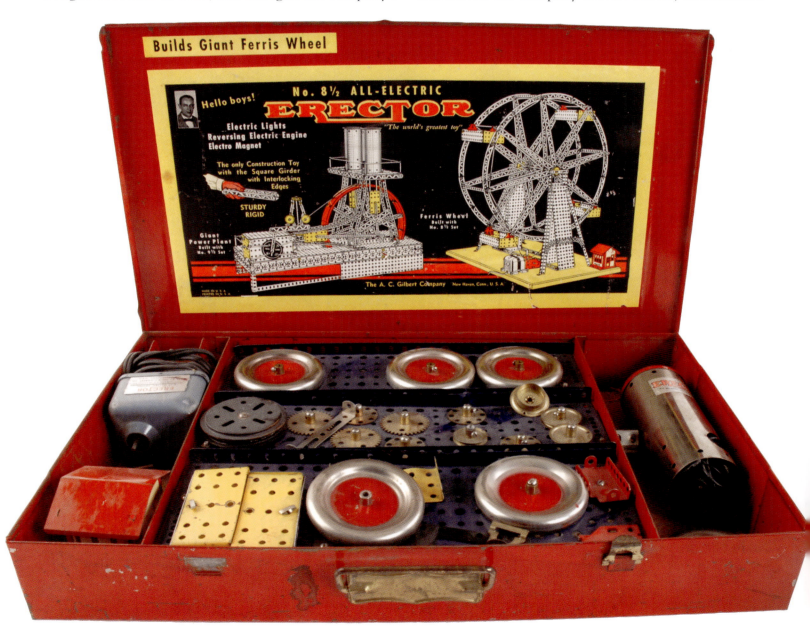

Erector sets came with instruction manuals.

H. C. WHITE POSTCARD PROJECTOR

The H. C. White Company of North Bennington, Vermont, made this "Radio Junior Postcard Projector," which dates from the 1920s and has an adjustable viewer and feet. Its tin plate body is litho printed in red, gold, and black. The postcard projector is an episcope, an optical device for projecting flat opaque images, like postcards, prints, and photographs. The postcard is placed upside down towards the rear of the viewer as the image is inverted by the projector's lens. An intense light, often from two sources, illuminates the object from the sides. Several companies printed postcards especially for these viewers, which were made by several American companies, including Buckeye Stereopticon Company and Mirroscope, both based in Cleveland, Ohio. H.C. White also made adult versions of the postcard viewer.

The lens is covered with a metal lid. The postcard projector is made from tin plate, which is lithographically printed.

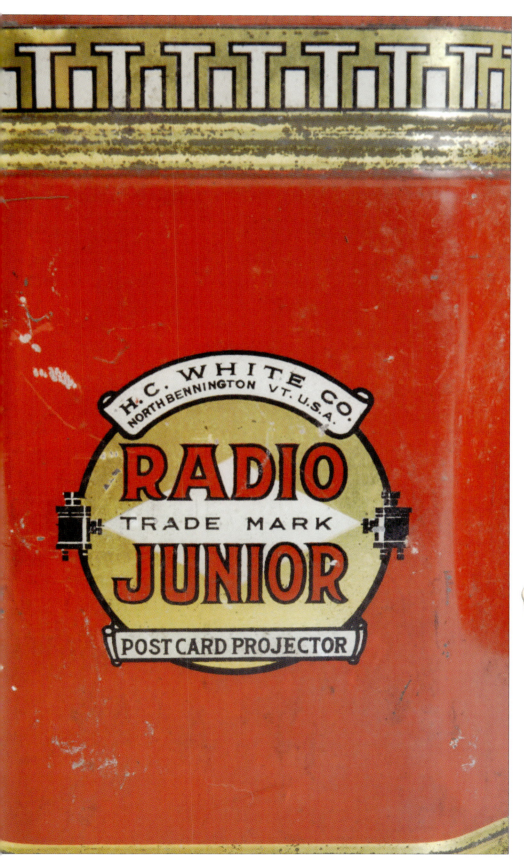

Above: H. C. White also made an adult version of the projector, the Radioptican.

Left: The "Junior Postcard Projector" dates from the 1920s. Several other makers made projectors of this kind.

MARX AMERICAN AIRLINES PLANE

This Marx American Airlines plane dates from around 1950 and is model NC-2100, "American Airlines Flagship Plane." The logo on the plane reads "Eagle and Wings over the World." The model is made from tin in two halves, has a wingspan of 27 inches, and is 21 inches long.

Marx made a line of several tin plate planes, including a P-34 fighter plane, some of which were labeled "Steelcraft." Several other toy manufacturers also made toy airplanes, including Buddy L, Keystone, Turner, and Wyandotte. American Airlines was incorporated in 1934, and was America's most popular airline by the end of the 1930s. American added Douglas DC-6 aircraft like this one to its fleet in the 1950s, fitted with Pratt and Whitney Double Wasp engines.

Above left: The logo on the side of the airline reads "Eagle and Wings over the World." The plane measures 21 inches in length.

Above: The DC-6 was Douglas's first pressurized aircraft.

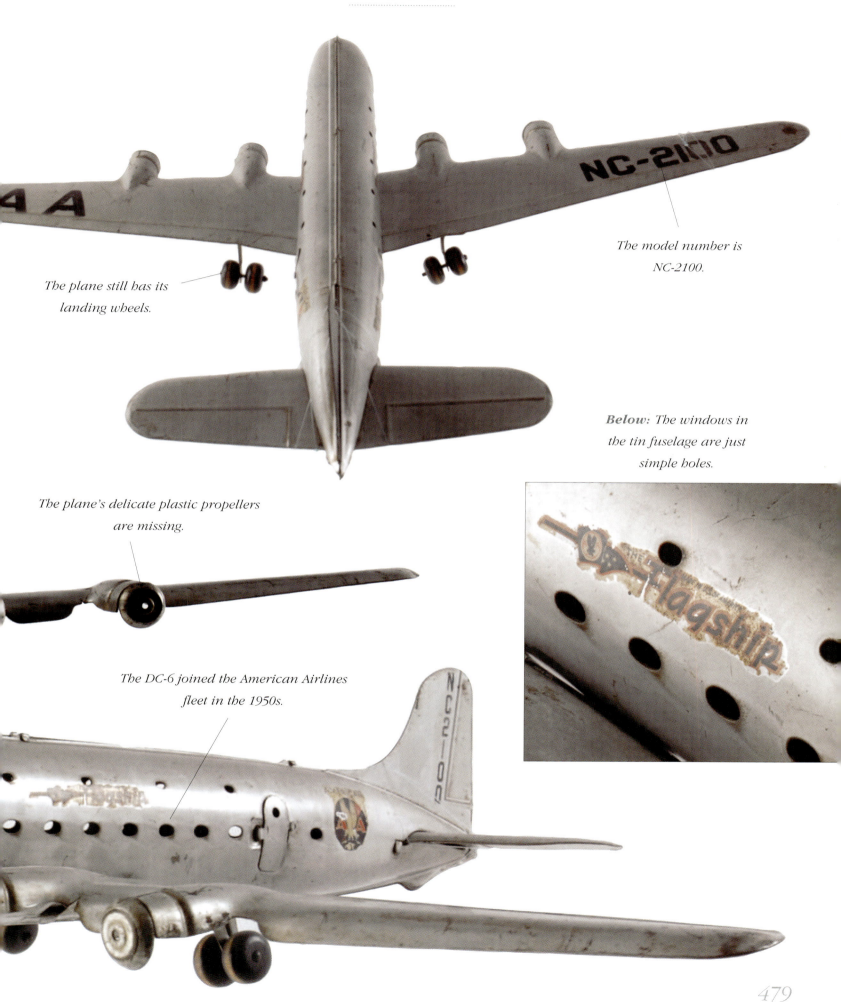

The model number is
NC-2100.

The plane still has its
landing wheels.

Below: The windows in
the tin fuselage are just
simple holes.

The plane's delicate plastic propellers
are missing.

The DC-6 joined the American Airlines
fleet in the 1950s.

Pan American World Airlines flew between 1927 and 1991. The airline has inspired a great deal of nostalgia for the era of elegant air travel.

MARX PAN AM CLIPPER

The Marx Pan Am Clipper is in the same style as the "American Airlines Flagship Plane," and also dates from the 1950s. Its fuselage is the same size, with a wingspan of 27 inches, and it is 21 inches in length. Like the American Airlines model it is a pressed tin toy, made in two halves, but is in better condition having retained its plastic propellers,

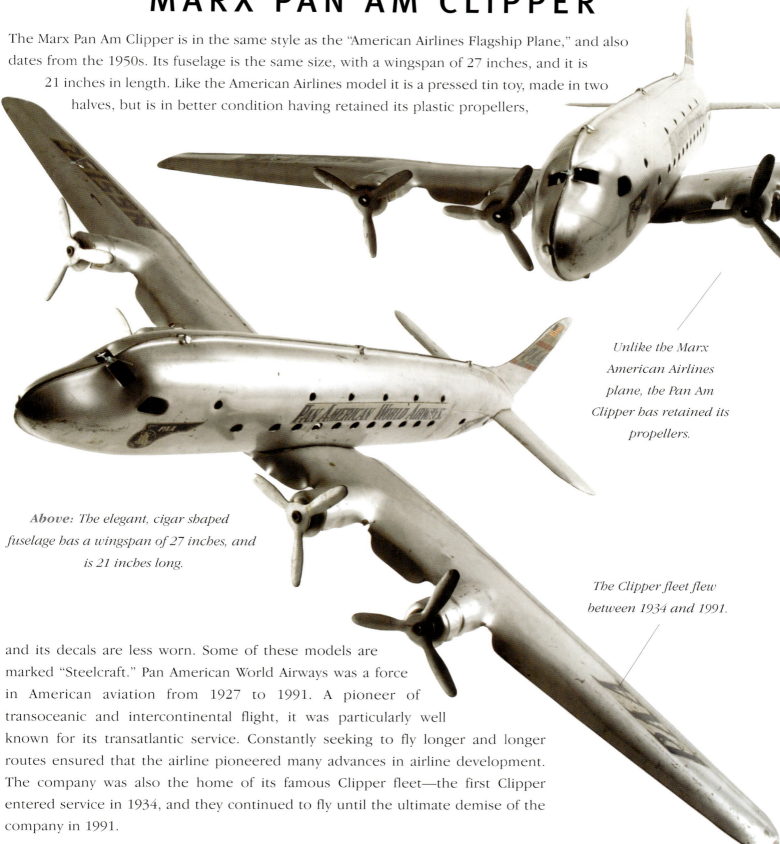

Unlike the Marx American Airlines plane, the Pan Am Clipper has retained its propellers.

Above: *The elegant, cigar shaped fuselage has a wingspan of 27 inches, and is 21 inches long.*

The Clipper fleet flew between 1934 and 1991.

and its decals are less worn. Some of these models are marked "Steelcraft." Pan American World Airways was a force in American aviation from 1927 to 1991. A pioneer of transoceanic and intercontinental flight, it was particularly well known for its transatlantic service. Constantly seeking to fly longer and longer routes ensured that the airline pioneered many advances in airline development. The company was also the home of its famous Clipper fleet—the first Clipper entered service in 1934, and they continued to fly until the ultimate demise of the company in 1991.

STEELCRAFT ARMY SCOUT PLANE

This orange and green Steelcraft NX 107 "Army Scout Plane" dates from around 1929, is 23 inches long and has a wingspan of 22½ inches. Steelcraft was best known for their early pedal cars—they were one of the five most active manufacturers in this field, together with American National, Gendron, Garton, and Toledo Wheel. Steelcraft also manufactured a range of other tin toys, including several aircraft. Some of their most famous and collectible models are their "Fighter Plane," with its 17-inch wingspan, and their "Mono Coupe Plane" of around 1935. The model planes were issued into a competitive field, dominated by Marx, but where Buddy L, Keystone, Turner, and Wyandotte were also active. There was a general fascination with the

Above: Steelcraft's NX 107 "Army Scout Plane" has become one of the most sought after aviation models of the 1920s.

Below: The plane's decals are in very good original condition.

The plane has green body and an orange tail.

Above: *In the 1920s, aviation was considered very exciting and glamorous. Charles Lindbergh's plane* The Spirit of St. Louis *was a small aircraft like this one.*

relatively new field of aviation in the 1920s and 1930s, and its glamour fed the popularity of model airplanes. Steelcraft was a brand name of the Murray company of Cleveland, Ohio. Such was the success of their Steelcraft range that the company moved to larger manufacturing premises in 1924. Murray continued to use the Steelcraft name until their demise at the end of World War II.

The wings have army decals.

FOUR EARLY CIVIL AIRCRAFT

Early twentieth century toy planes were produced in cast iron, die cast metal, and pressed steel. Aviation toys have become an increasingly popular collecting genre, and many enthusiasts specialize in early examples like these. Inspired by the glamour of the history of flight, toy manufacturers have launched models to capture aviation's defining moments. The Wright brothers constructed over 200 wing shapes before they were able to make the first sustained powered flight from Kitty Hawk, North Carolina on December 17, 1903. The technical advances to flight that were necessitated by World War I meant that post-

Above: Marx dominated the early toy airplane market, but it had several competitors.

Right: Early models of passenger airplanes have become increasingly sought after.

war planes were safer and much more capable—the Golden Era of flying had begun. Passenger flight was originally reserved for the privileged few, and was therefore very glamorous. But as World War II approached, passenger air travel became both more affordable and accessible.

CURTISS-TYPE MARX FIGHTER

Glenn Hammond Curtiss was one of the pioneering aviators and airplane designers of the early twentieth century. He famously said, "I sometimes think that the desire to fly after the fashion of the birds is an ideal handed down to us by our ancestors who... looked enviously at the birds soaring freely through space...

the late 1930s, and has a wingspan of 13 inches. Marx made several tin plate planes in this era, including several highly sought after models. These include the Douglas DC-6, which appeared with several aircraft liveries, including American Airlines and Pan American World Airways, and the P-39. Marx made plastic

This plane's propeller has survived.

This model was produced with either red or blue wings.

on the infinite highway of the air." As well as developing the first mass produced American aircraft engine, the Curtiss OX-5, Curtiss developed the flying boat. The Army Air Corps placed orders for a huge volume of aircraft in World War I, and Curtiss became rich. The Curtiss Company merged with Wright in 1929 to become Curtiss-Wright.

This Curtiss-based fighter plane shown here was launched by Marx toys as its P34 model. It dates from

airplanes in the post-war years, and some novelty items like the "Sparkling Jet Plane Friction Toy." The company's founder, Louis Marx, was born in Brooklyn in 1896. At the age of sixteen, he started his career in toys by working for the prestigious F. J. Strauss Company. Filled with energy and enthusiasm for the toy business, Louis became the manager of the company by the time he was twenty, but soon decided to venture out on his own.

Left and below: Curtiss was a pioneering aviator of the early twentieth century.

Below: Marx produced these little planes in the late 1930s, and sold thousands of them.

The plan has a wingspan of 13 inches.

This example has its original landing equipment.

U.S. ARMY PLANE N903

This Army N903 monoplane is a lithograph printed tin toy from the 1920s with very attractive graphics, including army stars. It has machine guns mounted on its high-mounted wings and is a single engine model marked Steelcraft. The Steelcraft toy company was best known for their pressed steel pedal cars, which were very successful during the 1920s. They were one of the most active manufacturers producing toys in this competitive field. But Steelcraft also manufactured a range of other desirable tin toys, including a range of early aircraft. Some of their most famous and collectible models are their "Fighter Plane," with its 17-inch wingspan, and their Mono Coupe reproduction aircraft, which dates from around 1935. Several famous tin toy manufacturers competed with Steelcraft in this field. The most pre-eminent among them was Marx, whose extensive range carried several model planes and aviation models, including the Universal Airport and various hangars. Buddy L, Turner, Keystone, and Wyandotte also made aviation-themed tin toys. Buddy L made the particularly charming "Catapult Hangar" in 1930, and Keystone offered an attractive Air Mail plane. Interestingly, Wyandotte's model airplanes were equipped with small wooden

The plane has machine guns mounted on its wings.

Below: This close-up shows the high quality of Steelcraft's lithography.

wheels. Most of these planes were of a similar size, with wingspans of between 13 and 22½ inches. Several Japanese tin toy manufacturers also offered lithographed model aircraft between the 1930s and 1950s, most of which were based on U.S.A.F. aircraft. They are now almost as collectible as their American contemporaries.

The tail is printed with the model number N903.

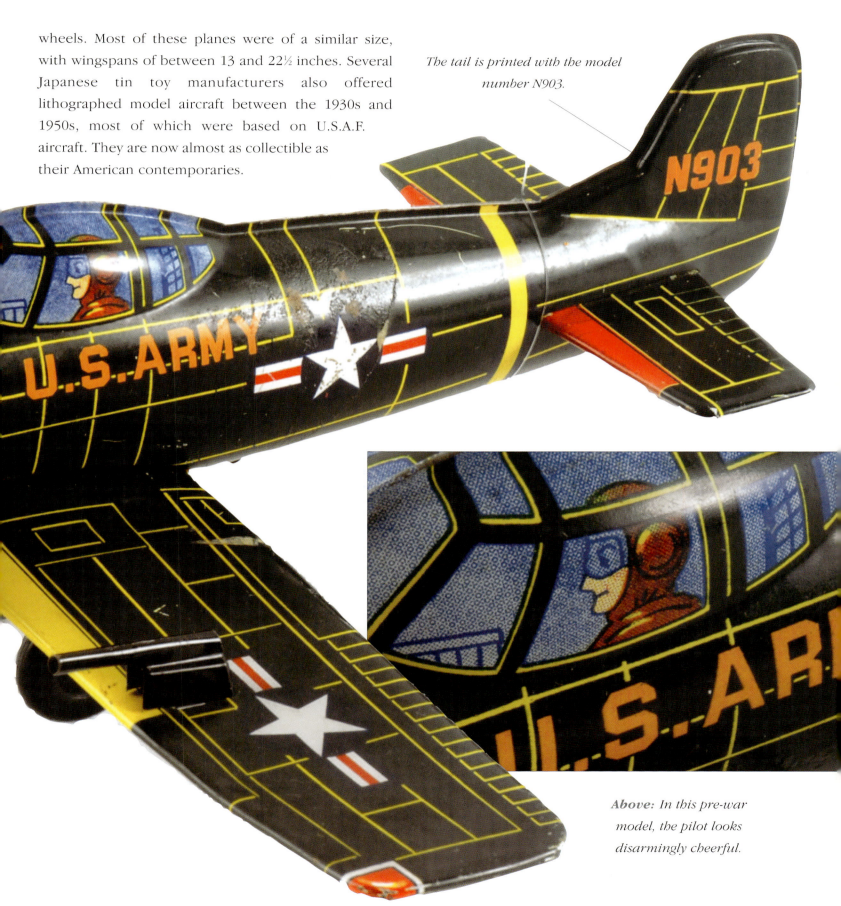

Above: In this pre-war model, the pilot looks disarmingly cheerful.

MARX BOMBER

This khaki-colored bomber is a wind-up toy from the post-World War II period, dating from the late 1940s. It has great graphics, featuring bombs and aggressive, war-like decals and is also equipped with a moving propeller, turning landing gear, and dual machine guns. The toy was made in America—the Marx logo appears on the top of the fuselage.

Marx wind-up toys mostly date from the company's pre-plastic, tin toy era. The Marx Merrymakers are some of the company's most famous tin toys. These toys were both creatively designed, and fantastically well engineered. The Marx company philosophy was that children enjoyed playing with replicas of vehicles they saw and knew about. Many children of the post-war era must have had parents who had served in one or other of the services, and were fascinated by the hardware they had used. Marx became the world's largest toy manufacturer in the post-war period, and produced an enormous range of mechanical boys' toys, ride-ons, play sets, dollhouses, and model trains. However, the 1950s was Marx's Golden Era.

Below: The bomber can be seen at the rear, wearing glasses and with a microphone.

This Marx model is a generic bomber plane.

This model is a twin engined plane.

Below: The styling of the plane's cockpit is reminiscent of the B52.

Right: The Marx company logo must be one of the most familiar in the vintage toy world.

FOKKER FRIENDSHIP

Toy companies like Hubley and A. C. Williams made cast iron planes like these between the 1930s and 1950s. The design of the Fokker F27 Friendship began in the 1950s as a replacement for the DC-3 airline—the prototype of the plane first flew on November 24, 1955. In 1956, Fokker signed a licensing deal with the American aircraft manufacturer Fairchild to manufacture the Fokker Friendship in America, and the first American-built Fokker first flew on April 12, 1958.

The plane seated forty-four passengers, and was delivered to Irish airline Aer Lingus in September 1958. This first plane was the first of 793 units built, making the model the most successful turboprop airliner of all time. The plane had a cruising speed of 322 miles per hour, and a range of 1,133 miles, and needed two or three crew members. Fokker went on to develop a replacement for the airliner, the Fokker 50, in the early 1980s.

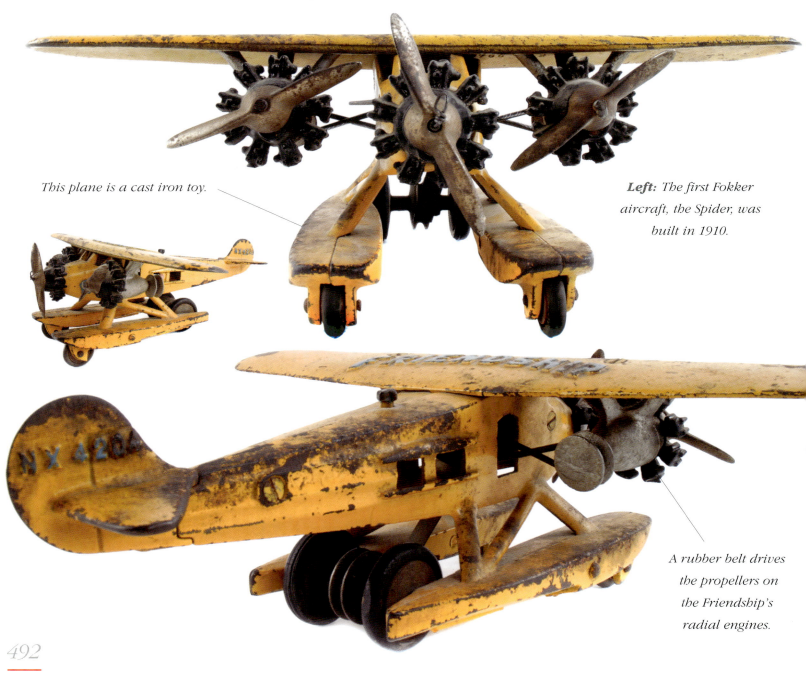

This plane is a cast iron toy.

__Left:__ The first Fokker aircraft, the Spider, was built in 1910.

A rubber belt drives the propellers on the Friendship's radial engines.

Below: *The Fokker has a turning cast iron propeller.*

Above: *The Friendship is an iconic aircraft.*

WOODEN MITCHELL B-25 BOMBER

This wooden replica of the Mitchell B-25 Bomber is enhanced with front machine guns, turret, top guns, and side guns. It dates from the late 1930s or early 1940s. The plane may well have been carved and painted by a father who had served on such an aircraft during the war. The B-25 Mitchell was a twin-engined medium bomber, manufactured in America by North American Aviation. John Leland Lee Atwood designed it. The plane first flew in August 1940, and was retired in 1979. The plane was used with devastating effect against German and Japanese targets in every combat theater of World War II. The aircraft was named in honor of General Billy Mitchell, a pioneer of the United States Air Force. It is the only American combat aircraft named after a specific person. Nearly 10,000 B-25s were constructed.

The top gun turret has two metal guns.

Right: The model is accurately painted to represent the window configuration of the B-25 bomber.

The wing is decorated with the U.S.A.F. star.

The fuselage also features a star.

Above: The model of the B-25 is very accurately shaped from softwood.

The painted twin engines lack propellers.

EARLY TOY AIRSHIP

The first toy airships (also know as blimps and dirigibles), were made from cast iron; they came from several early American toy manufacturers, such as Tootsietoy, Kenton, Champion, and A.C. Williams. Most date from the 1920s and 1930s and these models were usually a fairly consistent length of between roughly 5 and 6 inches. Slightly later toy airships like this one were made from pressed steel, and came from manufacturers such as Steelcraft. Later still, Mattel and other toy companies offered plastic blimps. A radio-controlled toy airship is now available, which actually flies—of course these metal versions could not.

There were no wheels on the original blimp.

The first rigid framed
airship flew in 1897.

The airship's gondola
is made from painted
pressed metal.

Below: This airship was originally designed as a
pull-along toy. Dents like these are common on
toy blimps.

STEELCRAFT GRAF ZEPPELIN

This pressed metal Graf Zeppelin was made by Steelcraft, and is a very rare toy indeed. German timber merchant David Schwarz invented the first rigid framed airship, powered by a 12 horsepower Daimler engine, and with three propellers. It achieved lift off on its first, tethered flight in 1897, but subsequently crashed. German military man Ferdinand Zeppelin took Schwarz's basic idea and developed it into a cloth-covered dirigible (blimp) with an aluminum frame. This airship, the LZ-1, made the first un-tethered airship flight on July 2, 1900, near Lake Constance in Germany. The Zeppelin flew for 17 minutes at a height of 1,300 feet. It was powered by two 15-cylinder Daimler engines, and had four working propellers and 17 hydrogen cells. It measured a massive 420 feet long, and 38 feet in diameter. Zeppelin founded an airship factory to manufacture his invention in 1908. The LZ-127 was the first commercial Zeppelin, with luxury passenger accommodation, including a gourmet dining saloon in its gondola. Zeppelin's 4,000 workers made 84 airships for the German government during World War I and constructed 129 between 1931 and 1935, during the Golden Age of airship travel. The Graf Zeppelin itself was built in 1928.

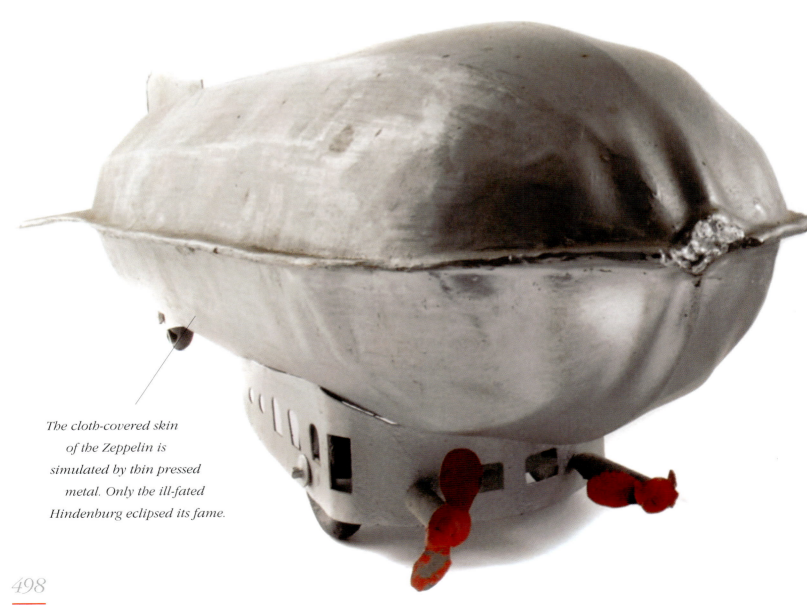

The cloth-covered skin of the Zeppelin is simulated by thin pressed metal. Only the ill-fated Hindenburg eclipsed its fame.

On the original Zeppelin, the framework was made out of aluminum. The original Schwarz blimp was made from wood.

Below right: The toy blimp is 6½ inches in diameter and 25 inches long.

JAPANESE-MADE TORNADO B-45

This replica North American Aviation Tornado B-45 was made in Japan. It served in the United States Air Force, so has "U.S.A.F." printed on the wings and the colorful graphics are blue, silver, and orange. The aircraft was one of America's first operational bombers to employ jet propulsion, and the first four-jet aircraft to fly in the United States, on February 24, 1947. Several versions of the original B-45 were manufactured. These included the B-45C with its special wing tips, and the photo-reconnaissance version, the RB-45C. The plane is now considered to be a light bomber. It was the first four-jet aircraft to drop an atom bomb and the first to refuel in mid air. The plane's top speed was 575 miles per hour; it had a flight ceiling of 45,000 feet, a range of 1,910 miles and flew with four crew members, the pilot,

The plane has U.S.A.F. decals.

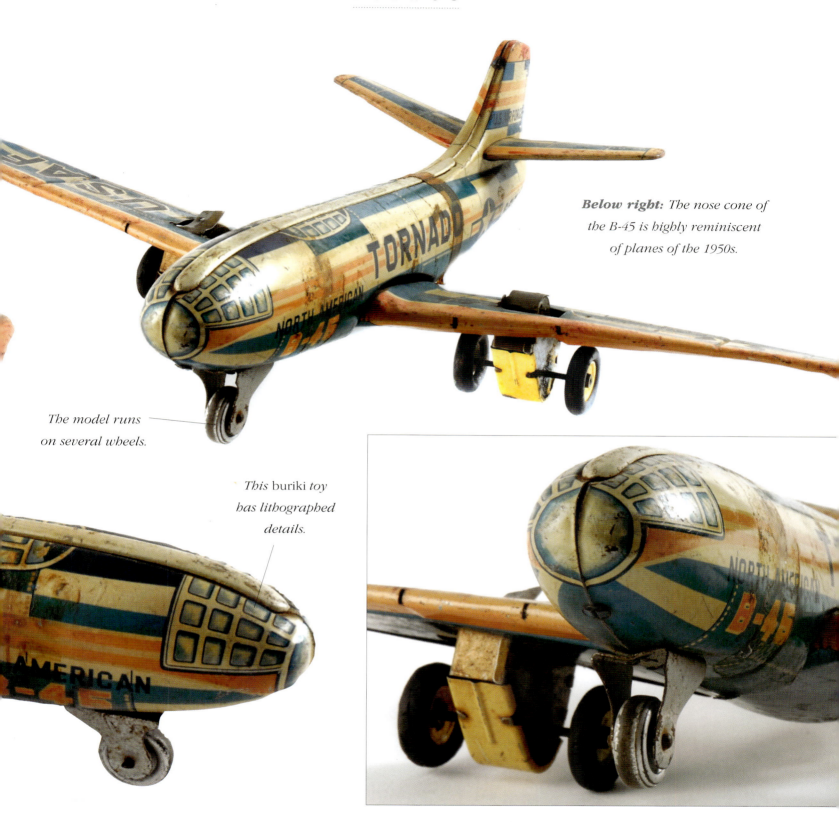

Below right: *The nose cone of the B-45 is highly reminiscent of planes of the 1950s.*

The model runs on several wheels.

This buriki toy has lithographed details.

co-pilot, navigator/bombardier, and tail gunner. Japanese *buriki* (tin plate) toy manufacturers of the post-war era were given a huge boost when the occupying American forces gave them permission in 1947 to resume production, and to export their wares to the United States. American children had been deprived of new metal toys in the war years when nearly all metal production was diverted to support the war effort. They were delighted to see a whole new range of toys on sale, including many friction models. Japanese toys of this vintage are usually marked "Foreign Made," rather than "Made in Japan."

SILVER EAGLE FLYING SHIP

This aluminum "Silver Eagle Flying Ship" is from the 1930s and is trademarked Ferdinand Strauss Inc., New York, U.S.A. This rare wind-up toy features an unusual shape and large propellers. Ferdinand Strauss was a French immigrant, who started as a toy importer in the early twentieth century and by 1914, had four toyshops in New York. Strauss was a founder of the mechanical toy industry in America, with a factory located in East Rutherford, New York. He was a major manufacturer of mechanical toys between 1914 and 1927, with a reputation for high quality and good design. Toys like the "Hornpipe Dancer" and "Silver Eagle Flying Ship" had clever and reliable mechanisms, and the 1925 catalog featured the "Dizzie Lizzie" auto and "Jenny the Balking Mule." The company went out of business at the end of the 1920s, but Strauss went back into toy manufacture between 1941 and 1946. Louis Marx started his illustrious career in toys working for Strauss at the age of 14, and soon became a manager in the company. Strauss's main business was supplying toys to the New York department store chain, Abraham Strauss. Marx, on the other hand, wanted to go into mass production, and supply playthings to the whole of the United States. In 1919, the two finally parted, and Marx went off to start his own company. Of course, we know that he was hugely successful, and ultimately bought out Ferdinand Strauss. At different times, Strauss and Marx are both referred to as America's "Toy King."

Above: The "Silver Eagle Flying Ship" is made from aluminum. It is trademarked Ferdinand Strauss, Inc. New York. U.S.A.

Right: *The shining "Silver Eagle" was one of Ferdinand Strauss's signature products, "Known the world over."*

The "Silver Eagle" has an unusual shape and a large wind-up propeller.

The model's wings are an extraordinary shape.

Note the large wheels.

503

DHL PLANE AND KENWORTH TRUCK

Several toy manufacturers have made toys based on the Kenworth truck, including Tonka and the All American Toy Company. This heavily decaled version has fantastic DHL-inspired graphics, and is extremely rare—it is estimated to be one of only three surviving examples. Kenworth manufactures medium and heavy-duty class 8 trucks and is based in Kirkland,

Washington, a suburb of Seattle. Two Seattle businessmen, Edgar Worthington and Harry Kent, founded the company in 1923. They combined both their names and resources to establish the company, capitalized with $60,000. They sold 80 trucks in 1924, and were the first American truck manufacturer to switch to diesel. Kenworth also invented the cab-over-

engine truck in 1957, and made school buses between the 1940s and 1957. PACCAR, the world's third largest truck manufacturer, and the owner of Peterbilt, now own the company. Kenworth has a reputation for making high quality vehicles, and has factories in the United States, Canada, Australia, and Mexico. The DHL plane, 00-DHM, the DHL World Wide Express, is a matching vehicle in the courier company's fleet.

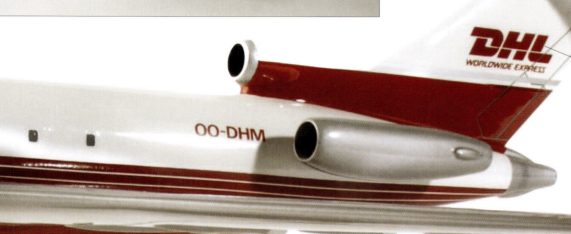

DHL, the international courier company, was founded by three business partners in 1969.

Above: The DHL company's first air run was between San Francisco and Honolulu.

Below left: This rare Kenworth DHL model is one of only three surviving examples.

FLYING TIGER LINE AIRCRAFT

This Flying Tiger Line plane was designed by Louis Marx and Company and manufactured in Japan under license (N447T). It is a lithographed tin toy dating from the 1950s and the decals read "Flying Tiger Line, INC, LIC-Gardner-Truesdell, INC." This particular example has retained its original box. The model is battery operated, and runs around on its wheels—the battery compartment is hidden underneath the plane. The rear tail section also opens and shuts to reveal the cargo inside, which consisted of tin boxes supplied with the toy. The plane measures 20 inches in length, and has a wingspan of 19 inches.

The Flying Tiger Line was a real American airline that was active between 1946 and 1989. Bob Prescott who lost his only son, Peter, in a plane crash, founded the company.

The plane's lithography reflects the skill of the Japanese manufacturer.

The battery compartment is located behind the front landing gear.

The plane runs on its wheels.

Above: *The Flying Tiger Line was a real life airline, active between 1946 and 1989.*

The rear tail section of the plane opens to reveal the cargo hold.

Right: The model measures 20 inches in length, and has a wingspan of 19 inches. It dates from the 1950s.

Above: The motor is located in metal housing between the two rear wheels.

TWA DC9 AND AMERICAN AIRLINES FLAGSHIP

The DC-9 Trans World Airlines plane on the right (model number N900TW) was made in Japan by the Y manufacturing company. The American Airlines flagship plane on the left (model number NC90425) is either a DC-4 or DC-6. Many toy collectors now specialize in the lithographed tin toys produced by Japanese manufacturers in the post-World War II years. Originally sold for modest prices (larger toys were offered at between $5 and $10), Japanese-produced model planes and automobiles were often quite amazingly detailed and creatively designed. Japanese-made toys are often labeled "Foreign Made," and are sometimes identified by special brand names given to them by the

This DC model, which is either the DC-4 or the DC-6, has four engines.

Left: The DC-1 came off the production line in 1933.

Below: The DC-9 has an elegant tail section.

TWA was acquired by American Airlines in 2001.

The iconic DC-9 first entered service in 1965. It was one of Douglas's most important aircraft.

Top left: The Japanese lithography is very accurate to the original plane.

American companies who commissioned them, such as Linemar, Cragson, or AH1. However, this one has the Japanese maker's initial, Y. At the peak of post-war tin toy production, there were over 200 active factories in Japan. They had been given a massive boost in 1947 when occupying American forces allowed them to restart toy production and export their products to America. By 1963, about 60% of the Japanese toy industry was making *buriki* for American consumers.

Donald Wills Douglas Sr. founded the Douglas Aircraft Company in Santa Monica, California, in 1921. Douglas planes circled the globe in 1924, to confirm a place in aviation history. The DC (Douglas Commercial) series, are generally considered the most important transport planes ever built. The DC-1 came off the production line in 1933. The DC-4 arrived in 1939, the DC-6 in 1946, and the iconic DC-9 in 1965. Douglas merged with the McDonnell Aircraft Corporation in 1967, and with Boeing's Commercial Airplane division in 1997.

AMERICAN AIRLINES PLANES

These three model American Airlines planes are all made of wood. They are based on three aviation workhorses from the 1930s, the Douglas DC-3, the Convair 580, and the Douglas DC-4 or DC-6, and are very charming models with a vintage feel.

American Airlines was formed by a series of mergers between 82 small American air companies, which were incorporated into a single entity in January 1930. The new airline had routes between Boston, Dallas, Chicago, Los Angeles, Dallas, and New York. Their first aircraft were the wood and fabric covered Fokker Trimotors, and the all-metal Ford Trimotors. In 1934, the company also began to fly Curtiss Condor biplanes, which were fitted with sleeping berths. E. L. Cord acquired the company in 1934, and renamed the American Airways Company, as American Air Lines. At this time, the company headquarters was at Chicago Midway International Airport in Chicago, Illinois. The

company worked closely with Douglas on the development of the DC-3, and when the planes were delivered, they started to use the term "flagships," to differentiate American from other airlines. The DC-3s also flew a three star Admiral's pennant.

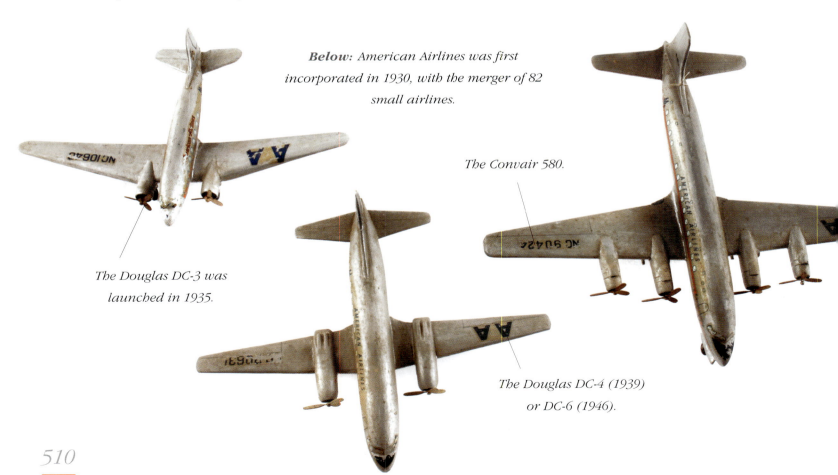

Below: American Airlines was first incorporated in 1930, with the merger of 82 small airlines.

The Convair 580.

The Douglas DC-3 was launched in 1935.

The Douglas DC-4 (1939) or DC-6 (1946).

Above: *The DC (Douglas Commercial)
line of aircraft is one of the most
important in aviation history. The DC-1
was launched in 1933, and the final mode,
the DC-10 in 1971.*

BOEING B-17 AND B-29 BOMBERS

These tin plate bombers date from the post-war years. The red and silver bomber on this page is the Boeing B-17 Flying Fortress, which was a four-engined heavy bomber developed by Boeing for the U.S. Army Air Corps (U.S.A.A.C.). Designed by Edwards C. Wells, the B-17 took its maiden flight in 1935. Between 1936 and 1945, a huge total of 12,731 B-17s were produced. They were heavily used in World War II, mostly for daylight precision raids on industrial targets in Germany. The plane also saw action in the Pacific and was finally retired in 1968.

The Boeing B-17 and B-29 were both four-engined heavy bombers.

Above: *The most famous B-29 was the* Enola Gay, *which dropped the atomic bomb "Little Boy" on Hiroshima on August 6, 1945.*

The orange plane above is a Boeing B-27 Superfortress. Almost commissioned by the USAAC, the B-29 was a heavy bomber four-propeller aircraft, one of the largest aircraft to see service in World War II. Its maiden flight in 1942, and 3,900 were built between 1943 and 1945. The unit cost of each B-29 Superfortress was $639,188.

This model B-17 has retained its moving propellers.

Both of these Boeing bomber models are from the immediate post-war years.

TEXACO TRUCK BANKS

The first money banks (or boxes) were simple pots in the fourteenth century. By the fifteenth century, money banks were made in various abstract shapes—eggs, balls, and domes—and had narrow openings for coins. By the nineteenth century, the boxes were made from a wide range of materials (including silver plated nickel), and most were molded into representational forms, such as animals and miniature safes. Twentieth century banks often had simple movements, such as the African who takes a coin to his mouth in his hand.

The banks here are part of Texaco's company history confirming its famously strong brand—in 2003, it was ranked as America's number one, built up over many decades of advertising and promotional activity. Texaco produced and sold many endorsed products through

The money bank slot concept dates from the fifteenth century.

Above: Texaco dates from the early days of the Texas oil boom. Joseph S. Cullinan and Arnold Schlaet founded the company.

Texaco's signature red livery.

The Texas Fuel Company dates from 1901.

their gas stations, including toy vehicles and several generations of banks like these Ertl-made ones. Texaco themed their gas stations from 1915, under the auspices of "ad man" Harry Tipper. The Texaco star dates from 1903—as Texaco's advertising manager D.P. Stewart wrote in 1947, "Our Company today has an emblem… which, all over the globe, means superior quality."

BANTHRICO BANKS

Banthrico banks likes these were offered as premiums by American businesses and financial institutions. The Banthrico company was established in 1931 when Jerome Aronson and Joseph Eisendrath bought the Banker's Thrift Corporation, a manufacturer of coin banks. The new owners abbreviated the company name to Ban-thri-co. Banthrico manufactured over 900 metal money banks in its long history, most of which had Banthrico embossed on their bases. A highly skilled workforce molded the banks from "white metal," an alloy of 95% zinc, and 5% aluminum. The banks were then electroplated and finished in clear lacquer. The banks often locked with individual keys, which were almost invariably lost. Banthrico produced many short orders of as few as 500 or 1000 units. Their designs included famous politicians, animals, birds, fish, household items, and bank buildings. Banthrico was sold to Toystalgia in 1985.

Above: *This line up of Banthrico car-shaped banks dates from the 1960s and 1970s.*

The banks are molded in "white metal" alloy.

Banthrico's skilled workforce created finely detailed molds.

The Banthrico logo is embossed on the bottom of the banks.

Many of these banks as business premiums.

ERTL TRUCK BANKS

Ertl made this collection of truck money banks. Famous for making all kinds of toy vehicles, Ertl is best known for its die-cast metal alloy collectible replicas of farm equipment and agricultural vehicles. The company is based in Dyersville, Iowa, which is also the home of the National Farm Toy Museum. The popularity of the company's toys is due to the fact that they are actually highly detailed scale models of popular vehicles. Ertl's slogan reflects its concern with accuracy and detail: "Ertl, just like the real thing, only smaller." Fred Ertl Sr. founded the company in 1945, and it soon became known for its miniature farm

Left: Ertl's truck money banks show the same attention to scale and detail as its conventional models.

Many of the trucks carry company endorsements.

Each truck has a coin slot somewhere in the top.

The Budweiser brand endorses this truck.

vehicles. The company made models of all the popular full-size brands, including John Deere, New Holland, and AGCO. The company is also well known for its model kits, which include kits based on licensed characters, such as Thomas the Tank Engine, and Star Wars. Through a series of acquisitions and mergers, Ertl has enhanced its market position, and now controls several famous toy brands, including Jada Toys, Maisto, Hot Wheels, Matchbox, Bumble Ball, and Thomas the Tank Engine and Friends ERTL Models. The company's magazine, launched in 1982, is called The Replica. Ertl is now owned by the RC2 Corporation. Since the 1990s, Ertl has made many of its toys in Mexico.

PHILLIPS 66 BANKS

These Phillips Petroleum banks were made by Ertl, with their usual concerned for real-life detail and scale. Like the money banks they made for Texaco, Ertl's Phillips Petroleum banks were sold as gas station premiums to build a company brand—Phillips 66 is a famous American gasoline brand and chain of gas stations. The Phillips Petroleum Company was originally founded in 1917. In 1927, they tested their new brand of petroleum on Highway 66 in Oklahoma, and decided to name the fuel for the iconic highway. The Phillips 66 shield logo, introduced in 1930, was based on the highway sign. It was originally black and orange, but the red, white, and black version, launched in 1959, is still in use. The first Phillips 66 gas station was opened in Wichita, Kansas on November 19, 1927, and the first Texan gas station at McLean in 1929. Both of these original gas stations have been preserved. One of Phillips strongest marketing strategies was its Highway Hostesses patrol. These ladies traveled the highways between the 1930s and 1960s, making random inspections of Phillips 66 gas station restrooms. Phillips was the second American producer to sell gas in all fifty states.

Above: The Phillips 66 shield logo was introduced in 1930, and is still in use today. This red, black, and white version dates from 1959.

Phillips merged with
Conoco in 2002 to
form ConocoPhillips.

SOUVENIR CORONATION MONEYBOX

This bank or moneybox was made to celebrate the coronation of King George VI and Queen Elizabeth of Great Britain on May 12, 1937. Oxo gave away the commemorative banks, which are made from lithographed tin plate. Oxo manufactures a famous brand of square beef stock cube, which remains in production today. This oval moneybox is printed the national emblems of the four countries that make up Great Britain, the English rose, Welsh daffodil, Scottish thistle, and Northern Irish shamrock. The tin has a removable lid and wide coin slot.

Left: *George VI and Elizabeth were the parents of the present Queen Elizabeth II.*

Below: *The moneybox originally contained six Oxo cubes.*

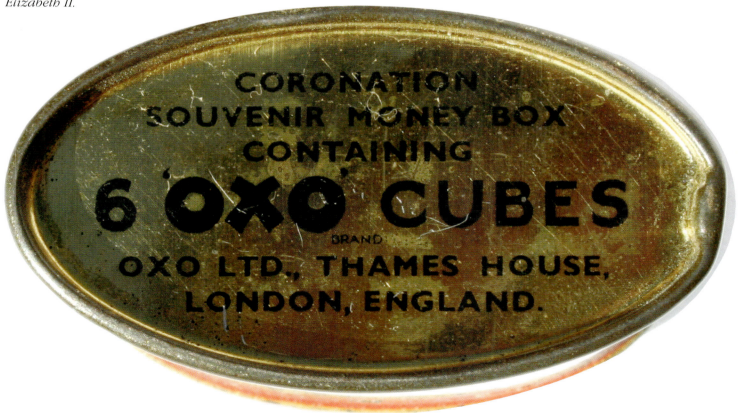

SAFE MONEY BANK

Although this safe-shaped money bank has a coin slot in its roof, it also has a fully opening door with locking mechanism and turn-able locking device. This tin plate toy measures approximately 5 inches high, 3 inches wide, and 2 inches deep and is stamped "foreign" on the bottom, which probably means it was made in Japan, and dates from around the 1930s. Its brand name, Orca, may be a reference to the famous whale, which is also large, powerful, and grayish. Charles and Jeremiah Chubb took out the first patent for a burglar-resistant safe in 1835. This English company was already a famous locksmith—in the 1820s, King George IV awarded

Above: *The door features a turning miniature locking device.*

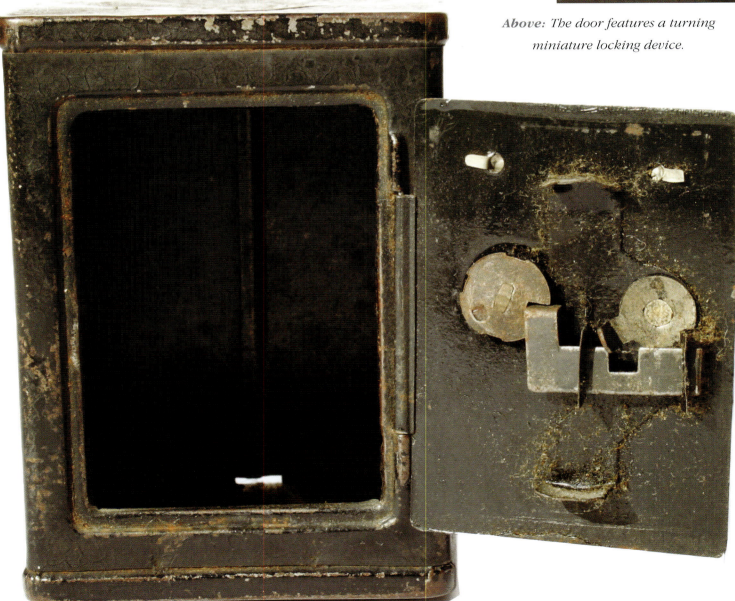

Right: The design of the safe reflects the weight and solidity of early full-size models.

Below: The safe has a coin slot in its roof.

Below: The "Foreign" stamp usually means the toy was made in Japan.

Chubb a special license, making them the sole suppliers of locks to the British Post Office and the Prison Service. Chubb opened the first safe factory in 1837. In 1851, they were commissioned to build a secure case for the Koh-I-Noor diamond, on display at the Great Exhibition held in London, England, at Crystal Palace .

MASON BANK BY SHEPARD

The iconic bank is imprinted with the words "Mason Bank." Made by Shepard Hardware, it dates from around 1887 and is a cast iron toy, painted red, gray, and orange. It shows two workmen building a chimney; one has a brick-carrying hod, while the other holds a cement trowel. The toy's smooth patina and signs of natural wear show that this is an original piece. Being early, rare, and sought after, the bank is now worth several thousand dollars.

Walter J. and Charles G. Shepard founded Shepard Hardware in 1866. The foundry originally made muffin pans and round broilers and was located in Buffalo, New York. Shepard began to manufacture cast iron banks in 1882. They produced many famous banks, both "still," and "mechanical," including the "Humpty Dumpty Bank" (1882), "Trick Pony Bank" (1885), "Stump Speaker Bank" (1886), "Circus Bank" (1888), "Santa Claus Bank" (1889), "Speaking Dog Bank," "Artillery Bank" (1892), "Jolly Black Man Bank," "Jonah and the Whale Bank," and "Leap Frog Bank." Several

Above: Shepard's cast iron banks are extremely well designed, and often contain an element of humor.

other companies also made cast iron banks at this time, including J. & E. Stevens, H. L. Judd, J. Barton Smith, Kyser & Rex, Blakeslee, Wagner & Zwiebel, Kenton Hardware, and John Harper. Shepard sold their bank making business in 1892, and some of their designs were later re-issued by J. & E. Stevens.

Right: The "Mason Bank" dates from the peak of Shepard's production.

STEVENS TAMMANY BANK

J. & E. Stevens of Cromwell, Connecticut, made this "Tammany Bank." Brothers John and Elisha Stevens founded the company in 1842 and it survived until the 1950s, making cast iron banks between 1870 and circa 1900. They developed a high reputation in this field, and their banks are now highly collectible. This bank is a mechanical, rather than "still" bank. The corrupt and greedy politician is constantly feeding himself. It dates

Right: This highly popular bank shows how New York viewed the Democratic Party in the 1870s.

from around 1873 and is around 5 inches high and 3 inches wide. The paint on this vintage toy is understandably worn—originally, it would have been brilliantly colored in black, gray, yellow, and red enamel. As well as using their foundry to make cast irons banks, J. & E. Stevens also made bell toy castings for both Gong Bell and Watrous. Elisha left the company in 1869 to found the Stevens and Brown Toy Company with George Brown, which survived until 1880. Tammany Hall was the Democratic Party political machine, which controlled the party's nominations and patronage in Manhattan from 1854. It was widely known that it used violence, intimidation, and widespread bribery to achieve its political goals.

Below: *The "Tammany Bank" was one of J. & E. Stevens most popular cast iron banks. It is still very highly sought after by collectors. Depending on condition, it can be worth hundreds, or thousands of dollars.*

This is a heavy, cast iron toy.

STEVENS CAT AND MOUSE BANK

J. & E. Stevens made this "Cat and Mouse Bank" in 1891. This version is 8½ inches tall, and 5½ inches wide, but the company also made a larger, 12-inch high model of the toy. If you put a coin into the bank slot, lock the mouse into position, and then press the level, the mouse disappears and then the kitten appears, holding the mouse. Mechanical cast iron banks like this one are highly regarded, and are worth several thousand dollars.

Founded in 1842, Stevens made cast iron hardware before it went into toy manufacture. As well as banks, they also produced a successful line of cast iron vehicle toys, including trucks, horses, and wagons. The company also became strongly associated with its long-running range of toy guns. It launched its first pea, pellet, and cap shooter in 1868 and by the 1880s, this firearm had been joined by a host of others, including the "Buffalo Bill," the "Bulls Eye," and the "Challenge." Stevens continued to develop variants on this theme for many decades. In the 1950s, they produced a range of four space guns—at the time, space toys had eclipsed the popularity of cowboy-themed playthings. The launch of these modern toys was actually a fruitless attempt to stave off financial ruin, and the company went out of business before they were able to market the final model, the "Cosmic Ray." Their entire range is rather roughly cast, and finished in a cheap silver paint finish which chips and wears very easily. It includes the "Jet Jr." and two "Space Police" models.

Left: The "Cat and Mouse Bank" mechanism still works perfectly, although it is nearly 120 years old.

Right: Stevens's castings are very attractive, and colored to appeal to children.

STEVENS CLOWN ON A GLOBE BANK

This red, white, and blue "Clown on a Globe Bank" was made by J. & E. Stevens around 1890. It is a mechanical, rather than "still" cast iron bank; the clown spins on his head. Clowns and circuses were popular themes for banks in the late nineteenth century, and several other American and European manufacturers produced banks on this theme. These included the "Circus Bank" issued by Shepard Hardware in 1888, the "Circus Ticket Collector Bank" made by the H. L. Judd Manufacturing Company in 1879, and the (very early) "Clown Bust Bank" launched by Chamberlain & Hill Ltd. in the 1820s. Stevens themselves manufactured several other circus-themed banks. These included their "Harlequin, Columbine, and Clown Bank" of 1877, and another version of the "Clown on Globe Bank" issued in 1890, where the clown is sitting on the globe.

Founded in 1842, Stevens made cast iron hardware before going into toy manufacture. As well as banks, they also made a successful line of cast iron toy vehicles, and became well known for a line of toy firearms. The firm was founded by two brothers, John and Elisha Stevens, in Cromwell, Connecticut, and became one of America's leading manufacturers of toy banks.

Right: Stevens made another version of the "Clown on a Globe Bank" in which the clown sits, rather than spins, on the globe.

Circus and clowns were a popular theme in the late 1800s.

TRICK DOG BANK

The "Trick Dog" is a very popular design for a coin-operated mechanical bank. The dog deposits the coin into the barrel after jumping through the hoop at the clown's request. Several manufacturers (including Shepard) made versions of this classic design, in different sizes and colors but retaining the basic barrel-clown-dog configuration. Most are around 7 to 8 inches tall, and 7 to 9 inches wide. The bases, which differ in color from blue, to buff, to red, to yellow, are sometimes hollow, and sometimes solid. The barrel is usually red, but may also be brown or green. The dog is usually black or brown. Only the clown himself remains almost completely unchanged in size, costume style, and facial expression; he is usually attired in some combination of red, black, and yellow, although the exact coloring of his outfit does tend to vary. The toy has become so iconic that modern versions are also now offered for sale. If anything, this has intensified the value of the early original pieces, which are worth hundreds or thousands of dollars, depending on their condition and rarity.

The dog deposits the coin into the barrel.

Below: Several versions of this bank were made, in a variety of colors.

Above: After depositing the coin in the barrel, the dog then jumps through the clown's hoop.

Shepherd also made their own version of this classic toy.

The colors of the base varied between blue, buff, yellow, and red.

535

ASTRO SPACE ROCKET BANK

This space rocket bank was one of several made in the 1950s and 1960s, when the interest in space toys was at its peak. This one is constructed from silver metal and plastic, and is 2 inches tall, and 3 inches wide at the fins. Its silver-blue band, trimmed with red, reads "Amarillo National Bank." Rocket banks like this one were commissioned as give-away items by many local banks, including the Perth Amboy National Bank of New Jersey, who also bought some of these rockets to give to their customers. The rocket fins are embossed "Astro Mfg." and "A Berzac Creation." American and Canadian patent numbers are also quoted. When you

put a coin in the slot, and press the red button, the coin shoots up to the top of the rocket. To retrieve the money, you needed to remove the red plastic rocket assembly underneath the rocket, which was key operated. Strato made another version of the space rocket bank in the 1950s, the "Rocket to the Moon Mechanical Coin Bank." This model was also cast in silvery metal, and came with a key. These space rocket banks were just one example of a huge range of space toys and models that flooded the market in the 1950s and 1960s. These included rockets, sputniks, Apollo rockets, rocket cars, flying saucers, space tanks, robots,

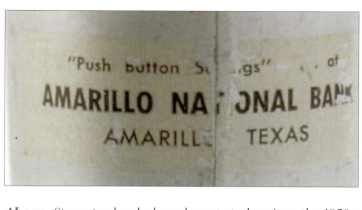

Above: *Space toy banks have been popular since the 1950s. The Kennedy Space Center currently sells the "NASA Space Shuttle Bank."*

Above: *Pressing the red button launches the coin to the top of the Astro Manufacturing rocket bank.*

moon rockets, space ships, rocket shooting fighters, and lunar transports. However, this is not the only connection between space and the world of play: the Slinky toy was part of the 1984 space experiment on the space shuttle, and Lego paid for 200 miniature aliens and a "Red Planet Protector" to be taken to the International Space Station to promote their "Life on Mars" play sets.

MARX MERCHANTS TRANSFER TRUCK

Among the many vehicles Marx made was the Marx Merchants transfer truck with the "NYS" logo, drawn by a team of two horses, and with solid metal wheels. The driver is appropriately uniformed to drive the gold-colored truck with its black details and blue-painted flatbed. Decorated with a delightfully rustic "Toyland's Farm Products" transfer, the toy is 10 inches in length. Below, the Marx Merchants transfer truck is parked next to a Toyland dairy truck, which—complete with its balloon tires—measures around 15 x 9 inches. This single horse-drawn, driverless, lithograph toy is a wind-up model and its red and black hubcaps are an added feature. The horse itself is gold, black, and red, with black-painted reins, and it draws a covered wagon. The models were both produced in the 1920s and 1930s.

Both below: Parked together, these two horse-drawn Marx trucks would have been a source of childish pride in the 1920s and 1930s.

Above: The rustic-styled "Toyland's Farm Products" transfer is very well preserved.

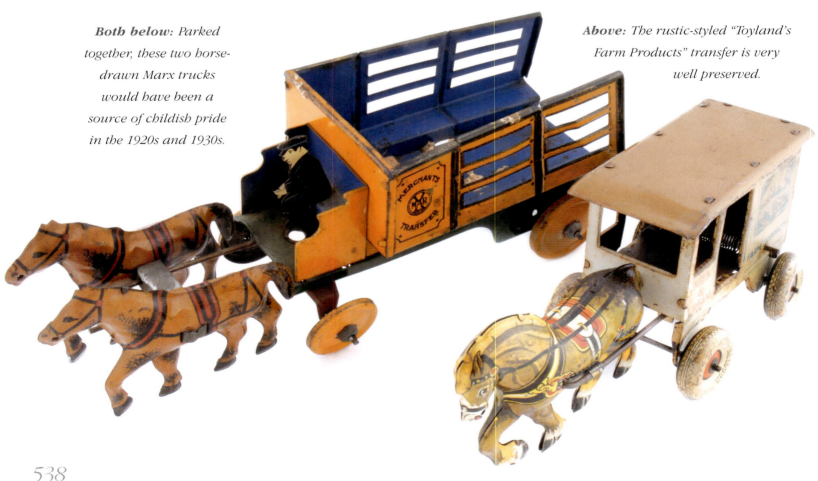

The driver wears the smart truck driver's uniform of the Marx Merchants.

Above: *The Marx Merchants transfer truck is a classically styled lithograph toy from the early twentieth-century, reflecting the horse-drawn era in which it was produced.*

STATE HI-WAY SET

Dating from around 1960, this Tonka B set of heavy equipment is designed for use by the "State Hi-Way Department." The serial number "975" is added to the transfer. There are five pieces in this lime green-painted set of road building toys: a dragline complete with low-boy; a bulldozer (complete with a broad curved vertical blade for clearing the ground); a crane with a lift-able bucket; a truck equipped with a steam shovel; and a huge motorized rototiller profiler, with a rotating blade designed to break up the ground. Originally competitive with manufacturers such as Buddy L, Marx, Nylint, Structo, and Wyandotte, high quality and innovative boys' toys like this set resulted in Tonka being inducted into the National Toy Hall of Fame (located in Salem, Oregon) on March 28, 2001.

Left: The low-loader is constructed complete with a working chain winch and fully working turning handle located on the pivoting joint between the truck and its trailer.

The rototiller has a rotating blade that would break up the ground beneath it.

The truck is equipped with a forward mounted steam shovel.

The low-loader has four pairs of rubber tires on the truck and trailer, and chrome effect bumpers.

Right: The "State Hi-Way Dept 975" transfer is proudly displayed by this high-quality set.

FOUR STEAM SHOVELS

This selection of four steam shovels all date from the 1940s, and this is an interesting collection of toys offered by highly competitive manufacturers. This collection demonstrates the popularity of this form of toy, which continues in similar forms even today as part of the standard offering of metal toys that are available to young boys.

The particularly robust-looking blue steam shovel was manufactured by Structo, and looks as though it would stand up to vigorous play. The red machine is from the Wyandotte Construction Company, and boasts rubber rather than solid wheels. The green "Lumar Contractors" model was made by Marx, and has the MAR logo.

The "Lumar Contractors" model has a wind-up hand winch.

The Wyandotte model has the remains of a piece of string.

The red steam shovel has the Wyandotte Construction Co. logo.

Above: *This collection of four steam shovels shows the universal popularity of this form, and how competitive manufacturers made different versions of the toy.*

Above: A detail showing the Wyandotte Construction Co. logo. This manufacturer was a major player in the construction of tin toys.

Above: The Structo Toys logo, and a detail showing the steam shovel's rubber tires mounted on solid metal wheels.

VINTAGE STEAM SHOVEL

This vintage steam shovel metal toy was manufactured by prestige maker Buddy L, sometime between 1921 and 1931. Constructed from heavy gauge metal, it has successfully stood the test of time and has obviously survived some vigorous play very well, although most of the original paintwork is worn away. This is a model of a true "steam" shovel. The pipe on the roof, and the hole in the "boiler," demonstrate that the original for the model was a coal-powered steam engine. The articulated arm of the shovel itself is raised by a handle-turned winch, which coils a roll of thin string. It

looks as though the string has been replaced, at least once, in the life of this venerable toy. It is slightly difficult to work out how a real-life operator would be able both to feed the boiler and raise the shovel at the same time! The roof of the steam shovel is constructed from a piece of genuine corrugated steel, and it has solid metal wheels.

The articulated arm of the shovel is raised by turning a winch, which coils a roll of thin string.

The curved roof of the vintage steam shovel is constructed from real corrugated steel.

Left: The back view of the steam shovel shows the hole where coal would have been shoveled to feed the boiler.

The stovepipe chimney would have belched smoke on the original.

VINTAGE STEAM SHOVEL

Like the vintage steam shovel on the previous pages, this toy was also manufactured by Buddy L, and is of a similar vintage. Buddy L toys are manufactured by the Moline Steel Company in East Moline, Illinois, founded by Fred A. Lundahl in 1910. Lundhal originally made automobile fenders and other stamped parts for the automotive industry, including parts for McCormack-Deering and the International Harvester Company, but his son, Arthur, was the inspiration behind the toys he began to make in 1921; "Buddy L" was Arthur's neighborhood nickname. Lundahl designed and produced an all-steel miniature truck, based on an

International Harvester model, using metal off-cuts. Despite a cool reception from the toy trade, Lundahl's Buddy L toys became the first all-American large pressed-steel toys. A year later, the company pulled out of car parts, and went into full-time toy production. By 1925, the company had twenty different models, including fire engines, moving vans, lumber trucks, sand loaders, overhead cranes, and tanker trucks. In 1926, the Buddy L Outdoor Railroad was added to the original lines, and ice trucks, tugboats, airplanes, ice trucks, and a bus were quick to follow. In 1930, the Moline Steel Company name was dropped, and it became the Buddy L Manufacturing Company.

This early steam shovel has an all-steel construction.

BUDDY L DREDGER

This Buddy L sand loader is a very heavy-duty toy. It is an early dredger with a chain craven wind-up mechanism, and dates from between 1925 and 1931. The movement is sophisticated, having both several gears and a brake lock. Like all Buddy L toys, the dredger was built out of steel, and constructed to survive the knocks of robust play. The dredger comes from an early Buddy L production era when some of the company's best ever models were offered to the toy-buying public.

Above: The sophisticated winding mechanism. Buddy L is famous for its highly detailed and functional construction toys.

The chain mechanism moves a sequence of sand buckets.

The steam shovel was a popular Buddy L model for several decades.

TONKA SAND LOADER

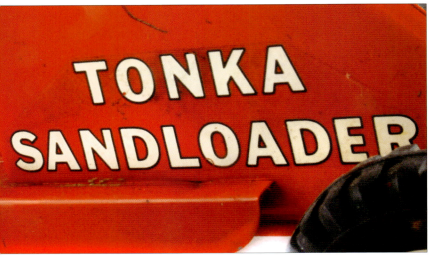

Tonka made the fine sandloader illustrated here. Mound Metalcraft (Tonka Toys) had started toy production back in 1946—the company had previously manufactured various metal hand tools, including rakes and shovels. The name "Tonka" was taken from the name of nearby Lake Minnetonka, which means "great" in the Sioux language. The company's first factory was based in the basement of a small schoolhouse in Mound, Minnesota, a small town near Minneapolis. Two of their first offerings were the No. 100 steam shovel, and the No. 150 crane and clam and the company unveiled their iconic Tonka trucks at the

Above: The "Tonka Sandloader" logo is applied to the truck as a transfer.

1947 New York toy fair. They continued to add many pressed-steel trucks and jeeps to their line in the 1950s and 1960s, and (including our sandloader) these models are now the most collectible Tonka toys, and

The trailer is equipped with a rubber belt to load the sand.

A lever moves the rubber belt in either direction.

Above: A robust side-positioned lever lifts the truck flatbed.

form the backbone of many serious collections. As well as being equipped with "Tonka Hydraulic" equipment the sandloader also has a moveable rubber loading belt fitted to its trailer, to load and unload the sand. A crank handle raises the flatbed of the truck itself, which has rubber tires on its solid metal wheels and a grey-painted metal fender. The cab has a clear plastic front windshield.

TWO DUMPER TRUCKS

These two dumper trucks are from two different manufacturers in direct competition, but despite this they are remarkably similar. The later version is from Buddy L, and Tonka made the earlier truck. Both are reminiscent of the ubiquitous Tonka trucks of the pre-war era, which were the inspiration for both models. The earlier example is an early Tonka truck, and the forerunner of a classic line.

Buddy L truck models went through several stages of improvement in the 1930s to make them more realistic to appeal to a sophisticated generation of toy buyers. This strategy worked and Buddy L became the leading American manufacturer of pressed steel toys in the decades up to World War II, with a reputation for producing large, high quality, pressed metal toys. When war broke out, the unavailability of steel for non-essential production meant Buddy L was forced to make a completely new range of wooden cars and trucks. They returned to more conventional materials after the war, but by that time—like many other toy manufacturers—they were using more plastic in their toy lines. However, it is pressed steel toys like these trucks that appeal to collectors and toy lovers the world over. These examples are un-restored, but it is possible to buy new transfers and decals, fenders, and headlights to replace Buddy L parts that are worn or missing.

The paintwork on this later example is mostly unscathed.

The metal hubs are fitted with deep tread rubber tires.

Above: The earlier truck (above) has a metal front grille, while that on the later one (below left) is white plastic.

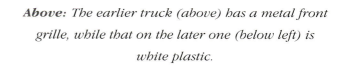

Above: Replacement Buddy L transfers are now available, but this one looks as if it is in pretty good condition.

TONKA AERIAL LOADER

Tonka made this magnificent aerial sand loader set (# 992) around 1955. It consists of several pieces that fit together to make a single, functional toy. The sand-loading crane itself runs on solid metal wheels along parallel tracks, which take it to drop its load into a frame-mounted sand hopper. The crane is painted red with a gray roof panel, solid metal wheels, and an opening for the "operator" to look out of. The bright metal crane bucket is attached with a clever system of pulleys, and can be raised and lowered as required.

The red metal hopper also runs along a lower set of parallel tracks, so that it can be positioned over the Tonka tipper truck that is waiting to carry a full load of sand onto a construction site. The unpainted "aerial loader" frame has rubber tipped feet. The post-World War II years saw a boom in the production of many different construction toys, produced by a variety of toy manufacturers. Their appearance reflected the building boom that was taking place in the 1950s, and demonstrated how children's toys can act as a

Below: The sand-loading crane runs on solid metal wheels on the top of the frame.

The Tonka dumpster was not part of the original set.

The hubs of the crane's solid wheels were originally painted red.

A pinned wheel is part of the sophisticated pulley arrangement.

***Left:** The decals and transfers on this toy have survived quite well.*

barometer of events in the adult world. The Tonka dumpster truck has some later attributes, such as a clear plastic windscreen and rubber tires on its solid metal wheels. This sophisticated set would have been a great opportunity to use a whole collection of other Tonka hardware.

EARLY TONKA TRUCK

The early Tonka truck featured on the previous pages being used with the aerial sand loader is shown in greater detail here. Its fairly rough appearance opens up an interesting subject that affects all classic toy collectors: condition. When buying toys at auction, or thumbing through works of reference, two condition guides are in general use: the alphanumeric condition guide, and the initial letter condition guide. Both use a letter/number shorthand to give an instant impression of a toy's condition. The very best condition that can be ascribed to a toy is "Mint" or "just like new." This refers to a brand new toy that has not been played with, and is still in its original packaging. Toys of this caliber are awarded the letter "M" or the alphanumeric code "C10." A toy in average condition might be described as "EX" (excellent), VG (very good), or "C8." In both cases, it would have minimal wear, be clean and well cared for, but would carry some evidence of having been played with. A toy in really poor condition might be described as "P" (poor) or "C5–C1" (useful for spare parts only). Our truck could fairly be defined as "G" (good) or "C7." It has seen heavy play, has some rust and is missing minor parts, and may be in need of some repair.

Right: The fairly rough condition of this early Tonka truck bears witness to the fact that it has been played with extensively. Many collectors have no problem with this level of condition.

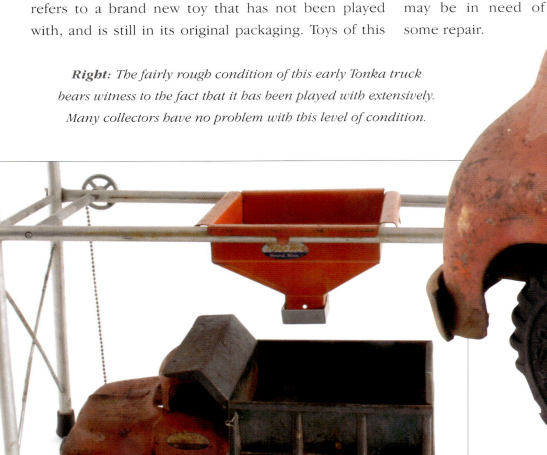

Many collectors prefer to see toys in their original paintwork, however worn, rather than having a shiny new livery.

MARX WIND-UP STEAMROLLER

This early Marx steamroller has been repainted in its current red and green livery. Although it is quite simply made it is certainly very charming and looks like it would have great play value, even though the simple corrugated metal roof has very sharp edges. The original key has survived and the mechanism is in full working order—a simple on/off lever located at the back in the "driver's" position operates the toy. The solid roller and back wheels give an authentic impression of weightiness, while the front smokestack looks as though it should be billowing with vapor.

Louis Marx and Company was founded in 1919 in New York, and their classic metal toys are some of the most sought after by collectors. The company's founder, Louis Marx, was born in Brooklyn in 1896. At the age of sixteen, he started his career in toys by working for the prestigious F.J. Strauss Company—Strauss made a wide variety of playthings for the Abraham and Strauss department stores. Filled with energy and enthusiasm for the toy business, Louis became the manager of the company by the time he was twenty, but soon decided to venture out on his own.

Above: *This view of the steamroller in profile shows the thin metal roof to advantage.*

The steamroller is equipped with two solid metal wheels at the back.

This is the original metal key—the steamroller is fully functional.

WYANDOTTE STEAM SHOVEL

This mounted digging machine was made by Wyandotte around 1952 but its transfers and decals are in excellent condition. The Wyandotte logo is clearly visible, and the toy's other decals proclaim the model to be from the "Sturdy Construction Company," and to be a "Diesel" model. The sides of the crane cab are decaled with a false "open" door that shows the operative hard at work in his overalls and cap. The graphics are in the popular red, gray, and navy color combination. This U.S.A.-made toy is a working model, and the rubber tires and wind-up boom add a degree of realism. It has a high quality, sturdy construction that has withstood the rigors of play over the years. Wyandotte, also known as the All Metal Products Company, was founded in the fall of 1921 in Michigan. From its inception, the company emphasized the use of mass production techniques and cheap raw materials, which included recycled scrap metal from the auto industry, and enabled Wyandotte to offer affordable and well-made toys to the market. They first began to produce pressed metal transport toys in the 1930s.

Below: This complete view of the steam shovel shows the red and blue digging arm in profile.

This handle cranks the
wind-up boom.

DIESEL

Above: *The charming decals are in excellent condition, and have withstood the test of time.*

STRUCTO STEAM SHOVEL

This is an early Structo steam shovel with track front and quad wheels and its brilliantly detailed steam shovel features a chain wind-up mechanism. The colorful yellow, navy, and black steam shovel itself was fully operational and came complete with a steam firebox positioned at the back of the model. The toy dates from the 1920s or 1930s, and was originally sold for the modest price of between $1.35 and $1.75, but is worth considerably more now. Three partners, Louis and Edward Strohacker and C. C. Thompson, founded the Structo Manufacturing Company in Freeport, Illinois in 1908. Originally, Structo produced ready-build construction kit auto toys and erector construction kits. The company are still in business today.

Left: The steam shovel's double front wheels are fitted with a realistic-looking articulated track.

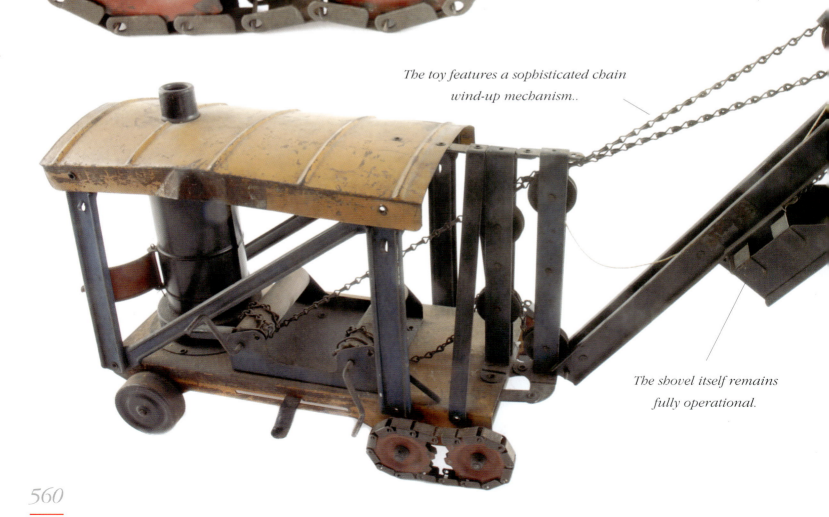

The toy features a sophisticated chain wind-up mechanism..

The shovel itself remains fully operational.

Right: This back view of
the steam shovel shows an
opening hatch to the firebox.

MACK STEAM SHOVEL TRUCK

This early Mack steam shovel truck was made by Chein Hercules, and is now a very rare toy indeed. The graphics on its wheels read "35 x 6 Made in USA." The toy was constructed with a winding mechanism to work the fully operational steam shovel—a crank handle is clearly visible; turning this raises or lowers the shovel.

J. Chein and Company was in production between 1903 and 1979, first based in New York City and then in Harrison, New Jersey. The company founder, Julius Chein, started out with a metal-stamping machine in a New York City loft and his first products were small tin prizes distributed in Cracker Jack boxes, and modest tin toys destined for five and dime stores. The company also made advertising tins, which have become hugely collectible—but even more desirable are Chein's early tin toys and tin banks. Much of the company's success was due to Julius Chein's decision to lithograph his toys. The company's last president, Robert Beckleman, said that Chein had the idea from a friend who worked for the American Can Company and persuaded Chein that lithography would look better on his toys than paint.

The robust truck has survived in perfect working order, but its paint finish has suffered.

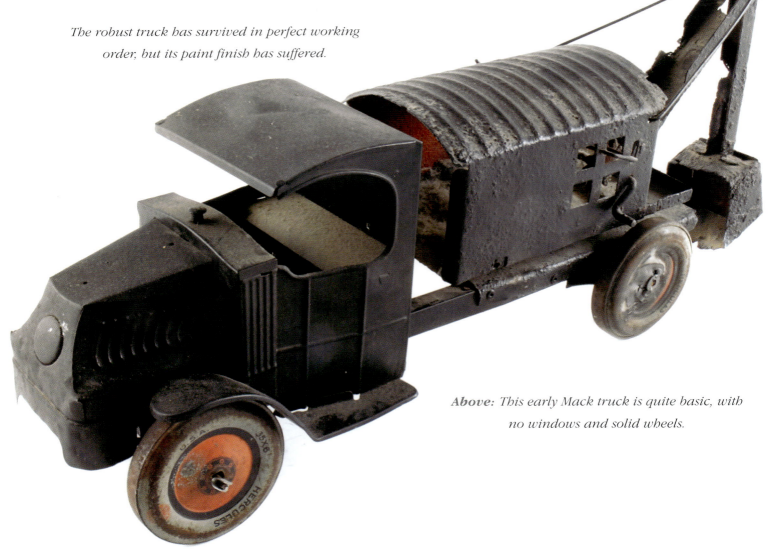

Above: This early Mack truck is quite basic, with no windows and solid wheels.

*The handle cranks the steam shovel,
which still works fine.*

*The wheel graphics are still legible:
"35 x 6 Made in USA."*

CEMENT MIXERS

This line-up of cement mixers shows how popular this form of construction toy became in the 1960s. The one on the left is a cement mixer #620 model, made by Tonka between 1962 and 1963. It is 14 inches long and retains its original red and white paint finish. It is equipped with metal fenders, a clear plastic windshield, and three pairs of plastic-hubbed wheels fitted with whitewall tires. The plastic cement mixer itself rotates fully. Tonka is now owned by Hasbro, but the metal toys the company produced between 1947 and 1963 are generally considered to be its most

The plastic cement mixer on this model rotates fully.

Above: *Tonka trucks of this vintage (early 1960s) are now very collectible.*

collectible offerings. Coming from this era makes this cement mixer particularly desirable.

The model on the right was made by Structo, and also has its original red and white paintjob, complete with "Structo Ready Mix" decals. Like its Tonka companion, the Structo cement mixer also dates from the 1960s and since it is of a similarly robust construction it has survived equally well. Like the Tonka, the truck is equipped with a metal fender, clear plastic windshield, and whitewall tires. It also has a fully rotating plastic cement mixer. Structo made something of a specialty of construction toys, offering several different models, including dump trucks, sand loaders, dirt haulers, and front-end loaders. They produced these alongside a range of general transport toys that included car haulers, fire trucks, livestock trailers, and cattle trucks.

The clear plastic windshield of this truck is still in place.

The "Structo Ready Mix" decal has survived for over forty years.

Above right: *Structo specialized in sturdy construction toys like the one shown here.*

Both cement mixers sport smart whitewall tires.

KEYSTONE STEAMROLLER

This Keystone steamroller was made by the Keystone Manufacturing Company of Boston, Massachusetts, where it was awarded model number "60." The red and black painted toy is around 26 inches long and although its construction is quite basic, the toy has a certain simple charm. The heavy-looking roller

Above: The decal shows manufacturer and model number.

appears effective when it rolls along, but the corrugated iron, yellow-painted roof has a rather sharp-looking edge.

The Keystone Manufacturing Company was founded by two brothers, Ben and Isidore Marks, in 1911. They started out making human hair doll wigs and celluloid dolls, but gradually diversified into other playthings. Keystone went on to have great success with movie tie-in toys that celebrated artists such as Charlie Chaplin. They began to produce metal toys in 1925—their first metal truck was based on a Packard Motor Company model, produced under licence. It was extremely successful, and led to a substantial diversification into all kinds of metal toys, including fire trucks, steam shovels, trains, and dump trucks. Their large range soon started to rival even Buddy L, the pre-World War II market leader.

KEYSTONE
STEAM ROLLER-60

Above: *This model has all the charm of Keystone's early metal toys. It is beautifully made and has lasted well.*

The steamroller's solid wheels convey the weight and power of the original.

CEMENT MIXERS

Here are two views of two popular cement mixers, one from Tonka and the other from Structo. Tonka introduced their first cement mixer, #120, in 1960; this model, #620, was introduced in 1962. Although the two models are very similar, the later version is instantly recognizable by its whitewall tires. Even if the issue date of this toy was not known, it could be identified by the logo. The original oval Tonka emblem,

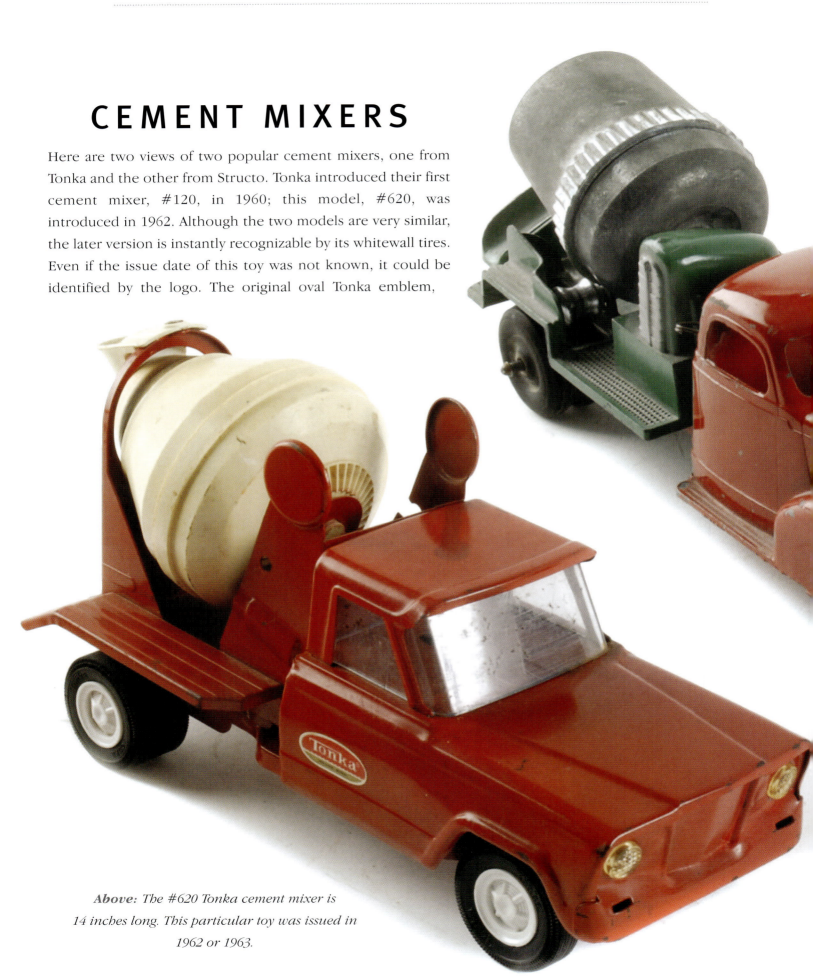

Above: *The #620 Tonka cement mixer is 14 inches long. This particular toy was issued in 1962 or 1963.*

introduced in 1947, was gold and blue with red script and white lettering and the Tonka brand name was written freeform, rather than in the typescript of later years. Originally, the words "Mound Metalcraft Inc. Mound, Minn." appeared in the bottom, blue part of the symbol. In 1956, although the original coloring and general appearance of the logo was retained, the wording in the bottom half was simplified to "Mound, Minn." In 1958, the top half of the oval was changed to white, but everything else remained the same. In 1962, Tonka

introduced a much more modern (but still oval) emblem. The original script lettering was changed to the cleaner, bolder typescript that Tonka uses to this day. The oval was now two thirds red (top), and one third gold (bottom), with the white Tonka emblem appearing on the red ground. The company used this logo from 1962 to 1973. Before 1970, "Mound, Minn." was written in black in the gold-colored area, but after 1970, this was altered to "U.S.A." A revised symbol appeared in 1974; it retained the oval shape and the red and white color scheme in the top part, but the lower area was now yellow instead of gold. In 1976, the oval became all red, and the lettering was reduced to just the Tonka logo itself, printed in white. As of 1978, the oval emblem was dropped altogether and the Tonka logo became red, designed into a simple white rectangle framed in yellow; this version is still in use today.

The other cement mixer comes from Structo, who are justifiably famous for their construction toys.

The Structo cement mixer has metal headlights.

The Structo has retained its metal bumper.

Both cement mixers are red and white.

TWO TRUCKS

These two models span nearly two decades in toy truck development. Buddy L manufactured the dark-colored army truck on the left in the 1940s. The truck originally had a canvas top, and was probably first retailed as part of a set of military vehicles. Army trucks were very popular in the 1930s, '40s, and '50s—many children who played with these toys must have had fathers in the armed services. Kingsbury and Keystone also manufactured army trucks and play sets during this time. Buddy L was founded by Fred

The Buddy L truck was part of the company's toy line-up in the 1940s.

The toy is in "VG" or "C8" condition.

Right: *The Buddy L army logo appeared on a whole range of military toys in this decade.*

Lundahl in the early 1920s, and named after his son, Buddy. The prototype toys he made for his son were so popular that Fred realized they had a great future. As his business grew, Fred kept a copy of almost every toy he manufactured. In the 1960s, this collection of over 1,000 Buddy L models was packed away and archived in a New Jersey warehouse and in 2001 they were sold at public auction. Almost all the toys were in mint condition, and in their original boxes. The highest price realized was over $40,000 for a coach bus from the late 1920s.

Structo made the metallic green dumper truck on the right, circa 1961. The company was well known for its live action steel trucks and road building toys. Structo Stamped Steel was founded in 1908, and taken over by an American toy company, Ertl, in 1974.

This Structo dumper truck has typical 1960's styling, and a very contemporary paint finish.

MARX AND WYANDOTTE TRUCKS

This tipper dump truck was made by Wyandotte, circa 1930. It has retained its original red and blue paint, and measures 20 inches in length. By 1929, Wyandotte was the world's largest manufacturer of toy guns, but had decided to reinvent their output and in the 1930s, they diversified into doll buggies, musical toys, games, wagons, plus a wide range of cars, trucks, and planes. Marx manufactured the red and blue builder's truck on the left. Louis Marx founded his toy company, Louis Marx and Company, in 1919, and set up his office at 200 Fifth Avenue in New York City. He began the business with no resources: no capital, machinery, products,

Below: Both of these blue and red trucks were built by highly successful American toy makers, who based their success on value for money.

The Wyandotte truck has rather more streamlined styling.

patents, or customers. Despite this, he immediately began to place orders for his toys with various manufacturers. His brother David joined him in the business in the early 1920s, and the two made a formidable team. Louis designed and marketed the toys, while David ran the operation. Between them, they grew the business into the world's largest toy manufacturer, basing their success on the maxim, "Give the customer more toy for less money."

HUBLEY BELL TELEPHONE TRUCKS

The Kiddietoy Division of the Hubley Manufacturing Company issued these two Bell Telephone trucks in the 1950s. They are fabricated from cast metal, with rubber tires, and the larger truck has dual wheels at the back and a wind-up mechanism for setting telephone poles. John E. Hubley established the company in 1894, in Lancaster Pennsylvania. They began by making equipment for electric toy trains, but diversified into toy autos in the 1930s. Hubley's slogan was "They're different."

Right: The original Bell Telephone Company was founded in 1878 by Alexander Graham Bell's father-in-law, Gardiner Greene Hubbard.

"Ma Bell" would have been proud of these well-maintained vehicles.

JAPANESE FORKLIFT

This forklift model "S1002" was made in Japan, and is a fully operational, battery-powered toy. This red, black, and silver model has a green, yellow, and black plaid-lithographed seat, while the pressed metal steering wheel and driver's footrest are painted black. It came equipped with a working fork-raising mechanism: a moveable gate suspended from a turning chain operates the forklift. The lifting mechanism itself is connected to a larger lever at the front of the vehicle, which rotates the chain. A lever positioned at the "driver's" left turns the toy on and off, engaging the battery power. The cast metal wheels are fitted with rubber tires. Originally inexpensive, imported Japanese *buriki* (tin plate) toys of this quality are now considered highly collectible and are worth quite a lot of money if they are in good condition.

Below: The forklift is equipped with a working fork-raising mechanism, operated by a moveable gate suspended from a turning chain.

The pressed metal wheels of the toy are fitted with rubber tires.

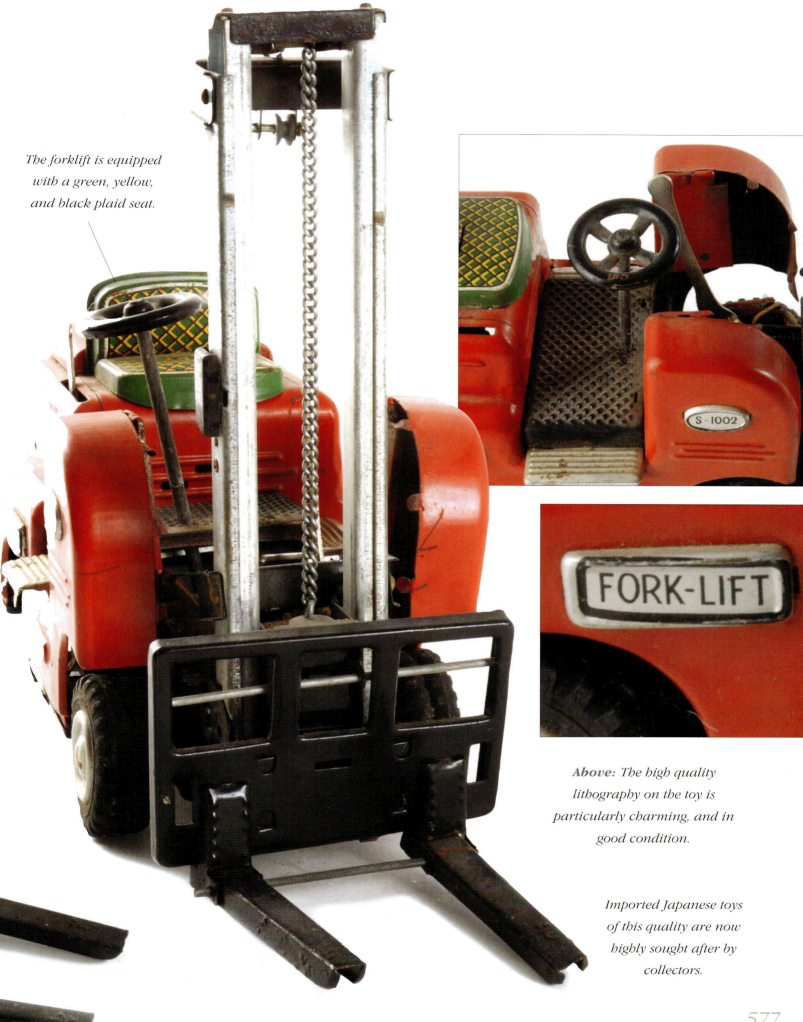

The forklift is equipped with a green, yellow, and black plaid seat.

S-1002

FORK-LIFT

Above: The high quality lithography on the toy is particularly charming, and in good condition.

Imported Japanese toys of this quality are now highly sought after by collectors.

BUDDY L TRUCK

This Buddy L wrecking truck is equipped with working headlights and its metal wheels are fitted with rubber tires. The truck dates from the 1930s, and is most probably a Buddy L Junior model. Fred Lundhal's first-ever toy was a miniature truck, which he based on an International Harvester model. Constructed in 1921, it was made from 18 and 20 gauge steel that he recycled from his company's scrap metal pile. By 1925, his range of toys had expanded to twenty items and as the decade wore on, Lundhal added more features, and greater realism to his models. He introduced the Junior line of trucks in 1930.

The Junior truck's bright blue paintwork has survived well.

Left: Buddy L was the pre-World War II market leader in pressed steel toys.

Right: Replacement decals can be sourced for Buddy L models.

LUMAR TRUCK

This red and gray Lumar dump truck was made by Marx, in around 1940. The decal on the doors reads "Lumar Contractors GVW 18,000, 11.00 x 20." Despite the Great Depression of the 1930s, Marx had thrived and built three new plants during this period, so by the late 1940s they were the world's biggest toy manufacturer.

The bumpers and headlights are pressed metal.

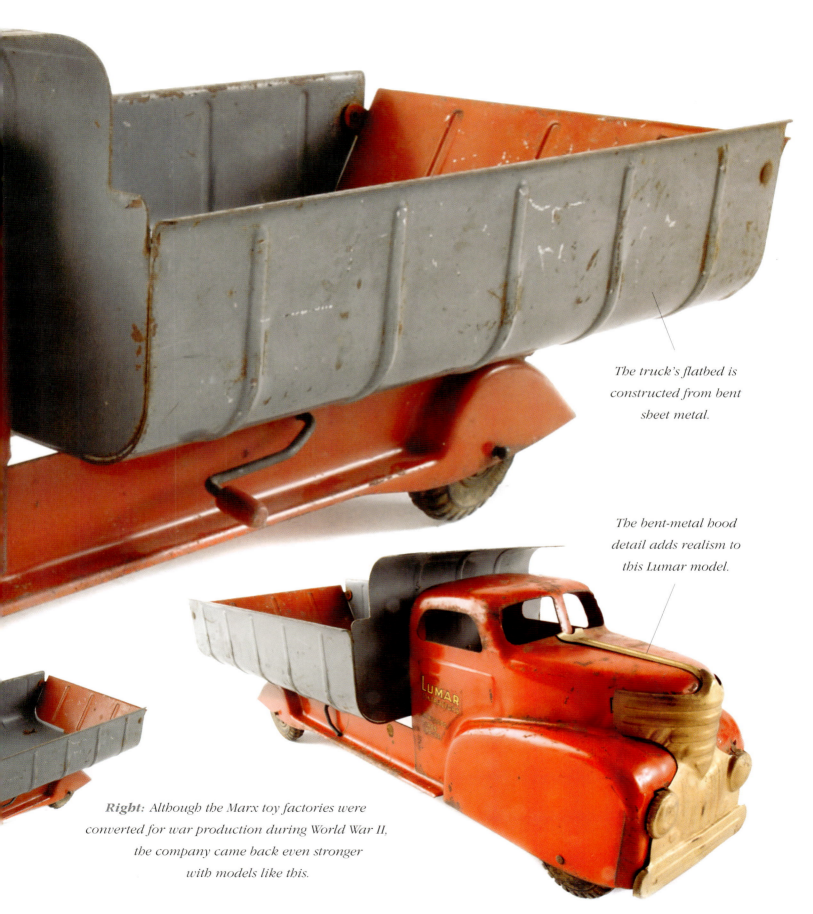

The truck's flatbed is constructed from bent sheet metal.

The bent-metal hood detail adds realism to this Lumar model.

Right: Although the Marx toy factories were converted for war production during World War II, the company came back even stronger with models like this.

ROBERTS AND STRUCTO TRUCKS

The front-end loader on the right was produced by Roberts in the 1940s. Roberts made several classic toys, including the "Big Toy" Super Stock Tractor, the litho-printed Magno Crane, and toy guns such as their Winchester Model 70. This front-end loader has classic red and yellow paintwork, typical of the period.

The tipper dump truck on the right is from the same era, but was manufactured by The Structo Manufacturing Company, established in 1908. It also has a red and yellow paintwork, with a logo on the doors. This six wheeler has duals on the back and is in fairly good condition, being complete with all six hubs, headlights, front bumper, hood, and tires—although it looks like the original tailgate is missing.

The scoop pulls over the cab to rest flat.

The scoop shown in the working position.

The Structo truck is in reasonable condition, but is missing some parts.

Above: *The axles have remained straight, and the flatbed turns on a pivot attached to the cab.*

The truck has a surviving logo on each door.

FARM SUPPLIES TRUCK AND KEYSTONE TIPPER

The yellow and blue farm supplies truck on the left was made by Buddy L in the 1940s. It is equipped with a manual dump.

The green and red tipper truck on the right was manufactured by Keystone, in around 1937 and came with working lights.

Above: This American-made Buddy L Farm Truck is constructed from pressed steel.

The Keystone Manufacturing Company developed from a partnership between two brothers, Ben and Isidore Marks, who founded the Marks Brothers Company in 1911. Originally, the company produced doll wigs and celluloid doll heads, but soon branched out into movie-making equipment. This led to the purchase of their rival company, the Pictograph Company of Manchester, New Hampshire in 1924. The merged companies were renamed the Keystone Manufacturing Company, and relocated to Boston, Massachusetts. Although Keystone continued to manufacture motion-picture toys, they saw the success other toy companies were having with model trucks and autos and added this line in 1925, basing their first models on Packard automobiles. They were built from 22-gauge steel, and well equipped with nickel hubcaps and radiator caps, see-through celluloid windshields, front cranks, headlamps, active steering, and (for an extra 50 cents) rubber tires.

This yellow truck has a manual dump.

Keystone's Packard models were so successful that they began to rival the achievements of market leader Buddy L.

FARM SUPPLIES

This later Keystone truck is fitted with rubber tires.

Above: *Although excellent products like this tipper truck were very popular with the public, Keystone went out of business in 1957.*

LAZY DAYS FARM TRUCK

The Lumar division of Louis Marx and Company manufactured this vintage tin truck, which is around 5 inches high and 17 inches long. Both cab and trailer are heavily lithographed with various details, including headlights on the cab, wooden slats on the trailer, and the "Lazy Day Farms Registered Stock" poster. This form of lithographed tin plate is inexpensive to produce, and fitted the Marx company ethos of providing good toys at competitive prices. "Give the customer more toy for their money" and "Quality is not negotiable" were the maxims on which Louis Marx had founded his business. The company became increasingly successful, and by 1921 they had taken over the manufacture of their own toys. Their high quality and modest prices enabled them to survive the ravages of the Depression, and they came back even stronger after World War II—when production resumed, Marks became the world's largest toy manufacturer and had a hugely diverse offering, including dollhouses, model cars and trucks, trains, toy guns, ride-on toys, and play sets. The 1950s was the Golden Era of the company's history—by 1955,

The "Lazy Day Farms Registered Stock" poster is lithographed.

Marx was manufacturing over 20 per cent of all the toys sold in the world. They distributed their products in Britain between 1937 and 1967 and also distributed toys made by foreign companies, including those made by Distler in Germany. The company's continued success led to the opening of more factories— they manufactured in ten countries, including Japan, where there was a tradition of making *buriki* or tin plate toys.

LAZY DAY FARMS

REGISTERED STOCK

TIRES 11.00 x 20
G.V.W. 42,000

The truck's tires are rated "11.00
x 20. GVW 42,000."

Above: Inexpensive but attractively designed toys
like this truck had enabled Marx to survive the
economic hard times of the Great Depression, and
go on to greater success.

587

KEYSTONE DUMP TRUCK

This black, pressed steel Keystone commercial dump truck has a crank start and is fitted with red and silver wheels. The truck measures approximately 6 inches high and 19 inches long and was probably manufactured by the company in the 1930s. Keystone's original toy truck, based on full-size Packard model, was launched in 1925 and so sturdy was its construction that a Keystone advertising campaign boasted that a 200-pound man could stand on the toy without damaging it. The company's reputation, sales, and market share all grew, and Keystone became a strong competitor for its rivals, including Buddy L. This popularity helped the company to survive the difficult trading conditions in the 1930s. Even during these hard times, the company's designers continued to evolve new products, including the "Siren Riding Toy" in 1934, and the "Ride 'Em Mail Plane" in 1936—the latter was affordably priced at $2.

This truck was built in Keystone's first decade as a manufacturer of toy vehicles.

A hand-operated lifting mechanism tips the flatbed.

Above: Considering the age of the toy, it is in reasonable condition.

The truck has a detailed radiator cap.

The crank handle actually turns.

Right: The Keystone Dump Truck logo appears on the side of the flatbed. It shows some wear, consistent with rigorous play.

KEYSTONE DUMP TRUCK

TURNER DUMP TRUCK

This Turner dump truck measures 26 inches in length. It has a red, yellow, and green paintwork, and its logos read "Copyright J. C. T. Company," "Turner Made in U.S.A.." The pictorial logo consists of a cheerful red-haired boy, who is sporting a checkerboard cap. The truck has rubber tires fitted to its metal hubs, and the headlights, hood ornament, and radiator grille are made from a single, separate piece of molded bright steel. A turning handle lifts the back of the truck to dump the contents. The John C. Turner Company, which was based in Wapakoneta, Ohio, constructed the toy in the 1930s.

John Turner founded the company that bears his name in 1915, and it was to survive both the Great Depression of the 1930s and World War II, until its

Right: The truck sports a logo on the cab doors of a red-haired boy wearing a checkerboard cap.

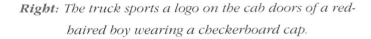

The hood is adorned with a pressed metal ornament.

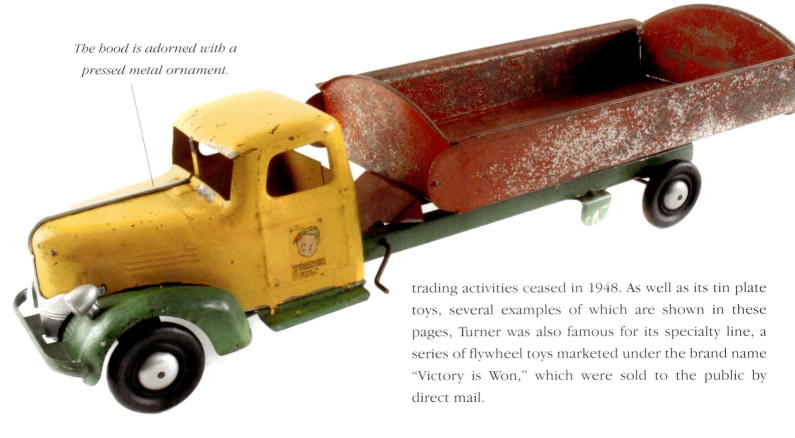

trading activities ceased in 1948. As well as its tin plate toys, several examples of which are shown in these pages, Turner was also famous for its specialty line, a series of flywheel toys marketed under the brand name "Victory is Won," which were sold to the public by direct mail.

Above: A hand-operated turning handle lifts the
back of the truck to dump the contents.

MARX HYDRAULIC DUMP TRUCK

Complete with its original black and créme paintwork, this truck is in very good condition. The logo on the truck door is completely accurate, this really is a "Hydraulic Dump" truck, made by Marx in the 1940s. The hydraulic tipping feature must have been really exciting to its original owner, giving the model an enhanced sense of realism. As well as manufacturing basic tin toys Louis Marx and Company always tried to give the customer extra features; sometimes their toys were wind-up, or had a special moving part, as this one does. The company was also good at making basic ideas fly—Marx reintroduced the yo-yo in 1928, and the toy sold well, even during the Depression years of the 1930s.

Above: The tipping back on this 1940s Marx truck is operated by a hydraulic mechanism driven by a crank handle.

Left: The "Hydraulic Dump" logo is completely accurate.

The vintage truck's paint is in good condition.

By the 1940s, rubber tires were a standard feature on quality toy vehicles.

Above: With the truck back in the "tipped" position, there is a clear view of the hydraulic assembly.

593

MARX SAND AND GRAVEL TRUCKS

Marx made these red and blue sand and gravel trucks, which also came fitted with a front scoop. They measure 11 inches in length without the scoop, and 16 inches with the scoop in place. The truck backs are printed tin plate and the cabs are molded plastic—this combination of different materials surely reflects the company's primary objective: to offer good toys at great prices. By the 1950s, Marx was the world's biggest manufacturer of toys, with sales in excess of $30 million, and 5,000 different products on offer. Louis Marx even made the cover of *Time Magazine* on December 12, 1955. In the accompanying article, he spoke about his tiny advertising budget of just $312—he was proud that his toys sold due to the legendary combination of Marx value and quality, and not because of advertising hype.

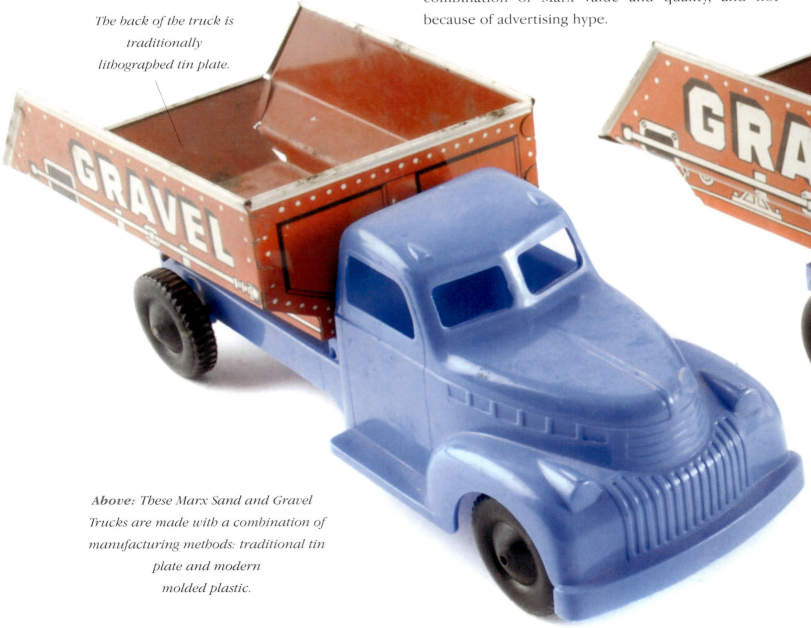

The back of the truck is traditionally lithographed tin plate.

Above: *These Marx Sand and Gravel Trucks are made with a combination of manufacturing methods: traditional tin plate and modern molded plastic.*

The trucks were just two of over 5,000 Marx products.

The axels are fitted with metal hubs and rubber tires.

Above: *This model also came with a front scoop, which extended its length to 16 inches.*

The high quality plastic molding shows precise details.

The plastic itself is colored blue.

595

TURNER TRUCK WITH BOWLING PINS

This Turner dump truck was manufactured in the early 1930s, and measures 15½ inches in length. It has rubber tires fitted to its red-painted metal wheels, and an open cab complete with a turn-able tin steering wheel. The cab is equipped with a curved metal running board on each side and the truck's semi-open back contains a collection of colored wooden bowling balls and pins. This is a friction flywheel toy, which was a very popular concept on model vehicles in the early 1930s. Despite its rather "played with" condition, it is a rare and collectible toy that is worth several hundred dollars to a serious toy collector. John Turner founded the John C. Turner toy manufacturing company in 1915, in Wapakoneta, Ohio. The town grew up on the trade route between Cincinnati and Detroit, and producing many other things apart from toys.

Despite its worn condition, this early Turner dump truck is highly collectible.

Above: *The truck very much reflects the real truck styling of the early 1930s, with its curving running boards, thin tires, and side-opening hood.*

597

SON-NY PARCEL POST VAN

SON-NY was the brand name for a range of mid-sized (up to 24 inches in length) motor toys, manufactured by The Dayton Toy and Specialty Company. The particular model shown here, the SON-NY parcel post van, is a very rare piece indeed and—despite its vintage condition—would command a value running into thousands of dollars on the collectors' market. It is 24 inches in length, and dates from the 1920s.

David P. Clarke founded the Dayton Toy and Specialty Company in Dayton, Ohio in 1909. He had previously established another toy company, D. P. Clarke, also of Dayton, in 1898; this company was re-

The back of the van has latticed sides.

Left: *The van has the large, thin wheels of full-sized vehicles of the 1920s.*

launched as the Schieble Toy and Novelty Company in 1909. Clarke's new venture specialized in pressed steel friction toys, marketed under the brand name SON-NY. In 1926, Clarke patented the "Gyro," which was a horizontal flywheel. The Dayton Toy and Specialty Company ceased trading in 1935, put out of business by the extremely difficult trading conditions of the Great Depression.

The roof is curved steel plate.

Despite its finish, the SON-NY van is highly collectible.

Right: *An interesting view of the pressed steel hood, radiator cap, and steering wheel.*

KEYSTONE DUMP TRUCK WITH SACKS

This green and tan pressed steel dump truck was made by Keystone and measures 26½ inches in length. It has a C-cab and a manual dump and is a valuable and highly collectible item. At first, Keystone manufactured toy motion picture machines (the Keystone Moviegraph), and produced children's comedy films. Their first venture into manufacturing pressed steel model vehicles was under license from Packard, making small versions of the company's production trucks—some of these were large enough to ride on.

Fierce competition with their main competitor, Buddy L, led Keystone to add many interesting refinements to their toy vehicles. These included nickel-plated hubcaps and radiator caps, engine cranks, transparent celluloid windshields, working headlamps, and rubber tires. Keystone trucks were also equipped with active steering and signal arms for "stop" and "go." Post-World War II, most of Keystone's toy manufacturing output was based on tools and dies that the company had acquired from the defunct Kingsbury toy division.

This Keystone dump truck is hauling a load of sacks.

BUDDY L RAILWAY EXPRESS

This Buddy L railway express was manufactured between 1926 and 1931 and has a black paint finish with large red wheels. The truck has an open cab, and the back has latticed steel sides. This toy is now a highly desirable collectors' item and could sell for several thousand dollars. It is remarkably similar in appearance to the SON-NY parcel post van (see page 598), and is of the same vintage. It has very similar curved running boards, an almost identical cab, steering wheel assembly, and shaped hood—the major visible difference is the contrast colored radiator grille and cap. The Railway

Express is an early Buddy L model. The company's first toy product, a pressed steel pick-up truck, had been launched only a few years earlier in 1921, but by the mid 1920s the Buddy L fleet had expanded to over thirty model vehicles, concentrating on cranes and other construction toys.

Right: This Buddy L railway express was one of a small fleet of vehicles the company had developed by the mid 1920s.

The van's paintwork has survived extremely well.

BUDDY L PULL TRUCK WITH DURYEAS' BOX

Buddy L manufactured this unusual pull truck with a conversation box in the 1930s. Along the side of the box is stenciled the words: "Duryeas'. Satin Gloss Starch Manufacturing by the National Starch Manufacturing. Glen Cove, Long Island. Since 1906."

The unique styling of the truck and box, together with the wooden truck bed, make this 19-inch long toy valuable and highly collectible. The National Starch Manufacturing Company was a real-life concern, which started business on Long Island in the late 1800s. It is mentioned in local records as planning to build a factory in the 1890s, and National Starch went on to become a major local employer. Duryeas' was the brand name of their premium starch; contemporary advertisements for it survive in publications such as *Lippincott's Monthly Magazine*. National Starch still survives today.

The charming "Duryeas' Satin Gloss Starch" logo.

Below: *The profile view of this extremely interesting and highly collectible Buddy L model.*

Above: *The front view of the truck shows the detail of the radiator grille and cap, the curvaceous running boards, and the narrow profile wheels.*

KEYSTONE U.S. MAIL TRUCK

This U.S. mail truck #45 was made by Keystone and is painted gold and black with red wheels. It is 26 inches in length and has a covered body with heavy grille work panels on the sides, ornamented with a "U.S. Mail" logo toward the front. The rear doors are fitted with a substantial lock and key and each truck was originally sold with its own set of mailbags, solid rubber balloon tires, and nickel-plated hubcaps. The headlamps are also finished in nickel, with their own lenses. The Keystone U.S. mail truck was also available in an alternative colorway of U.S. Government olive drab green.

The truck is painted in gold and black with red wheels.

Below: The "U.S. Mail" logo increased the truck's realistic play value.

Opposite: The truck's semi-open body is covered with heavy grille work. The steering wheel turns.

TWO BUDDY L WRECKING TRUCKS

These white and turquoise Buddy L wrecking trucks were made in the mid-twentieth century. The truck on the right is the "Fix My Flat Blue Wrecker Truck" from the 1960s, which was offered for sale in several different paint jobs. It is made from pressed steel, and has a working towing mechanism fitted to the back of the truck. A special logo also appears on the back, which reads: "Fix My Flat with Poly Tools." The truck is open-backed, and has a plastic light on the roof of the cab. Originally, it had clear

This early truck has a functional towing mechanism.

A crank handle winds the towrope onto the mechanism.

The Buddy L decal has survived in very good shape.

Above: The 1960s wrecker has a more complicated towing mechanism. The turquoise paint is in fine condition.

plastic windows. The truck has a separate, metal front fender. Although early Buddy L toys are the most desirable, toys from the 1960s are also highly collectible. Early toys were larger than the later models, and many were sturdy enough to ride—later toys were around half the size. The company offered a wide range of vehicles, including construction models, and Ford-based cars and trucks. Buddy L specialized in auto toys with moving parts, some of which were very elaborate, including working hydraulics. Before Fred Lundahl made toy vehicles from steel, most were constructed from wood or cast iron.

TWO WRECKING TRUCKS

These two wrecking trucks are of widely different vintages. The Japanese wrecker below left is made from tin, and painted in blue, red, yellow, and white. The great graphics add interest to this fascinating piece, which dates from the 1940s.

The Nylint wrecker, pictured right and below right, is made from plastic and metal, and dates from the 1990s. Bernard Klint of Rockford, Illinois founded Nylint Tool and Manufacturing in 1937. His uncle, David Nyberg, supplied his working capital and their names combined to form Nylint. They started to make toys in 1946.

Right: This Nylint wrecking truck

The Nylint decals are in virtually mint condition.

Japanese tin toys of this type are known as buriki.

Above: *Nylint referred to its first years in toy production as its "Wind-up Era."*

The towing assembly works with a crank handle, just like the earlier toy.

METALCRAFT HEINZ DELIVERY TRUCK

This Metalcraft Heinz delivery truck dates from around 1932. Its decals mention several of Heinz's original 57 varieties, including backed beans, bottled vinegar, and rice flakes. Metalcraft was based in St. Louis, Missouri, between 1920 and 1937, and the company originally produced playground equipment, including their "teeter-totters." They also made an extensive line of pressed-steel trucks, but

Left: Henry J. Heinz thought of the "57 Varieties" slogan in 1892, while riding the New York Railway.

This Metalcraft truck is simply made from pressed steel. Its decals make it special.

one of their greatest successes occurred when they acquired the rights to produce a pressed-metal airplane based on Lingburgh's *Spirit of St. Louis*, millions of which were sold. The company also produced a line of toy truck premiums. which were endorsed by various famous brands, which were known as their "Business Leaders," and this Heinz model is from this series.

Above: This truck came from Metalcraft's successful "Business Leaders" line, which celebrated the success of many famous American brands.

This early pressed-steel truck is equipped with rubber tires.

BUDDY L WILD ANIMAL CIRCUS ON WHEELS

This Buddy L "Wild Animal Circus" on wheels dates from the 1950s and is a tractor and trailer type truck assembly. Although the circus theme was quite unusual for Buddy L, it wasn't unique—they also produced a truck-mounted carousel on wheels. Their normal range concentrated on transport toys with more "adult" themes: the army, construction, farming, the fire service, and road haulage. The "Wild Animal Circus" truck stayed on Buddy L's product listing for several years. A later, white-painted version had the same three doors, marked Tony, Leo, and Jumbo. This was also made in metal and had active steering, but the cage also had a clear plastic top. Other manufacturers brought out circus themed models, including Kenton, who produced the "Overland Circus Bear Wagon". Buddy L toys were always sold on their quality and longevity, and they described their toys as being "guaranteed indestructible." The three hundred pound Buddy is reputed to have stood on every truck that came off the company's production line to test its durability. It was this care for quality that enabled Buddy L to dominate the pressed steel market. Sadly, pre-World War II metal drives meant many early Buddy L toys were melted down to support the war effort.

Below: Buddy L's concern for quality was preserved into its modern era of toy production. "Buddy L toys are the toughest toys on wheels."

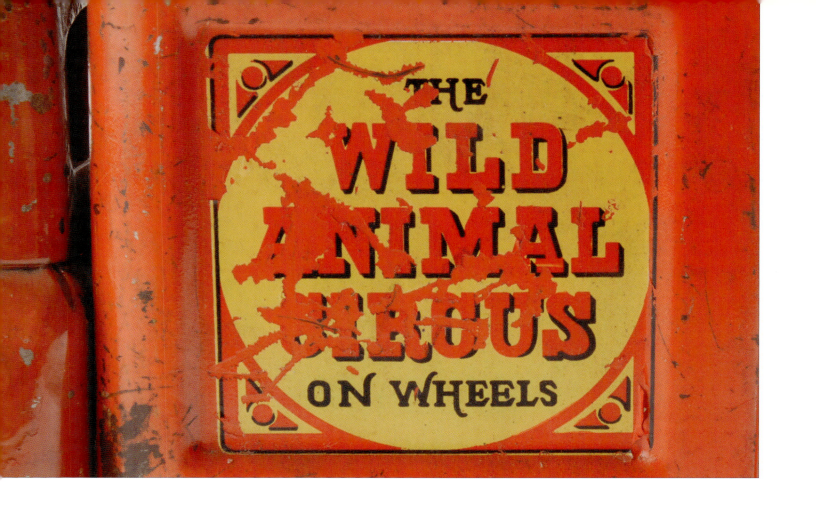

Right: *The truck has a canvas cover, mounted on a curved steel frame.*

STEELCRAFT MACK ARMY TRUCK

This highly collectible Steelcraft Mack army truck dates from the 1920s, and is around 26 inches in length. Steelcraft was a brand name of Murray, Ohio, originally a manufacturer of pressed steel parts for the automotive industry. In 1924 the company moved to a new factory located on 152nd Street, Cleveland, Ohio, where they began to manufacture pedal cars (for which they became particularly well known), and a range of other pressed steel toys. They continued to produce pressed steel goods at this site until the end of World War II.

The pressed steel molding is quite detailed.

This is now a highly valuable and collectible model, despite its condition.

Above: *The truck carries many of the details of full-size vehicles of this era, including the narrow-profile tires and running boards.*

615

NYLINT MOBILE HOME

This Nylint mobile home dates from circa 1964. The truck pulls a dual wheel trailer, and the whole assembly is around 30 inches in length. The piece has charming decals, including the "Mobile Home" decal on the trailer, and the "#6600 Nylint Mobile Home" decal on the truck. The model was produced during a cross-over period in Nylint's highly documented history between its "Ford Motor Company Era" and its "Mod Styling Era." In this latter phase, Nylint (originally Ny-Lint) removed the Ford logos from its pressed steel vehicles, but they remained heavily influenced by generic Ford styling. Like this mobile home toy, Nylint tended to give its models several action features that greatly enhanced their play value. Nylint finally filed for bankruptcy in 2001.

Below: During the 1950s and 1960s, Nylint's toys were often faithful reproductions of production vehicles.

Nylint are considered to be one of the best-ever American toy manufacturers.

Above: *The charming decal on the side of the trailer.*

NYLINT TRUCK AND TRAILER

This light blue and white Nylint truck and trailer set was manufactured in the early 1960s and comes from Nylint's Econoline range of toys, which were based on the Ford body of the same name. Although these toy trucks were remarkably similar to the real thing, many people actually preferred Nylint's styling to Ford's. Econoline was an extremely popular line of model vehicles that the Nylint company offered from 1962 to 1972. Early models have a Ford decal, but later this was replaced with an embossed and painted logo. On this

Below: *This Nylint truck came from their Econoline range.*

This is a later addition to the series. The generic Ford styling has been retained, but the logo has gone.

model, "Nylint" has replaced the Ford brand. The range included several variants, including an identical truck to this one but without the stake bed, and a fully covered-in model.

Right: This is a 1960s version of the Nylint logo. The company was originally called Ny-Lint.

This stake bed truck came with a trailer.

The trailer is hitched to the truck.

This color scheme is typical of the 1960s.

619

THREE JAPANESE TRAILERS

These three trailers were made in Japan, probably in the 1960s—such *buriki* toys were a popular import. The word *buriki* means "tin plate" in Japanese; it is derived from the Dutch word *blik*, which is short for *blikken speelgoed*, meaning "tinned iron." Until the 1870s, most tin imported into Japan was used to make oil cans, but Japanese manufacturers soon realized how popular imported tin plate toys had become, and began to produce their own. While the *blechspielzeug* toys of the German manufacturers were highly artistic, the Japanese toy manufacturers concentrated on making more conventional models, including rattles and toy rickshaws. Initially, the trade in Japanese toys was sluggish, but the introduction of printed tin plate, and clockwork technology from Germany, accelerated the success of the industry. The devastation of the German industry during the World War I left Japan as the center of tin toy production, but the effects of the World War II were equally destructive to the Japanese toy industry. The occupying American forces gave the Japanese toy industry permission to resume production in 1947, and to export its output, so from 1948, they began to export friction toys, including trains, fire engines, truck, and automobiles.

These models were probably specifically designed for the American market.

Above: *The trailers are painted and printed and had each has several moving parts, including window shutters.*

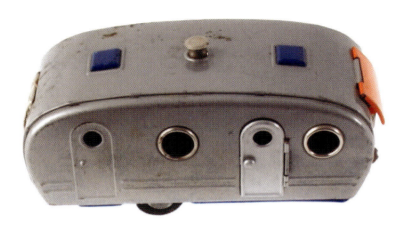

Below: The streamlined trailers have the classic lines and style of the 1960s.

THREE CAMPERS

These three camper trucks all date from the 1960s. The green and white pick up truck with cab-over camper is from Buddy L, and the two camper vans on the right are from Tonka. Before the war, Buddy L had been the market leader in pressed steel toys, but the shortage of metal during World War II not only led to many of their early toys being melted for scrap, but also meant that the company was reduced to making wooden cars and trucks during the war years. After the war, Buddy L re-introduced metal models to its line-up, but also began to make many components from molded plastic—this trend was adopted throughout the toy industry. This

This Buddy L truck and cab-over camper model comes from the company's post-war production, when more plastic was used in their toys.

The pick up truck body is made from pressed metal.

Above left: *The cab-over camper is equipped with clear plastic windows, and an opening door. It is in near perfect condition.*

particular camper truck is a classic "hybrid" toy, constructed from these two materials. The pick up truck is metal, and the cab-over camper is plastic. Tonka also made many versions of the camper during the 1960s and 1970s, reflecting the huge growth of the leisure industry in America. Many more people now had the time and a resource to travel, and the comfortable "camping" afforded by these mobile homes was highly appealing. As well as these two models, Tonka offered a pick up truck with a cab-over camper (model #530), and a Jeep camper. The model on the far right is Tonka's "Tiny Tonka Winnebago Camper Van," model #800. It is complete with the original Winnebago decals in green, and has free-turning rubber wheels fitted to its axles. Winnebago is the leading manufacturer of motor homes in America—it was established by John K. Hanson in Forest City, Iowa in 1958, and became Winnebago Industries in 1960. To maintain high quality standards, Winnebago manufactures almost every component for their motor homes, including the furniture and fittings. The company was immediately successful, and was launched onto the New York Stock Exchange in 1970. They manufactured their 100,000th unit in 1977, and their 200,000th in 1986. Winnebago now offers 12 models that range from around $59,000 for a budget "Access," to $299,000 for a luxury "Vectra." The company has maintained its enviably high reputation for quality, and is still based in Forest City, Iowa.

Below, center and right: Tonka made several version of their model camper, reflecting the growing popularity of these "RVs."

TWO OIL TANKERS

These two oil tankers are both highly collectible. The Structo Manufacturing Company made the model on the right in the 1950s. It is made from pressed steel and is complete with its original red livery and "Toyland Oil Co." decal, and, is equipped with rubber tires and a wind-up motor. Three partners founded Structo in Freeport, Illinois in 1908: brothers Louis and Edward Strohacker, and investor C.C. Thompson. They originally offered ready-built construction kit auto toys and erector construction kits.

The tin oil tanker on the right was built in China in the 1960s and is complete with its original cardboard box, in extraordinary condition. The cab is well made, and very attractively designed. When the Japanese tin toy industry began to fail in the 1960s, China stepped into the market. Originally, most Chinese tin toys were "cheap and cheerful," but the Chinese addressed their quality issues, and their toys were soon both robust and affordable. China is now the world's leading manufacturer of tin toys, and early examples of its export toys are becoming more sought after.

Below: The Structo Manufacturing Company oil tanker is in its original red livery and has retained its "Toyland Oil Co." decal.

Above right: Early export models from the Chinese tin toy industry, like this oil tanker, are now becoming more collectible.

The Structo truck looks more robust than the Chinese model.

Of the two models, the
Structo is more valuable.

BUDDY L OIL TANKER

This Buddy L oil tanker was built between 1925 and 1930, at the time when the company was still known as Moline Pressed Steel—it acquired its new name in 1930. The truck comes from an era when some of the most collectible, and highly desirable, toys from this premium manufacturer were manufactured. Their 1925 model range of twenty toy vehicles included fire engines, moving vans, tanker trucks, lumber trucks, overhead cranes, and sand loaders.

This toy is now worth at least $1,200, probably more.

Above: *This oil tanker comes from the more collectible Buddy L era. Many of these lovely toys were melted down to help the war effort, and this has increased their rarity.*

BUDDY
TANK LINE

*The tanker's headlights
have working light
bulbs.*

*The truck has
narrow profile tires.*

*The dark red paintwork is in relatively
good condition.*

NYLINT U-HAUL SET

This U-Haul set was made by Nylint around 1975. Unsurprisingly, the Nylint Tool and Manufacturing Company originally produced tools, but went on to use their extensive knowledge of manufacturing processes, and (in particular) precision die-making, to produce high quality toys at competitive prices. They first started manufacturing in 1937, having acquired the rights to produce two household items, a cheese

The U-Haul Truck is in excellent condition.

Above: *The U-Haul company originates from 1945. After the war, many people needed to move quickly and economically.*

slicer and a flour sifter. For several years, production was located at Barney Klint's home, until 1940 when the company could afford to build a small factory. Nylint knew that they needed to find new products to replace their original output, and conducted an extensive survey to see which area of production would be the most successful. They manufactured their first toy in 1945, an automatic spring-wind car, and it was introduced to the market in the following year, at the 1946 Toy Fair in New York City. Despite the model's high price of $3.98, Nylint sold 100,000 units over the time of the Fair. A lift truck, service cycle, street sweeper, and mobile pump soon joined the automobile.

Small trailers like these were the original U-Haul vehicles.

Above: *The Shoen family started U-Haul with a 1937 Ford and $5,000.*

NYLINT POWER AND LIGHT TRUCK

This Nylint Power and Light Company truck (Unit No. 3300) comes complete with a post-hole digging assembly and an on-board ladder and was made between 1959 and 1961. In Nylint's original incarnation as a tool manufacturer, the company had been stamping for various implement manufacturers and decided to make toy-sized versions of these products. This was the

Right: The brand name was originally written as Ny-Lint. Bernard Klint and David Nyberg founded the company in 1937.

The truck's decals have survived very well.

Below: The complicated post-hole digging assembly shows how much care Nylint took to make its toys genuine working models. They sometimes spent months designing new toys.

inspiration behind many of their early models, including the No. 1300 "Tournarocker," the No. 1400 "Roadgrader," the No. 1500 "Tournahopper," and the No. 1600 "Hough Payloader." Nylint took months to design new toys, ensuring that they were both a comfortable size for children's hands, and loaded with play value.

JAPANESE AUTOMOBILE CARRIER

This blue and red automobile carrier was manufactured in Japan, around the 1960s. The Japanese *buriki* (tin toy) manufacturers were given a massive boost in the post-war years, when in 1947 occupying American forces gave them permission to resume production and to export their wares to the United States. American children had been effectively starved of new metal toys in the war years, when nearly all metal production was diverted into munitions and the war effort. They were delighted to see a whole new range of toys on sale, including many friction models. Japanese toys were usually marked "Foreign made," rather than "Made in Japan." They included trains, fire engines, trucks, and automobiles, but as Japanese manufacturers became more ambitious electronic toys began to supersede friction and wind-up toys. This transition dates from the mid-1950s, and tin plate also became an increasingly popular material—by 1963, about sixty per cent of all the toys exported from Japanese were constructed from this material. However, this trend also became obsolete, and from around the mid-1960s the *buriki* tin plate toys gradually disappeared, having been replaced by cheaper plastic

The dark red truck is fixed to the automobile carrier.

Above: *The automobile carrier is equipped with a drop-down ramp for loading.*

AUTOMOBILE CARRIER

Below left: Tin toys like these were part of the final generation to come from Japanese manufacturers.

AUTOMOBILE CARRIER

and super alloy models. Japanese toy manufacturers from the *buriki* period include many famous names, including Masudaya, Nomura, Yoshiya, Masuya, Bandai, Sankei, Horikawa, and Yonezawa. Each had their own specialty, producing mechanical, battery-operated, wind-up, or friction toys. Some of these companies, including Masudaya and Bandai are still in business.

Yonezawa was Japan's biggest and most creative toy producer in the post-war period, but in the 1960s Japan's role in producing affordable tin toys was gradually taken over by China. Initially, there were suspicions about the quality of Chinese toys, but these were allayed as Chinese quality control was improved.

A.C. WILLIAMS AND ARCADE TRUCKS

A.C. William made the green c-cab, Mack-style truck on the left in the 1920s. John W. Williams founded the company in 1886, in Ravenna, Ohio, and produced cast iron toys between 1893 and 1923. These were mostly distributed by Woolworth, Kresge's, and other five-and-dime stores, and the company is still trading today.

Arcade made the red ice truck on the right sometime in the early 1940s. The Arcade Manufacturing Company was founded in 1868, in Freeport, Illinois, to make small cast iron machines, especially domestic appliances. Its range of coffee grinders was particularly successful and were made into the 1930s. Company founders Edgar and Charles Morgan designed many early products themselves. In the 1880s, Arcade decided to diversity into toy production and launched a line of cast iron models and playthings—they had their first notable success with their "Yellow Cab." Arcade gradually added to its toy range, achieving over 300 lines by 1939. These included a McCormick Deering tractor, a fire engine with firemen, various tractors, a Greyhound bus, a DeSoto Sedan, a Ford Coupe, and some farm animals.

Below: Despite its condition, this A. C. William truck shows its detailed moldings.

The truck was molded in two halves.

Cast iron meant few moving parts.

The Arcade ice truck has retained a little more paint.

Below: *The ice truck appears to have been cast in one piece.*

The truck's rubber tires are dry and cracked, but still turn.

ARCADE AND HUBLEY TRUCKS

The wrecker truck on the right was manufactured by Arcade and the company slogan, "They look real." told the whole story of their ambitions for their products. Founded by brothers Edgar and Charles Morgan in 1886, Arcade began as a novelty brass and iron foundry. The company began to look at producing toys very soon after its inception, in the 1880s, and continued manufacturing in this line until it ceased to trade in 1946. Its toys are now highly collectible; this wrecker is just one of an extensive range of playthings produced by the company. These included their most popular

models, Andy Gump and Chester Gump in his pony cart, and they also made toy banks, dollhouse furniture and ranges, and cast-iron penny toys. Although cast iron is very heavy, Arcade's toys have a certain lightness about them; they are surprisingly detailed and

Arcade began toy manufacture in the 1880s. Cast iron was widely used to create play models at this time, which are now highly collectible.

This early Arcade wrecker truck was cast in two halves that were then assembled together.

Above: Despite its sheer weight, this wrecker truck has a hand-operated tow mechanism, and plenty of play value.

attractive, with delicate moldings and flowing lines.

Hubley made the "Bell Telephone Mack Truck" on the right. The Hubley Manufacturing Company of Lancaster, Pennsylvania was founded in 1894 by John E. Hubley; the company also formed a toy manufacturing division, Lancaster Brand Iron Toys. Lancaster Brand's proud slogan was, "They're different!" The division began by producing electric toy train equipment and parts, but then Hubley bought the Safety Buggy Company in 1909 and moved into its premises. Deciding to widen their range, they launched a new range of toys—

their offering included a horse-drawn wagon, a fire engine, a circus trains, and a cap gun. By the 1930s, the toy division was headlining with model automobiles. Hubley managed to survive the Great Depression by switching to smaller and cheaper toys, and avoided the business failure that beset so many toy manufacturers in this era. Production was interrupted by World War II, since between 1942 and the end of the war iron production was diverted to the war effort, away from domestic production. The company later changed its name to Gabriel Industries, and became a trading division of CBS.

The towrope is equipped with a large towing hook.

Above: *Hubley's toy division, Lancaster Brand Iron Toys, manufactured this "Bell Telephone Mack Truck," with its white tires and red wheels.*

HUBLEY STEAMROLLER

This wonderfully detailed Army-green Hubley steamroller has a Huber logo on the side. The green version shown here is much scarcer—the model also came in red. It is an operational road roller with ornate nickel-plated wheels and driver, and it also has a rotating crank wheel with chain-driven steering. The castings are extremely accurate and crisp, and make this a stunning vehicle. It is 7½ inches long, and dates from around 1935.

The steamroller is finished in Army green.

Below: *The highly-defined Huber logo shows how crisp and detailed the casting is.*

The chains are linked to the steamroller's sophisticated steering mechanism.

MARX SPARKLING TANK

This attractive clockwork tin toy tank is a hybrid between a Sherman and a Chaffee M24. Marx marketed it in the late 1950s/early 1960s, a pivotal time in the development of the company, which was so successful in the 1950s that this time became known as the Golden Era. Although Louis Marx had hitherto rejected television advertising, he sponsored a blanket advertising campaign in the 1959 summer holidays, aiming to reach 27 million children. A company mascot, Magic Marxie, was invented especially for this hugely expensive campaign. Another factor in Marx's success at this time was its Japanese manufacturing subsidiary, Linemar, which also placed work with other Japanese manufacturers, including Marusan and T.P.S. The same Marx model was often manufactured by more than one plant.

An original box makes this toy even more sought after by collectors.

Marx bought several character licenses (including Popeye and The Flintstones), and was able to manufacture these high value toys in Japan, resulting in huge profits for the American parent company. This "Sparkling" tank owes its name to a small flint device that caused sparks to issue from the barrel as the tank rode forward. It bears the marking U.S. Tank Division. There is an on/off switch on the front apron and a permanently engaged wind-up key set in the front left hand track.

Right: The toy has a permanently engaged wind-up key set in the left front track.

"One of the Many Marx toys, do you have them all?" went the company slogan.

MARX G.I. JOE AND JUMPIN' JEEP

The "Jumpin' Jeep" is a lithographed tin toy by Marx that dates from the 1940s. It features four soldiers in leather flying hats, goggles, and dashing mustaches, armed with Browning machine guns, and comes with its original box, printed with Marx's New York City address and the words "Jumpin' action." It has a mechanism to make it jump as it is pushed along and is probably adapted from an earlier toy vehicle.

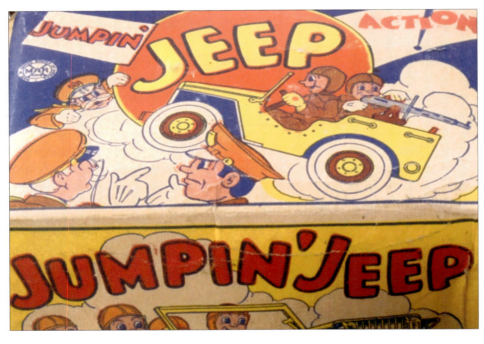

Above: The "Jumpin' Jeep" box is in exceptionally good condition, and increases the value of the 1940's toy considerably.

The "G.I. Joe" toy was probably manufactured by the Unique Art Company, a competitor of Marx, although the two companies enjoyed good relations and sometimes cooperated. Joe has two side wheel housings, disguised as dog carriers, and Sergeant's stripes. The Unique Art Company was founded in 1916 in Newark, New Jersey and, like Marx, the company originally specialized in wind-up mechanical toys—Sammy Bergman, Unique's president, was a good friend of Louis Marx. "G. I. Joe" was produced at a time when the two companies were working together; Marx provided distribution support and tooling for several Unique product lines.

Left: The Willys jeep on the "Jumpin' Jeep" box bears very little resemblance to the actual toy inside.

Tin toys like the "Jumpin' Jeep" were the backbone of the Marx company's output at this time.

The four soldiers carry Browning machine guns. There is a Marx logo on the front left side of the jeep.

The jeep makes a jumping movement as it is pushed along.

643

JOLLY JOE AND BLONDE LOCAL OLD JALOPY

These two lithographed tin toys were made by Louis Marx and Company. "Jolly Joe" is a wind-up motorized soldier with a mounted machine gun on the front of his car and dates from the 1940s. The machine gun also steers the front wheels and Joe's head rotates on a central spindle as the car goes along. His jolliness is demonstrated by a wide grin, but rather disconcertingly, his head is stamped in two parts down the middle of his face, giving him a slightly manic appearance.

The "Blonde Local Old Jalopy" comes from Marx's series of Crazy Cars and is a wind-up toy. The mechanism to drive the car is under the rear wheels and the front wheels pivot freely, allowing the toy to move erratically in any direction. It dates from the 1950s, and has amusing and rather suggestive decals, including "Exit" on the doors, "Step in here" on the running boards, and "No tight nuts allowed." These are both highly collectible Marx models, in excellent condition.

Above: The "Blonde Local Old Jalopy" has a permanent wind-up key.

Below: The car is covered in a selection of suggestive decals, like "The tin you love to touch" on the top, "Room on the top," and "Hi Ya, Babe." It has a fully equipped interior with two banks of seats.

The "Jolly Joe" lithographed jeep is decaled with an army star.

Above: *The head rotates on a central spindle as the car goes along. The front-mounted machine gun steers the front wheels.*

THREE TIN MOTORCYCLISTS

These three charming wind-up tin motorcyclists are from the heyday of American tin toy production. The police motorcycle was a particularly popular toy genre, made by several manufacturers, and toy police motorcyclists were usually seen on either Harleys or Indians. This Marx variation (on the right) has plenty of colorful lithography, in red, yellow, and blue. The policeman carries a sidearm and the toy is made completely from two pieces of tin put together, so that the back wheel is integral. The "Speed Boy Delivery" motorcyclist in the middle of the group is a wind-up toy and the motorcycle pulls a trailer. It was made by Marx around 1938, and is 9¾ inches long. The

Above left: The police motorcycle was a particularly popular toy genre.

The "Ice Cream Delivery" motorcycle has decals that read "Good flavor ice cream" and "Today, Strawberry."

The back motorcycle wheel is an integral part of the pressed metal toy.

Above: The "Speed Boy Delivery" motorcyclist is a pre-war wind-up toy, made by Marx.

three-wheeled toy is equipped with rubber tires and the front wheel turns. The red, white, and blue "Ice Cream Delivery" motorcycle on the left is in fantastic condition; its decals read "Good flavor ice cream" and "Today, Strawberry." This is a bump-and-go toy—when it bumps into an obstacle it backs up and takes off in another direction—made by the Unique Art Manufacturing Company of Newark, New Jersey, a company first established in 1916. Unique specialized in comic and animal characters.

TWO WESTERN TIN TOYS

The "Rodeo Joe Crazy Car" was made by the Unique Art Manufacturing Company of Newark, New Jersey and is marked "Made in U.S.A.. Patent pending." This wind-up tin toy features detailed graphics, with western styling themes, like the "leather" stitching, rope work lettering, the bucking horse on the front hood, and the longhorn cow on the grille.

The "Horse and Western Rider" is a tin litho, windup toy by Haji, which measures 6¼ inches high and 8 inches long. The Haji Mansei Toy Company was founded in Tokyo, Japan in 1951—they were a small toy maker that specialized in tin vehicles, such as tanks.

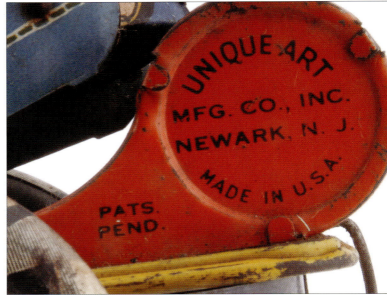

Above: The Unique logo is printed on the "Rodeo Joe Crazy Car" seat.

The "Horse and Cowboy" toy is unusual for Haji, as they specialized in making toy tanks.

Below: Everything with a western theme was popular in the 1950s, especially the cowboy outfit. Striped pants, Purina checks, cowboy hat, and leather gloves spawned thousands of dress-up toys.

Haji Mansei faded away in the 1960s.

Right: The blue jean-wearing cowboy rider sits on a red Indian style blanket. The toy is lithographically printed in brilliant colors that reflect the excitement of the popular cowboy theme.

HAJI BLACK DANCER ON A DRUM

Haji Mansei Toy Company was founded in Tokyo, Japan in 1951, and was a small toy maker that specialized in tin toy vehicles, particularly tanks, cars and planes. However, they also made this toy "Black Dancer on a Drum," a wind-up toy, fitted with an on/off switch, which measures 10½ inches in height. Haji was one of the almost two hundred Japanese toy manufacturers active in the post-war period. The occupying American forces encouraged a revival in toy production and Japanese manufacturers were allowed to export their wares to the toy-starved American market. American toy manufacturers like Marx placed work with Japanese manufacturers, and often developed their own factories in Japan—Marx owned the Japanese Linemar Company. As Japan was a low-wage economy in the post-war years, it was possible for American toy makers to make excellent profits on these toys. Haji made several highly collectible tin toys, including a space gun, the "Mechanical Donkey Express," and the "Select-O-Matic Jukebox Musical Bank." This toy was operated when a coin was dropped into it—a record then span and music played, and measured 4¾ inches high. Haji also made several larger-scale model Fords, including a car with an opening hood and spinning fan. The cars measure 11 inches in length.

Right: The pattern on the green and white plaid jacket is still quite clear.

Left: The drum on which the dancer stands is decorated with a frieze of similarly attired dancers.

Left: *The dancer wears a traditional straw boater, and a wide, lipsticked smile.*

Cheerful trousers in orange, red, and white pinstripes.

UNIQUE SKY RANGERS TOY

The Unique Art Manufacturing Company, whose registered offices were at 200, Fifth Avenue, New York, produced this unusual wind-up toy. The company was first established in the 1940s and was a successful tin toy manufacturer that specialized in inexpensive comic and animal character toys.

The Sky Rangers toy shown here is brilliantly lithographed in red, blue, and yellow. A Navy officer pilots the toy's plane, while more naval personnel climb the spiral stairs of the lighthouse. Unique became particularly successful in the 1940s, when they acquired the rights to the popular Li'l Abner Dogpatch Band comic strip; they released a special Li'l Abner toy in time for Christmas 1945, which featured a dancing Abner, with Pappy on drums, Mammy with a drumstick, and Daisy Mae playing the piano. Unique's President, Sammy Bergman, was a close friend of Louis Marx, America's greatest toy magnate, and the two companies both competed and cooperated with each other. In 1949, Unique also started to produce lithographed O gauge trains.

Below: The Sky Rangers toy is brilliantly lithographed in red, blue, and yellow.

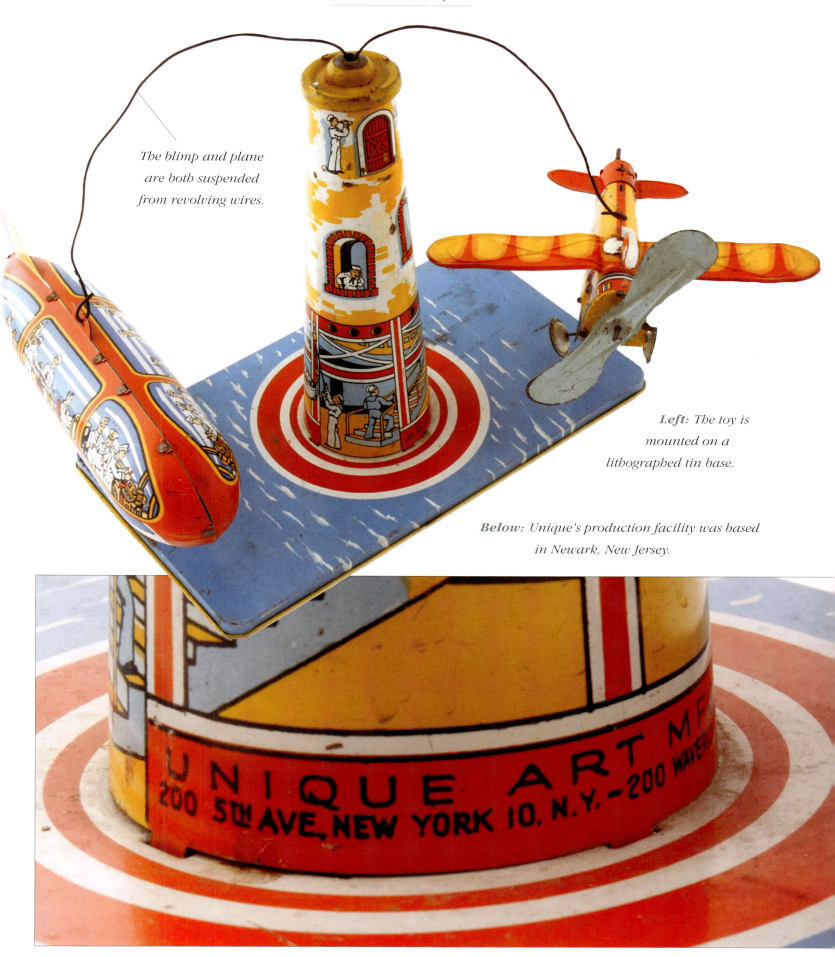

The blimp and plane are both suspended from revolving wires.

Left: *The toy is mounted on a lithographed tin base.*

Below: *Unique's production facility was based in Newark, New Jersey.*

CAPITOL HILL RACER

The Unique Art Manufacturing Company produced the "Capitol Hill Racer," shown here with its original box, a tin lithograph toy with a wind-up mechanism. Unique was founded in 1916, and one of its early products was a wind-up toy featuring two boxers. Like Marx, Unique was a price-conscious toy company, who offered their products at competitive prices. Unique's offices were located in New York, while its production facilities were located at 200 Waverly, Newark, New Jersey. The company was run by Sammy Bergman, who was a good friend of America's "Toy King," Louis Marx. Marx provided tooling to Unique and sometimes acted as a distributor for Unique's products, but after Unique began to produce lithographed tin toy trains in 1949, the company established a marketing arrangement with the Jewel Tea Company. Marx saw this as a betrayal of the cooperation between the two companies, and responded with aggressive

competition. Crushed by Marx's greater strength in the marketplace, Unique withdrew its trains in 1951. However, a tin typewriter toy that Unique launched in the early 1950s was hugely successful and took market share away from Marx. Marx immediately moved the production of its own typewriter toy to Japan to undercut Unique's price. It is unclear how Unique finally failed, but it had gone out of business by 1952.

Above: *The lithographic printing on this toy is in excellent condition.*

Right: *The toy is printed with several figures.*

CAPITOL HILL RACER

UNIQUE ART MANUFACTURING CO., Inc.

The original cardboard box is still with this toy.

The ramp is still complete.

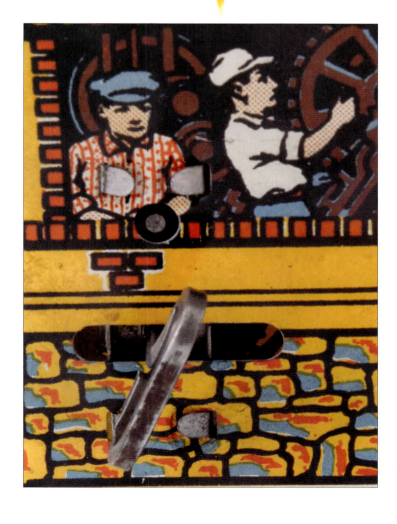

MARX DRUMMER BOY

The Marx company was established 1919 by two brothers, Louis and David Marx. The company funded itself in the early days by looking at toys already in the market place and finding a way of making them both better and more cheaply. Their stated mission was to provide more "toy for the buck" but with the proviso that "quality is not negotiable." Early on they bought the rights to two obsolete models made by employer Ferdinand Strauss, the "Alabama Minstrel" and "Zippo the Climbing Monkey," and with subtle changes they were able to turn them into hits.

By the late twenties both brothers were millionaires —Louis Marx was dubbed the 'Henry Ford of the toy industry.' The company continued until 1979 when he sold it to the Quaker Oats Company for $54 million. Although many Marx designs live on, none of the companies presently in existence have any direct links to the original company, and as a result, original Marx toys are much sought after by collectors.

The mechanical Drummer Boy featured here dates from 1936. His red tunic and yellow trousers reflect the bright costume of the Souza marching bands of the late nineteenth century. Made of pressed tin, a few turns on the clockwork key in his side propel his arms up and down rapidly allowing the drumsticks to contact the head of the drum to produce an audible clatter. This example of the toy is unusual as it still has its drum sticks intact—they are the first part to break off. The Marx trademark is on his lower back in the center of the white cross webbing. The feet of the toy are the same as the Marx walkers and some of the leg tooling was modified from the walking toys to build the drummer. This toy was made at the Marx plant in Erie, PA.

Right: Made of pressed tin, the drummer boy has a key in his side that winds up the mechanism.

Above: When the drum sticks hit the head of the drum they produce an audible clatter.

Left: The distinctive Marx trademark (Mar with a large X through the middle that resembled a railroad crossing sign). The toys are sometimes misidentified as 'Mar' toys.

Folded flaps hold
both of the tin-plate
sides together.
This allows access to
the inner workings
of the toy.

The mechanism
is clockwork. This
toy still has its key
and drum sticks.

ALPS LITTLE SHOEMAKER

This Alps-made shoemaker is a mechanical wind-up toy. As it says on the box, Alps made many wind-up tin dolls like this one, including the "Happy Fiddler Clown," "Reading Santa Claus," "Hobo Accordion Player," "Native American Drummer," and "Tin Marching Soldier." They also made rather

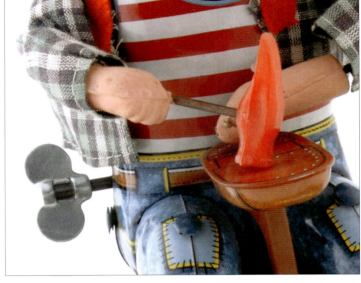

Right: The little shoemaker has his hammer in his hand, and is ready for work.

The toy has retained its original cardboard box.

anthropomorphic mechanical tin animals, such as a trumpet-playing monkey. Alps was a Japanese toy maker, whose highly distinctive logo makes their toys easy to identify. In the post-war years, Alps's main production was high quality battery-operated mechanical tin toys. Many of them had multiple actions—for example, their toy cars not only moved backwards and forwards, but also had a top that would roll down, and then go back up. This design quality and mechanical ingenuity made the toys highly popular, and for a time, they were in great demand. There were around 200 Japanese toy makers in the post-war period, and many (around 60%) specialized in tin toys. American manufacturers also outsourced some of their production to Japan, which enabled them to offer high quality toys at competitive prices. Despite their success as a toy maker, Alps switched to making consumer and industrial electronics in the 1970s, and continue in this field today.

Below: The shoemaker is outfitted in blue jeans, a striped shirt, and a plaid jacket.

MECHANICAL
LITTLE
SHOEMAKER

TRADE MARK
ALPS
MADE IN JAPAN

LITTLE
SHOEMAKER
504-2380

MARX ROLLOVER CAT

The rollover cat is busy pushing his ball; this is a Marx-made mechanical toy that dates from 1938. The key-operated tin cat holds onto his red ball as his tail turns in circles, making his body roll over and over. The cat is tiger striped, and is lithographed with a yellow ribbon around its neck, while the red ball is made from wood. There was also a slightly different version of the toy, which had a pink ribbon around its neck. Marx also made a very similar mechanical cat in 1940: a black cat, based on Figaro, the cat in Walt Disney's film *Pinocchio*, which was 5 inches long, and is also key operated. Released in 1940, Disney films of this era were some of the first to inspire spin-off toys. These Marx wind-up toys are from the company's era of classic, pre-plastic production. Some of the most memorable examples of these were the "Marx Merrymakers," which were amazing toys with remarkable engineering and design qualities—their incredible creativity is one of the things that made them so memorable.

The lithographed cat is printed in tiger stripes, and has a yellow ribbon.

The toy's red ball is made from wood.

Above: *The rollover cat is a key-operated mechanical toy from Marx's classic era.*

THREE MARX TIN TANKS

Marx made several tanks during its decades of production. The owner of the company, Louis Marx had served in the United States Army as a private during World War I—he attained the rank of sergeant before his discharge in 1918. Marx continued to show his fascination with the army by issuing many military inspired toys and the famous "Toycoon" also made a habit of befriending army generals, and naming his sons after them. Marx worked for a wood toy company for a year after leaving the army, where he revolutionized the product line, and increased sales tenfold. He and his brother David decided to start their own business in 1919; the business of his former employer, Straus, later failed and he bought the dies for the company's toys. He was a millionaire by the age of 26.

Below: Louis Marx was fascinated by military equipment, and model tanks often featured in his product line.

Left: Marx also made a famous "Rollover Tanks," with integral turrets.

Left and right: *These are wind-up lithographed tanks.*

ARCADE MCCORMICK DEERING THRASHER

This McCormick Deering Thrasher was made by Arcade in the 1920s. It is cast iron, and is painted gray, with red trim, crème wheels, and chrome trim, and comes complete with its original delivery chute. It is 9½ inches long, and has most of the other original equipment as well, including the tow bar, which was always unpainted. However, it is missing a bright metal tray at the front that helps to load the thrasher, and also the round black and yellow Arcade sticker that was fixed to the rear panel of the model.

Farm toys have been on the market since the 1920s, and this Arcade thrasher is an example of those early playthings. Hubley was also active in this field. Since the 1970s, farm toys have become the focus of many serious toy collections, and these models have become increasingly valuable. Adults and children alike enjoy the hobby, with modelers often displaying their toys in miniature farm scenes they have created. Almost invariably, the reason for collecting farm toys is nostalgia. Many farm

The metal tray used to feed the machine is missing from this model.

Above: McCormick Deering is one of the popular brands on which farm toys have been based. Others include Farmall, John Deere, Massey Ferguson, and International Harvester.

The narrow wheels were never fitted with rubber tires.

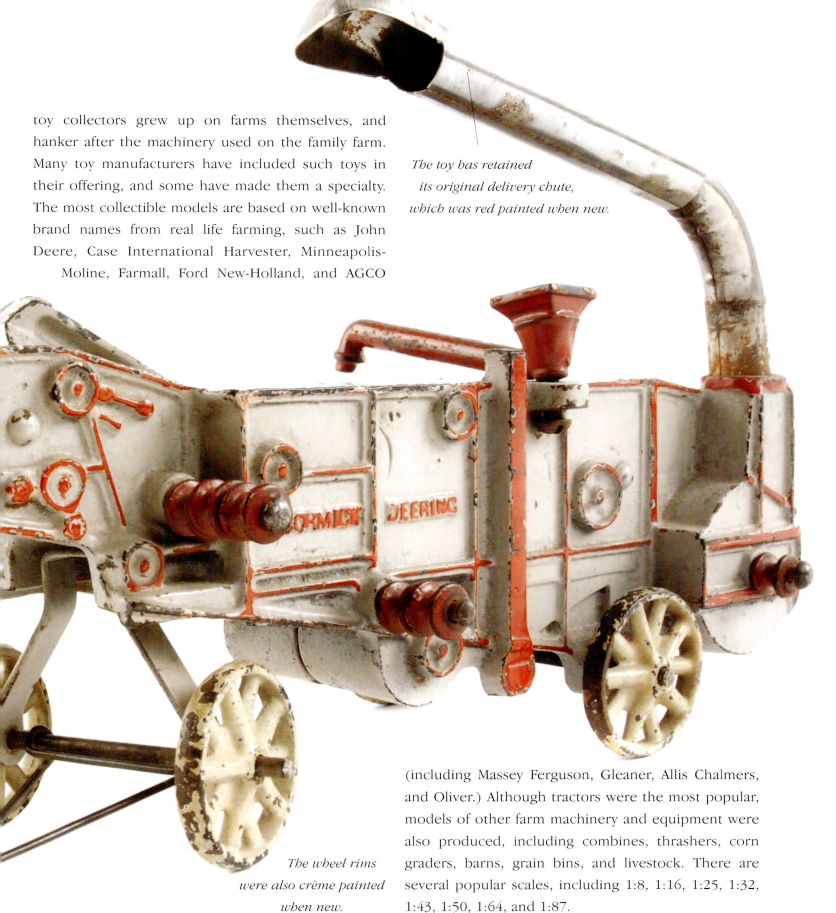

toy collectors grew up on farms themselves, and hanker after the machinery used on the family farm. Many toy manufacturers have included such toys in their offering, and some have made them a specialty. The most collectible models are based on well-known brand names from real life farming, such as John Deere, Case International Harvester, Minneapolis-Moline, Farmall, Ford New-Holland, and AGCO

The toy has retained its original delivery chute, which was red painted when new.

The wheel rims were also crème painted when new.

(including Massey Ferguson, Gleaner, Allis Chalmers, and Oliver.) Although tractors were the most popular, models of other farm machinery and equipment were also produced, including combines, thrashers, corn graders, barns, grain bins, and livestock. There are several popular scales, including 1:8, 1:16, 1:25, 1:32, 1:43, 1:50, 1:64, and 1:87.

ERTL JOHN DEERE B WITH COMBINE

This model is an all-original John Deere Model B tractor with combine, made by Ertl in the popular 1:16 scale. Ertl is one of America's most famous toy manufacturers, best known for its die-cast metal alloy collectibles of farm machinery and agricultural vehicles. Fred Ertl, Sr. founded the company in 1945, and worked there until his retirement in 1992. Ertl was originally located at Dyersville, Iowa, also home to the National Farm Toy Museum. The models were based on real life farm machines, including John Deeres, New Hollands, and AGCOs. In 1959, Ertl moved to larger facilities in Dyersville, Iowa. During its long history, Ertl has acquired several other toy manufacturers, including Carter Tru-Scale in 1971, and Structo Stamped Steel in 1974. Many of the most successful replicas are still in production, but since the 1990s, they have been made in Mexico.

The combine is chain operated.

Above: *The John Deere Model B tractor is still produced by Ertl.*

Above: *This view shows the delicate castings that make up the turning combine. Ertl's company slogan was "Ertl just like the real thing, only smaller."*

The model is finished in classic John Deere green.

This replica demonstrates Ertl's detailed, small-scale representations of farm machinery.

JOHN DEERE

The combine's tow bar attaches it to the tractor.

ERTL JOHN DEERE 4010 TRACTOR

Ertl made this John Deere 4010 die-cast replica tractor in the 1960s. The success of the company's toys had resulted in a move to larger production facilities in Dyersville, Iowa, and it is likely this model was made there. In 1967, the Victor Comptometer Corporation acquired Ertl, although Fred Ertl, Sr. retained his influence in the company. They began making plastic model kits in 1972, but these were not as successful as the company had hoped. Ertl retained its strong position in die-cast toys and replicas and this was confirmed by their acquisition of Structo Stamped Steel in 1974. Replicas of John Deere models have always done well for the company.

A hardworking blacksmith founded John Deere, after developing a polished steel plow in 1837. Although his invention was simple, it had a revolutionary effect on American agriculture, as the Midwestern farmers could now cut a clean furrow in the sticky soil of the prairies. John Deere established his company in 1838 and in 1863 produced a first ride-on model, the horse-drawn Hawkeye Riding Cultivator. The "leaping deer" trademark made an appearance in 1876. John Deere built a prototype engine-driven tractor in 1916 to compete with International Harvester, who had already entered the market.

Above: The two halves of this die-cast replica are easily visible. It is painted in John Deere's classic yellow and green livery.

Crisp die-castings detail the tractor's engine parts and "rivets."

The back wheels are fitted with deep tread rubber tires.

The steering wheel really turns on this model.

ERTL JOHN DEERE 5020 TRACTOR

The John Deere 5020 tractor was a later model than the 4020 and this is a detailed die-cast replica of the full-size version. John Deere is considered a "selling brand" for all kinds of toy farm equipment, and models like this one are highly collectible. Ertl first produced the 5020 in 1966, and a 1:16 scale replica was launched to celebrate the toy's fortieth anniversary in 2006. As well as the traditional green and yellow version, a gold painted edition was also offered. Seven years earlier, in 1999, Ertl was acquired by Racing Champions, a company formed by three partners, Bob Dodds, Boyd Meyer, and Peter Chung in 1989. The new company became known as Racing Champions Ertl. John Deere, by contrast, is a much older company—they launched the Model D in 1923, the first tractor to bear the John Deere name. It was immediately successful, and stayed on the company's product line for thirty years. The following year, International Harvester launched its Farmall tractor to compete with the Model D. Its wheels were widely spaced at the back, and close together at the front. By 1930, the Farmall had over 60% of the market.

The John Deere 5020 has unusually mounted lights.

The front axle still turns freely.

Above: *The 5020 shows the classic John Deere configuration of equally spaced wheels front and rear.*

Left: The paintwork, casting, and decals are all in reasonably good condition.

Below: Replacement yellow tractor seats are now available for Ertl models.

ERTL INTERNATIONAL HARVESTER COMBINE 915

When International Harvester launched its "15" series in 1968, the company had been building self-propelled combine harvesters for 26 years, and had more than 50 years' experience. The series included five different models; the 315, 615, 715, 815, and 915. This large range gave a wide variety of options and capabilities. The 915 was the largest machine in the series. In fact, it was the largest combine that International Harvester had ever offered and was also a highly sophisticated machine. The operator's cab was fully air conditioned, and equipped with an electronic digital monitoring system, while the gauges and controls were also

This model is the two-stack version.

The operator's cab window is cracked.

The model demonstrates the extreme width of the 915's combine.

Above: The Ertl replica has retained the International Harvester livery of red and white.

The combine could handle an eight row head.

specifically designed to be light and easy to use, even though the 915 was so large that it could handle an eight row corn head. Its modern controls also meant that the operator could position the grain spout hydraulically for easier loading. In real life, the 915 had a 150 horsepower engine, and a 146-bushel grain bin. Ertl's replica model reproduces all of the major features of International Harvester's full-size machine and also retains the exact color scheme of the original with its red and white livery.

ERTL FARMALL TURBO 1066

Ertl made this toy International Harvester Farmall tractor, with its wide front and metal canopy. The model was originally supplied in a blue cardboard box, which proclaimed "Real wide front wheel movement," "Real deep read rubber tires," "Real steering action," all of which claims were accurate. The International Harvester Company was formed in 1902, resulting from the merger of the McCormick Harvesting Machine Company and the Deering Harvester Company. From the beginning IH made gas-powered tractors, but they were enormous machines, with names like "Titan" and "Mogul." Two much lighter tractors, the 10-20 and 15-30 were later launched in 1915, but the company's real breakthrough came in 1924, when they introduced the first Farmall tractor. This was specifically designed to compete with John Deere's Model D and Ford's Fordson. By the 1930s, the Farmall had cornered 60% of the market.

The tractor wears the "IH" International Harvester decal.

The rear wheels have deep tread rubber tires.

Bright red is to
International Harvester
what green and yellow
are to John Deere.

Above: The Farmall 1066 Turbo model has a
white painted metal canopy.

ERTL INTERNATIONAL ROW CROP TRACTOR #415

This die-cast Ertl International Row Crop Tractor #415 has fixed steering, but the front axle and all four wheels turn freely. It is constructed in the popular 1:16 scale, and measures around 5 inches long, 2½ inches wide, and 3¾ inches high. A decal with the "International" logo appears on both sides, and the rear wheels have deep tread rubber tires.

The real #415 demonstrates one of International Harvester's important contributions to tractor design, in the way its wheels are mounted in a triangular arrangement, with a long back axle and short front one. This first appeared on the Farmall, launched in 1924 and designed to be used with all crops, including tall ones like cotton and corn. The Farmall was so successful that IH introduced several revised versions, including the #415. The original "tricycle" Farmall became known as the "Regular." 1939 was also when industrial designer Raymond Loewy gave IH's "letter series" of tractors a sleek new look.

The tractor's rear wheels are widely spaced and fitted with deep tread tires.

The #415 is painted in International Harvester red, and has a printed grille.

Above: *The #415 demonstrates International Harvester's most important contribution to tractor design, the "tricycle" wheel arrangement.*

SLIK-TOYS TRACTOR

The Lansing, Iowa, based company Armor Industries made Slik-Toys from 1938 to 1972, when they went into liquidation. During World War II the toys were wooden, mainly cars, trucks and tractors, made from scrap wood—off cuts 10–12 inches long. They reached a peak production of 30,000 toys a day.

When the war ended and metal became available again, production switched to aluminum because it was lighter and stronger than wood and with die-cast methods they could achieve much greater detail in the finished toys. Slik-Toys were available across the country but their manufacturing never moved out of Iowa. As the slogan went on the outer packaging of the tractors: "Ideal for the sandbox farmer." Our example is a generic tractor based on elements of the Case, John Deere and Farmall tractors of the late 1940s. The tractor is die-cast aluminum painted red, with black plastic wheels and steel spindles, dating it from the 1960s. It has a red matching plow. The toy is in its original box and is unused. The design of the box is typical of Slik-Toy in the 1960s with cartoon horses, cows, sheep, pigs and goats, along with the Armor Industries shield. It proudly proclaims "Slik Toys a great choice" and "Made in U.S.A.," something that would be a rare claim today.

Below: The art work on the Slik-Toys box is typical of the 1950s and 1960s with cartoon horses, cows, sheep, chickens, pigs and goats, along with the Armor Industries shield.

The 1960's model tractor has die-cast aluminum painted red, black plastic wheels with steel spindles.

Slik-Toys
from
Armor Industries, Inc.
LANSING, IA · (319) 338-4642

STRONG
DIE CAST
ALUMINUM
AND
STEEL
FARM
TOYS

MADE
IN
U.S.A

SLIK TOYS...
A
GREAT
CHOICE

Armor Industries · Lansing, IA 52151

Right: The toy is in its original box and is unused – it boasts "Slik Toys a great choice" and "Made in U.S.A."

Slik Toys is a brand name of Armor Industries.

Above: This example is a generic tractor based on elements of the Case, John Deere and Farmall tractors of the late 1940s. The tractor is die-cast aluminum painted red, with black plastic wheels on steel spindles dating it from the 1960s. It has a red matching plow.

LANZ BULLDOG 4016 TRACTOR

This Lanz Bulldog 4016 was made by Kovap Nachod of the Czech Republic, under license from John Deere, and is unusual in that it is a contemporary printed tin toy. The tractor is clockwork, and has a shiftable gearbox with three forward gears, neutral, and reverse.

Heinrich Lanz established his machine factory in Mannheim, Germany in 1859. Initially, he built engines and threshers, but soon started to make tractors. The legendary Bulldog range was introduced in 1921 and Lanz continued to make various Bulldog models (including the 4016) until 1956, when John Deere bought the company. The Lanz plant in Mannheim was bombed during World War II, but the re-built factory continues to make John Deere tractors.

Below: This contemporary Kovap Nachod toy is in mint condition.

The full-size Bulldog 4016 has exactly the same livery.

The Bulldog's front wheels are steerable.

The shiftable gearbox has three forward gears, neutral, and reverse.

AUBURN RUBBER TRACTORS

Auburn was an American toy manufacturer, originally founded in 1913 as the Double Fabric Tire Corporation, when its business was making tires for the Auburn Automobile Company. In the 1920s, the company became Auburn Rubber, and phased out its production of tires. They began to make toys in 1935, becoming the Auburn Rubber Toy Company, and continued to do so until the company ceased trading in 1969—except for during World War II, when they manufactured rubber soles for combat boots, and gaskets for "jerry cans." With its background in the rubber industry, it is hardly surprising that the company used its extensive knowledge of this material to make some highly unusual toys. These rubber and vinyl tractors date from the early days of Auburn's toy making. They were constructed in several different scales, including 1:32 and 1:42, and were based on tractors produced by several real life

These rubber tractors have rubber wheels.

This tractor has the wheel configuration of a Farmall.

Above: Auburn's background in rubber products inevitably led them to make toys in this material.

manufacturers. The company was actually best known for its line of miniature soldiers, which were based on men from both the European and American military services, and included some famous models such as the American Marines, and the English Palace Guards. The company produced many other rubber playthings,

The tractor drivers are also molded in the rubber.

The tractors were molded in colored rubber. Various details were highlighted in silver paint.

including a child's tool set, automobiles and trucks, train sets, farms and farm animals, motorcycles, flexible building bricks, and (perhaps rather disappointingly) a rubber pocket jack knife. But although rubber is the material most associated with Auburn, the company also made toys from other (more conventional) materials, including cast iron and plastic. In 1959, the company was sold, and Auburn's toy division moved to Deming in New Mexico.

WOODHAVEN TRACTORS

The Woodhaven Metal Stamping Company Incorporated of Brooklyn, New York, made these printed tin toy tractors in the 1920s and 1930s. They made a variety of tin toys, including a wind-up bubble blower, Chinese checkers game, and the St. Louis robot bus. The red tin tractor is shown with a driver wearing a yellow shirt, blue pants, dark boots, and a hat. This a wind-up toy, equipped with a belt driven wheel system.

The green tractor is a Fordson F, made in the 1920s. Henry Ford had an unsuccessful stab at tractor design in 1907, but in 1915 decided to

take the matter more seriously, and appointed a dedicated design team. Their brief was to design a tractor to be made using Ford's mass-production techniques. Ford intended to dominate the market with a well designed, competitively priced machine. A successful prototype was

The tin plate driver is smartly dressed.

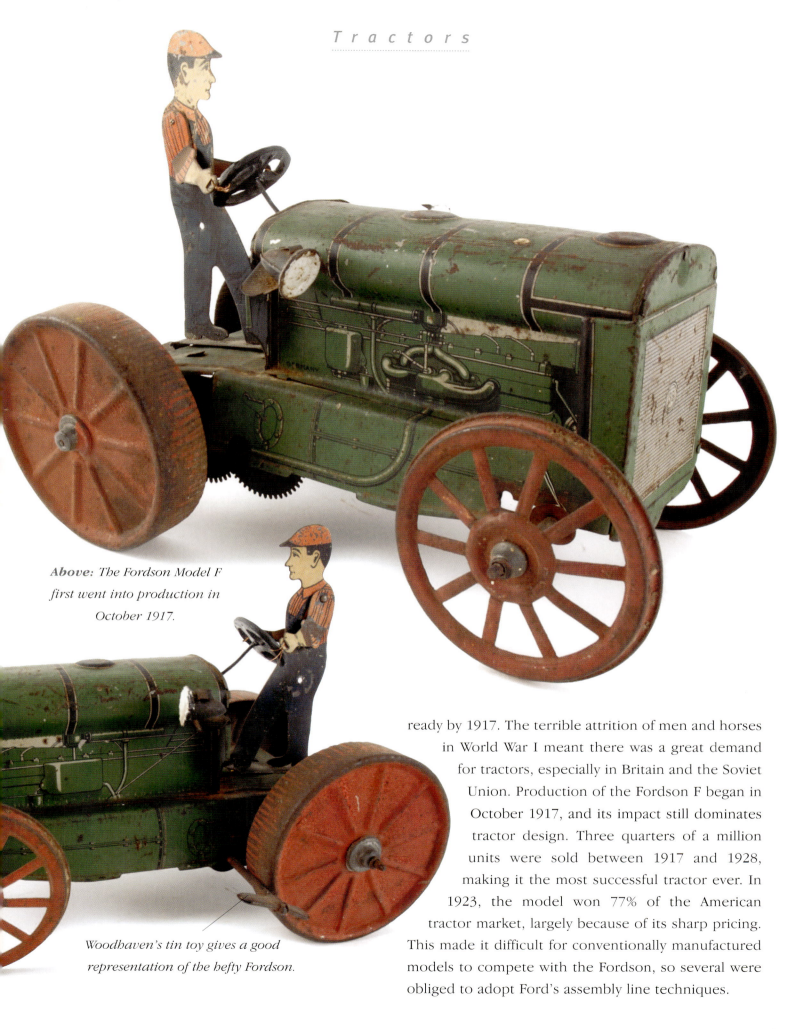

Above: The Fordson Model F first went into production in October 1917.

Woodhaven's tin toy gives a good representation of the hefty Fordson.

ready by 1917. The terrible attrition of men and horses in World War I meant there was a great demand for tractors, especially in Britain and the Soviet Union. Production of the Fordson F began in October 1917, and its impact still dominates tractor design. Three quarters of a million units were sold between 1917 and 1928, making it the most successful tractor ever. In 1923, the model won 77% of the American tractor market, largely because of its sharp pricing. This made it difficult for conventionally manufactured models to compete with the Fordson, so several were obliged to adopt Ford's assembly line techniques.

685

WILESCO WERKSTATT STEAM ENGINE

Model steam engines were extremely popular toys in the 1880s, right through until the 1960s. They were expensive, intricate and quite temperamental, and not really made for children at all—essentially, they were teaching aids for Victorians who were deeply interested in new technology. Most German model steam engines were made in the Nuremberg area, a center of precision manufacturing, and home to the finest metal workers in the country. In the pre-war period, there were eight major steam engine manufacturers based in the Nuremberg area. These

were: Bing, Carette, Doll, Falk, Krauss Mohr, Märklin, Plank, and Schoenner. Steam engines were also made in France and America. By the end of World War II, the German toy industry was virtually demolished, but the occupying American forces introduced the "tin toys for tinned food" program to encourage the resumption of toy production. "Made in Germany US Zone" was stamped on many toys of this era. Mamod and SEL were the biggest steam engine manufacturers during this period, but the toy itself was losing popularity fast. The steam engine enjoyed a brief revival in popularity

Left: *This intricate toy is equipped with a charming miniature steam gauge.*

Right: *Steam engines like Wilesco's were tiny testaments to the accuracy of German engineering.*

in the 1960s, and Wilesco was one of the most active manufacturers.

Wilesco was founded in 1912, and started by manufacturing kitchen utensils, diversified into making steam engine parts for Fleischmann, then started to produce their own engines circa 1950. Although Wilesco continued to produce steam engines until the 1970s, the market continued to decline.

WEEDEN STEAM ENGINE

Weeden Steam engines are now very collectible. Steam engine toys were very popular in the nineteenth century, and were made by several manufacturers including Märklin, Marx, and Bing. The Weeden Manufacturing Company, founded by William N. Weeden, was active in New Bedford, Massachusetts between 1883 and 1888. It specialized in producing working toy steam engines, as well as steamboats, fire engines, and miniature automobiles. Some of these were very intricate, while others were much more simple—all of them had steam-powered motors. Weeden also made several extremely rare clockwork tin mechanical banks, including "Ding Dong Bell" and the "Japanese Ball Tosser."

Below: Weeden were only one of several American toy manufacturers that manufactured steam engine toys in the late nineteenth century.

LIONEL TOWERS

As well as being the most famous American maker of toy electric trains, Lionel also made a series of wonderful trackside and station accessories. The model 394 Beacon Tower on the right has a single, electrified light, is white-painted steel, and has a black painted ladder. The Floodlight Tower on the right is also made from white-painted steel, with a black painted ladder, and has die-cast lamp heads and brackets. The electrified lights are fitted with six volt,

number 51 bulbs which are wired in pairs so that the tower can be operated at 12 volts. It was offered in the Lionel catalog between 1949 and 1956.

Joshua Lionel Cowen founded Lionel in 1903. Cowen was an electrical engineer, who was fascinated by this new power. Born in 1877, he started work for the Acme Electric Lamp Company of Manhattan while still in his teens, and soon started to experiment with battery-operated lamps in his spare time.

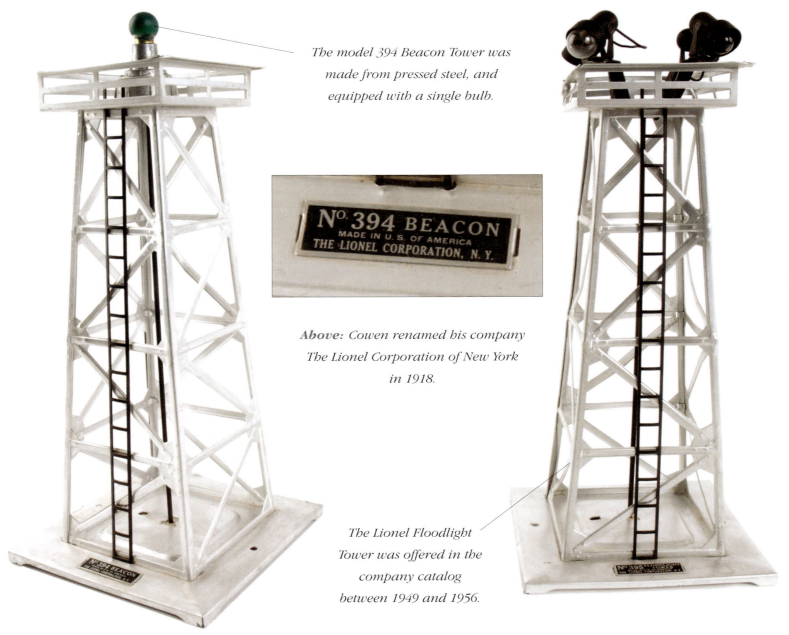

The model 394 Beacon Tower was made from pressed steel, and equipped with a single bulb.

No. 394 BEACON
MADE IN U.S. OF AMERICA
THE LIONEL CORPORATION, N.Y.

Above: *Cowen renamed his company The Lionel Corporation of New York in 1918.*

The Lionel Floodlight Tower was offered in the company catalog between 1949 and 1956.

LIONEL OIL DERRICK AND PUMPER

Since Lionel made many tank cars for its railways, including several, branded "Sunoco," in the early postwar years, it seemed perfectly logical to make oil derricks and pumpers to demonstrate a source for all this petroleum. Lionel offered the model 455 Oil Derrick between 1950 and 1954. It has a sheet metal base, and a pressed steel tower and the orange plastic generator is exactly the same as the one mounted on Lionel searchlight cars. The plastic pump casing is maroon, and the assembly is also equipped with a maroon pump jack. With typical Lionel ingenuity, an electric bulb is mounted beneath the base of the derrick, which heats the oil in the clear plastic tube, and causes it to bubble adding to the illusion that the derrick is actually pumping crude oil. A bimetallic strip triggered the pumping action. The toy was usually equipped with four turned, solid aluminum oil drums, which were placed under the tower, to the front of the oil pipe. The tower itself was sometimes also decorated with a small white-painted sign, which read "Sunoco Oil Derrick No. 455," especially in later versions. The toy was also offered with a dark green painted tower, and a matching upper platform (red on this version of the model).

The plastic pump casing and pump jack are maroon.

The Stars and Stripes flag is not original.

Above: *The oil in the clear plastic pipe was heated to make it bubble, so that it appears that the derrick is actually pumping crude.*

Left: *This example of model 455 has the original transfer printed on its red sheet metal base.*

MARX TRAIN AND DEPOT

This Marx Girard Depot was made for use with the company's tin trains. It was electrified, and was illuminated, with a whistling chimney. The station is made from lithographed tin, and has a gray and red simulated brick base and sides, with white trim, a gray roof with simulated shingles, and a simulated red brick chimney. It was usually supplied with the optional No. 1605 Marx Accessory Controller. A sign on the side reads "Railway Express Agency" and the front doors have a notice, which reads "Waiting Room." This lithographed tin plate toy train is likely to be pre-war, as Marx switched to making plastic trains after the war.

"Toy King" Louis Marx had first started to make toy trains back in the 1920s. They were so successful, that even during the gloomy days of the Great Depression, he was able to build a dedicated factory at Girard, Pennsylvania, to manufacture toy trains and accessories like the depot. During the company's most successful periods, Marx sold more toy trains than any other American toy company. Their first successful toy train was the Joy Line model, which was originally sold on commission for the Girard toy company. Marx then commissioned Girard to make a toy train for his company, and eventually purchased Girard. Marx's

Above: The Marx toy train factory was located at Girard, Pennsylvania.

Above: *Trains made at Girard were often sold through the Sears Roebuck magazine.*

trains were smaller and cheaper than those made by Lionel and American Flyer. Almost all of the Marx trains featured an open frame motor, and most had a copper shoe pickup assembly. The center rail pickup was also made from copper strip. Marx trains were designed and marketed to the mass market, and to younger children than those who were attracted to the Lionel and American Flyer models. Marx did also make some more expensive model trains, which were equipped with a smoker. This heated smoke fluid to make realistic looking steam. Until the late 1950s, Marx made their trains with a so-called "fat wheel." This made it impossible for their trains to negotiate the switches and crossovers of Lionel track.

MARX UNION PACIFIC TRAIN

This model is the Union Pacific UP M10005 Marx diesel wind-up train, and comes complete with a set of articulated cars. The train is constructed from lithographed tin plate, and the separate front grille is held on with metal tabs. The engine is equipped with four wheels, and is designed to run on "O" gauge track. This example is complete with the original wind-up key; a switch on the locomotive roof operates the wind-up power. Just like real Union Pacific trains, this wind-up toy sports a livery of Armor Yellow, Harbor Mist Gray, accentuated with a thin red band. Lettering and numbering is in red.

Union Pacific Railroad, headquartered in Omaha, Nebraska, is now the largest railroad network in the U.S.A. It owns and operates track in twenty-three

The lever controls the wind-up power.

The front grille is a separate piece of tin plate.

states, and covers most of central and west America. The company was first incorporated on July 1, 1862, when the dominant shareholder was Thomas C. Durant. Through a series of bankruptcies and acquisitions, the company succeeded in building some of the major rail routes across America. It operates its complicated system with hundreds of rail yards, and maintains its own functioning police department. Union Pacific's corporate motto is "Building America."

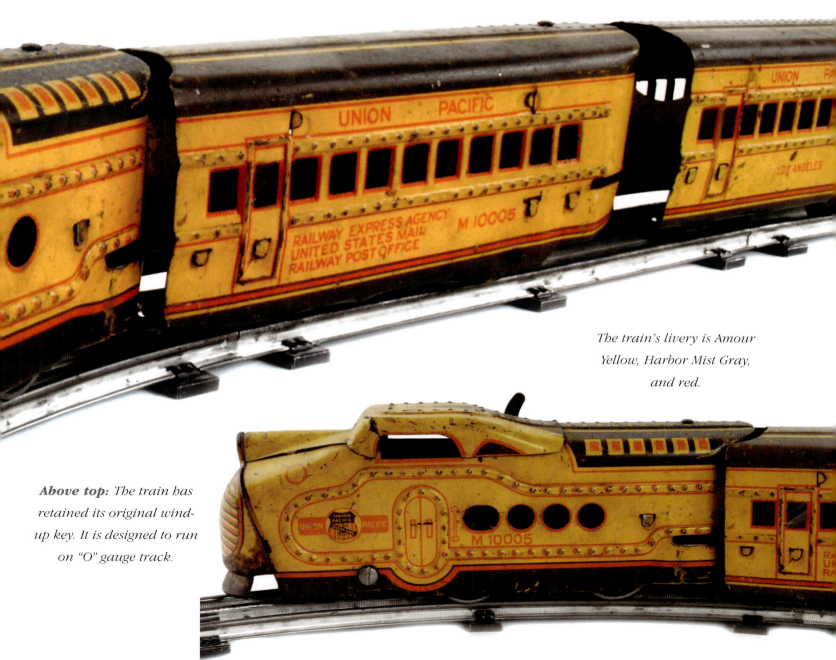

The train's livery is Amour Yellow, Harbor Mist Gray, and red.

Above top: *The train has retained its original wind-up key. It is designed to run on "O" gauge track.*

AMERICAN FLYER TRAIN

This American Flyer train is from around the 1940s. The engine is coupled to two passenger coaches and a goods van. The Milwaukee switcher works the Chicago-Milwaukee-St. Paul route.

American Flyer began as the Toy Auto Company in 1900, founded by William Hafner of Chicago, Illinois. The company initially specialized in manufacturing clockwork cars, and Hafner refined his clockwork mechanisms until they had an excellent reputation. In 1910, Hafner entered a partnership with William Coleman; the two men focused on making model trains, and renamed the company American Flyer. Although the model trains were the hub of the company's output, they also experimented with other toys, including four mechanical airplanes; "The Spirit of Columbia," "Lone Eagle," "Spirit of America," and "Sky King." In 1931, American Flyer dropped the planes and went back to trains and became increasingly successful. Their electric models (like this one) were directly competitive with Lionel's luxury models.

Above: This American Flyer model is designed to run on "O" gauge track.

Above: The train has an attractive livery of orange, red, and black, with gold lettering.

The carriages have two sets of double wheels.

Above: American Flyer was best known for the sophistication of its wind-up mechanisms, invented by the company founder, William Hafner. Hafner started a rival company, Overland Flyer in 1914, to compete directly with American Flyer.

LIONEL STEAM TRAIN

Lionel is certainly best known for its heavy, black model steam trains. The company had introduced zinc-alloy die-casting to its production process pre-World War II, but it took a few years to perfect the technique. Early die-cast engines were sometimes cast with impurities in the metal, which can cause problems for today's collectors—over the years, this faulty metal can "rot," and the models disintegrate. By the post-war period the problems had been resolved, and this method of casting enabled Lionel to produce highly accurate models that were also resilient. Lionel's famous air whistle was also introduced in the pre-war

years; a small electric motor forced air through two acoustic chambers to make a highly realistic sound. Lionel introduced its other famous trademark, puffing smoke, in 1946. Heating the company's SP smoke

The red light bulb simulates glowing coals in the boiler.

pellets made the smoke. The Magnetraction system appeared in 1950; this kept the train on the tracks, and increased the pulling power of the locomotive by using powerful magnets to attract the engine to the tin-plated steel track. The 1940s and 1950s were the heyday of full-size steam engines, and were also some of the best years in Lionel's manufacturing history.

LIONEL 2332 PENNSYLVANIA, 2442, AND 2443

The Lionel 2332 Pennsylvania engine was introduced in 1947, and was offered until 1949. It was Lionel's first electric locomotive of the post-war years, based on the famous GG1 locomotive of the Pennsylvania Railroad. It has a die-cast metal body, painted Brunswick Green, with five rubber-stamped stripes and lettering in gold paint that often oxidizes, and becomes silvery in appearance. A Pennsylvania Railroad decal appears between the engine windows. Detailed pantographs are mounted at either end of the locomotive roof and could be electrically wired. The engine was powered by a single motor, which drove the twelve nickel-rimmed wheels. Model 2332 was also equipped with a realistic-sounding horn.

Left: Lionel's Pullman 2442 car was offered for sale between 1946 and 1948.

Above: The 2332 is based on the GG1 locomotive of the Pennsylvania Railroad.

The 2442 Pullman carriage was also produced in 1947 and 1948, one of the 2000 series of sheet-metal passenger cars. They were available in blue with a silver roof, two-tone green with a darker green roof, and solid brown. 2443, in brown-painted steel to match the Pullman, is an Observation car, and was in production between 1946 and 1948. The door and window inserts are painted gray, and have celluloid strips in them. The car has white heat-stamped lettering, which probably means that it is Lionel's Type II version of this item as earlier versions had silver, rubber-stamped lettering. The Pullman and Observation cars can both be illuminated.

Above: The 2443 Observation car and the Pullman came packaged in Lionel's early post-war boxes.

The locomotive's pantographs could be raised and lowered.

LIONEL STEAM TRAIN PULLING STREAMLINED CARS

By 1948 Lionel wanted to update its image, and decided to follow the example of full-size railway car manufacturers. They introduced the 2400 series of streamlined passenger cars, based on the diesel-powered streamliners that were then being introduced onto America's railroads. Lionel adapted their designs from those of the Pullman-Standard car company— Pullman-Standard was one of America's most successful manufacturers of railway cars. Lionel's new series was a great success, and remained in production

for eighteen years. Only minor improvements, like the magnetic couplers of 1954, were made to the basic design. Pre-1959 cars are designated "Lionel Lines," while post-1959 cars are decaled for the Santa Fe railroad. Model 2421 Maplewood dates from 1950 or later, when the silver paintwork was introduced to 2400. The first 2421s were made for "O" gauge. The celluloid window strips had passenger silhouettes painted on them.

Right: The Maplewood 2421 car was in production between 1950 and 1953, when it was discontinued.

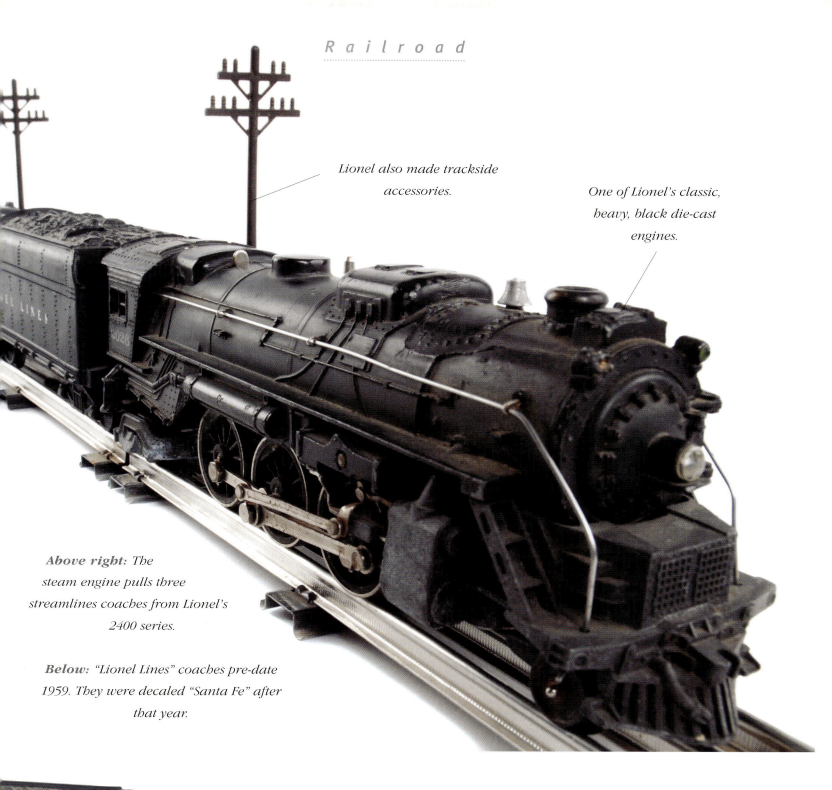

Lionel also made trackside accessories.

One of Lionel's classic, heavy, black die-cast engines.

Above right: The steam engine pulls three streamlines coaches from Lionel's 2400 series.

Below: "Lionel Lines" coaches pre-date 1959. They were decaled "Santa Fe" after that year.

IVES "G" GAUGE TRAIN

"G" gauge is a term used to describe a variety of popular larger-scale trains, built with widely differing proportions. The only two things that these model trains have in common are their track, and their proportions. "G" gauge trains all use Number One Gauge track, in which the running rails are positioned 1.77 inches apart. "G" gauge scale is 1:22.5, or 0.53 inches to the linear foot. Although this scale is now popular with collectors, only a few manufacturers, including American Flyer and Ives, have used it.

Edward R. Ives founded the Ives Corporation in 1868 and by the 1880s the company was a leader in the production of superb clockwork toys designed by the famous trio of Jerome Secor, Nathan Warner, and Arthur Hotchkiss. Many people credit the company with being the first true manufacturer of toy trains in America. They were the first to launch mechanical clockwork locomotives (back in the 1870s). Ives soon began to fit their clockwork motors into lithographed tin plate locomotives, and these became very popular. Some incorporated air whistles, and smoking stacks. Ives also made lithographed train stations, platforms, bridges, and signals.

Above: Model 4232 was produced by Ives, credited with being America's first toy train manufacturer.

Above: "G" gauge trains run on Number One Gauge track, and are made in 1:22.5 scale.

Above right: The Ives engine is made with wonderfully accurate details. Sadly, Ives went bankrupt in 1929.

Below right: The Ives Observation car is equipped with a viewing platform.

IVES STEAM LOCOMOTIVE

The first handmade live-steam toy locomotives were invented by European toy producers in the mid-nineteenth century. American toy manufacturers like Eugene Beggs, Weeden, and Garlick were soon offering live-steam models and they continued to do so into the 1920s. American Murray Bacon patented the first electric toy train in 1884, and Ives became the major American manufacturer. Initially, they faced stiff competition from German manufacturers, including Karl Bub, Märklin, and Bing, but the United States Government imposed tariffs on imported goods that helped American producers. Ives offered dozens of model steam locomotives, many of which had smoking stacks; originally, this was a simple "cigarette smoke"

system. Most Ives locomotives were based on full-size originals. Following the fashion, they switched from die-cast engines to lithographed tin plate, and became one of the most highly regarded producers of these toys, but they were overtaken by the success of Lionel in the 1920s, and taken over by Lionel in 1929.

Left: Ives was one of the best manufacturers of early electric trains.

Below: This locomotive is made from tin plate; cheaper to transport than die-cast toys.

Ives made trains for several track gauges.

Right: Lionel retained the proud Ives name until 1931, but it then disappeared forever.

LIONEL LINES ENGINE AND DEPOT

This Lionel engine 2055 is a 4-6-4 Hudson locomotive and shared a boiler casting with the 665, 685, and 2065. It was in production between 1953 and 1955 and has a die-cast body, Magnetraction, live smoke, and an operating headlight. The trailing truck is made from composite sheet metal and plastic construction—the engine was supplied with either the 6026 or 2046 tender, both lettered "Lionel Lines." The gondola car behind the tender is one of many produced by Lionel. Many were supplied with wooden barrels or plastic containers, and many were included with sets. The pre-war gondolas were made from pressed steel, while post-war models were injection-molded plastic.

Lionel also made depots, stations, and accessories.

Above: *The signal bridge has working lights.*

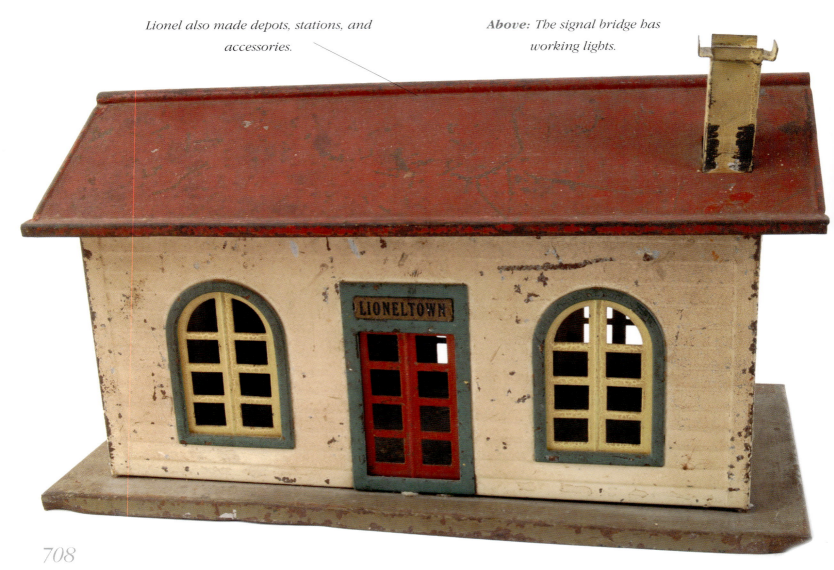

Lionel offered the signal bridge between 1952 and 1958. It could span two tracks, and had 6 inches of clearance under the bridge.

LIONEL RAILWAYS

Part of Lionel's great success lay in the wide variety of railway products they offered. These included steam, diesel, and electric engines, rolling stock, passenger cars, and trackside accessories—Lionel tank and vat cars were particularly popular. Four versions of the 2555 Sunoco deluxe tank car were offered, from 1946 to 1948. The tank and dome were painted shiny silver, and the truck had a Sunoco decal. The X3464 NYC operating boxcar was included in many sets, and offered for separate sale between 1949 and 1952. This truck is complete with its blue rubber man. For a brief period in the early 1950s, Lionel was the largest toy manufacturer in the world. Joshua Cowen resigned as chairman of the board at the end of 1958.

Below: Lionel offered many electrified trackside lamps. They also made several different versions of the tin plate station.

This is Lionel's automatic semaphore signal. As a train passes, the arm drops to a horizontal "Train Ahead" position.

Above: Lionel offered four versions of the 2555 Sunoco deluxe tank car from 1946 to 1948. This is the Type II variant.

Below: The X3664 NYC was included in many Lionel train sets. The body was molded from clear plastic and painted tan. The New York Central markings are heat-stamped in white.

The 8040 Engine is a classic heavy black Lionel engine. It has the perfectly detailed castings typical of Lionel locomotives.

LIONEL SANTA FE 2343

Lionel was relatively slow to embrace diesel locomotives and only a few examples were produced before World War II. Lionel introduced the F3 locomotive in 1948 and it was a great hit—the Santa Fe version was particularly popular, with its distinctive red, yellow, black, and silver livery. Several versions of this model were produced. The 2343 Santa Fe was a new version of the 2333 engine, equipped with Magnetraction and launched in 1950. During the first two years of production, the bodies were molded in black plastic, and painted in the Santa Fe livery. 1952 was its final year of production.

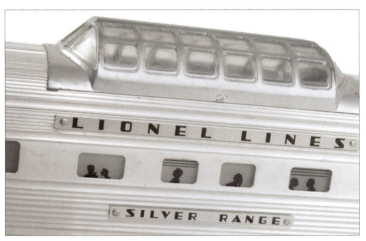

Above: The horn mountings were improved in the 2343 version of the 2333 engine.

The model number 2343 is embossed onto a small plastic plaque, which is then mounted on either side of the engine.

KARL BUB
TRAIN SET

Karl Bub of Nuremberg, Germany was active between 1851 and 1966 and specialized in high quality transportation toys. Their superb toys were originally enameled, but were later lithographed. They had a wonderful line of clockwork toys, including trains like the one shown here. Many Karl Bub toys reached the American market in the 1920s and 1930s through the company's exclusive U.S.A. distributor, F.A.O. Schwartz of New York City. KBN's trains were not actually "O" gauge, but can run on "O" gauge track. This clockwork train is a pre-war model, and operates through a fixed key. It is shown with a tender, brake car, and an ordinary passenger coach.

This slightly later KBN model is lithographed.

Left: Karl Bub took over the train manufacturing department of Bing in 1932.

Bub's model trains were at the high end of the toy market. In the 1920s and 1930s, F.A.O. Schwartz of New York City distributed them in America.

Above: Karl Bub founded The Karl Bub toy company in 1851. They made their first clockwork train in 1903. Bub production ceased in the early 1960s.

HORNBY "O" GAUGE TRAIN SET

Hornby is the most popular English brand of model train, and their toys remain highly collectible today. Frank Hornby—who has also invented the famous Meccano building sets in 1901—founded the company in 1920. Both Hornby trains and Meccano were manufactured in the same Liverpool factory. Hornby rapidly became the most successful brand of toy train in Britain and almost every little English boy had a Hornby train set, decorated with a selection of Hornby's excellent trackside accessories. The first "O" gauge trains were held together with nuts and bolts. Hornby trains were greatly improved in 1921, with the introduction of larger mechanisms, longer wheelbases, and larger wheels in the No. 1 Hornby Train set. This enabled trains to make longer runs, and gave them greater pulling power. Over the years, Hornby added hundreds of items to their train collection and in 1922, they opened a factory in Bobigny, France to make model trains for the French market. 1925 saw the introduction of electric trains to the Hornby range and the budget-priced M series was introduced in 1926. M models were made out of litho printed tin. Frank Hornby died in 1936, at the age of 72. The company continued to make "O" gauge models until 1964, after which they produced only "OO" and "HO" trains.

Above: *LNER stands for London and North Eastern Railway. Regional railways served Britain until the formation of British Railways in 1948.*

Above top: *The two brass topped rods controlled the movement of the trains.*

LIONEL LINES ENGINE AND CARS

This generic tin plate Lionel Lines engine probably dates from the 1940s. It is simply pressed, and cruder than the general run of Lionel production, but has some nice touches including the bright metal handrails on the engine, and the ornamental bell. The tin plate tender has a bright metal ladder and has "Lionel Lines" embossed on a plaque. Lionel production values tended to reflect the market conditions, availability of raw materials, and the trading health of the company itself, and so are somewhat variable in its later years of operation. The earlier models are much heavier and more robust, while the very late additions to the line were often quite flimsy plastic. The early items are more collectible.

Left: This engine is very attractively designed, and has a lot of play value.

Lionel trains are still in production.

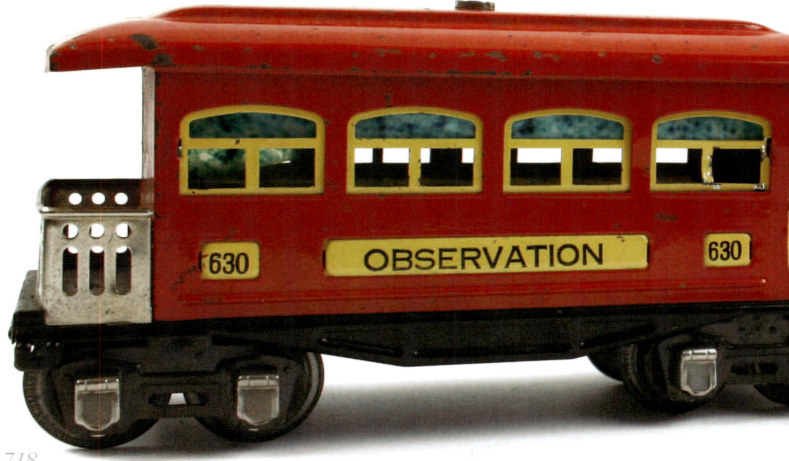

Above: This engine and tender are connected with a simple pin-operated coupling.

Below: Lionel often produced matching Pullman and Observation cars. These have celluloid windows.

BING LNER ENGINE AND HORNBY CARRIAGE

Gebrüder Bing was one of the famous tin toy manufacturers active around Nuremberg in Germany in the nineteenth and twentieth centuries. Two brothers, Ignaz and Adolf Bing, founded the company in 1863, originally to manufacture kitchen utensils. They diversified into toy trains in 1882, adopting Märklin's track gauges initially but adding "O" gauge models by 1895. The company produced their toys in the Nuremberg style. Steel sheets were lithographed with designs that were stamped out and assembled

Bing in the early 1920s. They opened a New York office between 1924 and 1935, but this did not help the company's fortunes. The market for their "1" gauge trains evaporated, and they re-gauged many models to the more popular "O" gauge. Competition in the American market was fierce, and Lionel squeezed Bing out of the market. The Bing family itself left the company in 1927—being Jews, they were forced to flee to England to avoid the rise of Fascism. The company went into liquidation in 1932, and sold its train tooling to rival Nuremberg toy company, Karl Bub.

with metal tabs and slots. This method was perfected by Bing and remained in widespread use until the 1950s, long after Bing itself had disappeared. Bing produced many trains for the American market in direct competition with Ives—German labor was cheaper than American, so Bing was often able to undercut prices. By 1914, Bing had 5,000 employees—by comparison, the famous German company Märklin had only 600 workers. The disruption of World War I, U.S. Government imposed tariffs, and increased labor costs in the post-war period conspired to undermine

Above right: Bing LNER (London North Eastern Railway) engine 4993 is a pre-war model, as is the Hornby coach.

Above: *Bing and Hornby both produced tin plate models in "O" gauge.*

HACHETTE HORNBY TRAIN

These Hachette trains are modern reproductions of Hornby "O" gauge tin plate railway items, based on their budget M series. Hachette is a hugely successful French magazine and part-works company that specialize in selling monthly magazines on various

Left: Hornby's budget-prices M series was introduced in 1926.

collecting subjects, with a premium attached to each. They issued a series of 55 train magazines, starting in 2002, and offered an enormous variety of Hornby-style models, including engines, tenders, tanks, carriages, and goods vans; the "Serie Hornby." The models carried the logos of the French railways, including SNCF, ETAT, and NORD. The rolling stock also carries the trademarks of various French products. The company had purchased the original stampings from the French Hornby factory, and even packed the trains in red cardboard Hornby boxes, with the company's classic black script. According to Hachette, the models were sold simply for collectors, but they said it would be easy to fit them with original M motors.

The Hachette series consisted of 55 magazines.

Below: *Although the trains are simply made, they are brightly printed and build up into an interesting collection.*

FABRIQUÉ POUR HACHETTE

3.1225

2528

HACHETTE STREAMLINER AND COACHES

The PLM streamliner was issued in two parts of Hachette's train collectors' series. The locomotive came with issue 43, while the tender came with issue 44. The two PLM coaches were attached to magazines 50 and 55 (the final part of the series). PLM stands for Paris-Lyon-Méditerranée, a railway company founded by Paulin Talabot (1799-1885) in 1858 and one of six railway companies that divided France into six regions. PLM operated in the south-east of the country and was absorbed in the French state railway system, Société Nationale des Chemins de Fer Français (SNCF) in 1938. Streamliners were fast, modern, lightweight trains introduced in the 1930s.

Left and right:
Streamlined engines added
a new glamor to rail travel.

PLM stands for Paris-Lyon-Méditerranée.

Below: *These articulated coached were issued with magazine numbers 50 and 55.*

METTOY SCHOOLS CLASS ENGINE AND PULLMAN CAR

Mettoy was established in Northampton, England in 1933 by German émigré Philip Ullmann. Ullmann had been running his own toy company in Germany, Tipp, for 21 years, so he had plenty of experience in the toy trade. In the 1940s and 1950s, Mettoy produced a range of die-cast model vehicles, which—although they were not particularly sophisticated—found a market niche. These railway pieces come from this time. As the company developed, Mettoy built a huge factory in Swansea, Wales, which employed 6,000 workers. The company was renamed "Corgi" in honor of the Queen's favorite breed of dog, and now specialized in making model cars—they were direct competitors of Matchbox and Dinky. Despite many decades of success, Corgi closed down in 1983. A new company, Corgi Classics Limited, was revived in the 1990s and has re-issued many iconic Corgi models.

Mettoy engines like this one are now rare and collectible. It was made in England.

Above: *George Pullman founded The Pullman Palace Car Company in 1862.*

PULLMAN

900

900

900

A simple coupling holds the engine and carriage together.

MÄRKLIN "HO" GAUGE RAILWAY

Märklin is one of the most famous ever German toy companies. Theodor Friedrich Wilhelm Märklin founded the company in 1859 and originally specialized in making dollhouse accessories, but released a first wind-up train in 1891. Märklin realized that, like dollhouses, train sets were brilliant marketing opportunities. Once the customer had made the initial purchase, the set could be built up over time by adding a whole variety of accessories. The company began to specialize in high-quality railway toys, and added many

trackside accessories to their offering. Märklin's influence on the model railway business has been huge. It invented almost every commonly used gauge, including "O" gauge (around 1895), and "HO" in 1935. Their diminutive "Z" scale, introduced in 1972 is the smallest scale commercially available. "HO" has a track width of 5/8 of an inch, exactly half that of "O" gauge; hence its name, half-O. Märklin continues to make "HO" scale trains to this day—the scale proved very popular, and was adopted by many other train

manufacturers, including Lionel, Fleischmann, HAG, and Roco. Vintage Märklin models have now become extremely collectible, to the point that the Märklin Museum in Göppingen was burgled, and more than 100 pieces, with an estimated value of one million euros were taken. Luckily, the items (some of which dated back to 1891) were recovered in March 2005.

Below: *The engine is Märklin Model 24158, the cattle car is 248847, and the Bordeaux car 4510.*

Right: *Märklin is thought to have invented "HO" gauge as early as 1895.*

This rolling stock dates from the 1950s.

"HO" GAUGE LAYOUT

This layout reflects how the "HO" gauge, invented by Märklin in 1935 soon became widespread. This hybrid arrangement consists of Lionel's Model 0625 steam train, decaled for the New York Central Railroad, a Tyco maintenance car, a C&O Coal car made by Revell in 1966, a Western Maryland coal car made by Marx, and a NYC caboose by Marx. Lionel was particularly involved in "HO," making a considerable range between 1957 and 1967, and again during the company's modern era. One of the most iconic engines in this scale is the Southern Pacific GS-4, which is from the modern production era. Although Lionel did not make as many accessories for its "HO" sets as for its "O" gauge production, the company did produce several very attractive and collectible models. These included the

0118 Engine House with whistle, the 0140 Banjo Signal, and the 0197 Radar Tower. Lionel's "HO" trains run on DC power, whereas some other manufacturers use AC for this scale. Marx also made a good range of "HO" models, which it sold successfully. These Marx "HO" sets sometimes came complete with scenery.

Below: *This maintenance car, complete with replacement track and spare wheels was made by Tyco.*

MAINTENANCE 932

NEW YORK CENTRAL

0625

The New York Central Railroad was the famous "Water Level Route."

Above: *The Lionel engine has the classic, massive feel of Lionel's high quality toys.*

Right: *In their Golden Era, Marx sold more toy trains than any other company.*

WE STE RN MA RYL AND

70 018

CAPY. 140000
LD.LMT. 155200   NEW 8-57   BLT-8-57   OU. FT. 2622
LT. WT. 54800   HT

TIN STREAMLINERS

These streamliners reflect the great popularity of streamline train travel. Introduced in the 1930s, streamliners brought a whole new glamor to train travel. Instead of hot, rickety, carriages, the streamlines were built for ease and comfort, with air-conditioned carriages, and fine foods served in the dining car. Streamline train travel actually became similar to air travel. The very attractive lithographed model 1006 is a representation of the famous Japanese Bullet Train. Known as *Shinkansen* in Japanese, the Bullet Train was the world's first train built specifically for speed. Construction started on the first section of Japan's

Left: *All three of these trains are made from lithographed tin plate, and have fabulous graphics.*

This toy probably dates from the 1960s.

high-speed rail network in 1959, which ran between Tokyo and Osaka, and was opened in October 1964, just in time for the Tokyo Olympics. It was an immediate success, and 100 million passengers had used the line by July 1967, one billion by 1976. The first trains ran at speeds of up to 125 miles per hour, but modern versions regularly run at speeds of up of 185 miles per hour. The Shinkansen trains have fabulous reliability—on average, they arrive within 6 seconds of their scheduled time.

Right: *The real Bullet Train drivers make a total of 160,000 high-speed trips each year.*

TWO PRESSED STEEL HILLCLIMBERS

These two pressed steel hillclimbers probably date from the early 1900s. Several manufacturers made toys like these, including Dayton and Republic, and they were particularly popular during the 1920s—a very splitting the train), attaching an additional engine, attaching a cable, or using geared steam locomotives. Hillclimber engines were yet another solution to this problem.

Below: This red and black engine has its original paintwork.

similar model appeared in the 1927 Butler Brothers catalog. These early toys are in reasonably good condition, in their original livery, and are now highly collectible. They reflect the real life problems of train operation: while trains have the ability to pull very heavy loads, this is only really possible while their tracks are fairly level. As soon as the gradient becomes pronounced, the tonnage that can be hauled is greatly reduced. Over the decades, many strategies were conceived to get around this problem. These included dividing the load (or

HILLCLIMBER TRAIN

This Red hillclimber train is made from pressed steel, and has its own tender. It is a very early toy, and probably comes from the very early 1900s. It has its original paint finish—although it is quite worn, many collectors prefer this played-with appearance to a refinished toy. Hillclimber toy trains were fitted with a heavy weight inside the body; once they had built up enough speed, the toy was able to climb an incline. Several manufacturers made models of this kind, but perhaps the Dayton Friction Works and Schieble Company were the most active in the field. Both launched several hillclimber friction locomotives in the early 1900s, and were fiercely competitive. Dayton's attractive red, black, and gold friction hillclimber train of 1909 was particularly popular, and several collectible examples have survived. This competition led to an acrimonious lawsuit mounted by Schieble, who disputed Dayton's right to use the term "hillclimber," as they maintained the term was their copyrighted trademark. Dayton remained firm—now owned by Clark, the company uses the term "hillclimber" to this day. Various manufacturers, including Dayton and Schieble, also fitted this system to model cars, wagons, and fire trucks.

This hillclimber is equipped with an elaborate pressed steel cowcatcher.

Above: Hillclimber models were equipped with a heavy weight inside the body cavity. When they built up enough speed, they could climb an incline.

MODEL STREETCAR

Several toy manufacturers made model streetcars like this early version, including LGB and Corgi. The streetcar was once the most popular form of transportation in America, the forerunner of today's mass transit systems, and most American cities, such as Pittsburgh, Washington, and New York had them. The original version was a horse-drawn "omnibus." The first ever omnibus worked on Broadway, starting in 1827 and owned and operated by entrepreneur Abraham Brower, who also helped to organize New York's first fire department. The revolutionary but simple concept behind streetcars was that they ran along designated routes, and charged low fares. Anyone who wanted to use the service simply raised their hand in the air. Horse-drawn streetcars ran in American cities until 1905; the first generation had steel wheels, and ran along rails rather than the street surface. However, these were still horse-drawn vehicles although various

Right: The unique concept behind streetcars is that they ran on designated routes, and charged low fares. This model is from an unknown maker.

experiments were made to find alterative forms of power, including steam. The first powered streetcars were cable driven and these finally left the horse-drawn era behind. They ran on motorized cables mounted in vaults under the track. Cable cars were first introduced in 1873, on the streets of San Francisco. Cable cars in their turn were superseded by an electrified system in the early twentieth century, and this streetcar model dates from then.

STEAM TRAIN NO. 999

This early model steam train has been repainted in its black and silver livery. It is a carpet train—it has no mechanism to propel it along. Although the maker of this toy is unknown, it is fairly safe to assume that it is a very early steam train toy, from the late nineteenth or early twentieth century—its excellent condition tends to belie its age. One of the earliest American manufacturers of toy trains was Althof Bergmann of New York City, active between 1867 and 1880. They were particularly renowned for both their carpet and clockwork trains. James Fallows and Son of Philadelphia, Pennsylvania, were another early maker of simple trains. A family-run company, their stamp read "IXL" or "I excel." Modern versions of these early carpet trains are still in production, almost all made in plastic, or sometimes wood, and aimed at younger children than these pressed steel versions. Manufacturers of these include Fisher-Price.

Above: The engine is number 999, and this is embossed into the pressed steel. The black and silver paintwork has been restored.

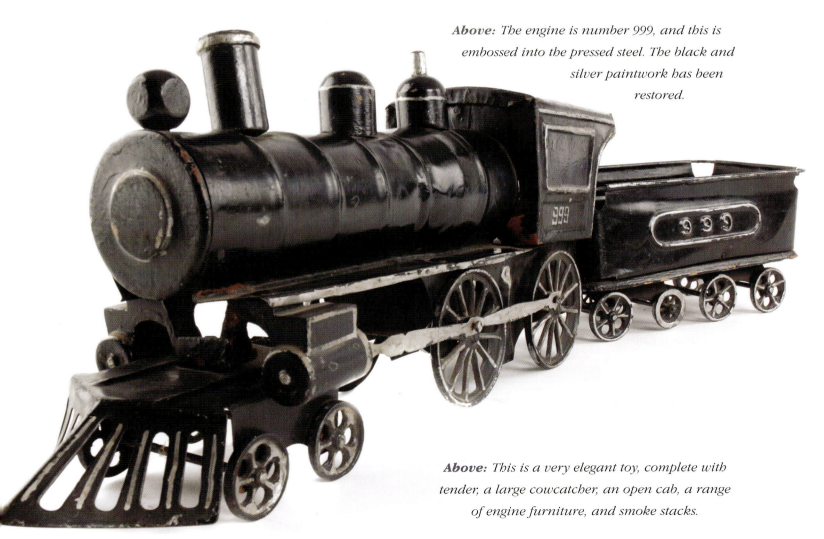

Above: This is a very elegant toy, complete with tender, a large cowcatcher, an open cab, a range of engine furniture, and smoke stacks.

ROCKET PATROL MASK AND SPACE GUNS

The rocket patrol mask and this selection of attractive tin plate space guns date from around the 1940s and are all highly collectible models. The "Atomic Flash" gun was made in America by J. Chein and Company. It is constructed from lithographed tin plate, with a friction operated light strip on either side. Julius Chein established his company in New York City in 1903 as a small metal stamping operation, whose main business was making tin prizes for Cracker Jack boxes and inexpensive toys for five and dime stores. They gradually evolved a line of more elaborate tin toys, and adopted lithographic printing from the canning industry. Their early models often had a "fun fair" theme, and included Ferris wheels, roller coasters, and merry-go-rounds. The company also made character toys, including Popeye and Mickey Mouse. Chein began to make space themed tin toys in the 1940s, including the "Atomic Flash" gun. Space toys reached the peak of their popularity in the post-Second World War years, up to the 1960s. A preoccupation with space exploration in these decades was reflected in a wide range of space-themed toys that became available, up to the moon landing in 1969. Japanese

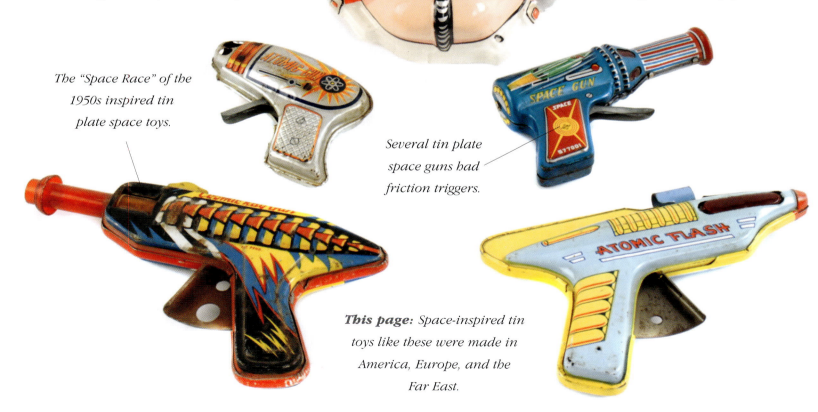

The "Space Race" of the 1950s inspired tin plate space toys.

Several tin plate space guns had friction triggers.

This page: *Space-inspired tin toys like these were made in America, Europe, and the Far East.*

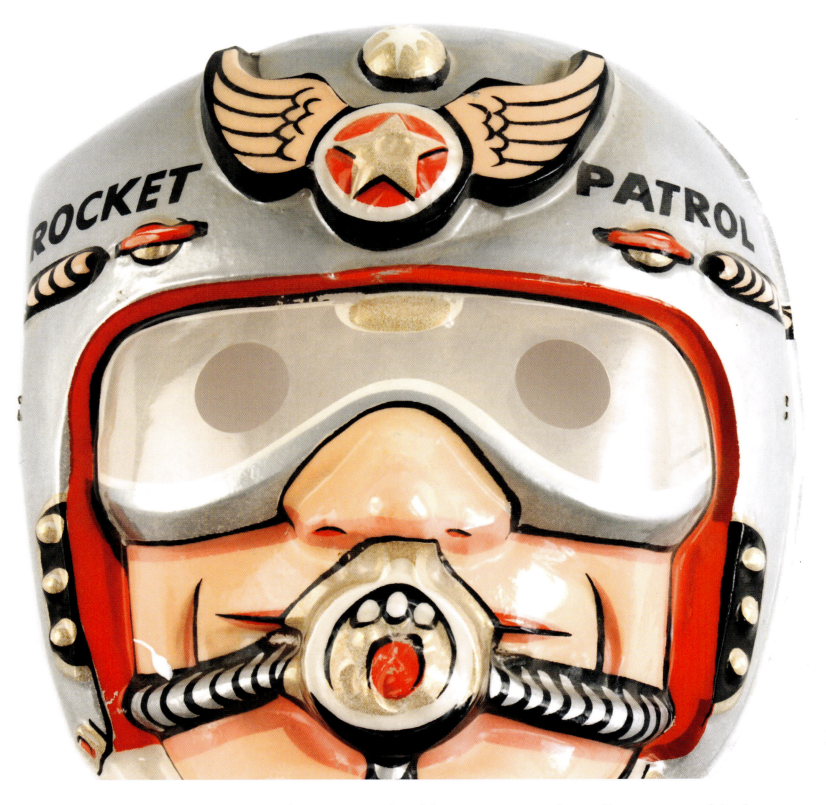

tin toy manufacturers produced a huge range of robots, rockets, flying saucers, and other futuristic spacecraft, many inspired by Hollywood science fiction movies of the 1950s. The toy industry followed their lead, but few showed the creative flair and imagination of the Japanese toy makers—Chein was one of the few American manufacturers to challenge the Japanese products. Julius Chein was killed in a riding accident in 1926, but the company continued to make high quality tin toys until it folded in 1979.

FOUR SPACE GUNS

These four space guns demonstrate how popular these toys were from the 1930s to the 1960s. The events of World War II, in particular, changed people's views of space and technology. Having witnessed V-2 rockets bombing London, and the effects of the atomic bomb, they also understood that science was not always a benign force. The beginning of the Cold War led to greatly increased sightings of UFOs, and many early television programs featured science fiction adventures. At least twelve toy ray guns were issued in the 1950s, based on science fiction soap operas.

Futuristic Products of Detroit manufactured the lustrous chrome-finished "Strato Gun" in 1953. When it was launched, it retailed for $2.49. Its box described the gun as a "Futuristic cap repeater… Earth's only interplanetary automatic cap gun…" As the gun's advertising slogan proclaimed, "Every kid in the Universe wants a Strato Gun."

The red enameled popper gun has space-inspired styling.

Pulling the popper gun's trigger results in a loud noise.

The "Strato Gun" uses conventional 10 shot foil caps.

Below: The "Buck Rogers
Disintegrator ZX-38" was Daisy's
third model in this line. It was
issued in 1935.

Like the "Strato," this gun
has "radical cooling fins."

The "Strato Gun" was 12 inches long, and featured "radical cooling fins." It was the subject of a patent issued by the United States Patent and Trademark Office to Sidney Wasserman and Allen M. Stevens for a "new, original, and ornamental design for a toy gun."

The "Buck Rogers Daisy Disintegrator" was an equally exciting toy: pulling the trigger launched a a barrage of fiery sparks, visible through the window on top of the gun. It measured 10½ inches in length. Daisy manufactured the gun in their Michigan plant and it was offered in two finishes, polished copper and a blued nickel effect. Daisy first made the "Disintegrator" in 1935, priced at 50 cents, and had first ventured into making Buck Rogers pistols in the early 1930s. The company collaborated with author Philip Francis Nowlan, and cartoonist Richard Calkins to redesign a whole range of Buck Rogers toys, which included guns, helmets, and holsters. Buck Rogers first appeared in 1926 in a pulp magazine called *Amazing Stories*. Rogers developed a large following through the comics

This is actually a conventional cap gun with space inspired styling.

The "Strato" measures 12 inches in length. It was first retailed at $2.49.

Above: *As the advertising proclaimed, "Every kid in the Universe wants a Strato Gun."*

and radio shows devoted to the character, and inspired a new genre of toy, the ray gun. Daisy launched their first Buck Rogers toy gun at Christmas 1933, and persuaded the Hudson department store in Chicago to run a special promotion, "Buck Rogers in the 25th Century," featuring a huge rocket ship and Martian figures. Macy's of New York ran the same promotion, and over 2,000 people queued to buy the gun, which was one of Daisy's most successful products—they were obliged to drive a truckload of them into New York every day from their Michigan factory. They also developed a holster and helmet to accompany it. The "Buck Rogers Disintegrator XZ-38" was the third model in the Buck Rogers series. It featured a fluted barrel, flamboyant fins, and the special spark effect. As well as being sold through stores, it was also merchandised as a Cream of Wheat premium in 1935, and a Popsicle premium in 1939. Daisy stopped making Buck Rogers guns in the mid-1940s.

The red enameled gun is a "popper." When the trigger is puller, it makes a loud bang. The gun has space-inspired styling.

The red popper gun is equipped with a gun sight.

The space-inspired styling of the popper makes it likely that the gun was manufactured in the 1930s.

Above: *Popular science fiction became a mainstay of the pulp magazines of the 1920s and 1930s. The popularity of this genre inspired many children's toys.*

ATOMIC ROBOT MAN AND SPACE DOG

Both of these Japanese toys are made from tin plate, and have wind-up motors. Japanese manufacturer KO made this "Space Dog" in the late 1950s. KO was a brand name of Yoshiya, a Japanese toy manufacturer active between 1950 and 1970. The company was also known as Kobe Yoko Ltd., and was a major toy manufacturer of the post war period of occupation. They specialized in mechanical and wind up models. Although well known for their robot toys, especially "Robby the Robot," the company also made many more conventional toys, including automobiles, fire pumpers, railways trucks and boxcars. The charming "Space

promotional item at the 1950 New York Science Fiction Convention. His box shows him striding through a decimated city, complete with atomic mushroom cloud. The first mass produced robot toy was "Lilliput," a boxy, yellow painted printed tin toy launched in the mid 1940s. Occupying American forces encouraged the Japanese tin toy industry in the post war years. General MacArthur was entrusted with re-establishing the Japanese economy, but did not want to establish industries that would compete with American companies. Several companies manufacture detailed reproductions of the "Atomic Robot Man."

The "Atomic Robot Man" dates from 1949.

The original box for the "Space Dog" has survived in excellent condition. Replicas are now available.

"Space Dog" was made by the Japanese manufacturer KO, also known as Yoshiya, and Kobe Yoko Ltd.

Dog" comes with his original box, and wind up key.

The "Atomic Robot Man" is reputed to be only the second robot toy to have been manufactured by the Japanese toy industry, circa 1949. He is 5 inches in height, and has a pinwheel walking mechanism. His arms hang loosely by his side. "Atomic Robot Man" was given out as a

This page: *"Atomic Robot Man" and "Space Dog" were both made by the Japanese toy industry during the post-Second World War occupation. General MacArthur encouraged the Japanese toy industry to rebuild.*

"Atomic Robot Man" is shown in his original tan paintwork.

"Space Dog" is in excellent, working condition, and is a valuable toy.

TWO ROBOTS

Japanese tin plate toys of the post-Second World War era are highly collectible. Their zany actions and outstanding colors are attractive and tin plate robots, in particular, have changed hands for many thousands of dollars. Not only did these toys help to rebuild the Japanese economy, they also soon surpassed the quality and inventiveness of tin plate toys from other countries. The tin robot on the right is the "Outer Space Conqueror" by Horikawa of Japan, circa 1959. The Horikawa Toy Company was the most prolific Japanese wholesaler of battery operated toys, also known by its SH trademark. Most of their toys were manufactured by the Metal House Company of Tokyo. Horikawa was famous for its seemingly infinite variety of square box-shaped tin robots with angular, prismic heads—they sold hundreds of different ones between the 1950s and 1980s and also marketed various rockets and space stations. They were so prolific that collectors are still identifying new models. Horikawa's robot line up included many iconic models, including "Mr. Hustler" (who did a disco dance routine), and their "Fire Robot" (model umber 1038). A tiny extension ladder and two small firemen were concealed in the chest of the "Fire Robot." He is also equipped with a separate remote control box—most of Horikawa's robots were fitted with a battery compartment at the back, concealed beneath a tin plate door. Although Horikawa is no more, Metal House continues to make limited edition robots for collectors.

The robot on the left is a later, plastic and metal toy. Plastic was a popular material for toys in the 1970s, and many earlier toys were redesigned in this less durable material. Robots like this are often difficult to attribute to a specific manufacturer. Since early robots have become so sought after, it is hardly surprising that replica robots are manufactured in huge numbers in Chinese toy factories.

Later plastic robot toys like this one are difficult to attribute.

Many early tin plate robots were redesigned as plastic toys in the 1970s.

Metal House made the "Outer Space Conqueror" for Horikawa.

Like the "Fire Robot," "Outer Space Conqueror" has an opening chest.

This robot has a concealed battery compartment in his back.

STAR WARS FIGURES

Since 1959, when Mattel launched its line of Barbie dolls, action figures have formed a significant sector of the American toy market. Hasbro borrowed Mattel's idea in 1964, and launched an action figure marketed specifically to boys, G.I. Joe. Another significant figure manufacturer was Mego—in 1972, they launched a range of figures based on various comic book heroes; Spiderman, Batman, and Captain America. When the *Star Wars* movie was released in May 1977, George Lucas offered Mego the rights to make the tie-in figures, but they and several other toy companies declined this offer. A relatively unknown manufacturer, Kenner, finally agreed to make the figures, which were launched in 1978. Kenner initially made their *Star Wars* figurines in two different sizes: 12 inches and 3¾ inches tall. The smaller version was much more popular, as they were more affordable, so the larger models were

Below: *Keener first launched its smaller scale Star Wars figures in 1978, alongside 12-inch tall versions.*

Right: *The original Jawa was launched with a vinyl (not cloth) cape. This version is very valuable.*

Above: *Hasbro now owns the rights to produce* Star Wars *character figures.*

Right: *Kenner finished production of the original* Star Wars *figures in 1985.*

later discontinued. Many other companies tried to copy Kenner's success by introducing their own movie-inspired figures, including ranges based on the *Star Trek* and *Buck Rogers* movies. However, even the huge success of Kenner's *Star Wars* figurines came to a natural end, and the line was cancelled in 1985, after they had been the backbone of the company's success for almost a decade.

In 1995, Kenner re-launched a slightly larger range of *Star Wars* figures, which were 4 inches tall. Hasbro merged with Kenner in 1994, and the new company offered figures based on the new *Star Wars* movie, "Episode I: The Phantom Menace." Like their earlier *Star Wars* offerings, these figures were also hugely successful, and are now highly collectible and very much sought after.

PALITOY STAR WARS TOYS

Kenner originated both of these toys for the American market—Palitoy was their British partner, who also marketed the Kenner *Star Wars* figures. Palitoy launched the X-Wing Fighter toy in 1980. It was based on a space vehicle featured in *Star Wars* "The Empire Strikes Back," but despite appearances, the toy was not equipped with any electronic features. The *Star Wars*

play sets debuted in 1978 with the release of the plastic "Death Star Space Station," a three-dimensional toy that required assembly. Palitoy is based in Coalville, Leicestershire. A. E. Kenner founded the company in 1919 but it is now a British subsidiary of General Mills. Kenner imported Palitoy's versions into Canada, re-boxing them for this market.

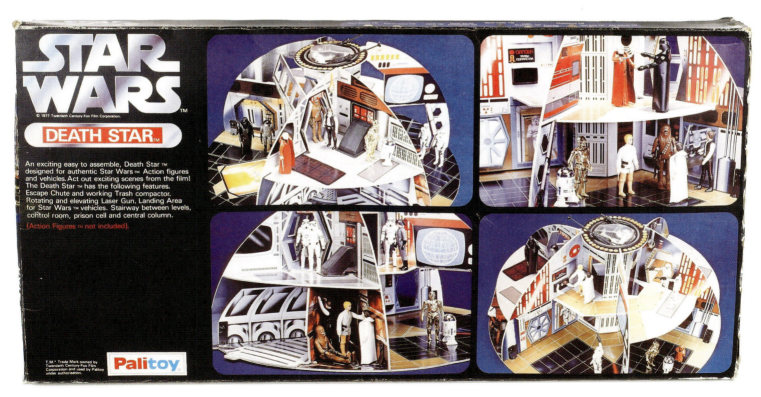

Left: *The X-Wing fighter was first launched in 1980.*

Above: *The "Death Star Space Station" is for use with Kenner's 3¾ inch high figures.*

ACKNOWLEDGMENTS

The publisher would like to thank the following for their help in compiling this book:

Tom & Wendy Beck – The World's Largest Toy Museum

J.P. Bell – Photography

Bud, Kobie and Dan – Marx Museum

D.T. Fletcher

Bob at BB Airguns

Amy Cannistraci, R. John Wright Dolls

Stephen Medina, Schylling Toys